THE POLITICS OF INTERNATIONAL ECONOMIC LAW

How do politics and international economic law interact with each other? Financial crises and shifts in global economic patterns have refocused our attention on how the fingerprints of the "visible hand" can be seen all over the institutions that underpin the rules of globalization. From trade and investment to finance, governments are under pressure to enforce, resist, and rewrite international economic law. Lawyers have seldom given enough attention to the influence of politics on law, whereas political scientists have had an on-again, off-again fascination with how the law influences relations among states. This book leads the way toward filling this interdisciplinary gap through a series of important studies written by leaders in the field on specific problems in international economic relations. The book demonstrates a variety of ways in which the international political–economic nexus may be researched and understood.

Tomer Broude is a Senior Lecturer with the Faculty of Law and Department of International Relations and Academic Director of the Minerva Center for Human Rights at the Hebrew University of Jerusalem. He is an expert in international economic law, particularly WTO and regional trade law, dispute settlement, investment, and development. He is the author of the book *International Governance in the WTO: Judicial Boundaries and Political Capitulation* (2004) and has coedited several other books, including *The Shifting Allocation of Authority in International Law: Considering Sovereignty, Supremacy and Subsidiary* (2008, edited with Yuval Shany); *Multisourced Equivalent Norms in International Law* (2010, edited with Yuval Shany); and *Law and Development Perspective on International Trade Law* (forthcoming, edited with Won-Mog Choi, Gary Horlick, and Y. S. Lee).

Marc L. Busch is the Karl F. Landegger Professor of International Business Diplomacy at the Edmund A. Walsh School of Foreign Service, Georgetown University in Washington, D.C., and an Adjunct Scholar at the American Enterprise Institute. He is an expert on international trade policy and law and the author of the book *Trade Warriors* and articles in the *American Journal of Political Science, American Journal of Sociology, British Journal of Political Science, Fordham International Law Journal, International Organization, Journal of Conflict Resolution, Journal of World Trade, World Politics,* and *World Trade Review.*

Amelia Porges practices law at the Law Offices of Amelia Porges PLLC, a law firm focused on WTO and international trade law. She is also a Professorial Lecturer at the Nitze School of Advanced International Studies of Johns Hopkins University, in Washington, D.C. She was the principal author of the sixth and final edition of the *Analytical Index/Guide to GATT Law and Practice*. She has authored many articles that have appeared as book chapters and law review articles on WTO and GATT dispute settlement, investment arbitration, trade in legal services, United States–Japan trade, and Japanese economic policy.

The Politics of International Economic Law

Edited by

TOMER BROUDE

Faculty of Law, Hebrew University of Jerusalem

MARC L. BUSCH

School of Foreign Service, Georgetown University

AMELIA PORGES

Law Offices of Amelia Porges PLLC

CAMBRIDGE
UNIVERSITY PRESS

CAMBRIDGE UNIVERSITY PRESS
Cambridge, New York, Melbourne, Madrid, Cape Town,
Singapore, São Paulo, Delhi, Tokyo, Mexico City

Cambridge University Press
32 Avenue of the Americas, New York, NY 10013-2473, USA

www.cambridge.org
Information on this title: www.cambridge.org/9781107003552

First published 2011

Printed in the United States of America

A catalog record for this publication is available from the British Library.

Library of Congress Cataloging in Publication data

The politics of international economic law / [edited by] Tomer Broude, Marc L. Busch,
Amelia Porges.
p. cm.
Includes bibliographical references.
ISBN 978-1-107-00355-2 (hardback)
1. Foreign trade regulation – Political aspects. 2. Investments, Foreign – Law and legislation – Political aspects. I. Broude, Tomer. II. Busch, Marc L. (Marc Lawrence), 1966–
III. Porges, Amelia.
K3943.G653 2011
343′.87 – dc22 2010037572

ISBN 978-1-107-00355-2 Hardback

Contents

Contributor List

Douglas W. Arner Director, Asian Institute of International Financial Law, Director of the LLM Programme and Professor, Faculty of Law, University of Hong Kong

Perry S. Bechky Visiting Assistant Professor, Seattle University School of Law, Washington State

Axel Berger Fellow, German Development Institute, Bonn, Germany

Tomer Broude Senior Lecturer, Faculty of Law and Department of International Relations, Hebrew University of Jerusalem

Marc Bungenberg Professor of Public Law, European Law, Public International Law, and International Law, Siegen University, Germany

Marc L. Busch Karl F. Landegger Professor of International Business Diplomacy, Edmund A. Walsh School of Foreign Service, Georgetown University, Washington, D.C.

Henry Gao Associate Professor, Faculty of Law, Singapore Management University, Rochor

Moshe Hirsch Hofmannsthal Professor in International Law, Faculty of Law, and Head of the Department of International Relations, Hebrew University of Jerusalem

Claire R. Kelly Professor of Law, Associate Director of the Dennis J. Block Center for the Study of International Business Law, Brooklyn Law School, New York

Yvonne C. L. Lee Assistant Professor, Faculty of Law, National University of Singapore, Pulau Bukom

Meredith Kolsky Lewis Senior Lecturer, Victoria University of Wellington Law School, New Zealand, and Co-Director, New Zealand Centre of International Economic Law

C. L. Lim Professor of Law and Associate Dean for Academic Affairs, the University of Hong Kong

Uche Ewelukwa Ofodile Professor, University of Arkansas School of Law, Fayetteville

Krzysztof J. Pelc Assistant Professor, Political Science Department, McGill University, Montreal, Canada

Lauge Skovgaard Poulsen Ph.D. Candidate, London School of Economics

Amelia Porges Professorial Lecturer at the Paul H. Nitze School of Advanced International Studies of Johns Hopkins University, Washington, D.C.

Kimberlee Weatherall Senior Lecturer, TC Beirne School of Law, University of Queensland, Australia, and Adjunct Research Fellow, Australian Centre for Intellectual Property in Agriculture

Acknowledgments

The editors thank all of the authors who submitted chapters for this book, as well as the other persons who contributed to the success of the November 2008 conference of the International Economic Law Interest Group of the American Society of International Law (ASIL): The Politics of International Economic Law: The Next Four Years. Taking place at a special, optimistic point in time, shortly after the U.S. presidential election of 2008, the conference benefited from the participation of many from Washington, D.C., and from far away, including our keynote and endnote speakers, Jennifer A. Hillman (World Trade Organization [WTO] Appellate Body Member and German Marshall Fund of the United States), Hon. William Frenzel (Brookings Institution), Prof. John H. Jackson (Georgetown University Law Center), Lucy Reed (ASIL and Freshfields, Bruckhaus, Deringer LLP), and Ambassador John K. Veroneau (Deputy U.S. Trade Representative [USTR]).

We also thank all those who authored conference papers or participated as discussants, including Padideh Ala'i (American University, Washington College of Law); Todd Allee (University of Illinois at Urbana–Champaign, Department of Political Science); Alberto Alvarez-Jimenez (University of Ottawa School of Law); Douglas W. Arner (Hong Kong University, Faculty of Law); Peter Bakstansky (New York, NY); Perry S. Bechky (University of Connecticut School of Law); Axel Berger (German Development Institute); Ljiljana Biukovic (University of British Columbia Faculty of Law); Yves Bonzon (World Trade Institute, Bern, National Centre of Competence in Research–Trade), Michael Bradfield (Jones Day LLP); A. Jane Bradley (Georgetown University Law Center); Marc L. Busch and Krzysztof J. Pelc (School of Foreign Service and Department of Government, Georgetown University); Marc Bungenberg (Ludwig-Maximilians University, Munich); Michael Castellano (Counsel and Senior Policy Adviser, Majority Leader Harry Reid, U.S. Senate); Sungjoon Cho (Chicago–Kent School of Law); Barnali Choudhury

(Pace Law School); Angelos Dimopoulos (European University Institute, Florence); Uche Ewelukwa Ofodile (University of Arkansas, School of Law); Steven Fabry (USTR); Michael Fakhri (University of Toronto Faculty of Law); Susan Franck (Washington & Lee University Law School); Ermal Frasheri (Harvard Law School); R. Michael Gadbaw (Georgetown University Law Center); David Gantz (University of Arizona Law School); Henry Gao (Singapore Management University) and C. L. Lim (Hong Kong University Faculty of Law); Robin F. Hansen (McGill University Faculty of Law); Moshe Hirsch (Hebrew University of Jerusalem Faculty of Law); Jorge L. Kamine (Skadden, Arps, Slate, Meagher & Flom LLP); Suzanne Katzenstein (Columbia University Department of Political Science); Claire R. Kelly (Brooklyn Law School); J. Patrick Kelly (Widener University School of Law); Yaraslau Kryvoi (Morgan Lewis & Bockius LLP); Rafael Leal-Arcas (Queen Mary University of London, School of Law); Yvonne C. L. Lee (National University of Singapore Faculty of Law); Meredith Kolsky Lewis (Victoria University of Wellington Law School); Dorotea López and Felipe Muñoz (University of Chile Institute of International Studies); Willajeanne F. McLean (University of Connecticut Law School); Patrick Meagher (University of Maryland IRIS Center); Joshua Meltzer (University of Michigan School of Law); James Mendenhall (Sidley Austin LLP); Kate Miles (University of Sydney Faculty of Law); Clint W. Peinhardt (University of Texas at Dallas, Department of Economic, Political and Policy Sciences); Colin B. Picker (University of Missouri–Kansas City School of Law); Lauge Skovgaard Poulsen (London School of Economics International Trade Policy Unit); Jenik Radon (Columbia University School of International and Public Affairs); Gustavo Ribeiro (Indiana University School of Law); Christopher M. Ryan (Shearman & Sterling LLP); Miriam Sapiro (Summit Strategies International LLC, Washington, D.C.); Deborah Siegel (International Monetary Fund Legal Department); Michael Smart (National Security Council, Washington, D.C.); Lars Thomann (University of Mannheim, Department of Political Science); Paul B. Stephan (University of Virginia School of Law); Joel P. Trachtman (Fletcher School of Law and Diplomacy, Tufts University); Edwin M. Truman (Peterson Institute for International Economics); and Kimberlee Weatherall (University of Queensland, TC Beirne School of Law).

We thank our conference host, the George Washington University Law School, including Dean Frederick M. Lawrence (Associate Dean for International and Comparative Legal Studies), Susan Karamanian, Professor Steve Charnovitz, and Silena Davis for their generous welcome to the conference and its participants.

We also thank Elizabeth Andersen, Sheila Ward, Nasser Qadri, and Scott Lyons of the ASIL for their unstinting support and administrative assistance for the conference and the activities of the Interest Group. We thank the members of the Conference Committee: Karen Bravo (Indiana University School of Law); Rachel Brewster (Harvard Law School); Marc L. Busch (Georgetown University School of Foreign Service); Steve Charnovitz (George Washington University Law School); Sungjoon Cho (Chicago–Kent School of Law); Steven Fabry (USTR); Susan Franck (Washington & Lee Law School); R. Michael Gadbaw (Georgetown University Law Center); Susan Karamanian (George Washington University Law School); Claire R. Kelly (Brooklyn Law School); Rafael Leal-Arcas (Queen Mary College, University of London); Simon Lester (Worldtradelaw.net); Joshua Meltzer (Washington DC); Krista Nadakavukaren Schefer (World Trade Institute, Bern); Sheila Ward (ASIL); and Richard Wilder (Microsoft Corporation). Julianne T. Zollinger of Georgetown University Law Center provided administrative assistance to Tomer Broude and the Conference Committee.

In addition, we appreciate the conference support provided by Cambridge University Press, Edward Elgar Publishing, Hart Publishing, and the *Trade Law Guide*, as well as the partnership of the Society of International Economic Law.

We also thank John Berger and his staff at Cambridge University Press for their continued support and guidance throughout the editorial and production phases of the book. Finally, we are grateful for the financial support of the Nathan and Judith Feinberg Fund at the Hebrew University of Jerusalem.

TB, MLB, and AP
Jerusalem and Washington, D.C.

1

Introduction

Some Observations on the Politics of International Economic Law

Tomer Broude, Marc L. Busch, and Amelia Porges

Politics is the art of looking for trouble, finding it everywhere, diagnosing it incorrectly and applying the wrong remedies.

– Groucho Marx

In times of crisis, we are forcefully reminded of the links between politics and international economic law.[1] Indeed, the meltdown in world markets has refocused attention on how the fingerprints of the "visible hand" can be seen all over the institutions that underpin the rules of globalization. From trade and investment to finance, governments are under pressure to enforce, resist, and rewrite international economic law. To be sure, the future of the Bretton Woods institutions is, itself, the subject of heated debate. For legal scholars and political scientists, this is fertile ground; lawyers have seldom given enough attention to the influence of politics on law, whereas political scientists have had an on-again, off-again fascination with how the law influences relations among states. This book is motivated by a deceptively simple question: How do politics and international economic law interact with each other?

[1] The term "international economic law" has by default usually been identified with the law of international trade regulation. Thus, despite its worthy ambitions of covering "a very broad range of subjects that concern the relation of law to international economic activity," the contents of the *Journal of International Economic Law*, for example, have predominantly been devoted to trade law issues (see http://jiel.oxfordjournals.org/). In this book we have adopted and pursued a broad understanding of international economic law as comprising those areas of international law related to the transnational movement of goods, services, capital, and persons, including (but not limited to) trade law, investment law, economic integration law, private international law, business regulation, financial law, tax law, intellectual property law, and development law.

CONTEMPORARY CONTEXT, ENDURING QUESTIONS

The prominence of international economic issues in the 2008 presidential campaign in the United States,[2] together with the global economic crisis that began to unfold at around the same time, inspired us to take stock of the ways in which politics shapes the legal frameworks within which international commerce takes place.[3] First, and most obviously, the crisis has reinforced the recognition of international economic interdependence. At the same time, however, it has also cast doubt on some of the institutional and normative underpinnings of liberal capitalism that have largely held sway since World War II.[4] If "[m]acroeconomics . . . was cast in the crucible of the [Great] Depression,"[5] then the economic turmoil of the early twenty-first century provides us, perhaps, with a new foundry in which to forge new solutions, new ideas, and new dynamics.

These are, after all, times characterized by changing politics, with novel yet insufficiently incorporated concerns and constituencies, such as the environment, energy needs, human rights, public participation, international equity, and a global economic map redrawn by the emergence of powerhouses such as Brazil, India, and China. We may also be witnessing the dawn of changed legal and institutional environments, with the multilateral Bretton Woods system. It has been amended in piecemeal style over the past few decades, and it has been viewed by some as no longer suited to the world's needs – hence the debate over Bretton Woods 2.0[6] and the replacement of the G-7. Clearly,

[2] See, e.g., the Clinton–Obama exchange on the future of the North American Free Trade Agreement (NAFTA) at the February 26, 2008, Democratic debate in Ohio (see transcript at http://www.cfr.org/publication/15604/); or the Obama–McCain exchanges on free trade agreements and labor and environmental clauses (e.g., see transcript of the third Presidential debate, October 18, 2008, Hofstra University, Hempstead, New York, at http://www.cfr.org/publication/17541/).

[3] The book consists of a selection of articles presented at the 2008 Biennial Conference of the American Society of International Law's International Economic Law Interest Group (ASIL-IELIG), held at George Washington University Law School, Washington, DC, November 14–15, 2008.

[4] This was most vividly expressed in the concession by Alan Greenspan, former Chairman of the U.S. Federal Reserve, that he had found a "flaw in the model" he had "perceived is the critical functioning structure that defines how the world works" in his October 23, 2008 testimony before the House Committee on Oversight and Government reform (see http://www.pbs.org/newshour/bb/business/july-dec08/crisishearing_10–23.html).

[5] Peter Passell, "A Nobel Award for a University of Chicago Economist, Yet Again," *New York Times*, October 11, 1995.

[6] Indeed, this possibility was made all the more tangible to the ASIL-IELIG conference participants, because by coincidence the G-20 Leaders Summit on Financial Markets and the World Economy, convened by then President George W. Bush to discuss steps necessary to produce

in these circumstances, any effort toward progress and change will require an improved understanding of the relationship between political dynamics and international economic law, an understanding to which this book hopes to contribute.

However, these momentous developments in global politics and economics provide only a general historical context for the inquiry into the interaction between politics and international economic law. To be sure, the links between them were pertinent before the crisis, and they will remain so long after it is over. Indeed, only one of the articles in this book deals directly with the political and legal reaction to the economic crisis, although surely an article on the topic of financial law would have been required with or without the crisis.[7] Rather, each of the selected contributions provides a detailed analysis of a discrete political process or phenomenon that relates to international economic law. In fact, several of the chapters look at political business being conducted far from the limelight in less-scrutinized areas of international economic law, such as the working methods of the United Nations Commission on International Trade Law (UNCITRAL),[8] the political use of technical rules of origin,[9] or economic agreements with small island states in the Pacific.[10]

That said, although the global economic crisis has confirmed and emphasized the importance of the links between politics and international economic law, this relationship is best studied by taking a look at several key thematic vignettes that, together, make up the global economy. Our book is organized in this way.

HOW DO POLITICS INTERACT WITH INTERNATIONAL ECONOMIC LAW? LET US COUNT THE WAYS . . .

This leads to our most central observation about the relationship between politics and international economic law: It is diverse. We find the diversity of the studies collected in this book to be rewarding not only because of the substantive richness it produces, but because it reveals processes that are

a "Bretton Woods 2.0," was held at the same time as the conference and only a few blocks away in downtown Washington.

7 See Douglas Arner, "The Politics of International Financial Law," Chapter 10, this volume.

8 See Claire R. Kelly, "The Politics of Legitimacy in the UNCITRAL Working Methods," Chapter 5, this volume.

9 See Moshe Hirsch, "The Politics of Rules of Origin," Chapter 13, this volume.

10 See Meredith Kolsky Lewis, "The Politics and Indirect Effects of Asymmetrical Bargaining Power in Free Trade Agreements," Chapter 2, this volume.

indicative of the ways law and politics interact on a regular basis. Put simply, the interaction between politics and international economic law is far from monolithic and cannot be reduced to a single set of principles or hypotheses.

Thus, from the outset,[11] our project was premised on a two-way street between law and politics. In one direction, politics sways the development of international economic law and its implementation. Although this should be obvious, it is still a controversial statement in a field such as international economic law, which has traditionally taken pride in its depoliticization.[12] Furthermore, although economic *policy* is clearly a political outcome, our interest lies in examining how politics can influence the making of the *law* and its materialization in action, or in the way politics determines legal outcomes. This distinction between policy and law is not necessarily a bright line – certainly not if one takes the law to be merely the ultimate expression of policy, or the translation of policy into official acts that direct behavior – but it is a necessary one, and it determines the focus of the studies included here.

As an illustration of this distinction, consider the political genesis of the North American Free Trade Agreement (NAFTA). A popular narrative is that the NAFTA was the result of an auspicious confluence between the political interests of Mexico's Salinas, Canada's Mulroney, and the U.S. administration under George H.W. Bush. As an explanation, this might shed some light on why the negotiating project was launched, but it cannot tell us much about the legal *content* of the agreement. Note that this is a difference not only in the level of detail of the explanation, but also in its subject. In one case, the question is "why is there law?" In other words, what were the political interests that led to a policy that required law making for its execution? In the second case, which interests us here, the question asked is "why is the law as it is?" That is, what were the political dynamics that led the law to gain its particular attributes? Thus, returning to NAFTA, we find that one book-scale study of the process has argued that these negotiations were shaped by "(1) asymmetries of power between the three states; (2) sharply contrasting domestic political institutions; and (3) differences in the nonagreement alternatives, patience, and risk orientations of the heads of government and their chief negotiators."[13]

In propositions such as these we can find contestable political explanations for the emergence of legal outcomes, and many of these are presented in

[11] For the original call for papers that framed the papers presented at the ASIL-IELIG conference, see http://www.worldtradelaw.net/asilielig2008.pdf.

[12] See Arie Reich, "The Threat of Politicization of the World Trade Organization," 26 *University of Pennsylvania Journal of International Economic Law* (2005) 779.

[13] See Maxwell A. Cameron and Brian W. Tomlin, *The Making of NAFTA: How the Deal Was Done* (Cornell University Press, 2000), p. 15.

the chapters that follow. Bismarck famously quipped that the less people know about how sausages and laws are made, the better they would sleep.[14] This easily applies to international treaties, decisions of international institutions, and rulings of international tribunals. Along these lines, the request we made of our authors was not to help explain why sausages are made (or what international economic law is for), but rather to engage in the explicit study of sausage making (the making of law and law-based behavior). This does not mean that just any technotactical, play-by-play description of the international law-making process satisfies this objective; only the political dimension of law making and legal practice is within our analytical focus.

Of course, just as politics influences the law, we expect that international economic law, and its various domestic and international arrangements, shapes politics at all levels. Most basically, the law can constrain politics: Procedural rules in decision-making bodies of institutions such as UNCITRAL,[15] or the division of legal competence among institutions and member states in the European Union (EU),[16] are examples of legal structures that determine the effective weight of political influence. Indeed, in these examples, we see that actors such as states or nongovernmental organizations take the rules of the game seriously, wrangling over procedure and legal authority because of the understanding that these might be the ultimate determinants of policy outcomes.

Political scientists, in particular, have been eager to theorize about the use of law as a constraint on policy. For example, in explaining free trade outcomes, scholars insist that elected officials are able to "tie their hands" by citing international legal authority – such as a likely reversal in World Trade Organization (WTO) dispute settlement and exposure to legal trade retaliation in denying requests for import relief demanded by protectionist constituents. The literature observes that preserving some flexibility for governments to provide short-term protectionism is key to getting members to join, but this just speaks to the faith in legal obligations as constraints on policy.

WHICH POLITICS? WHOSE LAW?

Beyond the "Marxian" definition of politics given in the earlier epigraph – Groucho's definition, that is – we left it to our authors to choose what kind

14 "Je weniger die Leute wissen, wie Würste und Gesetze gemacht werden, desto besser schlafen sie!"

15 See Kelly, *supra* note 9.

16 See Marc Bungenberg, "The Politics of the European Union's Investment Treaty-Making," Chapter 6, this volume.

of politics is most important, and their studies provide a wide range of understandings of politics. A number of contributions focus on power in the relations between states in the international economic arena,[17] or on the connection between economic policy and other political interests.[18] Still others look at the use of international economic law as an instrument of "higher" politics in foreign policy.[19] Some authors choose to examine how economic interests play out in international institutions,[20] whereas others see fit to analyze instances of so-called judicial politics and its interaction with state politics.[21] At times, political constellations serve as an independent, empirical variable,[22] whereas others see politicized economic relations as a subject of social critique.[23] Taken together, the chapters cover all levels of (inter-)governmental politics – global, regional, and domestic – as well as the political participation of nongovernmental organizations, and public legitimacy as a political factor.[24]

Although these diverse approaches reflect a high degree of multidisciplinarity, the majority of contributors are legal scholars rather than political scientists. This is remarkable given the ingrained inhibitions of international lawyers against acknowledging the role of politics in their profession. Martti Koskenniemi has written critically of the "flight from politics" that characterizes international law, where "the fight for an international Rule of Law is a fight against politics."[25] International economic law has been no exception to this flight, with the added convenience that, in their positivism, international lawyers could rely on the seemingly objective scientific-economic basis of "embedded

[17] See Lewis, *supra* note 11; Uche Ewelukwa, "The Politics of African Trade Negotiations in the WTO's Doha Round," Chapter 4, this volume; and Axel Berger, "The Politics of China's Investment Treaty-Making Programme," Chapter 7, this volume.

[18] See Kimberlee G. Weatherall, "The Politics of Linkages in U.S. Preferential Trade Agreements," Chapter 3, this volume; and Henry Gao and C. L. Lim, "The Politics of Competing Jurisdictions in WTO and RTA Disputes, and the Use of Private International Law Analogies," Chapter 12, this volume.

[19] See Hirsch, *supra* note 10; and Perry Bechky, "The Politics of Divestment from Sudan: Investment Decisions and Intersystemic Dialogue," Chapter 14, this volume.

[20] See Arner, *supra* note 8.

[21] See Gao and Lim, *supra* note 19; and Marc L. Busch and Krzystof Pelc, "The Politics of Judicial Economy at the WTO," Chapter 11, this volume.

[22] See Lauge Skovgaard Poulsen, "The Politics of South–South Bilateral Investment Treaties," Chapter 8, this volume.

[23] See Yvonne C. L. Lee, "The Politics of Sovereign Wealth Funds: Benign Investors or Smoking Guns?," Chapter 9, this volume.

[24] See Kelly, *supra* note 9.

[25] Martti Koskenniemi, "The Politics of International Law," 1(4) *European Journal of International Law* (1990) 4, p. 5.

liberalism."[26] Although "trade liberalization was embedded within a *political* commitment," its technical economics enabled a "forgetfulness or amnesia concerning the political foundation of the postwar trading regime."[27] The willingness to overcome this amnesia and recall the importance of politics in international economic law might be taken as a confirmation that "the liberal and pragmatic assumptions that have guided international economic law are increasingly beset with uncertainty, stemming from dilemmas in the study and practice of economics as well as from political disagreement and social discontent."[28] Renewed attention to politics is only a positive development, which will nurture and inform debates on future architectures of international economic relations.

At the same time, political scientists have traditionally been hesitant to engage with international law and legal process as an object of study, although over the past decade this has changed, as some of the contributions to this book vividly demonstrate. Indeed, political scientists and international lawyers "seem increasingly to see the same world outside their office windows,"[29] and this applies as well in the areas of international political economy and international economic law. Although this may not always generate true interdisciplinary research, it does, in projects such as this one, facilitate cross-disciplinary dialogue and exchanges on the interactions between politics and law.

On the backdrop of these observations, we now turn to a contextual summary of the book's contents.

CONTENTS OF THE BOOK

The book is organized under five thematic headings, covering trade agreements, investment protection treaties, international finance, dispute settlement, and foreign policy.

26 J. G. Ruggie, "International Regimes, Transactions and Change: Embedded Liberalism in the Postwar Economic Order," 36 *International Organization* (1982) 379; J. G. Ruggie, "Taking Embedded Liberalism Global: The Corporate Connection," in D. Held & M. Koenig-Archibugi (eds.), *Taming Globalization: Frontiers of Governance* (Cambridge Polity Press, 2003), p. 93.

27 Robert L. Howse, "From Politics to Technocracy – and Back Again: The Fate of the Multilateral Trading Regime," 96 *American Journal of International Law* (2002) 94, at 97.

28 Tomer Broude, "At the End of the Yellow Brick Road: International Economic Law Research in Times of Uncertainty," in Douglas Arner, Isabella Bunn, and Colin B. Picker (eds.), *International Economic Law: The State and Future of the Discipline* (Hart, 2008).

29 See Anne-Marie Slaughter, Andrew S. Tulumello, and Stepan Wood, "International Law and International Relations Theory: A New Generation of Interdisciplinary Scholarship," 92 *American Journal of International Law* (1998) 367, at 370.

A recurring theme in the first two parts is the role of power in international economic law making. These are exercises in the study of sausage making – sometimes with unexpected conclusions. Meredith Kolsky Lewis argues that the outcomes of asymmetrical trade negotiations between powerful actors such as the United States or the EU, on one hand, and weaker states, on the other, can indirectly prejudice the legal situation of even less powerful third parties in formally separate relationships or subsequent negotiations. For example, the terms of the Australia–United States Free Trade Agreement (AUSFTA),[30] in which Australia served as the weaker, "term-taking" party, have spilled over into the substance and procedure of regulatory coordination between Australia and New Zealand (a dyad in which Australia serves as the stronger party) under the Australia–New Zealand Closer Economic Relations Trade Agreement (ANZCERTA).[31] In an unrelated example, members of the Pacific Island Forum have had the legal options available to them in their negotiations with the EU effectively constrained by legal arrangements with Australia and New Zealand (the latter now serving as the stronger party). Thus, asymmetrical trade arrangements that might be justified under contract theory as freely entered into by both parties nevertheless suffer from flawed legitimacy, because they limit the legal options of third parties without their participation. Lewis sees this as yet another reason why the shift from multilateralization to bilateral or regional trade agreements is problematic.

Kimberlee G. Weatherall also focuses on the way in which politics trumps the text of trade agreements – in this case, the intellectual property rights chapters in U.S. free trade agreements. Her central thesis is that when politics and implementation are factored in, the copyright-related provisions in the AUSFTA – praised by U.S. copyright industry groups – actually achieved little of any significance to extend protection for U.S. right holders, and had unintended and undesirable consequences. By prescribing detailed rules requiring Australia to change its law to match U.S. statutory approaches, Weatherall argues, these provisions have led to resentment in Australia against U.S. dictation, creation of new exceptions to copyright to rebalance Australian law, and resistance to new remedies against online copyright piracy – in effect, delegitimization of strong copyright protection. If, instead of the standard model U.S. FTA intellectual property text, the AUSFTA had used a customized text limited to provisions addressing areas of substantive bilateral difference, the chapter would have generated less criticism and cost. Weatherall traces

[30] Australia–United States Free Trade Agreement (AUSFTA), entry into force, January 1, 2005, WT/REG184.

[31] Australia–New Zealand Closer Economic Relations Trade Agreement (ANZCERTA), entry into force, January 1, 1983, WT/REG111.

similar patterns emerging for the labor and environmental provisions in U.S. FTAs. In 2007, Congress demanded changes to Peru's environmental laws as a condition of approval of the Peru–United States FTA. Weatherall argues that Peru's legislation enacted to implement these changes has been problematic for human rights and the environment, and viewed as illegitimate; here, too, the U.S. agenda for foreign laws may backfire. She suggests that U.S. negotiators pay more attention to what can be achieved by trade agreements – and what cannot.

Politics can interact with international economic law making on several levels simultaneously. This is evident in a few of the volume's component articles, and it is drawn out clearly in Uche Ewelukwa Ofodile's article on the politics of African trade negotiations in the WTO's Doha Round. Ewelukwa provides a detailed analysis of central African proposals and positions in the Doha Round. On this basis, she explains that the political challenges faced by African trade negotiators lie on three levels. First, there is the long-standing face-off with developed countries, which need to be persuaded to change policies detrimental to African development; in this context, African states have to be careful not to trade away concessions too easily. Second, African states now have to consider their negotiating relationships with the emerging economic powerhouses who are no longer classified simply as developing countries, mainly China, India, and Brazil; these have become important markets as well as sources of investment, and their rise has significantly altered the political–economic map faced by African states. Third, there is the challenge of African domestic politics: Progress in trade negotiations is dependent not only on complicated external politics and diplomacy but also on the ability of African governments to enact significant domestic policy reforms, which entails political sacrifices. Ewelukwa's contribution also addresses forward looking, post-Doha steps to be taken by African states, but its significance in the context of this volume is that it provides a detailed case study of multilevel politics in international economic law making, within different power constellations.

Moving away from international trade agreements to the regulation of private international law, Claire R. Kelly examines the law-making process in a relatively understudied institution of international economic law: the United Nations Commission on International Trade Law. UNCITRAL does not deal with state-to-state issues, acting rather as a "soft" forum for the voluntary harmonization of national laws applying to private parties. Nevertheless, as Kelly shows in this case study, politics holds sway over negotiation processes, as France and the United States have significant differences over the formulation of UNCITRAL's rules of procedure, especially over the meaning of consensus, and the participation of nonstate actors. What is the political explanation for these clashing positions? Interestingly, its sources can be found in legal environments. On one hand, the United States and France have different legal traditions, not least in commercial law, and UNCITRAL, although soft law, might force a change upon them. Therefore, the preservation of particular national legal regimes becomes a political interest and UNCITRAL's rules of procedure become the rules of international law making. On the other hand – or in conjunction – the different national positions reflect diverging conceptions of the political legitimacy of the rules that will emerge from the process, with France focusing on state consent and the United States on nonstate participation. In discussing these competing explanations – each of which presents an interesting nexus between law and international politics, ever the contest over both power and legitimacy[32] – Kelly's contribution also shows a key difficulty in the work of any researcher interested in the politics of international economic law: namely the opaqueness of the interests and political processes that inform negotiating positions.

Similar expressions of power politics are evident in the studies relating to investment protection treaties. Marc Bungenberg, in his analysis of the development of EU investment treaty policy, presents a particularly complex, multilevel interaction between law and politics, engaging national interests, community interests, and global regulatory competition. To promote the protection of European investments abroad – in competition with U.S. and other investments – the EU will gain new legal competences under the Lisbon treaty, at the expense of member states that are loath to lose their powers. The Lisbon bargain grants unclear degrees of exclusive and shared competences between the EU and its member states. In aviation policy, the Commission managed to strong-arm states into accepting a de facto exclusive competence to conclude open skies agreements. Will it be similarly successful in the area of investment? This depends on the myriad legal and political factors that Bungenberg presents. He also discusses the politicization of the EU's Common Commercial Policy through linkage to external policy aims that will be evident in the interinstitutional political game, with the European Parliament's increased involvement already reflected in demands for human rights conditionality in investment protection treaties and chapters.

Axel Berger documents a remarkable turnabout in policy, impelled by economics and politics. Whereas developing countries have competed to sign a wave of similar bilateral investment treaties (BITs) with developed countries, China, India, and Brazil have had enough leverage to refrain from signing

[32] Inis L. Claude, *Collective Legitimation as a Political Function of the United Nations*, 20 *International Organization* (1966) 367, 368.

and have kept flexibility for their regimes as foreign direct investment (FDI) host countries. As Berger shows, until recently, China's treaties provided a low standard of substantive investment protection, and no, or limited, access to investor–state dispute settlement. However, as China has accumulated a trade surplus, and a large and growing flow of its own outward FDI, its treaty policy has followed, and the current Chinese model BIT is comparable with the admission-model BITs of European countries. China has hegemonically introduced these provisions in treaties signed with capital-importing developing countries as a "pro-active undertaking aimed at protecting Chinese outward FDI," and it has upgraded its treaties with developed countries (although still not taking on the same level of obligation as its developed country partners). Does this mean that the ongoing China–United States BIT negotiations will succeed? Berger finds their prospects still bleak, as China's recent change still leaves a substantial gap between the maximum China is likely to agree to and the minimum that the U.S. business and political community will accept.

Lauge Skovgaard Poulsen contrasts the design of South–South with North–South bilateral investment treaties (BITs). The question is whether South–South BITs are less deep than their North–South counterparts with respect to two key provisions: national treatment and the opportunity to repatriate profits. He finds that they are: BITs involving only poor countries are less likely to include national treatment terms, and more likely to impose restrictions on the repatriation of profits, than are BITs involving rich and poor countries. However, Poulsen insists that not too much should be made of this difference, because most-favored-nation provisions largely undermine any latitude that might have otherwise been derived from these differences in BIT design. He attributes this to developing countries' inability to cope with the complexity of these institutions, and their lack of a forward-looking strategy with respect to their design. One implication is that, given the web of South–South and North–South BITs in place, a multilateral effort, such as the ill-fated Multilateral Agreement on Investment, might have yielded much the same outcome in a more efficient manner.

In the shadow of the well-developed fields of international trade and investment protection, the study of interactions between law and politics in the field of international finance has been relatively ignored. However, the financial crisis of 2008, along with shifts in contemporary investment patterns, has shown that this neglect is unjustified. Yvonne C. L. Lee discusses the politics of sovereign wealth funds (SWFs), particularly the political aspects of "Western" reactions to the rise of "non-Western" SWFs as investors on a global strategic scale. Setting out the historical and legal contexts from a critical perspective, Lee shows not only how political considerations can override good economic sense, but also how political power differentials can influence the formation of international economic law. According to Lee, in its resort to sovereignty–security concerns and arguments, the SWF debate demonstrates a politicization – or deeconomization, if you will – of key global economic issues. At the same time, the economic theory that underwrites international economic law is itself not free of political considerations, reflecting Western neoliberal sensibilities. However, much of this is the result of protectionist economic concerns, couched in political rhetoric. A vicious circle between politics and economics therefore emerges, impeding the establishment of an international law norm governing SWFs and their investments. As a step toward building greater cooperation and achieving consensus, Lee proposes a practical and nondiscriminatory "best practices" type of regime for SWFs.

Douglas Arner sets out his own perspective on the financial crisis of 2007–2009, against the background of five central elements of economic cooperation – first, economic coordination; second, trade arrangements (including arrangements for trade in services); third, macroeconomic policy standard setting and monitoring; fourth, appropriate financial stability and development arrangements to prevent and resolve financial crises; and fifth, sustainable development. Arner tracks the handling of these elements through three eras of financial law, from the postwar era to the present. He tells the story of the financial crisis, from its roots, through the September 2009 economic summit at which the G-20 displaced the G-7. Arner argues that the outlines of a system are emerging, with the G-20 handling policy coordination (assisted by the United Nations, or UN, on climate change), the WTO handling trade, and the UN and multilateral development banks handling sustainable development coordination and assistance. In macroeconomic policy, the G-20 coordinates, the Financial Stability Forum makes international standards, and the International Monetary Fund handles monitoring (likely to shift to peer review in the Financial Stability Board); liquidity is still ensured through a patchwork of bilateral arrangements. Soft law cooperation has proved to be ineffective, but the G-20 is still unlikely to adopt a formal treaty on coordination, or to fold financial regulation into the WTO framework. The current global financial crisis marks the end of the period of hegemonic relations in international financial law, argues Arner, and a successor regime to ensure financial stability has yet to emerge.

The proliferation of international economic treaties over the past quarter century, both in investment and trade, has become a hallmark of the field, bearing with it a host of political questions. Why are these treaties made? How do they interact, in terms of institutional politics and values, with other regimes and with the multilateral level of economic regulation? What are the political forces, interest groups, and processes that influence their legal content? How politicized is their operation and implementation? What is their impact on political relations? We have already seen a number of contributions that address these questions in particular political contexts. Moreover, in trade, the rise of regional trade agreements (RTAs) has led to fragmentation within international economic law between the multilateral trading system (General Agreement on Tariffs and Trade–WTO), on one hand, and the bilateral and regional systems that constitute the "Spaghetti Bowl," on the other. In the area of trade dispute settlement, this produces a set of thorny legal questions relating to the allocation of jurisdiction between the WTO dispute settlement system and RTA dispute settlement, and the effect of rules and rulings produced under one treaty on the dispute settlement system of another.

Henry Gao and C. L. Lim explore this, discussing some of the ways in which doctrinaire legal questions intersect with sensitive political questions. On the legal side of things, they contend that the doctrinal approaches taken so far to this problem, both by the trade negotiators and trade tribunals (primarily the WTO dispute settlement system), as well as by researchers, build on a public international law toolbox that is ill-suited to the scale and nature of the problem. As an alternative, they propose a turn to a *private* international law toolbox, employing common conflict-of-laws techniques, specifically choice-of-law techniques, which would allocate jurisdiction and resolve questions of applicable law in similar ways regardless of the forum before which the dispute has been brought. Furthermore, the current situation of relative legal uncertainty is rife with disruptive political dynamics: institutional competition between the WTO and RTAs, unnecessary litigious tensions between states, and most centrally, clashes between trade law and value-based issue areas such as environmental protection and labor rights. Gao and Lim suggest that a private international law approach would circumvent – if not solve – these political difficulties and permit the economic legal system to function toward its goals. Of course this brings to mind Brainerd Currie's critique of the conflict-of-laws system as mechanistic, depriving judges of the power and capacity to adjudicate.[33] At the current stage of development of international economic law, however, this might be a necessary step.

The contribution by Gao and Lim demonstrates how "the politics of (international economic) law" encompasses international judicial politics, that is, the institutional political considerations that play a role in guiding both the

33 "No other goal being apparent, we have, in the construction of the machine, given uniformity of result primacy over all other considerations"; Brainerd Currie, *Selected Essays on the Conflict of Laws* (Duke University Press, 1963), p. 138.

outcomes and overt rationales of international tribunals. Nevertheless, judicial decision makers also have political stakes to consider vis-à-vis political institutions, other tribunals, disputants, states in general, and interested parties in the broadest of senses. Marc L. Busch and Krzysztof J. Pelc tackle some of these political relationships with the judiciary. In their article on the politics of "judicial economy" in the WTO, they delve into "sausage making," not of laws or treaties but of panel reports. Busch and Pelc analyze this little-known, but widely used, issue-avoidance technique by which panels rule not to rule on a given issue of law. Their analysis shows that WTO panels craft their rulings with a sophisticated eye turned not only to the litigants, but to the wider membership. Busch and Pelc find that panels are more likely to exercise judicial economy where nondisputing governments, intervening as third parties, offer "mixed" as opposed to partisan testimony. The key is that, because this testimony comes at the expense of influencing which side prevails, it is taken as a credible signal of the WTO membership's ambivalence about the precedential value of a broader (as opposed to a more narrow) ruling. In this sense, the practice of judicial economy reveals that international economic tribunals are politically savvy.

The final contributions discuss the use of international trade and investment law in the pursuit of noneconomic foreign policy. Moshe Hirsch focuses on a legal device with obvious political uses: the rules of origin used to determine where products legally originate, for the purposes of trade regimes that discriminate based on product origin. An origin rule can send a message about political claims – as when the EU refused to accept products made in Israeli settlements in the Gaza Strip as "Israeli" for the purposes of trade benefits. Technical and incomprehensible origin rules are often manipulated to favor or disfavor particular exporters; the WTO Agreement on Rules of Origin cannot effectively prevent such tactics, and it does not cover the fast-growing network of rules of origin for preferential trade agreements. Hirsch urges enhanced discipline to curb political manipulation and promote stability in commercial relations. Nonetheless, he also urges exceptional action to permit desirably political origin rules, such as rules that allow content in Egypt and Israel to cumulate for purposes of preferential access to the U.S. market, building economic cooperation between former political enemies.

Perry S. Bechky examines the politics of divestment, with a focus on U.S. divestment from Sudan and Iran. As in Bungenberg's examination of the EU's investment policy, the politics–law interaction in this area takes place on three levels: global, national (federal), and state. At the global level, one state's decision to divest may prove ineffective if not supported by other states, who may in fact challenge the legality of such measures under international economic law principles (such as in the WTO). The political game Bechky focuses on is within the United States. Some U.S. states have pushed the envelope of their authority into foreign policy through the use of their economic power to invest; this has met with legislative debates at the federal level, particularly in legislative debates in Congress, whether state divestment should be encouraged or rather preempted. In the case of Sudan, these have resulted in the Sudan Accountability and Divestment Act, known as SADA,[34] which is federal legislation that establishes a space of "dialogic federalism" in which states can express their foreign policy preferences under the aegis of the federal – in spite of the Administration's protest in the form of a Presidential "signing statement" that the SADA is without prejudice to the federal government's "exclusive authority to conduct foreign relations."[35] In the case of Iran, Bechky suggests, this meeting of minds and interests between states and Congress might not overpower the President. In short, this study shows that the determinative politics of divestment – a significant issue in international economics – are ultimately local.

UNDERSTANDING THE POLITICS OF INTERNATIONAL ECONOMIC LAW: THE WAY FORWARD

The chapters collected in this volume provide an indication of the many ways in which politics inform international economic law, and vice versa. As already noted, this interaction is far from monolithic. "Theories of everything" might be helpful in shaping world views, but they will never capture the complexities of legal and institutional structures that populate the global economy. This does not mean that the study of the politics of international economic law is an eclectic, undisciplined area of research. On the contrary, there are many organizing principles that can easily be discerned, such as the respective roles of economic and political power, interest groups, legal competence, and so on. If, however, we are to extract a single lesson from this collection of studies, it is that any understanding of the politics–law nexus must rely on detailed, rigorous, and empirical research, even if its focus is on the law. We hope the chapters included in this volume will prove inspirational in this regard.

34 Pub. L. No. 110–174, 21 Stat. 2516 (2007).

35 "Statement by President George W. Bush upon Signing S. 2271," 43 *Weekly Compilation of Presidential Documents* 1646 (December 31, 2007).

PART I

THE POLITICS OF LAW MAKING IN INTERNATIONAL TRADE

2

The Politics and Indirect Effects of Asymmetrical Bargaining Power in Free Trade Agreements

Meredith Kolsky Lewis

1. INTRODUCTION

The World Trade Organization (WTO) has been, and continues to be, shaped in its agreements and institutional foci in significant part by political pressures emanating from its members, particularly those able to wield the most influence. Rather than being an institution with the singular focus of achieving free trade among all members, the WTO comprises a complex set of agreements, many of which represent a politically driven compromise among members as to how to manage trade rather than to liberalize it.[1] Although the state of WTO liberalization reflects positions agreed to in part as a result of political realities, the reach of politics is more significant in the context of bilateral trade negotiations. Indeed, what members cannot accomplish through the WTO they may try to achieve through free trade agreements (FTAs), particularly with politically or economically weaker trade partners. In the case of the United States, FTAs have been used as an opportunity to impose provisions favored by domestic constituents – such as strengthened intellectual property provisions and labor and environment clauses – that it has not been able to get WTO members to agree to collectively in the multilateral forum. A similar phenomenon has occurred with respect to the European Union (EU)

[1] See, e.g., Bagwell and Staiger, "Reciprocity, Non-Discrimination and Preferential Agreements in the Multilateral Trading System," National Bureau of Economic Research Working Paper 5932 (1997), at 1 (noting that the GATT establishes goals of reciprocity and nondiscrimination, but not of free trade).

Note: I owe thanks to the participants of the ASIL International Economic Law Interest Group 2008 Biennial Conference for their feedback on this chapter, and particularly owe gratitude to Joel Trachtman for his helpful comments. I also thank the editors and peer reviewers of this volume for their valuable suggestions.

and its FTA partners.[2] For countries with less bargaining power, the WTO's multilateral setting provides some buffer from power politics[3] in the form of the consensus decision-making practice[4] and the disproportionate number of developing and least-developed countries. Countries with limited bargaining power will often find themselves in a relatively more vulnerable position in the bilateral or even plurilateral context.[5] For poorer countries, this may translate into giving significant concessions in FTA negotiations out of concern that aid or other preferential treatment will be withdrawn.[6]

In critiquing FTAs as a negative for the multilateral trading system, commentators have addressed numerous issues, including the potential for such agreements to be more trade diverting than trade creating;[7] that FTA negotiations necessarily detract resources and attention from multilateral negotiations;[8] that the plethora of regional arrangements is undermining the most-favored nation (MFN) principle;[9] and arguments that particular agreements have unfortunate

[2] Harpaz, "When East Meets West: Approximation of Laws in the EU-Mediterranean Context," 43 *Common Market L. Rev.* (2006) 993, at 999 (discussing the expectation by the EU that in connection with its European Neighbourhood Policy, its Mediterranean neighbors will unilaterally "approximate" or align their legislation to some degree to that of the EU rather than having the parties engage in a cooperative process of give and take).

[3] See Mattoo and Wunsch-Vincent, "Pre-empting Protectionism in Services: The GATS and Outsourcing," 7 *J. Int'l Econ. L.* (2004) 765, at 787 ("in a world of unequal bargaining power, multilaterally agreed formulae ... are likely to produce a more favourable outcome for the weaker party than bilateral negotiations.").

[4] See Abbott, "A New Dominant Trade Species Emerges: Is Bilateralism a Threat?," 10 *J. Int'l Econ. L.* (2007) 571, at 583 (arguing that "weaker actors have a better chance to have their voices heard, and their policy choices taken into account" in the multilateral consensus-based system).

[5] See, e.g., Hirsch, "The Sociology of International Economic Law: Sociological Analysis of the Regulation of Regional Agreements in the World Trading System," 19 *Eur J. Int'l L.* (2008) 277, at 295–296 (identifying the social conflict conception of international economic law as disfavoring FTAs because developing states will achieve better outcomes through the collective action of the WTO than through FTA negotiations that will reflect the power asymmetries between the parties). Bagwell and Staiger conclude that FTAs prevent the implementation of an efficient multilateral agreement based on the GATT pillars of nondiscrimination and reciprocity. See Bagwell and Staiger, "An Economic Theory of GATT," Wisconsin Madison – Social Systems Working Paper 15 (June 1998), at 33.

[6] For example, as will be subsequently discussed, the Pacific Island Forum (PIF) countries signed the PACER agreement with Australia and New Zealand in part out of fear that the latter would terminate the agreement known as SPARTECA, pursuant to which the PIF countries receive largely duty-free access to the Australian and New Zealand markets and do not have to provide preferential market access in return.

[7] J. Viner, *The Customs Union Issue* (1950).

[8] See, e.g., Abbott, *supra* note 4, at 581.

[9] See, e.g., Sutherland et al., "The Future of the WTO, Addressing Institutional Challenges in the New Millenium," Report by the Consultative Board to Director-General Supachai Panitchpakdi (2005).

terms such as TRIPS-plus provisions (where TRIPS stands for the Agreement on Trade-Related Aspects of Intellectual Property Rights). To these critiques this chapter adds an additional reason to disfavor FTAs by arguing that FTAs can have a further negative effect of constraining the future policy choices of countries that are *not* party to the original FTAs and therefore did not have the opportunity to negotiate or bargain with respect to terms that later end up having spillover effects on these nonparties.

This chapter argues that in addition to the direct impacts of political pressure the weaker party to an FTA experiences in the form of "take it or leave it" terms, those terms can also cause additional difficulties in an indirect way, including those for nonparties to the agreement, by effectively constraining policy choices outside the context of the original FTA. In this context "weaker members"[10] can include developed countries as well when their FTA partners are more powerful,[11] as is the case with Australia relative to the United States and to some degree New Zealand relative to Australia.[12]

This chapter uses examples from Oceania to illustrate the negative externalities that earlier-negotiated FTAs can have on nonparties to those agreements. Using two specific regional examples as illustrations, the chapter argues that, as

[10] In this chapter the term "weak" is used to describe countries with relatively less bargaining power in trade negotiations than the countries with which they are negotiating, and "strong" or "powerful" is used to describe countries with relatively more bargaining power.

[11] See, e.g., Abbott, *supra* note 4, at 571, noting that the "PTA negotiating environment strongly favors powerful economic actors like the United States and European Union, which are largely dictating terms to developing (and developed) countries." See also Harpaz, *supra* note 2.

[12] For examples of developed countries in the "weaker country" position, see, e.g., Crump, "Global Trade Policy Development in a Two-Track System," 9 *J. Int'l Econ. L.* (2006) 487 (identifying examples of Singapore capitulating to demands of Australia; Singapore giving in to demands of the United States; and Australia reluctantly accepting terms dictated by the United States in their respective FTA negotiations). Crump provides a useful example in the context of the types of rules of origin (ROO) provisions chosen in various FTAs. In 1983, New Zealand and Australia chose a value-added ROO system for their trade agreement (the Australia New Zealand Closer Economic Relationship Trade Agreement, or ANZCERTA). Subsequently, when Australia negotiated its FTA with Singapore, Singapore pushed for a change in tariff classification or transformation measure for ROO, but Australia insisted on the value-added ROO methodology used in ANZCERTA. On the flip side, when Australia later negotiated its FTA with the United States and was the weaker of the two parties, it capitulated to U.S. demands for the type of ROO methodology Australia had rejected when it had been proposed by Singapore. Ibid., at 502. The phenomenon of FTA provisions having spillover effects for others is akin to findings of "regulatory export" from stronger to weaker countries, in which the United States and the EU tend to be the exporters and a wide range of other countries the importers. See, e.g., Raustiala, "The Architecture of International Cooperation: Transgovernmental Networks & the Future of International Law," 43 *Va. J. Int'l L.* (2002) 1; Slaughter, "Sovereignty and Power in a Networked World Order," 40 *Stan. J. Int'l L.* (2004) 283, at 293–297 (discussing Raustiala's findings).

a result of the power imbalances in many FTA negotiations and of path dependence among FTAs, the terms agreed to in earlier FTAs can subsequently constrain negotiating space and policy options for other trading partners and political allies.[13]

In the first case, Australia succumbed to the United States' superior bargaining power in the Australia–United States Free Trade Agreement (AUSFTA)[14] negotiations by agreeing to various exceptions to liberalization commitments and to terms with which it was not happy. The success of U.S. pressure has resulted in changes in Australian law. Although these changes clearly have direct effects on Australia, they also have repercussions for New Zealand, because under the Australia–New Zealand Closer Economic Relations Trade Agreement (ANZCERTA or CER) and related treaties,[15] Australia and New Zealand engage jointly in certain regulatory activities and seek broadly to create a harmonized business environment.[16] Thus, Australia's agreement under the AUSFTA to impose heightened intellectual property protections and to enact regulations on pharmaceuticals has potential indirect effects on New Zealand, which does not impose such protections or regulations. Although New Zealand would not otherwise adopt such regulations, it will now be futile on the part of New Zealand to try to persuade Australia to revert to its previous regulations, because of the bind established by the AUSFTA terms all but imposed by the United States.[17]

In the second illustrative case, Pacific Island Forum (PIF) members have very little bargaining power relative to Australia and New Zealand, and they have had agreement terms essentially dictated to them by their larger, wealthier neighbors.[18] The terms of the Pacific Agreement on Closer Economic Relations (PACER)[19] are now resulting in the PIF countries' experiencing pressure

[13] In addition to these effects there are, of course, the more visible examples of U.S.- or EU-drafted template agreements being virtually imposed upon future generations of partners to trade and investment agreements.

[14] Australia–United States Free Trade Agreement (AUSFTA), WT/REG184, entry into force January 1, 2005.

[15] The ANZCERTA comprises a number of instruments, including the Trans-Tasman Mutual Recognition Arrangement, the Trans-Tasman Travel Arrangement, and several other documents; these may be accessed at http://www.mfat.govt.nz/Foreign-Relations/Australia/1-CER/0-cer-timeline.php.

[16] Australia New Zealand Closer Economic Relations Trade Agreement (ANZCERTA), WT/REG111, entry into force January 1, 1983.

[17] This can also be seen as a form of path dependence. For a discussion of sequencing path dependence see Hathaway, "Path Dependence in the Law: The Course and Pattern of Legal Change in a Common Law System," 86 *Iowa L. Rev.* (2001) 601, at 617–622.

[18] In particular the Pacific Agreement on Closer Economic Relations, discussed herein.

[19] See the Pacific Agreement on Closer Economic Relations, made at Nauru, August 18, 2001, entry into force October 3, 2002, which is discussed herein. PACER is an umbrella agreement

from these traditional allies[20] and are constraining the PIF countries in deciding how to approach negotiations with the EU to form potential economic partnership agreements.[21]

The negative externalities that result when FTA terms are imposed by stronger FTA partners on weaker ones create legitimacy concerns about FTAs above and beyond those already identified in the literature. It is problematic that countries not party to an FTA or its negotiations nonetheless find their policy options negatively constrained. This is an issue the WTO has not considered, but it would be worthy of attention in the context of attempting to reform General Agreement on Tariffs and Trade (GATT) Article XXIV.

2. THE AUSFTA AND ITS INDIRECT IMPLICATIONS FOR NEW ZEALAND

After several years of negotiations, the AUSFTA came into effect on January 1, 2005. Although the agreement was widely supported by Australian businesses, the negotiating process[22] and substantive provisions have been criticized on a number of grounds. The most frequent criticisms have been addressed at the TRIPS-plus intellectual property provisions the AUSFTA contains, provisions relating to Australia's Pharmaceutical Benefits Scheme, and the effects these provisions collectively may have on the availability of low-cost pharmaceutical products in Australia.[23] However, the agreement has also been criticized more

rather than an FTA itself. It contains provisions relating to the formation of the Pacific Island Countries Trade Agreement (PICTA), and in this way Australia and New Zealand, although not parties to PICTA, have influenced that agreement by means of the PACER Agreement. For the text of PACER see http://www.forumsec.org/UserFiles/File/PACER_Text.pdf.

20 See generally Kelsey, "Big Brothers Behaving Badly: The Implications for the Pacific Islands of the Pacific Agreement on Closer Economic Relations (PACER)," Interim Report, commissioned by the Pacific Network on Globalisation (2004).

21 See Part III of this chapter.

22 See, e.g., Mitchell, "The Australia–United States Free Trade Agreement," in Laurence Boulle et al. (eds.), *Challenges to Multilateral Trade: The Impact of Bilateral, Preferential and Regional Agreements* (2008) 115, at 117–118 (criticizing the limited parliamentary scrutiny treaties receive in Australia, and the limited role interested stakeholders had in the treaty negotiating process).

23 See, e.g., Faunce, Johnston, and Bambrick, "The Trans-Tasman Therapeutic Products Authority: Potential AUSFTA Impacts on Safety and Cost-Effectiveness Regulation for Medicines and Medical Devices in New Zealand," 37 *Victoria U. Wellington L. Rev.* (2006) 365 (hereinafter Faunce et al., "Trans-Tasman"); Faunce and Lexchin, "'Linkage' Pharmaceutical Evergreening in Canada and Australia," 4:8 *Australia and New Zealand Health Policy* (2007), accessible at http://www.anzhealthpolicy.com/content/4/1/8 (hereinafter Faunce and Lexchin, "Evergreening"); Mercurio, "The Impact of the Australia–United States Free Trade Agreement on the Provision of Health Services in Australia," 26 *Whittier L. Rev.* (2005) 1051; Chalmers, "Evergreen or Deciduous? Australian Trends in Relation to the 'Evergreening' of Patents," 30 *Melb.*

generally as being a bad deal for Australia. Andrew Mitchell put it bluntly:

> The AUSFTA provides an illustration of the outcomes that countries with relatively little bargaining and economic power can expect from an FTA with the US. It also serves as a warning of how even an economically successful developed country may end up sacrificing its welfare, public policies, and democratic processes in a dogged pursuit to cement relations with the United States, in a manner that would be unlikely in the vigorous negotiating environment of the WTO.[24]

One might dismiss such criticisms on the basis that Australia was aware of its limited bargaining power and nonetheless determined that it was worthwhile to enter into an FTA with the United States, even though it had to accept certain terms it did not like. Although this may be the case, this chapter focuses on a separate point: that Australia's decision to accept the U.S.'s terms in the AUSFTA affects not just Australia but also its neighbor across the Tasman. To the extent that the AUSFTA results in higher prices for pharmaceuticals in Australia, for example, New Zealanders' access to affordable pharmaceuticals is also potentially at stake as a result of the relationship between Australia and New Zealand that was established in the Australia–New Zealand CER and its flow-on agreements. In particular, because Australia has committed to certain provisions in the AUSFTA, it will seek to have relevant arrangements with New Zealand conform to its existing commitments. New Zealand is thus a victim of path-dependent externalities in the form of regulations Australia has agreed to adopt by virtue of its negotiations with the United States – negotiations in which New Zealand had no opportunity to participate.

A. *AUSFTA and Pharmaceuticals Trade*

The AUSFTA has the potential to affect Australian pharmaceutical prices in a couple of ways. First, certain TRIPS-plus intellectual property provisions have implications for medicines.[25] In particular, relative to TRIPS, the agreement

U. L. Rev. (2006) 29; Kingsbury, "Intellectual Property Provisions in Bilateral and Regional Free Trade Agreements: What Should New Zealand Expect from a New Zealand/United States Free Trade Agreement?," 10 *NZ Bus. L. Q.* (2004) 222.

[24] Mitchell, *supra* note 21, at 116.

[25] The AUSFTA intellectual property commitments are in Chapter 17 of the agreement and in accompanying side letters. Provisions with specific implications for the provision of low-cost medicines include AUSFTA Art 17.9.8 (effectively extending the patent term for pharmaceuticals); AUSFTA Art. 17.9.7 (limiting compulsory licensing of patented pharmaceuticals to the extent provided in TRIPS); and AUSFTA Art. 17.9.4 (limiting parallel importing). See also Kingsbury, *supra* note 23, at 233.

provides narrower avenues for allowing compulsory licensing; an expanded scope for what is patentable; and minimum and extended terms of data protection and data exclusivity. It also prohibits parallel importation.[26] It additionally contains an "evergreening" notification provision,[27] which requires that drug manufacturers be notified of any upcoming generic drug entry into the market, and further requires that approval be denied to such generic drugs when a patent is "claimed" by a manufacturer that has not "consented or acquiesced" to the entry into the market of the generic drug.[28] Although Australia introduced anti-evergreening provisions along with the AUSFTA implementing legislation to combat the possibility that this provision would lead to an increase in drug prices, such provisions were strongly criticized by the United States and it remains to be seen what would happen if a dispute arose over the operation of the Pharmaceutical Benefits Scheme.[29]

In addition to the TRIPS-plus provisions, the AUSFTA requires regulatory dialogue between the U.S. Food and Drug Administration and the Australian Therapeutic Goods Association to speed up approvals of "innovative" medical products and emphasizes a linkage between innovation and high-quality health care.[30] Pursuant to AUSFTA, Australia had to make changes to the Pharmaceutical Benefits Scheme, including adding a review procedure of the Pharmaceutical Benefits Advisory Committee (PBAC) drug-listing rejections.[31] Although no changes were directly required to Australia's system of reference pricing, the United States had as a negotiating goal that that system be dismantled.[32] Because of this, concerns have been raised that the combination of the various requirements will ultimately force Australia to abandon this cost-effective measure of setting drug prices.[33]

[26] Lopert and Rosenbaum, "What is Fair? Choice, Fairness, and Transparency in Access to Prescription Medicines in the United States and Australia," 35 *J. L. Med. & Ethics* (2007) 643, at 650 n. 50.

[27] AUSFTA Art. 17.10.4(a) and (b).

[28] Ibid.; see also Faunce et al., "Trans-Tasman," *supra* note 23, at 368–369 for a discussion of evergreening.

[29] Faunce et al., "Trans-Tasman," *supra* note 23, at 371–372. In the event a dispute were to arise, Faunce argues that to the extent the AUSFTA is textually ambiguous, Australia could rely on the anti-evergreening amendments as evidence of its expectation that Art. 17.10.4 would not lead to higher pharmaceutical prices under the Pharmaceutical Benefits Scheme. See ibid. for a discussion of the merits of the potential legal arguments that could be raised.

[30] AUSFTA Annex 2C(1), 2C(4).

[31] Faunce, "Reference Pricing for Pharmaceuticals: Is the Australia–United States Free Trade Agreement Affecting Australia's Pharmaceutical Benefits Scheme?," 187:4 *Med. J. Australia* (2007) 240, at 240–242.

[32] Ibid.

[33] Ibid.

B. CER – A *Unique Relationship*

Australia and New Zealand have a long history of economic partnership. They entered into a limited trade agreement in 1933,[34] and they subsequently formed the original "NAFTA" – the New Zealand Australia Free Trade Agreement – in 1965.[35] This agreement removed 80 percent of the tariffs on trans-Tasman trade, but some restrictions remained. The remaining barriers included Australia's closed market for New Zealand dairy products and New Zealand's quantitative restrictions and various export incentives. In the early 1980s, agreement was finally reached to remove these obstacles and the countries entered into the highly comprehensive ANZCERTA (commonly referred to as CER) in 1983.

The parties subsequently entered into a protocol to accelerate the removal of all tariff barriers by 1990, which was a number of years earlier than called for in the CER Agreement.[36] In connection with CER, the two countries have gone well beyond tariff liberalization and have contemplated – and in some cases already enacted – various forms of regulatory harmonization with respect to customs and quarantine procedures.[37] In 1993, the two countries entered into the Trans-Tasman Mutual Recognition Arrangement (TTMRA), which provides (subject to limited exceptions) that goods that may lawfully be sold in either country may be lawfully sold in the other,[38] and (also subject to limited exceptions) that an individual licensed to practice a given occupation in one of the countries is entitled to practice the equivalent occupation in the other country.[39] Although therapeutic goods legislation (such as Australia's Therapeutic Goods Act 1989 and New Zealand's Medicines Act 1981) is currently exempted from the TTMRA, the TTMRA provides that it is a goal to ultimately incorporate therapeutic goods into the agreement.

CER is a unique arrangement, among other reasons, because it has led to a significant degree of harmonization between Australia and New Zealand.[40]

[34] Trade Agreement of September 5, 1933.

[35] New Zealand Australia Free Trade Agreement, August 31, 1965.

[36] Protocol to the Australia New Zealand Closer Economic Relations Trade Agreement on Acceleration of Free Trade in Goods, Art. 1.1.

[37] See, e.g., Exchange of Letters and Joint Understanding of Harmonisation of Customs Policies and Procedures, August 16, 1988; Protocol on Harmonisation of Quarantine Administrative Procedures to the Australia New Zealand Closer Economic Relations Trade Agreement, August 18, 1988.

[38] Trans-Tasman Mutual Recognition Arrangement Part IV, accessible at http://www.dfat.gov.au/geo/new_zealand/ttmra.pdf.

[39] Ibid., Part V.

[40] See, e.g., Rennie, "Competition Provisions in Free Trade Agreements: Unique Responses to Bilateral Needs or Derivative Developments in International Competition Policy," 15 *Int. T.L.R.* (2009) 57, at 64 (noting unique harmonization provisions of ANZCERTA).

It was formed with the belief that agreeing to joint procedures and practices would reduce transaction costs and enhance economic growth for both economies. Although there is often an expectation that the unified practice will more strongly resemble whatever Australia's system has been, rather than New Zealand's,[41] New Zealand presumably has been willing to accept this bias in the instances where it has signed on to specific harmonization measures, in part because of the similarities between Australia and New Zealand's regulatory approaches. However, New Zealand would have made its decisions based on Australia's regulatory standards and procedures at the time. New Zealand likely would not have contemplated that Australia would subsequently significantly alter certain parts of its regulatory framework pursuant to a future FTA, rendering aspects of its regulatory structure significantly different from their previously similar approach. Nevertheless, because of New Zealand's relatively weaker position with respect to Australia – and Australia's relative lack of bargaining power vis-à-vis the United States – Australia accepted the terms of AUSFTA notwithstanding its commitments under ANZCERTA and the implicit assumptions (of similar regulatory approaches) underlying those commitments.

C. AUSFTA *Implications for New Zealand*

As already noted, Australia and New Zealand have engaged in a range of harmonization efforts as a result of specific CER commitments or more indirectly as a result of the general integration goal of CER. To the extent that Australia has changed or will change certain of its regulatory frameworks pursuant to its obligations under the AUSFTA, New Zealand may find itself under pressure to do the same in the future. The most salient example of this phenomenon lies in the context of the regulation of therapeutic products (comprising medicines, medical devices, and complementary medicines and dietary supplements that have therapeutic uses).[42]

In December 2003, New Zealand and Australia entered into an agreement to negotiate the creation of a joint agency to be called the Australia New Zealand Therapeutic Products Authority (ANZTPA), which would replace Australia's Therapeutic Goods Authority and New Zealand's equivalent, the Medicines and Medical Devices Safety Authority (known as Medsafe).[43] ANZTPA would

41 Compare Harpaz, *supra* note 2, with respect to EC–Israel relations.

42 See generally Faunce et al., "Trans-Tasman," *supra* note 23.

43 Agreement between the Government of Australia and the Government of New Zealand for the Establishment of a Joint Scheme for the Regulation of Therapeutic Products (September 9, 2003), accessible at http://www.anztpa.org/about/treatytext.pdf.

create harmonized regulations for therapeutic products that would apply to both countries. An eventual ANZTPA has been seen by both countries as "a significant step in the further development of a single economic market."[44]

ANZTPA was to have been created by 2006, but the New Zealand Labour-led government (which was subsequently replaced in 2008 with a National-led coalition) did not have the numbers necessary in Parliament to pass a version of the requisite legislation that would satisfy all interested parties.[45] In 2007, the project was officially placed on hold.[46] Nonetheless, the original agreement remains in place and the bill will be revisited once sufficient votes are available.[47]

In this context, significant concern was voiced in New Zealand that ANZTPA would inherit the heightened intellectual property obligations and pharmaceutical manufacturer protections that the United States imposed on Australia's Therapeutic Goods Authority by means of the AUSFTA.[48] New Zealand's Health Committee raised these concerns – and those of New Zealand's Pharmaceutical Management Agency (Pharmac) – in its 2004 report on ANZTPA:[49]

> Pharmac noted a number of concerns . . . including possible increases in the cost of generic drugs . . . and possible increases in patent terms for medicines. In its written submission to us, Pharmac noted that . . . the cost of these latter increases as a flow-on effect of the free trade agreement between Australia and the United States of America could amount to between $85 million and $135 million over 3 years.

As of this writing, it remains to be seen whether Pharmac and the New Zealand Health Committee's concerns will keep ANZTPA on the back burner

44 See "Australia and New Zealand Closer Economic Relations (CER) Ministerial Communique" (December 11, 2004), accessible at http://www.dfat.gov.au/geo/new_zealand/anz_cer/cer_communique_2004.html.

45 New Zealand has a Mixed Member Proportional representation system of government similar to that used in Germany. Therefore unless one political party wins an absolute majority of seats, there is a coalition government comprising two or more parties. Although the members of the coalition will often vote together, this is not the case on every issue. See, e.g., http://www.elections.org.nz/voting/mmp/.

46 State Services Minister Annette King, "Therapeutics Products and Medicines Bill on Hold," Press Release (July 16, 2007), accessible at Http://Www.Beehive.Govt.Nz/Release/Therapeutics+Products+And+Medicines+Bill+Hold.

47 Ibid.

48 Faunce et al., "Trans-Tasman," *supra* note 23, at 367.

49 New Zealand Health Committee, "International Treaty Examination of the Agreement Between the Government of New Zealand and the Government of Australia for the Establishment of a Joint Scheme for the Regulation of Therapeutic Products," (June 2004) 3, quoted in Faunce et al., "Trans-Tasman," *supra* note 23, at 367.

indefinitely. Given the support among some members of Parliament, it seems more likely that at some point the legislation will be passed, the treaty signed, and ANZTPA will become a reality. However, in either case, the terms the United States extracted from Australia in the AUSFTA will affect New Zealand. If plans for ANZTPA were scuttled as a result of the AUSFTA, this would mean that New Zealand felt it had to abandon a harmonization effort it otherwise intended to pursue. If, as is more likely, ANZTPA ultimately comes into being, the effects for New Zealand may be more significant, because it might need to adopt the AUSFTA standards to effectuate the authority – and see costs increase as a result. The political reality for New Zealand is, unfortunately, that Australia will likely be able to dictate the terms of ANZTPA by virtue of its preexisting commitments under the AUSFTA – commitments to a trading partner more powerful than New Zealand. This is a concrete example of a negotiation phenomenon that Oona Hathaway has explained in terms of sequencing path dependence: "The power to set the agenda can thus become, in a very real sense, the power to determine the result."[50]

Thus, in the absence of AUSFTA, New Zealand and Australia had similar regulatory approaches to pharmaceuticals and likely could have harmonized their regulatory schemes relatively easily. Now, however, New Zealand finds itself in a very different situation as a result of the spillover effects of the AUSFTA – an agreement to which it is not a party, in which it had no negotiating role, and from which it receives no benefits.

New Zealand may be faced with preordained AUSFTA terms in a different context as well. The United States is currently seeking to join the Trans-Pacific Strategic Economic Partnership Agreement (also known as the P-4 Agreement), which now comprises New Zealand, Chile, Singapore, and Brunei Darussalam.[51] Initial negotiations on financial services and investment have already been conducted. Further negotiations, geared toward having the United States join the agreement in its entirety, as well as the additional participation of Australia and Peru, were scheduled to occur in March 2009. These negotiations have been put on hold temporarily while the Obama administration conducts a review of its trade policy and decides which of the various FTA negotiations initiated by the Bush administration it wishes to continue to pursue. Although these negotiations have therefore been temporarily delayed, it seems likely this is merely procedural and that the Obama administration will decide to resume the negotiations. With the United States already having

50 Hathaway, *supra* note 17, at 618–619.

51 The Trans-Pacific Strategic Economic Partnership Agreement, WT/REG229 S/C/N/394, entry into force May 28, 2006.

concluded FTAs with Australia, Peru, Chile, and Singapore, it seems highly likely that the United States will expect New Zealand and Brunei Darussalam to agree to at least some of the measures found in the FTAs the United States has with the other expanded P-4 agreement partners.[52]

The AUSFTA therefore provides an example of an FTA in which the weaker party, Australia, has capitulated to TRIPS-plus provision and other terms that WTO members collectively have successfully resisted incorporating into multilateral trade agreements. This may be a bargained-for exchange in the case of Australia and the gains it sought to obtain under the AUSFTA, but the bargaining process did not take into account the negative externalities of these terms impacting New Zealand. It is problematic that New Zealand finds itself with unexpected, undesirable regulatory choices as a result of political power being exercised in an agreement it had no role in negotiating.

Although New Zealand may be the victim of path dependence and FTA politics in the case of flow-on effects of the AUSFTA or in the case of the P-4 expansion, it is on the other side of the equation in the role of a "big brother behaving badly"[53] in the context of the Pacific region, as is discussed in the following section.

3. PICTA, PACER, AND THE ECONOMIC PARTNERSHIP AGREEMENTS: PACIFIC ISLANDS NATIONS BETWEEN A ROCK AND A HARD PLACE

Pacific Islands countries have had historical ties to Europe as a result of colonization, and to Australia and New Zealand largely as a result of sheer proximity.[54] Many countries in the Pacific are a part of the ACP group of countries (Africa, Caribbean, and the Pacific) that comprise former European colonies. The ACP group historically benefited from preferential access to European markets based on the colonial relationships. However, providing preferential access to former colonies to the exclusion of other developing countries was recognized to be a violation of the MFN principle enshrined

[52] Rennie, *supra* note 40, at 71 (noting the path-dependent nature of bilateral FTA provisions whereby terms become a reflection of common practice rather than the particular needs of the parties). In the case of pharmaceuticals protection, the United States has negotiated similar terms to the AUSFTA provisions in its FTA with Korea.

[53] See, generally, Kelsey, *supra* note 20.

[54] The Cook Islands, Niue, and Tokelau are part of the Realm of New Zealand. The Cook Islands and Niue are in free association with New Zealand. Tokelau has taken steps toward free association but has less autonomy than the Cooks or Niue. See http://www.gg.govt.nz/role/constofnz.htm for information regarding New Zealand's constitutional structure.

in GATT Article I. Article I provides in relevant part that "any advantage, favour, privilege or immunity granted by any contracting party to any product originating in or destined for any other country shall be accorded immediately and unconditionally to the like product originating in or destined for the territories of all other contracting parties."[55] It is inconsistent with the MFN principle for Europe to give preferential tariff access to ACP countries while not providing this same access to other WTO members.[56] Furthermore, providing the ACP countries with comprehensive market access to the EU under the arrangements established under the Lomé Conventions did not create a free trade area or areas pursuant to Article XXIV because of the nonreciprocal nature of the arrangements.[57]

As a result of the MFN-inconsistent nature of the historical preferences, the EU sought and successfully received a waiver from the GATT and later the WTO that permitted it to maintain its preferential treatment of the ACP countries notwithstanding its obligations pursuant to Article I GATT, within the Lomé framework. This waiver was extended in 2000, but it ultimately expired in December 2007. As a result, the EU, on the one hand, and the ACP countries, on the other, have had to decide what, if anything, will replace the historical preferences. Without any new agreements, the waiver would expire and the EU would then need to apply its tariff schedules on an MFN basis with respect to the ACP countries. Although other exceptions would apply in certain instances and for certain products by means of the Generalized System of Preferences (GSP) schemes for developing countries and Europe's Everything but Arms program for least developed countries, this coverage would not be comprehensive. For example, sugar, which is one of Fiji's most important exports and which is currently the subject of a protocol to promote such

55 General Agreement on Tariffs and Trade (GATT) Art. I.1.

56 The long-running EC–Bananas dispute has highlighted this inconsistency. See "European Communities – Regime for the Importation, Sale and Distribution of Bananas," WTO Doc. WT/DS27/R/USA (May 22, 1997), panel report.

57 The EC had also attempted to argue to the contrary in the second GATT panel examination of the EC's bananas program. The panel (whose report was not adopted) stated that the lack of reciprocal trade liberalization obligations made the Lomé Convention arrangements "substantially different from those of a free trade area, as defined in the Article XXIV:8(b)." See "EEC – Import Regime for Bananas," WTO Doc. DS38/R (February 11, 1994), panel report, para. 159. The panel noted that if such arrangements did fall within Article XXIV:8(b) there would have been little need for the contracting parties to reach decisions regarding Generalized System of Preferences schemes and the Enabling Clause. Ibid., para. 162. For a detailed discussion of the GATT-era panel reports in the Bananas dispute, see J. H. Mathis, *Regional Trade Agreements in the GATT/WTO: Article XXIV and the Internal Trade Requirement* (2002), at 88–97.

exports,[58] is not included in the EU's GSP scheme.[59] Rather than broaden its GSP scheme coverage to enable the ACP countries to maintain their nonreciprocal market access to the EU, the EU instead proposed that it enter into a series of economic partnership agreements (EPAs) with the ACP countries (in six regional groups)[60] to take the place of the waiver. The concept was that the EPAs would satisfy the definition of free trade areas under GATT Article XXIV,[61] and therefore the tariff treatment granted under such agreements would not need to be extended to other WTO members on an MFN basis and would not be subject to waiver approval. Thus the ACP countries would be able to maintain their existing preferential access to the EU market.

A difficulty for the ACP countries, however, has been that acceding to the EPAs would require them to provide substantial, comprehensive market access to the EU. Previously, under the waiver, the EU provided preferential market access to the ACP states, but it did not demand reciprocal market access in return. Thus, the ACP countries have been faced with a choice: Should they sacrifice their preferential access to the European Union but maintain their own tariffs on goods originating from its members, or should they instead opt to enter an EPA, thus formalizing their preferential access to the European Union but at the cost of having to provide significant new market access in return?[62]

To complicate matters further for Pacific Island countries, once the EU made clear its intention to replace ACP preferences with reciprocal trade arrangements in the form of EPAs, Australia and New Zealand orchestrated the Pacific Agreement on Closer Economic Relations, known as PACER, which

58 The ACP/EU Sugar Protocol is an agreement by which the EU agrees to purchase set quantities of sugar from the ACP countries. It was originally annexed to the Fourth ACP/EU Lomé Convention. Upon the expiry of the Lomé Convention, the protocol was subsequently incorporated into the Cotonou Partnership Agreement, June 23, 2000.

59 See, e.g., Curran, "Response to the Article 'Are the Economic Partnership Agreements a First-Best Outcome for the ACP Countries?' Perez, R. (2006) 40(6)," 41 *JWT* (2007) 243, at 244 (noting that certain products important to ACP countries are excluded even from proposed GSP-plus formulations).

60 There is a Caribbean group, Central African group, East and Southern African Group, South Africa Development Community group, West African group, and a Pacific group.

61 Article XXIV:8(b) defines a free trade area as "a group of two or more customs territories in which the duties and other restrictive regulations of commerce ... are eliminated on substantially all the trade between the constituent territories in products originating in such territories."

62 One analysis has suggested that ACP countries would be better off declining to enter into EPAs and relying instead on the EU's GSP scheme (in the case of developing countries) and Everything but Arms program (in the case of least developed countries). See Perez, "Are the Economic Partnership Agreements a First-Best Optimum for the African Caribbean Pacific Countries?," 40 *JWT* (2006) 999.

calls for fundamental changes to the relationship between the Pacific Islands Forum or PIF countries on the one hand and Australia and New Zealand on the other. If an EPA with the EU is entered into, the PIF countries will likely trigger obligations under PACER to begin negotiating an FTA with Australia and New Zealand. Indeed, several meetings of the PACER parties were held in 2008 and 2009 to discuss when and how to commence negotiations for a future agreement, which is being referred to as "PACER-Plus."[63]

The PIF countries have reason to want to avoid triggering these negotiations. Although the Pacific's imports from Europe are not particularly substantial,[64] they are much more significant from Australia and New Zealand. For example, in 2007, New Zealand exported NZ $786.5 million in merchandise to PIF countries.[65] Likewise, Australia's exports to the Pacific are substantial and significantly in excess of its imports from the region.[66] It has been predicted that, should the PIF countries have to lower their tariffs on goods entering from New Zealand and Australia, there will be significant losses of revenue. This lost tariff income – estimated as approximately U.S. $110 million – will represent losses of up to 12 to 19 percent of national income for some PIF countries.[67] In addition, some forecast that upward of 75 percent of Pacific manufacturing will have to cease operations under PACER-Plus.[68]

A. *Historical Preferences from Australia and New Zealand*

Not unlike the arrangements the EU had with the ACP countries pursuant to the Lomé Conventions, New Zealand and Australia have long been providing

63 For a discussion of these meetings see Pacific Institute of Public Policy, "PACER Plus: The Art of Negotiation," Briefing Paper (May 2009), accessible at www.pacificpolicy.org.

64 Approximately 3 percent of Pacific imports come from the EU. See the European Commission, Directorate-General for Trade and Directorate-General for Development, "Trading for Development: An European Union–Pacific Economic Partnership Agreement," (2007), at 5, accessible at http://trade.ec.europa.eu/doclib/docs/2007/june/tradoc_134815.pdf.

65 Nearly half of this total went to Fiji. See Ministry of Foreign Affairs and Trade, "Key Pacific Issues – Trade" (August 20, 2009), accessible at www.mfat.govt.nz/Foreign-Relations/Pacific/Trade/index.php.

66 Close to half of the Solomon Islands' imports come from Australia; in 2001–2002 this represented AU $64 million in trade, whereas the Solomons only exported AU $2 million in merchandise to Australia. In 2002–2003, Australia exported AU $38 million to Kiribati but only imported a negligible AU $285,000 in merchandise from Kiribati. See Kim, "Howard's Pacific Colonialism: Who Benefits?," Centre for Research on Globalisation–Global Research (July 27, 2005), accessible at http://www.globalresearch.ca/index.php?context=va&aid=742.

67 Ibid., at 2.

68 See, e.g., Cordemans, "Pacific Islands Bullied by Australian, NZ Trade Officials, Say Experts," *The Epoch Times* (May 30, 2009, quoting Pacific Network on Globalisation statements that 80 percent of manufacturing could close down).

preferential treatment to Pacific Island countries. The South Pacific Regional Trade and Economic Cooperation Agreement (SPARTECA), which came into force in 1981, is a nonreciprocal agreement among the members of the South Pacific Forum[69] that provides duty-free access into Australia and New Zealand markets for goods from PIF members.[70]

It is unclear how it came to pass that SPARTECA was able to be notified to the GATT as a partial scope agreement pursuant to the Enabling Clause.[71] The Enabling Clause allows for certain arrangements that would not otherwise be permissible under GATT Article XXIV. In particular, the Enabling Clause is the legal basis in the WTO for GSP schemes. It also permits regional arrangements among developing countries, and the Global System of Trade Preferences pursuant to which various developing countries provide reciprocal trade concessions to one another.[72] However, the Enabling Clause does not permit agreements whereby developed countries give nonreciprocal preferences to subsets of developing countries, outside of the GSP context. This has been precisely the problem with the EC's long-standing preferences granted to the ACP states, and why waivers have been necessary in order for the EC to provide preferential, nonreciprocal treatment to the ACP countries.[73]

Notwithstanding the scope of the Enabling Clause, however, SPARTECA was notified pursuant to the Enabling Clause even though it involves the developed member countries of Australia and New Zealand providing nonreciprocal preferential market access only to the Pacific Island countries. Unlike the EC's Lomé and Cotonou arrangements, there is no apparent expiration

[69] The original members of SPARTECA were Australia, New Zealand, and the members of the South Pacific Forum – the Cook Islands, Fiji, Kiribati, Nauru, Niue, Papua New Guinea, Solomon Islands, Tonga, Tuvalu, and Western Samoa. SPARTECA Article XIV.1.

[70] The text of SPARTECA may be found at, inter alia, http://www.worldtradelaw.net/fta/agreements/spartecafta.pdf.

[71] "SPARTECA Enabling Clause Preferential Arrangement," GATT Doc. L/5100 (February 20, 1981).

[72] "Decision on Differential and More Favourable Treatment, Reciprocity and Fuller Participation of Developing Countries," GATT Doc. L/4903, BISD 26S/203 (November 28, 1979).

[73] The initial waiver was granted by the GATT contracting parties on December 9, 1994, just prior to the entry into effect of the WTO, to the preferences the EU was granting to ACP countries pursuant to the Fourth Lomé Convention. This waiver was extended on October 14, 1995 until February 29, 2000, "EC – The Fourth ACP-EC Convention of Lome – Extension of Waiver – Decision of 14 October 1996," WTO Doc. WT/L/186 (October 18, 1996). At the Doha Ministerial Conference a further waiver was granted to permit the EU to continue providing preferences pursuant to the interim Cotonou Agreement until December 31, 2007; "Ministerial Conference – Fourth Session – Doha, 9–14 November 2001 – European Communities – The ACP-EC Partnership Agreement – Decision of 14 November 2001," WTO Doc. WT/MIN(01)/15 (November 14, 2001). See also Nwobike, "The Emerging Trade Regime under the Cotonou Partnership Agreement: Its Human Rights Implications," 40 *JWT* (2006) 291, at 294 n. 24.

date for SPARTECA's status.[74] Thus, for many years the PIF countries have received unilateral trade preferences from Australia and New Zealand. Once it became clear the EU was going to attempt to negotiate EPAs with the Pacific ACP countries, however, Australia and New Zealand developed an interest in reciprocal relationships as well.

B. *PICTA and PACER*

PACER is an agreement among Australia and New Zealand, on the one hand, and the fourteen countries then comprising the Forum Island Countries[75] (Cook Islands, Federated States of Micronesia, Fiji Islands, Kiribati, Republic of Marshall Islands, Nauru, Niue, Republic of Palau, Papua New Guinea, Samoa, Solomon Islands, Tonga, Tuvalu, and Vanuatu), on the other.[76] PACER is described as an umbrella agreement under which the Pacific Island Countries Trade Agreement (PICTA)[77] and other arrangements fall; it is not intended in and of itself to be a trade agreement that requires notification pursuant to GATT Article XXIV.[78]

At present the agreement is asymmetrical, providing that Australia and New Zealand will maintain "all existing arrangements with respect to market access" for any Forum Island Country until such time as "that particular Forum Island Country has concluded new and/or improved trade arrangements providing equal or better access to" Australia and New Zealand's markets.[79] Forum Island Countries are not expected to make any immediate market access concessions to Australia or New Zealand; instead, the agreement contemplates that these countries will integrate among themselves first, in the form of

74 See also Onguglo, "Developing Countries and Unilateral Trade Preferences in the International Trading System," in M. R. Mendoza, P. Low, and B. Kotschwar (eds.), *Trade Rules in the Making: Challenges in Regional and Multilateral Negotiations* (1999), accessible at http://www.wto.org/English/tratop_e/devel_e/sem01_e/ongugl_e.doc (referring to SPARTECA and GSP as permanent exceptions under the Enabling Clause).

75 The Forum Island countries are also referred to as the Pacific Islands Forum (PIF) members.

76 The Pacific Islands Forum suspended Fiji from its membership on May 2, 2009. See, e.g., Cordemans, *supra* note 68.

77 PICTA is an agreement among the Forum Island countries; neither Australia nor New Zealand is a party.

78 PACER Article 3.7(a) makes this statement: "This Agreement is not intended to be: a customs union, an interim agreement leading to the formation of a customs union, a free trade area, or an interim agreement leading to the formation of a free trade area notifiable under Article XXIV of the General Agreement on Tariffs and Trade." Article 3.7(b) further explains that the agreement is not intended to be an agreement notifiable under Article V of the General Agreement on Trade in Services (GATS).

79 PACER Article 5.3.

PICTA.[80] However, eight years after PICTA comes into force, negotiations will begin "with a view to establishing reciprocal free trade agreements between the Forum Island Countries and Australia and New Zealand."[81] Consultations leading to negotiations to form a reciprocal trade agreement with Australia and New Zealand can be triggered earlier, however, if a Forum Island Country enters into a trade agreement (as defined by GATT Article XXIV:8) with a developed non-Forum country with a per capita GDP higher than the lowest per capita GDP of a developed Forum member,[82] or if all the PICTA countries jointly enter into negotiations to form a trade agreement with one or more non-Forum members.[83] It is these provisions – drafted with the EU's EPA plans in mind – that seem to have served as significant motivation for Australia and New Zealand to negotiate this agreement.[84]

PICTA came into force in 2003. Accordingly, the Forum Island Countries are to begin consultations with Australia and New Zealand by 2011 with respect to negotiating an FTA. However, should the Pacific ACP states enter into an EPA before then, negotiations with Australia and New Zealand will have to begin at that time. Further complications arise for the three Pacific ACP states (Federated States of Micronesia, Palau, and Marshall Islands) that have a Compact of Free Association with the United States. As with PACER, the Compact requires that the United States should receive market access as favorable as that provided to any other country.[85] Thus, for these three countries, any EPA assessment must take into account the extension of duty-free access not only to Australia and New Zealand but to U.S. exports as well.[86]

C. *Pacific Islands in the Balance*

The PIF countries now find themselves in a difficult position. Their ACP preferences have expired, leaving them with the choice of negotiating an EPA or relying on alternative sources of preferences. The former is fraught

80 PACER Article 4.1.

81 PACER Article 5.1.

82 PACER Article 6.3(b).

83 PACER Article 6.4.

84 For example, Australia's national interest analysis of PACER emphasizes the benefit of getting MFN treatment if Forum Island countries negotiate an FTA with a developed country with a higher GDP than Australia or New Zealand; see http://www.aph.gov.au/House/committee/jsct/12March2002/pacernia.pdf.

85 See, e.g., Compact of Free Association between the Federated States of Micronesia and the United States (as amended 2004), Title 2, Art. IV, Section 243.

86 Dearden, "The Interim Pacific Economic Partnership Agreement," DSA European Development Policy Study Group Discussion Paper No. 36 (March 2008), at 4. See also http://www.forumsec.org.fj/_resources/article/files/FAQ%20-%20PICTA%20&%20PACER.pdf.

with difficulty – the EPA should ideally be an agreement that is sufficiently comprehensive to satisfy Article XXIV but not so comprehensive as to trigger obligations under PACER. This is a combination that may not be feasible.[87] Thus, there is a real risk that if an EPA is entered into, preferential access will also have to be extended to Australia and New Zealand a number of years earlier than it otherwise would. As already noted, Pacific Island countries do not import much from Europe, but they do import significant volumes from Australia and New Zealand. Entering into reciprocal trading arrangements with Australia and New Zealand would entail lowering tariffs on products from these countries, which would have significant consequences for the small local economies.[88] The other option is to decline to negotiate an EPA. On the export side of things, Europe is not a major export market for most Pacific Island countries; however, they still do not want to lose their preferential access. The EU's GSP scheme does not cover certain important exports for Pacific economies, such as sugar, and it is unlikely it would be willing to dramatically expand its GSP scheme as such preferences have to be offered on a generalized basis to all similarly situated developing countries.[89] In this way, declining to enter into an EPA would have potential negative consequences for export volumes.

The Pacific Island countries have next to no bargaining power when dealing with their stronger regional partners, Australia and New Zealand. Not only are Australia and New Zealand the main export markets for these economies, but they are the source of many imports. Pacific Island nations receive a great deal of their financial assistance from Australia and New Zealand, and many of their citizens attend school or work (or both) in these developed neighboring countries. Thus, although the PIF countries entered into PACER with New Zealand and Australia, this does not mean all parties saw the agreement as equally beneficial. Indeed, the Forum countries felt significant pressure to

87 This may not be impossible, however. Whether it is due to poor drafting or intentional design, PACER appears to give some wiggle room to the Forum Island countries to negotiate an agreement with the EU that would not trigger obligations to negotiate with Australia and New Zealand, but only if the EPA covered trade other than goods, i.e., services and investment. Although the EU agreed to begin EPA negotiations within these sectors, it is clear it wants to have goods incorporated into an agreement, whether that be in the form of an EPA or a separate goods arrangement. See Articles 5 and 6 PACER; Kelsey, "Free Trade Agreements – Boon or Bane? Through the Lens of PACER," 37 *Victoria U. Wellington L. Rev.* (2006) 391, at 398–400 (explaining the lack of clarity in these provisions and the implications of the potential interpretations).

88 Tariffs provide between 20 and 50 percent of government revenue for the Pacific Island countries. See Kelsey, *supra* note 87 at 412.

89 See "European Communities – Conditions for the Granting of Tariff Preferences to Developing Countries," WT/DS246/AB/R (April 7, 2004), Appellate Body report.

enter into PACER. Although the Forum has proven a useful entity for Pacific Island members in the context of their multilateral trade concerns, it is less helpful in the regional context when it is members of the Forum itself – Australia and New Zealand – that are pushing difficult decisions.[90]

4. CONCLUSION

The multilateral trading system provides a better prospect than do FTAs for weaker countries to obtain meaningful trade access to their stronger trading partners' markets.[91] Furthermore, weaker countries may be less susceptible to political pressures in the multilateral context where they constitute a majority than in the bilateral or plurilateral setting. Path dependence is also more of a problem in the bilateral–plurilateral context, where "cookie cutter" agreement provisions can easily become default rules. Notwithstanding most WTO members' preference for the multilateral forum, given the uncertain timing and scope for a completed Doha Round, it is likely that the next several years will see members continue to flock to enter into new bilateral and plurilateral arrangements. Developing and developed countries alike, no matter how committed to the WTO in theory, will feel the need to enter into FTAs at a minimum to avoid losing their comparative advantage as their trading competitors pair up with common export target countries.[92]

Unfortunately, as this chapter has shown, the political influence stronger countries can exert in bilateral and plurilateral negotiations not only has direct effects on the weaker parties to the negotiations, but can also have flow-on effects for countries not directly tied to the agreements. Unfavorable provisions arise initially out of the political dominance of stronger negotiating partners such as the United States, the EU, and – relative to the Pacific – Australia and New Zealand. Although these provisions are perhaps problematic for the multilateral trading system as they proliferate, in the first instance they

[90] Bowman, "The Pacific Island Nations: Towards Shared Representation," in P. Gallagher, P. Low, and A. L. Stoler (eds.), *Managing the Challenges of WTO Participation* (2005), Case Study 33 (discussing the benefits for the Pacific Island WTO members of having the Pacific Islands Forum Representative Office to assist with participating in WTO negotiations and resolving disputes on a regional rather than a country-specific basis).

[91] But see Blum, "Bilateralism, Multilateralism, and the Architecture of International Law," 49 *Harv. Int'l L. J.* (2008) 323, at 339–343 (identifying instances when bilateral settings may be more advantageous for weaker states than multilateral settings).

[92] For a discussion of this phenomenon see Lewis, "The Free Trade Agreement Paradox," 21 *NZ U. L. Rev.* (2005) 554; Lewis, "The Prisoners' Dilemma and Free Trade Agreements: An Application of Game Theory to Trade Liberalization Strategy," in Boulle et al. (eds.), *supra* note 22, at 21–39.

were accepted by the weaker parties to these trade agreements and thus may seem legitimate. However, as the two examples provided demonstrate, such provisions can have impacts outside the parameters of the original agreement. These negative externalities are not the result of a bargained-for exchange. As FTAs continue to proliferate, we can expect political influence to continue to have ripple effects far beyond the scope of any given agreement. This creates legitimacy concerns, because it is not equitable for FTAs to constrain the policy options of countries that are not party to those agreements, whether through path-dependent externalities of boilerplate provisions or, as demonstrated through the examples of AUSTFA and PACER, through more particularized dynamics existing between trading partners. In contemplating potential reforms to GATT Article XXIV, WTO members should address the fact that political asymmetry in FTA negotiations produces negative externalities on third parties to FTAs, and that these externalities further undermine the legitimacy of such agreements in general.

3

The Politics of Linkages in U.S. Preferential Trade Agreements

Kimberlee Weatherall

1. INTRODUCTION

Recent U.S. trade agreements have been characterized by the incorporation of increasingly detailed standards backed up by provision for their enforcement. This trend continued right up to the last days of the Bush Administration, with Democrats insisting on the addition of new, more specific labor and environmental provisions to agreements then before Congress.[1] Under the new Administration there has been no apparent inclination to resile from this approach; if anything, the preference appears to be for "more of the same." The 2009 President's Trade Policy Agenda states an intention to maintain "strong standards of social accountability" by "[b]uilding on the provisions concerning labor in some of [the United States'] FTAs."[2] U.S. Trade Representative Ron Kirk more recently has promised a new focus on enforcement, stating in an important speech that "[r]ealizing the potential benefits of trade pacts depends largely on whether we're willing and able to enforce [the negotiated] rules."[3] This approach, although suggesting a shift in focus, does not seem to imply any fundamental rethinking; for the Administration, the provisions found in past agreements remain a baseline.

It is easy to see the attraction of detailed standards. In the 1980s, frustration with worldwide intellectual property (IP) protection led American policy-makers to link the grant of trade benefits to countries' adoption of higher

[1] United States Trade Representative, May 10, 2007 Bipartisan Trade Agreement, available from the USTR Web site at http://www.ustr.gov/assets/Document_Library/Fact_Sheets/2007/asset_upload_file127_11319.pdf. The genesis of these provisions is discussed in detail in I. M. Destler, "American Trade Politics in 2007: Building Bipartisan Compromise" (2007), Peterson Institute for International Economics Policy Brief Number PB07-5, May 2007.

[2] United States Trade Representative, *The President's Trade Policy Agenda* (2009).

[3] United States Trade Representative, Speech delivered July 16, 2009 at the Mon Valley Works – Edgar Thomson Plant, Pittsburgh.

IP standards. This occurred in trade preference systems, then in the WTO negotiations,[4] and, more recently, in bilateral preferential trade agreements (PTAs) – or, as they have been known, free trade or trade promotion agreements. U.S. PTAs include IP chapters that, over time, have come to resemble U.S. legislation. Although these chapters have plenty of critics, most focus their ire on the detrimental impact of stronger IP law on developing countries, seeming to view the chapters as wins for the United States, and a successful "export" of U.S. law. Commentators and policymakers tend to assume that the more detailed the provisions, the more effective they are likely to be in achieving U.S. objectives. Moreover, the apparent success of the IP strategy has led some commentators to suggest it should be emulated in environmental policy, labor policy, or both. Among other benefits, such provisions could provide certainty, detail, and teeth, and they might make supporters out of groups, such as environmentalists or labor activists, who are usually critical of trade liberalization.

This chapter suggests that the United States should be cautious both about extending the level of detail in its trade agreements concerning nontariff barriers to trade and in seeking strenuously to enforce the detail already there. Contrary to popular American belief, there is reason to believe that the detailed IP provisions not only are failing to achieve their purported objectives but even are undermining the political and strategic goals of the United States, and harming the interests of the very industry stakeholders who push for them. As I have explored in earlier research with a colleague,[5] summarized here, the IP provisions of the Australia–United States Free Trade Agreement (AUSFTA) achieved relatively little of any significance to extend protection for U.S. IP owners, had unintended and undesirable consequences, and created a political backlash against IP protection. They also harmed the United States' political capital in Australia, which is directly contrary to the U.S. goal of using trade agreements to promote alliances. Moreover, there is reason to believe that similar dynamics will develop if comparable chapters are developed on environmental protection and labor rights. This chapter explores early evidence from the implementation of the United States–Peru Trade Promotion Agreement (Peru TPA), showing that, like the IP provisions of the earlier PTAs, the detailed environmental provisions of the Peru TPA are generating both unintended consequences and a political backlash.

4 P. Drahos with J. Braithwaite, *Information Feudalism: Who Owns the Knowledge Economy?* (2002).

5 R. Burrell and K. Weatherall, "Exporting Controversy? Reactions to the Copyright Provisions of the US-Australia Free Trade Agreement: Lessons for US Trade Policy," 2 *University of Illinois Journal of Law, Technology and Policy* (2008), at 259.

The evidence and arguments presented in this chapter should prompt a reassessment, on the U.S. side, of the real costs and benefits of its counterproductive negotiating stance, and they suggest that caution will be required in taking too harsh a stance on enforcement.

2. U.S. APPROACHES AND OBJECTIVES

A. *Describing the U.S. Approach*

To date, IP has been in the vanguard of moves to push detailed U.S. standards on "behind the border" issues in trade negotiations. Early agreements, such as the North American Free Trade Agreement (NAFTA; 1994) or the Jordan FTA (2000), included basic examples of IP chapters at a low level of detail. They were mostly concerned with requiring signatories to enforce their own legal standards and comply with specified international agreements, although they also added a number of more specific provisions, such as NAFTA Article 1705(1), to address particular matters not addressed in multilateral treaties.

As time has gone on, more and more of these specific provisions, inserting IP rules over and above multilateral commitments, have been included in U.S. PTAs, using increasingly elaborate language. These IP rules are set out in a standard template developed through successive U.S. agreements, and they tend to be based closely on American domestic law and regulation.[6] These moves find their Congressional imprimatur in the legislation granting trade promotion authority, such as that passed in 2002, in which Congress directed the United States Trade Representative (USTR) to ensure "that the provisions of any multilateral or bilateral trade agreement governing intellectual property rights that is entered into by the United States reflect a standard of protection *similar to that found in United States law* [emphasis added]."[7] The USTR appears to have interpreted this as requiring that the agreements

6 Very detailed procedural provisions always accompany the substantive obligations discussed here. Such procedures can be of very real significance: see P. Drahos, T. Faunce, M. Goddard, and D. Henry, "The FTA and the PBS," Evatt Foundation Paper, available at http://www.evatt.labor.net.au/publications/papers/126.htm. They are not, however, the focus of this chapter.

7 Bipartisan Trade Promotion Authority Act of 2002, §2102(b)(4)(A)(i)(II), Pub. L. 107–210 (August 6, 2002), codified at 19 U.S.C. §3802(b)(4) (negotiating objectives). Trade promotion authority (TPA) – formerly known as "fast track" authority – is legislation that binds Congress to timely consideration, and a straight up-or-down vote, on trade agreements negotiated by the Executive on the basis of the authority. The most recent TPA granted by Congress to President George W. Bush expired in July 2007 without renewal: Bipartisan Trade Promotion Authority Act of 2002, Pub. L. 107–210 (August 6, 2002), codified at 19 U.S.C. §3802. As to the requirement of Congressional approval for PTAs, see 19 U.S.C. §3805(a)(1)(D).

should result in *laws* that will be similar to U.S. law. The provisions in the IP chapters addressing copyright in the online environment and enforcement (in AUSFTA, Articles 17.4.7 and 17.11), for example, are particularly conspicuous for the fact that their details correspond so closely to certain domestic U.S. laws.[8]

In addition, all the recent U.S. PTAs also include one-sided "side letters" or annexures in which the non-U.S. party commits to specific actions on issues of concern to the United States. For example, all of the recent PTAs include side letters dealing with the system for managing the removal of infringing copyright material online. Some go even further: For example, in KORUS, the (still-pending) PTA with South Korea, there are two side letters in which South Korea commits to setting up a division or joint investigation team specifically to address online piracy, prosecuting people providing services to facilitate infringement, and taking action to reduce book piracy on university campuses. No equivalent obligations fall on the United States.

B. *General and Specific U.S. Goals in PTA Negotiations*

An important question is whether the United States is gaining the benefits anticipated from the kinds of provisions just described, and what costs the approach entails. The first step in answering this question is to establish the goals of the United States in negotiating PTAs – acknowledging that, as Feinberg has pointed out,[9] we cannot talk about "U.S. trade policy" as if the actors involved held a single, unified vision: The goals of the Administration or individuals within the Administration are not necessarily the same as those of members of Congress, nor of industry stakeholders. Nevertheless, there are a series of objectives that have been identified in USTR and Congressional statements on the PTAs, as well as submissions and comments by stakeholder groups. Those goals are both economic and political, and they relate to the negotiation of agreements overall, as well as more specific chapters.

To take the political goals first, bilateral PTAs were explicitly used by the Bush Administration to achieve strategic and foreign policy goals: to build coalitions,[10] and to strengthen relationships with allies and offer "rewards"

8 The Digital Millennium Copyright Act 1998 (codified at 17 U.S.C. §512 and following, and 17 U.S.C. §§1201 and following). Indeed, the PTAs even reflect political compromises reached between U.S. stakeholders in the Act, such as the individually negotiated exceptions to certain copyright provisions; compare 17 U.S.C. §1201(d) – (j); AUSFTA Article 17.4.7(e).

9 R. E. Feinberg, "The Political Economy of United States' Free Trade Agreements," 26 *World Economy* (2003), 1019 at 1038.

10 G. White, "Free Trade as a Strategic Instrument in the War on Terror? The 2004 US–Moroccan Free Trade Agreement," 59 *Middle East Journal* (2005) 597; H. Rosen, "Free Trade

for support.[11] These kinds of political goals formed a common thread during the debate over the extension of trade promotion authority in the Trade Act of 2002,[12] and in Congressional debate over particular agreements. One example of this use of PTAs may be seen in Australia's case, where both the Administration and members of Congress saw the AUSFTA as a reward, or less patronizingly, a "thank you" for Australia's participation in the Iraq war.[13] At a formal political level, a U.S. PTA increases political interactions: By instituting annual meetings of government officials, PTAs create a forum to discuss trade and the state of the relationship.[14] More generally, a PTA may bring countries together by increasing economic integration and business links between the two countries.

In economic terms, U.S. policymakers have identified a number of objectives. At the highest level of generality, the PTAs are said to expand the scope of trade liberalization on a theory of "competitive liberalization," promulgated by former U.S. Trade Representative Robert Zoellick. According to Zoellick, PTAs could be "staging grounds," allowing two willing parties to negotiate faster, deeper trade liberalization, which was impossible to achieve in a multilateral forum.[15] A further economic goal is to reduce the "transaction costs" of trade by harmonizing regulation in a range of behind-the-border areas such as investment, quarantine rules and the like: first with individual trading partners, but perhaps with a more long-term goal of building a common set of standards among U.S. PTA partners that may be converted into plurilateral

Agreements as Foreign Policy Tools: The US–Israel and the US–Jordan FTAs," in Jeffrey Schott (ed.), *Free Trade Agreements: US Strategies and Priorities* (2004), 51.

[11] A. Capling, "Preferential Trade Agreements as Instruments of Foreign Policy: An Australia–Japan Free Trade Agreement and Its Implications for the Asia Pacific Region," 21 *Pacific Review* (2008) 27.

[12] See, e.g., 147 Cong. Rec. H8972–02, 8973 (Reynolds); id. at H8974 (Dreier).

[13] This can be seen in statements made during the Congressional debates. See, e.g., Dreier (150 Cong. Rec. H5660–07, 5662); Linder (id. at 5664–5665); Crowley (id. at 5665); McDermott (id. at 5668); Dunn (id. at 5700–5701); Shaw (id. at 5708); Cunningham (id. at 5709); Kolbe (id. at 5711–5712); Bereuter (id. at 5717–5718); Alexander (150 Cong. Rec. 8178–01, 8188); McCain (id. at 8199, supporting despite misgivings about the agreement overall); Clinton (id. at 8206); and Dodd (id. at 8214, despite misgivings on the pharmaceuticals provisions).

[14] See, e.g., Australia–United States Free Trade Agreement, Chapter 21; Singapore–United States Free Trade Agreement, Chapter 20; United States–Peru Trade Promotion Agreement, Chapter 20.

[15] F. Bergsten, "Toward a Free Trade Area of the Asia Pacific," *Petersen Institute for International Economics Policy Brief in International Economics No. PB07–2* (2007); F. Bergsten, "China and Economic Integration in East Asia," *Petersen Institute for International Economics Policy Brief in International Economics No. PB07–3* (2007); B. Hoekman and D. Vines, "Multilateral Cooperation: What Next?," 23 *Oxford Review of Economic Policy*, 311. Garnaut and Vines refer to this view as one that "used to be" held: R. Garnaut and D. Vines, "Regional Free-Trade Areas: Sorting Out the Tangled Spaghetti," 23 *Oxford Review of Economic Policy* (2007), 508.

or even multilateral agreements.[16] Through bilateral negotiations, the United States has been able to secure more detailed provisions and hence, at least apparently, more harmonization of regulatory regimes.

These, then, are the general political and economic goals of the U.S. PTAs. Such general goals, however, do not entirely explain the detail found in the IP chapters.[17] We must therefore recognize a second level of objectives, those concerned with furthering the specific objectives of securing market access and regulations that will be advantageous to U.S. industries.[18] In IP, the specific interests of U.S. IP-dependent industries are (broadly) threefold: (1) securing higher standards of protection in trading partners' IP law so as to provide tangible gains to IP owners through new (exploitable) rights and hence raised profits; (2) increasing the ease of enforcing rights and thus hopefully reducing infringement; and (3) reducing the costs of enforcement to U.S. industry by shifting them onto other actors such as the governments of trading partner states.[19] It is these goals, both general and specific, against which the achievements and benefits of the U.S. PTAs should be judged.

One obvious objection may have occurred to the reader. The actors involved in U.S. trade policy are not all rational actors promoting the welfare of the United States in some objectively defined way; in fact, actors such as individual

[16] A set of countries in the Asia–Pacific Region that are parties to U.S. PTAs (along with some other countries in the region) are, at the time of this writing, considering the possibility of constructing a plurilateral agreement, tentatively known as the Trans-Pacific Partnership, which has the potential to "multilateralize" some U.S. PTA provisions and reduce transaction costs and barriers to trade among a group of countries. Although success is by no means guaranteed even with the U.S. PTAs in place, because there are differences between the U.S. PTAs negotiated to date, the existence of those U.S. agreements does potentially set some kind of baseline for negotiation.

[17] Even the goal of harmonizing regulation does not entirely explain the detail in the U.S. chapters: As we will see in looking at the IP chapter, for example, the goal of "harmonization" appears to apply mostly to parts of U.S. law that increase IP protection; there is little effort to harmonize those parts of IP law that protect the interests of users. Thus the kinds of details found in the IP chapters must be explained by reference to industry interests.

[18] The term "U.S. industries" here refers to the IP-dependent industries such as the entertainment and music industries and the pharmaceutical industry. There are other U.S. industries that might disagree with the IP standards in the U.S. PTAs: U.S. technology companies, for example, such as Apple, Inc. or Google, Inc., who have often vocally supported exceptions in areas such as copyright, because those exceptions are important to aspects of their business. These opposing U.S. interests have not historically been represented in committees that advise USTR on U.S. PTAs; nor is it clear that many have strong incentives to oppose the current approach: Google and Apple must already comply with U.S. law in the United States; the additional costs of doing so overseas, particularly in smaller trading partners, are likely to be limited.

[19] These claimed benefits of the IP chapters are summarized in the reports of the Industry Trade Advisory Committees on negotiated PTAs.

stakeholder groups and even USTR officials may have personal or institutional interests not necessarily consistent with the broader economic and political interests of the United States. In other words, the stated goals of the U.S. PTAs may not correspond to the "real" goals motivating the individuals involved. Thus commentators have argued that particular stakeholder representative groups have "captured" the USTR,[20] and hence that the detailed provisions are a direct translation of stakeholder goals. Indeed, we can take this argument further, and distinguish between the interests of IP-owning industries and the interests of their representative bodies. To take one example, the Recording Industry Association of America may wish to have copyright provisions in a trade agreement as a tangible outcome of its lobbying, *even if* such provisions provide little tangible benefit or raised profit. It could also be argued that USTR negotiators have their own personal interests in ensuring that trade agreements pass Congress, and they may include provisions to neutralize opposition or to build coalitions of Congressional support for PTAs. These two arguments are related: Support for a PTA will be easier to obtain if stakeholder representatives' demands, however unreasonable, are met.

The purpose of this chapter, however, is not to explain why IP chapters have become detailed[21] but to consider, in as objective a manner as possible, whether the detailed U.S. provisions can be *justified* by reference to their stated economic and political goals, and to make an argument that the USTR, and the various stakeholders, as rational actors, ought to reconsider their approach, in light of the costs here identified. Industry stakeholders ought, in their own interests, to adjust their approach according to the external costs and benefits to them of the detailed provisions embodied in recent U.S. PTAs. Negotiators within the USTR and members of Congress ought to take into account the full range of costs and benefits to stakeholders in particular and more general U.S. interests: One would hope (even if somewhat naively) that the USTR would resist negotiating treaties that will harm U.S. interests overseas while achieving nothing of value for industry stakeholders.

C. *Were These Goals Achieved?*

Having identified the goals, the next step in a cost–benefit analysis of the U.S. approach to negotiating PTA provisions on behind-the-border issues is to determine what the United States gained. The core of my argument here is that it is not sufficient to look at the agreement text, link it to U.S. laws and

[20] Drahos with Braithwaite, *supra* note 4.

[21] For that, see Drahos with Braithwaite, *supra* note 4.

stated goals, and assume that the United States "got what it wanted." We also need to look in more detail at what, in substantive, practical terms, was actually achieved for the benefit of U.S. industries when that text was implemented in domestic law. The case study chosen for such a detailed consideration here is the implementation of the IP chapter of the AUSFTA.

Of the goals identified in the last section, only some are relevant; no one thinks, for example, that an IP chapter will strengthen political alliances. The main benefits that *might* be achieved are, as already mentioned, threefold: raising IP protection in such a way as to provide tangible gains to IP owners; harmonizing law and practice and thus reducing global IP management costs; or building a platform of agreements with individual countries with a view to eventual embodiment of the same standards in one or more multilateral agreements. A detailed analysis showing just how doubtful the gains are may be found in an earlier article,[22] but it can be summarized here.

Despite long and detailed provisions setting out what copyright, patent, and trademark law must protect and the scope of rights to be granted, few of the IP provisions of the AUSFTA *as implemented* raised standards of protection in Australia, or broadened IP owner rights. Vast swathes of the chapter simply match existing Australian law, restate provisions from other IP treaties to which Australia was already a party,[23] or state obvious features of any reasonably advanced common law legal system, such as remedies to be made available to IP owners (injunctions, damages, and the payment of legal costs; see Article 17.11). Admittedly, some provisions did grant to IP owners some rights they did not previously have, which might conceivably increase profits, such as extending the copyright term for an additional 20 years (Article 17.4.4), providing for patent term extension (Article 17.9.8), preventing the reuse of clinical test data by generic manufacturers seeking regulatory approval to sell pharmaceuticals (Article 17.10),[24] and some provisions narrowing exceptions to patent rights (Article 17.9.7). Beyond these narrow areas, however, assertions

22 Burrell and Weatherall, *supra* note 5.

23 Including various provisions from other treaties in the AUSFTA does bring those provisions within the jurisdiction of bilateral dispute resolution (Chapter 21). However, even that could have been achieved more simply, by having the parties agree to implement the relevant international treaties (rather than restating full text). In some cases, a provision from a multilateral treaty is repeated with a very small change; cf. TRIPS Article 46 (giving courts discretion to require destruction of materials the *predominant* use of which is to make infringing products) vs. AUSFTA Article 17.11.10 (taking out "predominant"). Given judicial discretion, the substantive difference is marginal at best and most likely irrelevant, and might benefit an IP owner once in a period of years in a small jurisdiction like Australia; such benefit must be balanced against the various costs discussed later in this chapter.

24 These laws provide a de facto extension of the monopoly over those pharmaceuticals and agricultural chemicals.

by American commentators and peak bodies that U.S. IP owners obtained real benefits as a result of AUSFTA do not bear close examination. For example, U.S. commentators referred to AUSFTA as extending criminal liability for IP infringements and strengthening anticircumvention provisions that prohibit the "hacking" of technical protections for copyright works. In fact, the only actual extensions in either of these areas to existing Australian law were to private, noncommercial, personal acts,[25] which, given limited prosecutorial and policing resources, are never likely to be detected or, even if they are detected, are unlikely to excite prosecutors to take action. As a result, it is not particularly likely that IP infringements will be reduced by such a move.[26]

It might be objected that even if AUSFTA did not *raise* IP protection, it at least "locked in" existing high levels of protection and will thus prevent "backsliding." This argument, too, is weak, for a number of reasons. First, the agreement says little, in many cases, about exceptions, thus leaving some room for Australia to reduce IP owner rights subject only to existing, very general limitations found in international treaties.[27] Second, the benefits to the United States or U.S. interests of locking in a given model of IP law are questionable given the notorious rate at which both technology and law evolve. Even in the few short years since AUSFTA, there have been significant revisions of trademark law in the United States and copyright law in Australia,[28] and proposals for patent reform in both countries. As technology, too, has evolved it has arguably become less clear that the AUSFTA provisions are appropriate to protect IP owners' interests; exceptions appropriate at an early stage can become problematic for IP owners subsequently. For example, the provisions on online service provider (OSP) liability for copyright infringements are built on the assumption that OSPs are unable to monitor infringements passing over their networks. As technology raises the potential for more filtering, it becomes less clear, at least in the eyes of IP-dependent industry stakeholders, that OSPs like Verizon should be absolved of all responsibility for monitoring their services – as required by AUSFTA under Article 17.11.29(vii).

Nor did AUSFTA in fact achieve harmonization of IP laws in areas of real practical significance for international trade or IP owners. For example, the greatest IP-related legal barriers to free movement of legitimate goods

[25] Australian law already criminalized distribution; cf. the now-repealed §132(2)(b) of the Copyright Act of 1968 (Cth) with the postimplementation §§132(5DB) and 132(5DC). The pre-AUSFTA criminal provisions caught all acts of commercial copying and commercial possession for the purposes of sale or hire; see §§132(1)(b) and 132(2A)(a).

[26] Further analysis and examples are provided in Burrell and Weatherall, *supra* note 5.

[27] In particular TRIPS Articles 13 (copyright), 17 (trademark), and 30 (patent) impose some limits.

[28] See the Trademark Dilution Revision Act of 2006 (United States); Copyright Amendment Act of 2006 (Australia).

across borders arise where rights expire at different times, meaning goods legitimately made in one country cannot be exported to another. This is particularly problematic in these days of online transactions. European Union members recognized this by harmonizing copyright terms early in the formation of their common market. Despite provisions dealing with copyright term, it expires at different times in Australia and America in many cases, including the many productions by employees.[29] To take another example, U.S. OSPs would have benefited from a strong effort to harmonize their legal liability for wrongs committed by using their facilities. Again, though, differences arose in implementation: Australia applied the quite detailed AUSFTA provisions creating so-called safe harbors to a narrow subset of service providers – leaving major players such as Google, Inc. without protection. Furthermore, no effort was made to look at OSP legal risk beyond copyright, despite the fact that Australia's defamation law, for example, has caused problems for the U.S.-based news provider Dow Jones.[30] In some areas, AUSFTA actually increased differences between Australian and U.S. copyright law: For example, to comply, as required by AUSFTA, with a World Intellectual Property Organization Treaty on Performers and Phonograms, Australia introduced a whole raft of performers' economic and moral rights that have no equivalent in U.S. law and that will require adjustments to standard industry contracts.[31] In sum, there is little reason to think that IP owners face lower transaction costs post-AUSFTA.

A third touted "benefit" of the detailed IP provisions of the AUSFTA to U.S. interests is that it constitutes a plank in a broader U.S. trade strategy, the ultimate goal of which is to "multilateralize" the IP standards preferred by the United States by means of a "global IP ratchet."[32] On this argument,

[29] Australian copyright in employees' works endures for the life of the author plus 70 years: See the Copyright Act of 1968 (Cth) §33 (if anonymous, the term will be the usual term for anonymous works, namely 70 years from publication: §34). In the United States, copyright in "works made for hire" endures for a term of 95 years from the year of first publication, or 120 years from the year of creation, whichever expires first: 17 U.S.C. §302(c).

[30] Dow Jones & Company, Inc v. Gutnick, 210 CLR 575 (2002), where the High Court held that an Australian court could exercise jurisdiction to allow a plaintiff to sue a U.S.-based company for defamation promulgated via an online subscription service (the servers were based in the United States).

[31] Note that the Australian moral rights provisions require very specific consent on the part of the performer to acts that might otherwise infringe their rights: See the Copyright Act of 1968 (Australia) §195AXJ.

[32] P. Drahos, "BITs and BIPs – Bilateralism in Intellectual Property," 4 *Journal of World Intellectual Property* (2001), 791; P. Drahos, "The Global Ratchet for Intellectual Property Rights: Why It Fails as Policy and What Should Be Done about It," *Paper for the Open Society Institute* (2003); B. Mercurio, "TRIPS-Plus Provisions in FTAs: Recent Trends," in L. Bartels & F. Ortino (eds.), *Regional Trade Agreements and the WTO Legal System* (2006), 215.

each similar IP chapter in a U.S. PTA is a stepping-stone toward its eventual consolidation in multilateral agreements.

But there are problems with this argument too. Historically, IP standards incorporated in multilateral treaties have been closer to the *lowest* common denominator of laws among trading partners, rather than the highest: The fact that Australia has higher than average levels of protection will not make multilateralization of those standards any more likely in the face of lower levels in other (politically significant) countries. Nor are these other more powerful countries more likely to sign up to a set of standards as a result of the actions of minor players such as Australia, Morocco, Chile, and Oman. Further, the level of detail in the PTAs is simply "unmultilateralizable" – the provisions are so closely based on U.S. law that they will inevitably be unacceptable to major players such as Europe, Brazil, China, or India. Europe, for example, has its own detailed regimes for digital copyright law, with a series of different exceptions and other provisions to protect consumers that are not compatible with the model that constitutes the most detailed part of the IP chapters in the U.S. PTAs. Thus these most objectionable of the PTA provisions are not likely ever to be embodied in a multilateral agreement. Finally, obligations the United States might want to multilateralize, such as the requirement to have a statutory (prefixed) damages system for copyright and trademark infringements, were not included in AUSFTA (presumably owing to Australia's objection).[33] If the ultimate objective is multilateral agreement, then a chapter with provisions representing common ground with other significant powers like Europe would be more useful. Such provisions would have the advantage of being less detailed, and thus less politically costly to negotiate. In sum, then, it is highly questionable whether the IP chapters of AUSFTA achieved any of the touted benefits – or, to the extent that IP owners have benefited, those benefits appear to be quite marginal.

However, an obvious objection to this line of argument is that Australia, as a developed country with a common law system, is a special case and therefore an inadequate case study. In this view, the detailed provisions of the U.S. IP chapters may have more force and more effect in developing countries such as Morocco or Oman, or countries with quite different systems, such as Peru or South Korea.

There are three responses to this argument. First, it is an argument for more tailoring: Provisions unnecessary in the AUSFTA should not have been included, particularly, as will be subsequently argued, if they had significant

33 See AUSFTA Article 17.11.7; compare this to the Singapore PTA, which does include statutory damages: United States–Singapore Free Trade Agreement (2003), Article 16.9.5.

costs. Second, it is simplistic to assert that the benefits of detailed IP obligations will be greater in developing countries. Even if a U.S. PTA does succeed in placing higher standards "on the books" in a developing country, this will have tangible little benefit to IP owners unless those rights are actually enforceable and enforced. As the United States has recently learned in its WTO dispute with China, bringing a claim based on failure to enforce standards in a trade agreement is very difficult.[34] Further, as Daniel Gervais has recently pointed out, even developing partner countries are increasingly finding ways to exploit what policy flexibility they have in IP (and related) law to lessen any perceived negative impact of these laws ("calibration").[35] The AUSFTA provisions discussed earlier clearly demonstrate that even the most detailed treaty provisions can change when translated into domestic law. We should therefore be hesitant to assert that the benefits to the United States from the IP provisions of AUSFTA were uniquely low. An analysis similar to the one conducted in earlier work with Robert Burrell would need to be done for other trading partners.[36] Third, insofar as the benefits to IP owners *are* greater in the case of developing countries, in that there are more radical and effective legal changes bringing about stronger IP protection, so too will be the costs. The deeper the changes to its domestic laws a country must implement to comply with an agreement, the greater local resentment is likely to be. As I argue in the text that follows, the IP provisions generated a great deal of resentment in Australia, but Korea had protests in the streets – and some of them raised issues of IP among the many other issues.[37]

Another obvious response to the analysis here is that the IP provisions must be achieving some ends desired by U.S. industry peak bodies, who can be

34 WTO, China – measures affecting the protection and enforcement of intellectual property rights – Report of the Panel, WT/DS362/R (January 26, 2009). Significant elements of the U.S. case were rejected, in particular a challenge by the United States to China's thresholds for criminal actions against counterfeiting and piracy. The WTO Panel decision will likely make it more difficult to challenge enforcement levels in other countries even under the U.S. PTAs: The same reasoning arguably applies to the term "significant" and even the term "willful" (and "piracy" could also be interpreted differently in different countries, if one applied the Panel's reasoning).

35 Gervais' work is, as yet, not published in article form, but see D. Standeford and K. Mara, "TRIPS May Evolve To Keep Pace with Modern IP Concerns," *Intellectual Property Watch*, October 24, 2008. My own discussions with people involved in this field make it clear that negotiators make efforts to learn from predecessors: Korean negotiators, for example, paid careful attention to what concessions or variations Australia negotiated.

36 Burrell and Weatherall, *supra* note 5.

37 This assertion is a little flip: It must be acknowledged that the Korean protests over the U.S. PTA were fueled by local political issues and concern over beef safety, with the U.S. PTA and its IP provisions a convenient hook.

assumed to act rationally in their members' interests in lobbying for such provisions. There are a number of answers to this objection. First, close analysis of the costs and benefits of an agreement following its implementation will not necessarily be conducted by industry peak bodies, who will, by the time implementation processes are complete, be busy with the next issue or negotiation. In any event, peak bodies in particular may hesitate to acknowledge problems with agreements: As recipients of funding from industry participants, their incentives will be to present any text achieved as a win. Further, as will become clear in the text that follows, the harms caused by the IP provisions are spread: There are costs to general U.S. political capital and some costs to industry stakeholders themselves, and such general costs are likely to be of less concern to industry stakeholders than they should be to the USTR.

3. THE POLITICAL COSTS OF THE U.S. APPROACH AND THEIR SOURCES

A. *Recognized and Unrecognized Costs of the U.S. Approach*

Having cast doubt on the benefits of the detailed IP provisions of the U.S. PTAs, we must turn now to their costs. Certain costs of the U.S. PTAs are well recognized in the literature. For example, economists have highlighted problems such as trade diversion and distortion,[38] and the inefficiency caused by proliferation of preferences and rules of origin of such complexity that they are, themselves, a trade barrier.[39]

Politically, it is argued that PTA negotiations divert attention from multilateral negotiations[40] and cause resentment in excluded countries.[41] Capling has also noted that there has been relatively little analysis of the extent to which PTAs in fact strengthen political ties, despite the fact that commentators have identified some reasons for doubt. In fact, Capling argues, PTAs can exacerbate existing political tensions between countries by creating another field of competition: For example, consider the impact of growing numbers of PTAs in the Asia-Pacific region on the long-standing tension between Japan and China.[42] There are also domestic political costs. Within partner countries, there may be resentment from industries excluded from the benefits of a

[38] J. Viner, *The Customs Union Issue* (1950); J. Bhagwati, *Free Trade Today* (2002), 108–111.

[39] Bhagwati, *supra* note 38; D. A. Irwin, *Free Trade Under Fire* (2nd ed. 2005); C. L. Davis, "Overlapping Institutions in Trade Policy," 7 *Perspectives In Politics* (2009), 25.

[40] Capling, *supra* note 11; Bhagwati, *supra* note 38; Garnaut and Vines, *supra* note 15.

[41] R. M. Campbell, (1929), "Empire Free Trade," 39 *The Economic Journal* (1929) 371.

[42] Capling, *supra* note 11.

PTA (e.g., the Australian sugar industry), and from industries that suffer from the increase in competition. In South America, for example, there has been fear that competition from U.S. imports would devastate local agriculture.[43] All these represent political costs, which have an impact on whether a U.S. bilateral trade agreement will build positive political relations with a partner country. Trade agreements are hard; displacement is real, and it has observable and public political costs. Nonetheless, these are *general* costs arising from the existence of the agreements. What is not sufficiently recognized – and what this chapter now seeks to describe in relation to AUSFTA – is the set of costs generated by the U.S. approach of including *detailed* regulation of domestic issues in the name of reducing nontariff barriers to trade, which can only be understood by engaging with the implementation process in partner countries.

As my colleague and I outlined in more detail elsewhere,[44] U.S. audiences often fail to appreciate the extent to which the drafting and detail of the IP chapter of the AUSFTA generated a negative reaction in Australia. In my personal experience, American commentators, if they have thought about the agreement at all, tend to think it was good for Australia. However, mainstream Australian media coverage of the agreement generally was negative, and in relation to the IP provisions, it was *universally* negative, even among commentators supportive of AUSFTA.[45] The chapter was labeled "pernicious," "market closing,"[46] a reason for not accepting the agreement,[47] "a major concern," "dangerous," and "one of the worst aspects of this deal." Many of the critics were not the so-called usual suspects but rather people not normally concerned with IP: union officials, state governments, former political leaders

43 Congressional Research Service, *Congressional Research Service Report No. RL32770: Andean-US Free Trade Agreement Negotiations*, March 14, 2006, available at http://www.wikileaks.se/leak/crs/RL32770.pdf.

44 Burrell and Weatherall, *supra* note 5.

45 See, e.g., Henry Ergas, "Patent Protection an USFTA Complication," *Australian Financial Review*, February 24, 2004; Brian Toohey, "Brothers in Arms, Not Trade," *Australian Financial Review*, March 6–7, 2004; Shane Wright, "The Free Trade Agreement – It's All Politics," *Australian Associated Press Financial News Wire*, July 30, 2004; John Garnaut, "What's the Big Deal?," *Sydney Morning Herald*, July 31, 2004; Peter Martin, "The FTA Clause that Stifles Creativity," *Sydney Morning Herald*, April 14, 2004; "Paying the Price of Free Trade," *Canberra Times*, July 27, 2004. Even the conservative broadsheet *The Australian*, generally supportive in its coverage of the AUSFTA, published critical articles relating to copyright: see, e.g., Bruce McCabe, "FTA Leaves Us Second Among Equals," *The Australian*, August 31, 2004; and, in an otherwise positive editorial, it had little or nothing favorable to say about the copyright provisions: "Making the Case for the US Trade Deal," *The Australian*, July 27, 2004.

46 P. Dee, *The Australia–US Free Trade Agreement: An Assessment*, June 2004, available at http://www.aph.gov.au/senate_freetrade/rel_links/dee_fta_report.pdf.

47 P. Urban, "No Free Trade in So-Called Free Trade Agreement," *Sydney Morning Herald*, July 19, 2004.

and senior judges, and senior academic economists and economics editors of the main broadsheet newspapers.[48] Their concerns were not only the immediate costs of the new rules, but also the loss of sovereignty and control over matters of economic and social policy.

The structure of the IP chapter was a key reason that well-informed public figures of all stripes reacted this way. Everyone could find something to hate, and its very detail suggested a patronizing American attitude, as if Australia was an IP dilettante to be lectured and dictated to, to be told how to run a legal system or how to manage its innovation policy and its criminal justice system. Even if you could excuse the template text as not being aimed at Australia, the attitude of "only the American system will do" emerges also in the way such matters were handled in correspondence. For example, following the Australian implementation, the USTR *insisted* that the new Australian law relating to temporary copies in copyright was inadequate and must be amended, threatening to hold up the whole agreement – thus reinforcing the impression that copyright law making had been handed to a foreign power.

The detailed, standard-form nature of the provisions also had further observable effects. Because of the level of detail, and the number of (small and large) changes that needed to be made to Australian law in a short time, ordinary processes of legislative consultation and compromise were bypassed. Further, the level of detail also heightened the risk that U.S. law would itself be found wanting by the standards of the agreement, and hence that the United States would be perceived as hypocritical. The belief that the United States would simply ignore the treaty if it proved inconvenient had already been expressed in the media, and even in Parliament.[49] This risk soon eventuated: In 2008, a U.S. Appeals Court specifically held noninfringing the very copies that the United States had been so insistent on ensuring were covered by Australian copyright law.[50] Although this may seem, and in practical terms probably was, inconsequential, the lack of consistency with AUSFTA did not go unnoticed in Australia. Of course, criticism of the United States for hypocrisy in its trade

[48] See sources cited in Burrell and Weatherall, *supra* note 5, 280–283.

[49] Bruce McCabe, "FTA Leaves Us Second Among Equals," *The Australian*, August 31, 2004; for Parliament, see, e.g., Commonwealth of Australia, *Parliamentary Debates*, House of Representatives, August 12, 2004 at 33018 (Katter, Independent). This impression was not helped by a letter from the USTR to the Chairman of the House Ways and Means Committee, which stated that "no trade agreement can prevent the US Congress from changing US law by passing another law": Robert Zoellick, "Letter to the Chairman of the Ways and Means Committee the Hon. William Thomas," July 13, 2004. Similar comments have been made by Members of Congress; see, e.g., 150 Cong. Rec. H5666–07 (Dreier).

[50] Cartoon Network LP, LLLP v. CSC Holdings, Inc., 536 F.3d 121 (2nd Cir. N.Y. August 4, 2008).

policy is scarcely new.[51] Many critics have pointed out that the prominent refusal by the United States to comply with WTO rulings has damaged its standing in the international community. The point here is that the United States' own strategy heightens the risk of hypocrisy.

All of these problems, and discussions, and criticism, have fueled anti-Americanism and have cost the United States political capital in Australia.

What is more, a full accounting of the costs of AUSFTA must recognize the political costs and unintended consequences for IP owners in implementation. In some cases, we had some new and unexpected laws, such as a whole new regime of performers' economic and moral rights that imposed direct costs (in terms of changing contracts to manage moral rights) for certain copyright industries. More dangerously, AUSFTA caused an anti-IP backlash. To legislatures and other political actors in Australia, the changes required by the AUSFTA in copyright and patent law all appeared to be strengthening IP rights – and thus upsetting Australia's own "balanced" regime. Two parliamentary committees that reviewed the AUSFTA recommended adjustments in the other direction to "restore" the balance. As a result, the government promised to find ways to lessen the impact of the agreement, and Australian users in 2006 gained a raft of new free exceptions to copyright, for personal copying, for parody and satire, and more for libraries and educational institutions.[52] The IP chapter also galvanized a series of groups not previously involved in opposing extensions to IP, and it ensured the general public would view Australian IP law as Americanized, contrary to local interests, and too strong. These developments have arguably made it harder to achieve other reforms to IP law considered more important by IP-owning stakeholders, such as anti-camcording laws to increase penalties for people filming commercial movies in cinemas, or "three strikes" laws to require online service providers to police infringements. In other words, the marginal successes achieved in the AUSFTA and the anti-IP political backlash they engendered have been factors standing in the way of reforms that would provide real advantages to U.S. IP owners.

The magnitude of these political costs and the amount of resentment caused by the IP chapter should not be overexaggerated. No one could claim that

[51] Bhagwati, *supra* note 38, 53–54.

[52] Copyright Amendment Act of 2006 (Australia), Schedule 6. There were also attempts to balance the changes in patent law: For example, as required by the FTA, Australia introduced provisions to allow patent holders to be notified of applications to obtain marketing approval for drugs that might implicate a patent, but at the same time enacted punitive provisions to ensure that patent holders could not abuse that system: see U.S. Free Trade Agreement Implementation Act of 2004 (Cth), Schedule 7, §§26B–26D.

Australia will refuse the next U.S. request for military assistance because the U.S. insisted on restrictive and insulting IP provisions; and there were many sources of Australian umbrage arising from AUSFTA, particularly in relation to agriculture. Some of the more extreme reactions to the IP chapter were due, no doubt, to anti-Americanism that was a feature of the Bush era. The point, however, is that the U.S. drafting approach evident in the IP chapter had noticeable, and sustained, political downsides for the United States, contributing in a significant way to beliefs about American high-handedness. These costs have been underappreciated in the United States, no doubt because much of the time American commentators have little reason to engage with the details of implementation.

The point too is that much of this political cost, to the United States and to IP owners, could easily have been avoided without compromising the achievement of substantive benefits to U.S. IP owners. The USTR could have asked its stakeholders to identify those areas where there were real and important differences between Australian and American law. A shorter chapter that took out detailed and repetitive provisions that added nothing to Australian law; that affirmed both countries' commitment to international treaties; and perhaps addressed a few confined areas where there were substantive differences would have generated significantly less criticism and cost, and it could have been justified to stakeholders, Congress, and any future negotiating partners on the basis that Australia already provided strong protection to IP.[53]

4. EXTENDING THE LESSONS OF THE AUSFTA

The argument presented in Burrell and Weatherall and summarized herein was an argument against extending the U.S. approach in IP in new PTAs.[54] This warning is important: In IP, there is reason to think that the United States will continue to demand detailed and substantive rules, both bilaterally and in the context of negotiations toward an Anti-Counterfeiting Trade Agreement between the United States, EU, Switzerland, Japan, Australia, South Korea, New Zealand, Mexico, Canada, Jordan, Morocco, Singapore, and the United Arab Emirates. I asserted earlier in this chapter that the level of detail that can be negotiated among major players will be considerably less than has been

53 At present such an approach may be inconsistent with The Trade Act of 2002, 19 U.S.C. §3802(b)(4), which requires that the *agreement* (not the law in the partner country) "reflect a standard of protection similar to that found in United States law." This is an argument for changing the Trade Act provision in the future as part of a rethinking of U.S. bilateral policy.

54 Burrell and Weatherall, *supra* note 5.

seen in the U.S. PTAs; it will be interesting to see what emerges from these negotiations.

More significant would be if the IP drafting approach were to be emulated in other behind-the-border areas such as future labor or environmental chapters. Such a move, although consistent with the general trend mentioned in the introduction, would still be a shift. Although labor provisions have been part of U.S. trade agreements since the NAFTA, Congress' negotiating objectives in both these areas have, to date, been more aspirational than those relating to IP: They have directed the USTR to "promote respect for worker rights and the rights of children consistent with core labor standards of the ILO"; "ensure that a party to a trade agreement with the United States does not fail to effectively enforce its environmental or labor laws"; strengthen capacity; and "reduce or eliminate government practices or policies that unduly threaten sustainable development."[55] These aspirational provisions on labor and the environment were necessary to gain support for President George W. Bush's trade promotion authority early in his presidency.

Academics and policy commentators in recent times have explicitly or implicitly made the link with IP in suggesting the expansion of labor and environmental provisions. Drezner is most explicit: In a book published by the Council on Foreign Relations he advocated two possible routes for promoting "fair trade" issues. The story he tells matches closely to what happened in the 1980s in IP: tightening the links between regulatory standards and the Generalized System of Preferences (GSP),[56] or including demands for improved labor conditions or environmental protection in PTA negotiations. This is "*déjà vu* all over again": IP policy was first linked to trade by means of the Caribbean Basin Initiative and subsequently the GSP.[57] All we need is a reference to "standards similar to those found in US law" in the trade legislation to complete the picture.

Further, a variety of forces over the past two decades have pushed in this direction: increases in trade (and hence adjustment costs); the inclusion of other behind-the-border issues like IP, raising the question why labor and the environment should be excluded; more integration of low-wage countries into the global trade system; and the increased mobility of capital, giving rise to a fear of a regulatory "race to the bottom."[58] Partly as a result of all of these

55 Bipartisan Trade Promotion Authority Act of 2002, §2102(b)(4)(A)(i)(II), Pub. L. 107–210 (August 6, 2002), codified at 19 U.S.C. §3802(b)(11).

56 D. Drezner, *U.S. Trade Strategy: Free Versus Fair* (2006), 69–70.

57 Drahos with Braithwaite, *supra* note 4.

58 K. Elliott, "(Mis)Managing Diversity: Worker Rights and US Trade Policy," 5 *International Negotiation* (2000) 97–127.

shifts, and out of a desire to protect local jobs, American voters overwhelmingly support inclusion of minimum labor and environmental standards in trade agreements. There can be little doubt that some will also continue to push for the inclusion of more detailed, and more enforceable, labor and environmental rules in the U.S. negotiating template because a trade linkage comes with "teeth."[59]

Nevertheless, the dynamic here is not the same as it is in IP. For one thing, American business interests are likely to oppose the expansion of labor and environmental provisions, creating a domestic opposition largely missing from the IP arena. Second, in both labor and the environment, unlike IP, law-making power is not exclusively federal, which creates difficulty for USTR negotiators wanting to push detailed standards. Third, unlike IP, where U.S. law tends to provide for higher standards than those found in international treaty obligations, in both labor and the environment it has been argued that U.S. law falls short, for example, of International Labour Organization treaties. Finally, commentators such as Elliott and Destler have in the past said that "other nations simply will not agree to amend their laws affecting their people as part of trade agreements with us."[60]

Admittedly, too, at the time of writing, the Administration appears to be shifting its focus away from negotiating new agreements, toward enforcement of existing trade obligations. U.S. Trade Representative Ron Kirk, in a recent speech, suggested that the United States would be looking at the enforcement of rules in existing agreements.[61] Because the labor and environmental standards in existing agreements are drafted in general terms, they are unlikely to be the target of early enforcement attempts: This may mean less attention on these social issues and their relationship with trade in the short term.

Nevertheless, it is undeniable that there is a general trend toward more detail. Bolle has traced the incremental development of labor provisions since NAFTA.[62] Similar growth may be seen in relation to the environmental provisions. The Chile PTA, concluded in 2003, required only that Chile enforce its own environmental laws. When the Peru PTA was scheduled to come before Congress in 2007, it already contained more extensive provisions than Chile;

59 On the arguments against trade sanctions to achieve ends in environmental and social policy, see Bhagwati, *supra* note 38, 79–80.

60 I. M. Destler, "Getting Back on Track," *The New Democrat*, January 1, 1998; Elliott, *supra* note 58.

61 United States Trade Representative, *supra* note 3.

62 M. J. Bolle, "Overview of Labor Enforcement Issues in Free Trade Agreements," *Congressional Research Service Report* No. RS22823, February 29, 2008; also K. A. Elliott, "Appendix A: Treatment of Labor Issues in US Bilateral Trade Agreements," Appendix A to Destler, *supra* note 1.

in addition, to pass through Congress, it was amended to comply with the fiercely negotiated May 10 agreement, which, at the insistence of Democrats, requires even more specific environmental and labor provisions.[63] The purpose of the May 10, 2007 Agreement, as it is known, was to secure Congressional approval for pending PTAs following the expiry of the Bush Administration's trade promotion authority.[64] Further, President Obama has been explicit in his desire to "build on" (i.e., expand) existing labor provisions, has referred to the Peru PTA as a guide for the future, and during his campaign raised the possibility of moving the side agreements on labor and environmental provisions in NAFTA into the main agreement.[65] Recent reports suggest that leading Democrats "are already signalling that they want to push for even stronger protections on labor and the environment in particular."[66] There have been various attempts at legislation, including the Trade Reform, Accountability, Development and Employment Act of 2009, which, although not at the level currently found in the Trade Act on IP, would require high standards in both labor and environmental law in core text, subject to the full dispute resolution provisions of future agreements.

This all suggests that if, or rather, when, U.S. attention turns to the negotiation of further agreements, labor and environmental provisions are likely to be escalated, even if only for the purposes of neutralizing opposition. Although we may not yet see an "IP" level of specificity in labor or the environment, we may see more than Destler or Elliott would have predicted at the turn of the present century. Furthermore, although such an approach might not be *favored* by American business, it is also possible that opposition will be reduced in recognition of the political demand for *some* provisions, provided that, like the Peru PTA, they require no change to existing U.S. standards and laws.[67]

[63] Including a fully enforceable commitment that countries will adopt, maintain, and enforce in their laws and practices the five basic international labor standards, stated in the 1998 ILO Declaration on Fundamental Principles and Rights at Work; a new, fully enforceable, binding commitment prohibiting countries from lowering labor or environmental standards in a manner affecting trade or investment; new limitations on prosecutorial and enforcement discretions; and a fully enforceable commitment to adopt, implement, and enforce in laws and practice obligations under seven common major multilateral environmental agreements, including the Convention on International Trade in Endangered Species of Wild Fauna and Flora, 1973, and the Montreal Protocol on Substances That Deplete the Ozone Layer, 1987.

[64] Although the agreement failed to secure Congressional approval for the Colombian or South Korean agreements, as other issues were involved: See "Padilla Warns against Passage Of China Bill, Protectionist 'Surge'," 26(45) *Inside US Trade*, November 14, 2008.

[65] *New York Times*, April 20, 2009.

[66] *Inside US Trade*, March 6, 2009.

[67] Destler, *supra* note 1.

Assuming that is correct, the second question is whether such a move would give rise to minimal benefits and significant political costs, as we have seen in IP. On the one hand, there are reasons for optimism. IP is often seen as a corporate welfare scheme, benefiting only foreign corporate interests, and thus will tend to have few supporters in the countries party to U.S. PTAs. On the other hand, labor and environmental regulations may garner support from local unions, environmental activists, and other such interested parties and politicians in trading partner countries. Indeed, *including* such provisions may turn groups that would otherwise be free trade opponents into supporters or at least neutral entities.[68] Such groups may even welcome a trade agreement because it can expand local support for labor and environmental regulations. Other industries that benefit from the PTA, fearing loss of PTA benefits, may support compliance with environmental laws that would otherwise be of no interest to them.[69]

Local support, however, is likely to depend on whether the negotiated rules are sensitive to local concerns, and reflect the priorities desired by local groups, or whether, in contrast, they undermine existing local initiatives. Bhagwati has pointed out the conceptual error of assuming that the price of pollution or the appropriate labor conditions are identical in vastly differing countries. As he points out, if country A has cleaner air and worse water than country B, then given equal willingness to address environmental issues, country A will tax water pollution more, and air pollution less, than country B. It is by no means clear that the issues that will concern the United States (or U.S. environmental groups, or U.S. voters) will be the most pressing even for environmental or labor activists in any given trading partner. If the United States makes determinations of good policy based on American rules, or uses a "template" approach as it has in IP, local support may not be forthcoming.

Further, there *is* early evidence of a dynamic of unexpected consequences, avoidance, and minimal implementation of the environmental provisions in the Peruvian PTA. According to reports, to enable the timely passage of the detailed laws required under the U.S. PTA, in December 2007 the Peruvian Congress passed Law 29157, which, for 180 days, delegated to the Executive

[68] This happened among environmental groups in relation to NAFTA: As Destler outlines, the inclusion of the NAFTA side agreements split environmental groups, with some supporting; see Destler, *American Trade Politics* (4th ed 2005), 224.

[69] Verifor, "Trade Liberalisation and Forest Verification: Learning from the US-Peru Trade Promotion Agreement," Verifor Briefing Paper, February 2009, available at http://www.verifor.org/RESOURCES/briefing-papers/9-perutradeliberalisation.pdf.

the authority to legislate on a range of topics related to the agreement. This was necessary because of the scope of changes required to bring the PTA into effect. By the end of June 2008, Peru's President had approved more than ninety legislative decrees, many controversial, for a range of reasons.[70] First, there have been criticisms of the process: Civil society groups have denounced the way in which the decrees were produced without public consultation.[71] Like the Australian IP laws that came out of the AUSFTA, these laws lack legitimacy. Second, it appears that, again like the AUSFTA, there have been some attempts at avoidance of PTA standards: The Peruvian Congress the passed labor laws inconsistent with the labor obligations of the FTA as laid out in a May 10, 2007 agreement; in what sounds like avoidance of the agreement, it also amended forestry laws to exclude large swathes of rain forest from the definition of forest land, thus denying it the kinds of protection intended by the PTA.[72] These various changes were a cause of riots in Peru by indigenous groups, causing NGOs to write to Secretary of State Hilary Clinton, asking her to clarify whether the contested decrees were necessary under the Peru PTA.[73] It is even the case that, just as the United States can be accused of hypocrisy in its handling of IP laws, so too can it be accused in labor laws, where, as Destler points out, "while there is little opposition in the United States to having partner nations upgrade their labor practices, there are concerns … over what some label a 'boomerang' effect: that such provisions, in the standard 'reciprocal' form embodied in trade agreements, might come home to impact US labor practices."[74]

70 Laws in dispute included Legislative Decree 1090, the new forestry law, and Legislative Decree 1064, which would allow the government to grant corporate contracts on communal indigenous lands without consultations; Legislative Decrees 1020 and 994, which encourage private ownership of agricultural lands, and Legislative Decree 1089, allowing temporary sale of rural land for oil and mining extractions; and Law 29338, which would change Peru's water management and distribution regime. The extent to which the various laws can be directly traced to the U.S. PTA may be in dispute; however, their linking with the U.S. PTA process and passage under Executive power delegated to pass the Peru PTA ensures that they will be perceived as being linked to the PTA, thus increasing the political costs of the PTA.

71 Ironically, the United States has "expressed concern" about the lack of "outreach" to civil society groups during the legislative process: This is ironic given that it is U.S. insistence on changes prior to bringing the PTA into effect that creates the urgency justifying such a process: see 27(15) *Inside US Trade*, April 17, 2009.

72 "Schwab Certifies Peru FTA Despite Labor Complaints from Key Democrats," 27(3) *Inside US Trade*, January 23, 2009; see also 27(2) *Inside US Trade*, January 16, 2009.

73 NGO Letter to Secretary of State Hilary Clinton, June 19 2009, available at http://www.earthworksaction.org/pubs/JUN)(NGO-letter-US-rePeru.pdf.

74 Destler, *supra* note 1.

Thus, like the AUSFTA, the agreement may have had unintended consequences, and the political reaction to the agreement and its strictures was not, perhaps, in accordance with U.S. goals. We should not draw too much from these early developments, but it at least suggests that we should not be too hasty to conclude that more detailed text on environmental regulation will operate as expected once the domestic political and legislative process gets underway.

As for the question of whether the benefits would be greater for stakeholders and the United States than in IP, it is, of course, difficult at this point in history to downplay the importance of achieving environmental goals.[75] Here, however, the trade economists sound a note of caution. One problem is inefficiency: Tying trade to social and regulatory concerns, as Bhagwati has pointed out, distorts both. Inevitable concessions are made on the questions of social and environmental policy in order to reach agreement, and thus "we underachieve both trade liberalization and progress on social and human rights and on environmental objectives."[76] In the case of the Peru PTA, it appears that special powers given to government to implement the agreement were used to roll back local protections for indigenous groups and the environment and to wind up local institutions previously providing for consultation.[77]

The best way to test some of these questions will be to examine, over the next few years, the reception and application of the Peruvian provisions. What we can say is that, despite the long-standing difficulties of extending labor and environmental provisions in U.S. PTAs, we cannot dismiss out of hand the possibility that the United States could be tempted to extend its past, damaging approach from IP to these new policy areas. Nor can we pretend that such provisions will be unproblematic or guaranteed to achieve their goals once they are translated through local political processes into domestic law. Perhaps the benefits will outweigh the costs on a global scale. At the very least, however, an awareness of the way that implementation plays out should be part of the

[75] I acknowledge, but cannot really address here, the argument that environmental provisions in trade agreements are aimed at achieving protectionism rather than environmental goals. The assumption is that when the United States exports certain environmental standards by means of trade agreements, those provisions *in the United States* do have environmental goals, whatever the individual motivations of those who push for them in trade agreements.

[76] Bhagwati, *supra* note 38; J. Bhagwati, "Free Trade: What Now?," Keynote Address delivered at the University of St. Gallen, Switzerland, on May 25, 1998, on the occasion of the International Management Symposium at which the 1998 Freedom Prize of the Max Schmidheiny Foundation was awarded.

[77] "Peru's Congress Extends Session to Finalize FTA before Bush Leaves," 26(51) *Inside US Trade*, December 26, 2008. Disbanded institutions included CONAFOR, that is, the National Forestry Advisory Council, which provided for some civic participation in forestry policy, and INRENA, that is, the National Institute for Natural Resources, which, according to reports, was monitoring and publishing information about forestry resources in Peru, albeit imperfectly.

discussion, and caution should be exercised about what can be achieved by extraordinarily detailed provisions, of the IP style, in PTAs.

In short, we need to stop assuming that good (or detailed) text equals good trade or policy results: Reality and careful analysis of what happens "after the agreement" will provide us with a more nuanced understanding of what can be achieved by trade agreements – and what cannot.

4

The Politics of African Trade Negotiations in the WTO's Doha Round

Uche Ewelukwa Ofodile

1. INTRODUCTION

Launched on November 14, 2001, the Doha Round of multilateral trade negotiations has experienced a lot of bumps and setbacks along the way.[1] In late July of 2008, the Doha Round collapsed yet again after disagreement over trigger levels for special safeguard mechanisms (SSMs).[2] The Doha Development Agenda (DDA) was supposed to put development at the center of trade negotiations and address the needs and concerns of developing countries.[3] However, the failure to meet the deadlines set out in the Doha Ministerial Declaration and subsequent deadlines, and entrenched North–South divide over important issues in the agricultural negotiation, cast serious doubt on the commitments of World Trade Organization (WTO) member states to a true development-oriented outcome. Given the proposals on the table, important issues that have been left out of the discussions, and new trade-distorting and trade-restricting measures emerging in many industrialized economies in the

[1] Launched in September 2001, the Round ended in a deadlock at the Fifth WTO Ministerial Conference in Cancun, Mexico in 2003. In July 2004, WTO member states agreed on a text – the July Framework Agreement, or the July Package – that clarified the modalities for negotiation. Although some measure of progress occurred at the Sixth WTO Ministerial Conference resulting in the 2005 Hong Kong Ministerial Declaration, the deadlines set in the Hong Kong Declarations were all missed. On July 27, 2006, the Director-General of the WTO, Pascal Lamy, called for trade talks to be suspended because, in his view, there was need for reflection and quiet diplomacy.

[2] Report to the Trade Negotiations Committee by the Chairman of the Special Session of the Committee on Agriculture, Ambassador Crawford Falconer, WTO Doc Job(08)/95 (August 12, 2008).

[3] World Trade Organization, "Hong Kong Ministerial Declaration 2005," WT/MIN(05)/DEC (adopted December 18, 2005): "We emphasize the central importance of the development dimension in every aspect of the Doha Work Programme and recommit ourselves to making it a meaningful reality, in terms both of the results of the negotiations on market access and rule-making and of the specific development-related issues set out below."

wake of the global financial crisis, it would appear that the development objective of the Doha Round has been significantly watered down if not completely abandoned. With continuing delays in negotiations and as the development dividend of current proposals comes under increasing scrutiny, countries in sub-Saharan Africa (SSA), particularly the least developed countries (LDCs) among them,[4] must begin to explore alternative paths to improving their trade performance and meeting their development objectives.

For Africa as a whole, several questions must be asked. Will the Doha Round provide real opportunities for advancing the continent's trade and development interests? Does the Doha Round have the potential to address, in a meaningful and comprehensive fashion, the major impediments to African trade? Assuming that the much-vaunted goals of the Doha Round are not realized, does Africa have alternative pathways to achieving economic growth, improving trade performance, and fostering long-term sustainable development? Assuming that the Doha Round is revived, what should be the strategy of SSA countries going forward?

These questions are pertinent because discussions about the DDA are now occurring against the backdrop of four crises that have hit SSA countries very hard: a financial crisis, a food crisis, a commodity crisis, and a fuel crisis. For SSA countries, the global economic crisis makes a meaningful deal in the Doha Round all the more imperative.[5] The world is now experiencing the worst global economic crisis since the depression – a crisis that is now destabilizing a growing number of developing countries and is pushing tens of millions of people in the global South below the poverty line.[6] SSA countries have felt the impact of global financial crisis.[7] Growth in SSA fell from nearly 7 percent in 2007 to under 5.5 percent in 2008 and just 1.5 percent in

[4] *Facts About Least Developed Countries (LDCs)*, UN-OHRLLS, http://www.unohrlls.org/UserFiles/File/Publications/Factsheet.pdf, accessed October 24, 2008.

[5] This point is reflected in the Declaration and Decision of Heads of State and Government of the African Union in Addis Ababa on the international financial crisis and the need to conclude the Doha Development Round. See "Addis Ababa Declaration on the International Financial Crisis," Assembly/AU/Decl. 2(XII) (February 3, 2009). See also the communiqué on the impact of the global economic and financial crisis on trade and development in Africa, issued during the fifth ordinary session of the African Union Conference of Ministers of Trade held in Addis Ababa, Ethiopia, March 16–20, 2009.

[6] Paul Richter, "Economic Crisis Threatens to Destabilize Developing Countries," *Los Angeles Times*, October 27, 2008, available at http://www.latimes.com/news/nationworld/world/la-fg-crisis27-2008oct27,0,5121157.story.

[7] The International Monetary Fund (IMF) projected that global output will contract by about 1.25 percent in 2009. Unfortunately, a 1 percentage point decline in world growth is associated with a drop of about 0.5 percentage point in GDP growth for SSA countries; see IMF, *Regional Economic Outlook: Sub-Saharan Africa 2009* 3 (2009).

2009.[8] For the first time in fifteen years, per capita income in Africa fell in 2009. The African Development Bank estimates that the African continent will lose about $251 billion in 2009, and $277 billion in 2010 export revenues as a result of the crisis. As a result of the crisis, countries in Africa are experiencing a major decline in the external demand for their exports,[9] a contraction in international finance, a decline in capital inflows (particularly foreign direct investment, or FDI) to the continent, a sharp global decline in the price of export commodities such as oil, coffee, cocoa, and cotton, significant reduction in remittances, and rising protectionism in rich countries as a variety of new trade-distorting and trade-restricting measures emerge despite pledges by the Group of Twenty Finance Ministers and Central Bank Governors to the contrary.[10] The hardest hit countries have been the net oil importers and the net food importers on the continent. To mitigate the impact of the crisis and reduce the risk to future crisis, experts call for measures aimed at expanding trade and expanding trade finance – and these require speedy conclusion of a pro-development Doha Round.

This chapter argues that, going forward, SSA countries must adopt five strategies. First, they must continue to question the commitment of the industrialized countries to the development aspect of the Doha Round by highlighting domestic laws and policies in these countries that are at odds with real commitment to a true development outcome. New trade-restricting and trade-distorting measures in some industrialized countries in the form of increase

[8] Ibid. at 13. Although the IMF projects that growth in SSA will recover to about 3.75 percent in 2010, this remains to be seen, and such a level would still be below the precrisis level.

[9] In 2009, the WTO downgraded its forecast for the year and estimated that the volume of world merchandise export will fall by 10 percent. The export of developing economies was expected to decline by 7 percent and was expected to have devastating consequences for the poorest countries, particularly those dependent on primary commodity export because falling world prices were compounding the decline in export volumes. See World Trade Organization, "Report to the TPRP from the Director-General on the Financial and Economic Crisis and Trade-Related Developments," WT/TPR/OV/W/2 (July 15, 2009), paragraph 30 (hereinafter "WTO's Financial Crisis Report").

[10] According to the WTO, 2009 witnessed slippages toward more trade-restricting and trade-distorting policies. See World Trade Organization, WTO's Financial Crisis Report. In April 2009, G-20 leaders meeting in London reaffirmed their commitment, until the end of 2010, to "refrain from raising new barriers to investment or to trade in goods and services, imposing new export restrictions, or implementing World Trade Organisation (WTO) inconsistent measures to stimulate exports" and to "rectify promptly any such measures." They also pledged to "minimise any negative impact on trade and investment of our domestic policy actions including fiscal policy and action in support of the financial sector" and promised "not [to] retreat into financial protectionism, particularly measures that constrain worldwide capital flows, especially to developing countries." See G-20 Declaration "Global Plan for Recovery and Reform," April 2, 2009, available at http://www.londonsummit.gov.uk/resources/en/PDF/final-communique.

in the initiation of trade-remedy investigations, increase in the number of new tariffs, and nontariff measures affecting agricultural trade, contradicts avowed commitment to a true development round.[11] For example, a 2009 report from the WTO reveal that in the wake of the crisis, the European Community (EC), the United States, and Switzerland all introduced new agricultural export subsidies on dairy products, despite commitment in the Doha Ministerial Declaration and subsequent WTO ministerial declarations to eliminate agricultural subsidies.[12]

Second, African countries must also continue to put forward concrete proposals that have the potential to advance the continent's vision of development, and they must adopt a strong defensive posture in negotiations to ensure that they do not accept new commitments that are inimical to their interests. Third, African countries must rethink their relationship with advanced developing countries (ADCs) such as China, India, and Brazil. Even while attempting to strengthen trade and investment relations with the ADCs, African leaders must seek to win real concessions from these countries and must guard against negotiation postures that undermine the continent's long-term economic and strategic interests. Fourth, African leaders must also embark on serious domestic reform aimed at addressing internal obstacles to trade and development and must devote renewed attention to regional integration.

Finally, African countries must increasingly call attention to the systemic costs of a failed Doha Round. Consequences of failure are legion and include the following: increased poverty, particularly in LDCs; renewed pessimism in developing countries about the role of trade in development and the benefits of free and open markets; backpedaling on trade liberalization policies, which causes serious damage to the WTO's credibility; and growth in the number of people and groups isolated and disengaged from the multilateral trading system and hostile to the capitalist global society of the twenty-first century and the countries that are seen to be pushing the capitalist agenda. These costs cannot be easily discounted by industrialized countries because they have implications for their national security and the global war against extremism.

This chapter is in seven parts. Part 2 discusses the promise(s) of the DDA. Part 3 reviews the process of the Doha Round talks in terms of the participation of African countries in the negotiation process. Part 4 evaluates key proposals that African countries have tabled in the course of negotiations and reviews the current status of these proposals. Part 5 discusses, from the perspective of SSA

[11] According to the WTO, trade in agricultural products and textile and clothing have been among the sectors most affected by new protectionist measures. See WTO's Financial Crisis Report, *supra* note 9, paragraph 8.

[12] Ibid., paragraph 35.

countries, the major obstacles and challenges to achieving a development-oriented outcome in the DDA negotiations. Part 6 evaluates a possible post-Doha plan of action for Africa. Some concluding observations are offered in Part 7. SSA countries are by no means homogenous. The heterogeneity of SSA countries means that any potential gains or losses from the Doha Round will not be evenly distributed. Consequently, a one-size-fits-all approach to negotiation or trade policy is neither wise nor workable in the region.

2. THE PROMISE AND POSSIBILITIES OF THE DDA

Launched in 2001, the Doha Round promised to place the needs of developing countries at the center of multilateral trade negotiations.[13] Although the term "development" was not defined in the Doha Ministerial Declaration or any subsequent document and although no binding commitments were undertaken regarding possible outcomes, good-faith promises were made and there was wide expectation that the concerns of developing countries regarding the functioning of the multilateral trading system would be taken seriously. Member states of the WTO promised to "continue to make positive efforts designed to ensure that developing countries, and especially the least-developed among them, *secure a share in the growth of world trade commensurate with the needs of their economic development*,"[14] and they specifically hinted that enhanced market access, balanced rules, and well targeted, sustainably financed technical assistance, and capacity-building programs were among the likely outcome of negotiations. Regarding LDCs, the member states recognized "the particular vulnerability of the LDCs and the special structural difficulties they face in the global economy," and consequently they committed to "addressing the marginalization of LDCs in international trade and to improving their effective participation in the multilateral trading system."[15]

Undoubtedly, the Doha Ministerial Declaration was a carefully crafted political response to the "legitimacy crisis" that has dogged the WTO since its inception. For developing countries in general and African states in particular, promises of accommodation and reform of the multilateral trading system are not new. The DDA must therefore be evaluated against the backdrop a string of failed initiatives and proposals aimed at addressing the concerns of

[13] World Trade Organization, "Doha WTO Ministerial Declaration," WT/MIN(01)/DEC/1 (November 20, 2001), available at http://www.wto.org/english/thewto_e/minist_e/min01_e/mindecl_e.htm. ("The majority of WTO members are developing countries. We seek to place their needs and interests at the heart of the Work Programme adopted in this Declaration.")

[14] Ibid., paragraph 2 (emphasis added).

[15] Ibid., paragraph 3.

developing countries regarding the design and operation of the multilateral trading system. The DDA must also be evaluated against the backdrop of the disappointing implementation of the Uruguay Round agreements, and the real possibility that developing countries may, once again, be pressured into making commitments that they neither understand nor are ready for. Although there is now an extensive literature on the potential gains from trade, whether countries in Africa have benefited in the past or are likely to benefit in the future remains controversial and is a factor that must be borne in mind by African trade negotiators going forward.

Despite past disappointments, African countries embraced the DDA for obvious reasons. Compared with foreign aid, trade is now viewed as a more realistic and more sustainable means of alleviating poverty.[16] Africa represents the largest number of both developing countries and LDCs and is thus facing numerous development-related challenges.[17] Compared with other regions, only a handful of countries in the continent are on track to meet the millennium development goals of halving poverty by 2015. Given decline in overseas development aid,[18] concerns about the burden of unsustainable debt, low rates of FDI, and poor human development indicators, external trade provides an opportunity for Africa to stimulate economic growth and generate much-needed resources.[19] Going into the negotiations, African leaders clearly hoped that greater integration in the multilateral trading system would help reverse the continent's dismal economic performance of the past two decades. Africa attracts less than 1 percent of global investment, and it "is the only major region to see per capita investment and savings decline since 1970."[20] Although net FDI flow to Africa increased from an average of $11.9 billion in the period from 1998 to 2001 to $18.1 billion in the period from 2002 to 2005 – a result of growing ties with Asia – FDI flow into the continent is heavily concentrated in the extractive industries and in only a few countries within the continent. In terms of Africa's participation in the global trading system, the records are equally discouraging. Africa's share of world export is insignificant

[16] Kevin Watkins and Penny Fowler, *Rigged Rules and Double Standards: Trade, Globalisation and the Fight Against Poverty* (2002).

[17] "Report to the Trade Negotiations Committee by the Chairman of the Special Session of the Committee on Agriculture, Ambassador Crawford Falconer," WTO Doc Job(08)/95 (August 12, 2008).

[18] According to a 2002 report by the G-8, the total net Official Development Assistance (ODA) to Africa has fallen from previous levels of U.S. $17 billion to U.S. $12 billion in 2002. See G-8 Africa Action Plan Highlights, Kananskis Summit, Canada, June 26–27, 2002, available at http://www.state.gov/e/eeb/rls/othr/11511.htm (accessed October 31, 2008).

[19] Economic Commission for Africa, *Economic Report on Africa 2008* 6 (2008).

[20] G-8 Africa Action Plan Highlights, *supra* note 18.

and has been in steady decline – from about 5.5 percent in 1975 to about 2.5 percent in 2002.[21] Worse, "there has been little progress in improving [Africa's] international trading environment."[22] Although Africa has 13 percent of the world population, the continent's export accounts for only about 1.6 percent of the global trade. Regarding agriculture, a sector where the continent arguably enjoys some comparative advantage, the continent's share of exports dropped from about 8 percent in 1971 to about 3.4 percent in the time frame from 1991 to 2000.[23]

3. AFRICA AND THE DDA NEGOTIATION PROCESS

The Doha Ministerial Declaration promised that trade talks would be conducted "in a transparent manner among participants, in order to facilitate the effective participation of all." [24] Compared to the Uruguay Round negotiations, African countries are undoubtedly more involved in the DDA negotiations.[25] With forty-two countries in the WTO, Africa represents the single largest bloc of countries in the WTO, and effort has been increasingly directed toward better coordination and cooperation in trade negotiation. The African Group, comprising about forty-one countries, has been active in negotiations.[26] The LDC Group has also been active in presenting the position of its members.[27] Countries in Africa have also sought to strengthen their alliances with other developing countries and have not hesitated to pursue common interests and positions with other countries within the Group of Ninety (G-90), the Group of Thirty-Three (G-33), and the Group of Twenty (G-20) developing blocs.[28] As part of the effort to enhance their participation in the trade negotiations, African countries adopted a common position on key issues and set out development objectives and benchmarks for the continent. Specific proposals

[21] Saswati Bora, Antoine Bouët, and Devesh Roy, "The Marginalization of Africa in World Trade", IFPRI Research Brief No. 7 (2007).

[22] Economic Report on Africa 2008, *supra* note 19, at 14.

[23] G-8 Africa Action Plan Highlights, *supra* note 19.

[24] Doha Ministerial Declaration, *supra* note 13.

[25] Edwini Kessie and Yvonne Apea, "The Participation of African Countries in the Multilateral Trading System," paper on file with the author (observing that unlike in the past, African countries "are now relatively active in the work of the WTO").

[26] For countries that are part of the Africa group see http://www.wto.org/english/tratop_e/agric_e/negoti_groups_e.htm.

[27] See http://www.wto.org/english/tratop_e/agric_e/negoti_groups_e.htm. For a current UN list of LDCs, see http://www.un.org/special-rep/ohrlls/ldc/list.htm.

[28] For a list of the different groups that have emerged in the course of the DDA negotiations, see WTO, Groups in the Agriculture Negotiations, available at http://www.wto.org/english/tratop_e/agric_e/negoti_groups_e.htm.

covering most areas under negotiation were tabled[29] and common positions on the LDCs' agenda were also adopted.[30] In documents such as the Cairo Declaration and Road Map on the Doha Work Programme (June 5–9, 2005), the Arusha Development Benchmarks (November 21–24, 2005),[31] the Arusha Declaration and Plan of Action on African Commodities, the Kampala Ministerial Statement (2004), the Kigali Consensus (May 27–28, 2004),[32] and the Nairobi Ministerial Declaration on the Doha Work Programme (April 12–14, 2006),[33] African leaders sought to effectively frame the issues of importance to the continent and articulate the continent's position on these issues.

Despite a demonstrated commitment to the trade negotiation process, three factors continue to undermine Africa's efforts at effective participation. First, lack of human and material resources remains a major problem for many countries. Second, broader systemic issues, particularly the skewed structures of global economic governance, pose an ongoing challenge for the continent. A final issue of concern is the problem posed by the so-called Lamy Triangle negotiations. By all indicators, human and financial constraints remain major impediments to the capacity of most countries in Africa to negotiate effectively. The continent still lacks the three core sets of competencies required for effective participation in multilateral trade negotiations. These sets of competencies, according to Blackhurst, Lyakura, and Oyejide, are these:

> A country's resident delegation in Geneva, skilled in negotiation and diplomacy... key staff in home capitals with analytical and policy-making skills who provide direct operational support and guidance to the resident delegation... the more general personnel requirement, in the form of technical, legal, political and legislative skills, which are distributed among the various trade policy institutions in the country to contribute to effective participation in the WTO process by implementing the country's commitments.[34]

[29] Kessie and Apea, *supra* note 25 (attributing the change in attitude of African countries to their strong conviction that increased participation in the multilateral trading system was crucial to the long-term effort to reverse the continent's marginalization in the global trading system).

[30] See The LDC Ministers' Declarations adopted at Zanzibar (2001), Dhaka (2003), Dakar (2004), and Livingston (2005).

[31] The Arusha Development Benchmark for the Sixth WTO Ministerial Conference in Hong Kong, China. AU Conference of Ministers 2nd Extraordinary Session, November 22–24, 2005, Arusha, United Republic of Tanzania.

[32] See ICTSD, "African Trade Ministers Adopt 'Kigali Consensus' On Ongoing WTO Talks," *Bridges Weekly Trade News Digest* 8(19), June 2, 2004.

[33] *See* The Nairobi Ministerial Declaration on the Doha Work Program, TI/TMIN/MIN/Decl. (IV). AU Conference of Ministers of Trade, 4th Ordinary Session, April 12–14, 2006, Nairobi, Republic of Kenya.

[34] R. Blackhurst, B. Lyakura, and A. Oyejide, "Improving African Participation in the WTO," Paper Commissioned by the World Bank for a Conference at the WTO, September 20–21, 1999.

To ensure better outcome from trade negotiations, the analytical skills and negotiation capacity of policymakers and trade negotiators have to be strengthened. However, African countries will also have to address more basis obstacles to effective trade negotiation, such as the big and unexplained chasm between their delegates in Geneva and relevant staff in home capitals. For the most part, African trade delegates in Geneva are overwhelmed and do not appear to receive much-needed operational support from the home capitals. The lack of involvement of the private sector in trade policy–making on most countries on the continent is also a huge problem. With the possible exception of South Africa, private sector activity is grossly limited, and the private sector is neither involved in trade policy–making nor plugged into the trade negotiation discussions. Most countries in the continent lack a sizeable pool of small and medium enterprises; private sector activity is largely dominated either by large multinational corporations or by small businesses operating in the informal sector.[35] Unfortunately, few countries in SSA have made serious efforts to inform, engage, and actively involve the private sector in trade policy discussions and rule making.

Africa's underrepresentation and lack of real involvement in the key structures of global economic governance is also a problem. According to the 2008 Economic Report on Africa, "African countries still lack fair representation on the decision-making organs of international institutions."[36] A survey of Africa's LDCs found that two-thirds of the respondents expressed the view that the current structure of global economic governance does not allow for their effective participation in the decision making and norm setting of key financial, monetary, and multilateral trading institutions.[37] The continent's lack of meaningful participation in the key institution for global development and financial rule making inevitably affects the continent's participation in the DDA negotiations; oftentimes important trade-related and trade-impacting issues are framed, decisions taken, and norms adopted in settings other than the WTO. The recent global financial crisis and the response to the crises by the G-20 is an example.[38] Virtually the entire continent of Africa is excluded from G-20 deliberations, despite the wide-reaching impact of decisions taken

[35] Arieff, Weiss, and Jones, *The Global Economic Crisis: Impact on Sub-Saharan Africa and Global Policy Response* 5 (August 25, 2009).

[36] Economic Report on Africa 2008, *supra* note 19, at 16.

[37] Ibid.

[38] In the wake of the Asian Financial Crisis in 1997, the G-20 Finance Ministers and Central Bank Governors group was established in 1999 to bring together major advanced and emerging economies to stabilize the global financial market. It is estimated that, collectively, the G-20 economies comprise 85 percent of global gross national product, 80 percent of world trade, and two-thirds of the world population. See http://en.wikipedia.org/wiki/G-20_major_economies.

by the group. Not surprisingly, in the wake of the global financial crisis, African states are asking for a greater voice in international financial decision making. In the 2009 Addis Ababa Declaration on the International Financial Crisis, African heads of state reiterated earlier calls "for an in-depth reform of the global financial system, based on an inclusive approach which fully integrates, in all legitimacy, the voice of Africa"[39] and called for "a real voice to be given to Africa in the reform of the international financial institutions."[40] They also reaffirmed that "Africa must be fully represented in deliberations on the financial crisis while calling for the G20 framework to be revised to include all the Member States of the United Nations System."[41]

The Lamy Triangle – the triangle consisting of the European Union (EU), the United States, and ADC countries such as India, China, and Brazil – is a concern and raises troubling questions regarding transparency and inclusiveness of the DDA negotiations. Although the outcome of negotiations among the countries that are in this triangle has implications for SSA countries, the latter are completely shut out of the process. Repeated pleas by SSA countries for transparency and inclusion in negotiation have been ignored. Even while acknowledging that meetings on a horizontal level are important, in a March 26, 2010 report to the Trade Negotiation Committee, the WTO Director-General still encouraged meetings "in smaller groups *in variable geometry* and bilateral contacts," which he considered "necessary and essential – within specific areas."[42]

In conclusion, compared to their level of involvement in past trade negotiations, African countries are more engaged in the Doha Round. For SSA countries, effective participation in trade talks is seriously hampered by a host of factors, including, shortage of skilled personnel, complexity of existing rules, lack of full information on the rules, weak institutional infrastructure in the capitals, and the high cost of maintaining missions in Geneva.[43] Although efforts have been made to provide support to aid developing countries in trade

[39] See "Addis Ababa Declaration on the International Financial Crisis," Assembly/AU/Decl. 2(XII), *supra* note 5, paragraph 12.

[40] Ibid, paragraph 18.

[41] Ibid, paragraph 13.

[42] World Trade Organization, "Stock-Taking Ends With Collective Determination to Start Building Global Doha Package," 2010 news item, March 26, 2010. Available at: http://www.wto.org/english/news_e/news10_e/tnc_dg_stat_26mar10_e.htm.

[43] "Integrating Least Developed Countries into the Global Economy: Proposals for a Comprehensive New Plan of Action in the Context of the Third Ministerial Conference," adopted at the Coordinating Workshop's Final Plenary, June 25, 1999; "The Challenge of Integrating LDCs into the Multilateral Trading System: Coordinating Workshop for Senior Advisors to Ministers of Trade in LDCs in Preparation for the Third WTO Ministerial Conference," Sun City, South Africa, June 21–25, 1999.

negotiations, these are not enough to overcome fundamental inadequacies and asymmetries in access to information and resources; many governments still report an immense need for technical assistance in the areas of trade negotiation techniques.[44]

4. THE DDA NEGOTIATIONS: PROPOSALS BY AFRICAN COUNTRIES

This section focuses on two aspects of the DDA negotiations: the agricultural sector and the development agenda.[45] Going into negotiations, African countries adopted both offensive and defensive strategies. Offensively, the strategy was to seek greater market access in industrialized countries for agricultural products, tackle long-standing barriers to the continent's export in the form of export subsidies and domestic support, and push for greater commitments with respect to the development agenda. Defensively, the strategy was to prevent or at least curtail preference erosion, minimize Africa's liberalization commitments through special and differential treatments in key sectors, and ensure protection for LDCs and net-food-importing countries.

A. *Agriculture*

Article 13 of the Doha Ministerial Declaration commits WTO members to comprehensive negotiations aimed at "substantial improvements in market access; reductions of, with a view to phasing out, all forms of export subsidies; and substantial reductions in trade-distorting domestic support." Article 13 also explicitly states that

> special and differential treatment for developing countries shall be an integral part of all elements of the negotiations and shall be embodied in the schedules of concessions and commitments and as appropriate in the rules and disciplines to be negotiated, so as to be operationally effective and to enable developing countries to effectively take account of their development needs, including food security and rural development.

For SSA countries, therefore, a development-oriented agricultural negotiation must at the very least address four issues: domestic support and export subsidies,

[44] See, e.g., Trade Policy Review Body, "Trade Policy Review: Report of Madagascar," WT/TPR/G/197.

[45] In terms of their respective contribution to Africa's GDP, the service sector had the largest share in 2006 (44.7 percent), followed by industry (41.5 percent) and agriculture (13.8 percent). The manufacturing sector accounted for only 10.9 percent of Africa's GDP in 2006, down from an average of 12.8 percent in the period 2000–2005. See, generally, Economic Report on Africa, *supra* note 19.

market access, export competition, and sensitive and special sectors. Although, on average, Africa's access to foreign markets is better than that of America, Asia, or the Pacific, startling and disturbing wide variations exist among African countries. Studies reveal that only twenty-one African countries have better access than the world average. In contrast, thirty-two countries in Africa have less favorable access to foreign markets compared to the world average; thirteen of these countries face an average duty on export that is greater than 10 percent.[46] Malawi, a LDC, face an average tariff of 23.1 percent on its exports.

Cotton is also a real issue that must be addressed in the DDA negotiations. Cotton has become the litmus test of the commitment to a true development round, Pascal Lamy rightly noted. To countries in West and Central Africa (WCA),

> [t]he elimination of subsidies for cotton production and export is the only specific interest of WCA cotton-producing countries in the Doha Round. Any outcome of the negotiations that does not help to ensure respect for the principles of free trade and competition in global trade in cotton will be seen by the WCA countries as unbalanced, unfair and contrary to the objectives approved by all the Member countries at Doha.[47]

1. Relevance of Sector

Agriculture constitutes the backbone of most economies in Africa and "is an important key to unlocking progress in the Trade Round."[48] The agricultural sector accounts for about 17 percent of the continent's gross domestic product (GDP), 60 percent of the total labor force, and 20 percent of the total merchandise export.[49] In rural areas, agriculture supports about 70–80 percent of the total population. Agriculture also has serious implications for food security and livelihood in the continent.[50] Food import into Africa is on the rise and food insecurity is greatest in the continent. In the year 2000 alone, Africa spent an

[46] Antoine Bouët, Santosh Mishra, and Devesh Roy, "Does Africa Trade Less than It Should, and If So Why?," IFPRI Discussion Paper 00770 (May 2008).

[47] TN/AG/GEN/4 (May 16, 2003).

[48] Dr. Kipkorir Aly Azad Rana, WTO Deputy Director-General, "Prospects for the Doha Trade Round and Steps by African Countries to Draw on the Post-Doha Trading System," address at the 2004 Conference of African Ministers of Finance, Planning and Economic Development, Kampala, Uganda, May 21–22, 2004.

[49] New Partnership for Africa's Development, *Comprehensive Africa Agricultural Development Programme*, paragraph 1.1.1. (2003), hereinafter "CAADP."

[50] From 1990 through 1992, about 173 million people in Africa were chronically hungry. Between 1979 and 1999, the number had jumped to 200 million people or 28 percent of Africa's population. About 28 million Africans faced food emergencies in 2001 – a result of factors such as drought and strife; see ibid.

estimated U.S. $18.7 billion on food imports.[51] Unfortunately, the agriculture sector in Africa has consistently underperformed. Since 1960, imports of agricultural products have been rising faster than exports and "Africa as a whole has been a net agricultural importing region since 1980. Agriculture accounts for about 20 percent of total merchandise exports from Africa having declined from over 50 percent in the 1960s."[52] In short, because agriculture-led development "is fundamental to cutting hunger, reducing poverty . . . generating economic growth, reducing the burden of food imports, and opening the way to an expansion of exports,"[53] negotiation on agriculture has serious implication for Africa. In the WCA region, cotton plays an important and strategic role in poverty alleviation and overall economic development; about 5 to 10 percent of the GDP of Benin, Burkina Faso, Chad, Mali, and Togo comes from cotton, and at least thirty-three African countries are cotton producers and net exporters.[54]

2. Key African Proposals

African countries have sought to ensure that the development concerns of the continent are placed at the heart of the agricultural negotiations. Individually and collectively, SSA countries submitted about twenty proposals. Offensively, African countries call for greater market access, the elimination of destructive tariffs and nontariff barriers, and substantial reduction in domestic and export subsidies. Regarding market access, African countries are seriously concerned about tariff peaks and tariff escalation.[55] Subsidies by developed countries are also of concern;[56] most member countries of the Organization for Economic Cooperation and Development (OECD) still maintain high protection against

[51] Ibid., at 2.

[52] Ibid.

[53] Ibid., at 2.

[54] WTO/Sub-Committee on Cotton, "Summary Report on the Tenth Meeting of the Sub-Committee on Cotton Held on 2 March 2006," TN/AG/SCC/R/10 (October 6, 2006).

[55] See "Common Position of the Member States of the West African Economic Monetary Union (WAEMU) in the Multilateral Trade Negotiations on Agriculture," G/AG/NG/W/188 (September 26, 2002).

[56] The consequences of export subsidies, Namibia rightly notes, is that "is that all efforts made by countries such as Namibia are futile and hinder the very policies aimed at alleviating poverty and improving the livelihood of the rural population." See "Proposal by Namibia," G/AG/NG/W/143 (March 23, 2001). See also "Ministerial Statement," Thirty-Seventh Session of the Commission/Conference of African Ministers of Finance, Planning and Economic Development, Kampala, Uganda, May 21–22, 2004 (hereinafter "Kampala Ministerial Statement). Kampala Ministerial Statement, paragraph 6 ("For Africa, the adoption of market-distorting subsidies by our OECD partners is a core issue in multilateral trade negotiations.").

agricultural exports from Africa.[57] If OECD countries were to eliminate the U.S. $300 billion of subsidies they provide to their farmers each year, this would result in significant gains for developing countries, studies have found. The World Bank puts the income that would accrue to developing countries as a result of elimination of export subsidies at between U.S. $150 and U.S. $400 billion. African countries therefore call for a substantial reduction of export subsidies and their eventual elimination.[58] On this issue, the position of net-food-exporting countries in the continent (e.g., South Africa) is understandably at odds with that of net-food-importing countries in the region (e.g., Congo). Domestic support is also an issue. African countries propose for developed countries to reduce them significantly from their current levels. Additionally, they propose the tightening of the "green box" criteria for developed countries to ensure that it is not or is minimally trade-distorting and they call for modalities to include disciples to prevent box shifting. Overall, SSA countries have underlined the importance of meeting the Doha Round objective of real reductions in trade-distorting domestic support.

Defensively, African countries are demanding protection for sensitive and special products, are pushing for the establishment of a realistic special safeguard mechanism,[59] are calling for meaningful negotiation on commodities, and are stressing the need to resolve issues relating to net-food-importing developing countries and LDCs.[60] They want credit for unilateral liberalizations they have already carried out[61] and want to be exempted from making reduction commitments on key staples.[62] They believe that obligations to be

57 Yongzheng Yang, "Africa in the Doha Round: Dealing with Preference Erosion and Beyond," IMF Policy Discussion Paper, PDP/05/8, at 8 (2005).

58 See "The Proposal by Congo," G/AG/NG/W/135 (March 12, 2001). See also "Proposal by Namibia," G/AG/NG/W/143 (March 23, 2001).

59 See "G33 Proposal on Special Safeguard Measures," JOB(05)/92 (June 3, 2005); "Joint Communication from the G-33, African Group, ACP, and LDCs on Special Products and the Special Safeguard Mechanism," TN/AG/GEN/17 (May 11, 2006).

60 See "Modalities for Negotiation on Agricultural Commodity Issues: Proposal Submitted by the African Group to the Special Session of the Committee on Agriculture," TN/AG/GEN/18 (June 8, 2006).

61 See "Proposals by African Group," G/AG/NG/W/142 (March 23, 2001), and "Proposal by Kenya," G/AG/NG/W/136 (March 12, 2001).

62 Sandra Polaski, *Agricultural Negotiations at the WTO: First, Do No Harm*. Carnegie Endowment for International Peace, Policy Outlook, June 2005, observing that the defensive concern "is grounded in the risk that large numbers of subsistence farmers and farm workers will see their income plummet if their countries are forced to reduce agricultural tariffs covering the crops that they grow." This risk, Polaski notes, "arises because producers in other countries may be able to produce the same crop more cheaply owing to economies of scale, greater mechanization, differences in input costs, a more favorable climate, or other advantages in addition to the impact of subsidies."

undertaken by African countries should be proportional and commensurate with their level of development and, specifically, support full exemption of LDCs from any reduction commitments in agriculture.[63] African countries are also concerned about preference erosion and have put forth proposals that call for the margin of preference to be maintained and "made binding."[64] With respect to domestic support, they call for the creation of a "development box."[65]

Regarding cotton, a June 10, 2003 proposal submitted by President Blaise Compaore of Burkina Faso on behalf of the Cotton-Four (Benin, Burkina Faso, Chad, and Mali) led to the launch of the Cotton Initiative. The proposal called for (a) "[r]ecognition of the strategic nature of cotton for development and poverty reduction in many LDCs," (b) a "complete phase-out of support measures for the production and export of cotton," (c) the "[e]stablishment at Cancún of a mechanism for phasing out support for cotton production with a view to its total elimination (early harvest), and (d) transitional measures for cotton producers in LDCs in the form of financial compensation to help affected countries offset the income lost income until cotton production support measures have been completely eliminated.[66]

Overall, African countries have sought to address barriers to industrialized countries' markets while resisting the pressure to commit to further tariff reductions. They have also sought more flexibility and discretion in the use of public policies needed to enhance their prospects for industrialization, export and production diversification, and overall development. In the Kampala Ministerial Statement, African Ministers of Finance, Planning, and Development expressed concern at the unbalanced state of the global trading system and the insistence by industrialized countries that developing countries substantially reduce tariffs, noting that in many countries in the continent, "political support to cutting tariffs can only come after significant improvement in access to OECD markets that may offset the potential economic dislocation, as workers are laid off, factories closed down and government revenue diminished."[67]

[63] The Arusha Development Benchmark, *supra* note 31, paragraph 13.

[64] See "Proposals by African Group," G/AG/NG/W/142 (March 23, 2001). See also "Proposal by Kenya," G/AG/NG/W/136 (March 12, 2001).

[65] *See* G/AG/NG/W/142, Ibid.

[66] "Poverty Reduction: Sectoral Initiative in Favour of Cotton: Joint Proposal by Benin, Burkina Faso, Chad and Mali," TN/AG/GEN/4 (May 16, 2003). See also, "Poverty Reduction: Sectoral Initiative in Favour of Cotton. Joint Proposal by Benin, Burkina Faso, Chad and Mali: Proposal on Implementation Modalities," TN/AG/GEN/6 (August 4, 2003).

[67] Kampala Ministerial Statement, *supra* note 56, paragraph 9.

3. Current State of Play

What, if any, are the main achievements of the agricultural negotiation to date? In general, progress has been slow.[68] The need for countries to protect sensitive products was recognized in the "July Package of 2004," although there was no agreement on the scope or scale of protection that would be permissible.[69] At the WTO Ministerial Conference in Hong Kong in 2005, a decision was reached in principle to abolish all agricultural export subsidies by 2013.[70] It is doubtful that the 2013 goal will be met, given the unrestrained practice of box shifting and wide disagreement on the modalities for the elimination of the different subsidies. In addition, renewed application of agricultural subsidies by the EU, United States, and other industrialized countries in the wake of the global economic crisis suggests that Doha commitments may be ineffective in constraining the trade practices of the big economic powers.[71]

At the Ministerial Conference in Hong Kong, it was also decided that LDCs would not be required to undertake reduction commitments. Developed members, and developing-country members in a position to do so, committed to provide duty-free and quota-free (DFQF) market access for products originating from LDCs under at least 97 percent of tariff lines. Experts question the decision to limit the DFQF concession to 97 percent of the tariff lines, given that often what is excluded is products for which LDCs have the most comparative advantage and the most to gain from the DFQF

[68] Not surprising, in 2005, Burkina Faso decried the lack of progress regarding the issue of cotton in the WTO and expressed concern for the worsening situation of cotton producers. See "Ouagadougou Declaration on the Cotton Situation since the Adoption of the July Package: Communication from Burkina Faso," N/AG/SCC/GEN/1 (April 7, 2005).

[69] Annex A, paragraph 41, makes this statement: "Developing country Members will have the flexibility to designate an appropriate number of products as Special Products, based on criteria of food security, livelihood security and rural development needs. These products will be eligible for more flexible treatment. The criteria and treatment of these products will be further specified during the negotiation phase and will recognize the fundamental importance of Special Products to developing countries."

See the text of the July Package – "The General Council's post-Cancún decision, decision adopted by the General Council on 1 August 2004," WT/L/579 (August 2, 2004). Available at http://www.wto.org/english/tratop_e/dda_e/ draft_text_gc_dg_31july04 _e.htm. On August 1, 2004, WTO members agreed on the text of the General Council's decision on the Doha Agenda work programme (the July Package), which contains frameworks and other agreements designed to focus the negotiations. The framework for negotiation in agriculture is dealt specifically dealt with in Annex A of the document.

[70] Hong Kong Ministerial Declaration, *supra* note 3, paragraph 6 ("We agree to ensure the parallel elimination of all forms of export subsidies and disciplines on all export measures with equivalent effect to be completed by the end of 2013").

[71] WTO's Financial Crisis Report, *supra* note 9.

treatment.[72] Furthermore, to be successful, some advanced developing countries will need to commit to the DFQF initiative. Studies have found that extending the geographic coverage and number of preference-granting countries to include BRIC countries (i.e., Brazil, Russia, India, and China) would benefit African countries the most.[73]

On cotton, little progress had been made on either the trade or development aspects of the Cotton Initiative, although the General Council reaffirmed the importance of the initiative in the July Package.[74] On the trade policy side, African states are still waiting for progress on important market access issues and resolution on the subsidies issues. In the Hong Kong Ministerial Declaration, member states reaffirmed their commitment to "having an explicit decision on cotton within the agriculture negotiations and through the Sub-Committee on Cotton ambitiously, expeditiously." Specifically, developed countries committed to eliminate "all forms of export subsidies for cotton" in 2006 but to date have yet to do so. In March 2005, the WTO Dispute Settlement Body adopted Panel and Appellate Body reports on the U.S. Upland Cotton case, which found certain aspects of the U.S. cotton subsidies regime

[72] Oxfam has noted that products in which LDCs are most competitive such as textile and clothing comprise less than 3 percent of all tariff lines and could easily be excluded from benefits. See Oxfam International, "Empty Promises: What Happened to 'Development' in the WTO's Doha Round," Oxfam Briefing Paper (July 16, 2009). See also Antoine Bouët and David Laborde, "Eight Years of Doha Trade Talks: Where Do We Stand," IFPRI Issue Brief 61, p. 7 (November 2009), observing that the benefits of the DFQF Initiative "are likely to be drastically reduced by the exclusion of 3 percent of products." In comparison, a study by the IFPRI suggests that a 100 percent DFQF scenario will benefit Asian LDCs significantly by reducing the current preferential margins available to African countries in the United States under the African Growth Opportunity Act (AGOA). See Valdete Berisha-Krasniqi, Antoine Bouët, David Laborde, and Simon Mevel, "The Development Promise: Can the Doha Development Agenda Deliver for Least-Developed Countries?," IFPRI Note 14, p. 7.

[73] Berisha-Krasniqi et al., ibid., arguing that although a 100 percent DFQF regime is in the interest of Asian LDCs, "African countries will draw more benefits from a geographic extension of this regime to BrIC countries."

[74] In the July Package, the General Council did the following: (a) "recognize[d] the importance of cotton for a certain number of countries and its vital importance for developing countries, especially LDCs," (b) pledged that it will be addressed ambitiously, expeditiously, and specifically, within the agriculture negotiations, (c) declared that the Special Session of the Committee on Agriculture "shall ensure appropriate prioritization of the cotton issue independently from other sectoral initiatives," (d) decided that a subcommittee on cotton will meet periodically and report to the Special Session of the Committee on Agriculture to review progress, (e) restated that negotiations on cotton "shall encompass all trade-distorting policies affecting the sector in all three pillars of market access, domestic support, and export competition," and promised that coherence between trade and development aspects of the cotton issue will be pursued. See the text of the July Package – "The General Council's post-Cancún decision," WT/L/579 (August 2, 2004), namely the July Decision on the Development Assistance Aspects of Cotton.

in violation of WTO rules.[75] Although the decision was a victory for cotton producers in developing countries, the failure of the United States to comply with relevant aspects of the decision remains a problem and demonstrates the challenges that developing countries that attempt to utilize the dispute settlement mechanism face. On the development aspect of the Cotton Initiative, some symbolic progress has been made. For example, in March 2004, the WTO Secretariat organized a workshop on cotton in Cotonou to address the development-assistance aspect of the Cotton Initiative, but few concrete measures were adopted at this meeting.[76] In November 2004, the Committee on Agriculture Special Session established the Subcommittee on Cotton.[77] The Subcommittee was expected to "work in depth on all trade-distorting policies affecting the sector in all three pillars of market access, domestic support and export competition." Unfortunately, the last time this Subcommittee met appears to be in 2006.[78] Underscoring the low priority accorded development-related questions in DDA negotiations, cotton was not even discussed during the July 2008 mini-ministerial meeting in Geneva.

SSA countries will consider the Doha Round a failure unless key issues in the agricultural negotiations – domestic support and export subsidies, market access, export competition, and sensitive and special sectors – are addressed. For Africa, the adoption of market-distorting subsidies by the continent's OECD partners "is a core issue in multilateral trade negotiations."[79] Even if African countries succeed in their push for greater market access, they must address supply-side constraints to export if they are to maximize the opportunities presented by any improved market access. Presently, studies suggest that the benefit of improved market access will only accrue to the few countries in the continent that are net exporters of agricultural products.[80] Unfortunately, a majority of SSA countries are net food importers and are likely to suffer as world food prices rise.[81]

[75] United States – Subsidies on Upland Cotton, DISPUTE DS267.

[76] WTO African Regional Workshop on Cotton in Cotonou, Benin, March 23–24, 2004, "Report by the Secretariat," WT/L/587 (November 17, 2004). The goal of the workshop, jointly organized by the World Bank and the IMF, the WTO Secretariat, was to bring together the trade and development communities to consider the development assistance aspects of the cotton initiative. The workshop brought together eighteen multilateral institutions, Canada, China, the European Communities, Japan, and the United States, and the thirty African countries.

[77] Establishment of the Sub-Committee on Cotton: Decision adopted by the Committee on Agriculture, Special Session on November 19, 2004, TN/AG/13 (November 26, 2004).

[78] Work Program of the Sub-Committee on Cotton, adopted on March 22, 2005, TN/AG/SCC/1 (March 29, 2005).

[79] Kampala Ministerial Declaration, *supra* note 56, paragraph 6.

[80] Economic Report on Africa 2008, *supra* note 19.

[81] Yang, *supra* note 57, at 8.

B. *The Development Agenda*

Conceptually, the development dimension of the DDA is broad and covers issues such as technology transfer,[82] technical assistance and capacity building,[83] special and differential treatment (SDT) in WTO agreements,[84] and special provision and protection for LDCs.[85] Although the Doha Ministerial Declaration promised negotiations on some of the development issues, for example, the SDT provisions, for other issues an agreement was reached simply to examine them in working groups under the auspices of the General Council.[86]

1. Relevance and Scope of Issue

The development dimension is important to SSA countries and is necessary if they are to successfully implement existing obligations, effectively participate in the multilateral trading system, and benefit from the global trading system.[87] Technical assistance and capacity-building initiatives is very important to SSA countries and is needed to address a host of supply-side constraints to the continent's export. Globally, Africa is an underexporter.[88] However, recent

[82] Doha Declaration, *supra* note 13, paragraph 37.

[83] Ibid., paragraph 38, noting that technical cooperation and capacity building "are core elements of the development dimension of the multilateral trading system" and stressing that the delivery of WTO technical assistance "shall be designed to assist developing countries and least-developed countries and low-income countries in transition to adjust to WTO rules and disciples, implement obligations and exercise the rights of membership."

[84] Ibid., paragraph 44.

[85] Ibid., paragraphs 42 and 43.

[86] To be examined in working groups under the auspices of the General Council are issues such as trade, debt, and finance (paragraph 36 of the Doha Declaration) and trade and technology transfer (paragraph 37 of the Doha Declaration).

[87] Kampala Ministerial Statement, *supra* note 56, paragraph 10, observing that more progress is needed on SDT because African countries require "more flexibility and discretion in the use of public policies to enhance their prospects for industrialization, diversification of production and exports, and overall development."

[88] The question whether or not Africa is an undertrading continent is very controversial. On the one hand are those that argue that Africa is undertrading and has missed out on globalization (e.g., Sachs and Warner 1997 and Subramanian and Tamirisa 2001), and on the other hand are those who argue that Africa is not undertrading and may even be overtrading given income levels, country sizes, and geography (e.g., Coe and Hoffmaister 1998, Foroutan and Pritchett 1993, Rodrik 1998). See generally J. D. Sachs and A. M. Warner, "Sources of slow growth in African economies," 6(3) *Journal of African Economies* (1997) 335–376; A. Subramanian and N. Tamirisa, "Africa's Trade Revisited," IMF Working Paper No. 01/33 (2001); D. T. Coe and A.W. Hoffmaister, "North–South Trade: Is Africa Unusual?," IMF Working Paper No. 98/94 (1998), available at http://www.imf.org/external/pubs/ft/wp/wp9894.pdf.; F. Foroutan and L. Pritchett, "Intra-Sub-Saharan Trade: Is it Too little?," 2(1) *Journal of African Economies* (1993)

studies suggest that accounting for transportation and communication infrastructure reduced the undertrading effect for Africa, underscoring the need for assistance in the area of infrastructure development.[89]

SDT provisions are also equally important to countries in SSA. As originally conceived, SDT provisions were essentially an acknowledgment that, relative to industrialized countries, developing countries are at very different stages of economic development, have entirely different capacities as compared with developed countries in taking on multilateral commitments and obligations, and thus need accommodation in global trade rules.[90] As a package, SDT provisions have usually included better market access for developing countries' exports, a lower level of obligations for developing countries, policy space, transition periods, and technical assistance. Although in the past fifty years the multilateral trading system achieved some milestones in terms of effort to accommodate developing countries,[91] the perceived erosion of SDT provisions in Uruguay Round agreements – a shift in emphasis from enhanced market opportunities to grants of transition periods and technical assistance – is a concern for SSA countries.

2. Key African Proposals

It is widely acknowledged that existing SDT provisions in key agreements were added during Uruguay Round negotiations as afterthoughts simply to pacify developing countries without much consideration about their potential impact on development. No mechanisms were ever put in place to track progress and determine if stated objectives were being achieved. SSA countries, together with other developing countries, have long expressed concern at the erosion of SDT provisions in the Uruguay Round agreements[92] and the fact that the

74–105; D. Rodrik, "Trade policy and economic performance in Sub-Saharan Africa," NBER Working Paper No. 6562 (1998).

89 Bouët, Mishra, and Roy, *supra* note 46.

90 See "Proposal for a Framework Agreement on Special and Differential Treatment.: Communication from Cuba, Dominican Republic, Honduras, India, Indonesia, Kenya, Malaysia, Pakistan, Sri Lanka, Tanzania, Uganda and Zimbabwe," WT/GC/W/442 (September 19, 2001).

91 Milestones achieved during this period include the following: (a) the modification of Article XVIII of GATT in 1954–55 to include Article XVIII-B; (b) the establishment of the U.N. Conference on Trade and Development and the creation of the Committee on Trade and Development in the GATT in 1964; (c) the addition of Part IV on Trade and Development to the GATT in 1965; and (d) the adoption of the Enabling Clause in 1979.

92 Developing countries were concerned by the fact that the Uruguay Round agreements shifted the thrust of SDT from enhanced market opportunities and ample policy space to grants of transition periods and technical assistance. See "Proposal for a Framework Agreement on Special and Differential Treatment: Communication from Cuba, Dominican Republic,

existing provisions are legally useless as they did not go beyond a best endeavor promise.[93] Also of concern is the lack of any mechanism to ensure effective implementation of SDT provisions. African countries want SDT provisions to be fully incorporated into the architecture of WTO rules rather than exist as afterthoughts.[94] In a 2002 communication, SSA countries expressed disappointment with the nonbinding language of the SDT provisions in the Uruguay Round agreements and called for these provisions to be clarified, made legally enforceable, and, in some cases, extended.[95] Collectively, they assert the need for amendment of the SDT provisions to convert nonmandatory provisions into mandatory ones or alternatively the need for authoritative interpretation of these provisions to achieve the desired result.[96] Submissions by the African Group address agreement-specific concerns as well as several cross-cutting issues. Regarding cross-cutting issues, the African Group called for "[c]lear legal rights to enforce the provisions as binding obligations," "provisions setting out the details and mechanisms for implementing and complying with the binding provisions," "[a]ppropriate institutions to determine issues concerning implementation and compliance with the obligations, and to make authoritative recommendations that Members are to comply with," effective monitoring mechanisms, and regular evaluation of SDT in the Committee on Trade and Development, the General Council, and the Ministerial Conference.[97] SSA countries are concerned that the global crisis will lead to significant decline in aid flow.[98]

Infrastructure, particularly energy and transport, remains a major obstacle to Africa's competitiveness, according to the 2009 African Competitiveness Report. SSA countries have consistently identified the need for increased financial assistance for countries that will experience adjustment cost and the

Honduras, India, Indonesia, Kenya, Malaysia, Pakistan, Sri Lanka, Tanzania, Uganda and Zimbabwe," WT/GC/W/442 (September 19, 2001).

93 WT/GC/W/442 (September 19, 2001).

94 See "Special and Differential Treatment Provisions: Joint Communication from the African Group," TN/CTD/W/3 (May 24, 2002).

95 See "Special and Differential Treatment Provisions: Joint Communication from the African Group in the WTO," TN/CTD/W/3/Rev. 2 (July 17, 2002).

96 Ibid.

97 Ibid, calling for a "Special and Differential Treatment Monitoring Body [to] be established under the Committee on Trade and Development." See also "Special and Differential Treatment Provisions: Joint Communication from LDC Group," TN/CTD/W/4 (May 24, 2002); "Special and Differential Treatment Provisions: Joint Communication from the African Group in the WTO," TN/CTD/W/3/Rev.2 (July 17, 2002).

98 Arieff, Weiss, and Jones, *supra* note 35, at 12, observing that "[m]ost observers believe that while most aid levels will not be impacted by the crisis in 2009 and 2010, they may drop in 2011 and 2012 as developed countries experience continued fiscal strains and political pressures to balance budgets."

need for technical assistance for trade capacity building and improvement of the continent's competitiveness as one of the priority areas for Africa.[99] They have emphasized "the need for a new institutional framework and a clear mechanism for managing all the assistance and capacity building programmes within the WTO."[100] They have also stressed both "the centrality of adequate and predictable development assistance for trade capacity building for African countries" and the need for a firm commitment to expand development assistance for trade capacity building in all African countries.[101]

3. Current State of Play

Regarding SDT provisions, in Paragraph 44 of the Doha Ministerial Declaration, member states "reaffirm[ed] that provisions for special and differential treatment are an integral part of the WTO Agreements," agreed "that all special and differential treatment provisions shall be reviewed with a view to strengthening them and making them more precise, effective and operational," and endorsed the work program set out in the Decision on Implementation-Related Issues and Concerns. However, not much progress has been achieved in this area. Although the vulnerability of LDCs is widely acknowledged, there are significant obstacles to successful negotiation on SDT. The very idea of special treatment goes against the core fundamental principles underpinning the multilateral trading system. As Dr. Kipkorir Aly Azad Rana put it, "[t]here are significant challenges in this area; where the objective is to ensure that countries have flexibility and policy spaces, but in a manner that is in accordance with a non-discriminatory, rule-based multilateral trading system."[102]

Not surprisingly, little progress has been made on the SDT front. The 2001 Decision on Implementation-Related Issues and Concerns left three instructions for the Committee on Trade and Development (CTD). First, this committee is "to identify those [SDT] provisions that are already mandatory in nature and those that are non-binding in character, to consider the legal and practical implications for developed and developing Members of converting [SDT] measures into mandatory provisions, to identify those that Members consider should be made mandatory, and to report to the General Council with clear recommendations for a decision by July 2002."[103] Second, the

[99] The Arusha Development Benchmarks, *supra* note 31.
[100] Ibid., paragraph 9.
[101] Ibid., paragraph 11.
[102] Ibid.
[103] World Trade Organization, "Decision on Implementation," WT/MIN(01)/17 WT/MIN(01)/17 (decision of November 14, 2001), paragraph 12.1(i).

committee is to "examine additional ways in which [SDT] provisions can be made more effective," and "to report to the General Council with clear recommendations for a decision by July 2002."[104] Third, the committee was instructed "to consider . . . how special and differential treatment may be incorporated into the architecture of WTO rules."[105] In 2004, the General Council merely reaffirmed that SDT provisions are an integral part of the WTO agreements and instructed the Committee on Trade and Development "to expeditiously complete the review of all the outstanding Agreement-specific proposals and report to the General Council, with clear recommendations for a decision, by July 2005." SSA countries are still waiting for tangible outcomes in this area.

The Hong Kong Ministerial Declaration provides the mandate for the Aid for Trade Initiative (AfT). In paragraph 57 of the declaration, member states welcomed the discussions of Finance and Development Ministers in various fora on expanding the AfT and identifying the broad objectives of the AfT,[106] and they stressed that the AfT "cannot be a substitute for the development benefits that will result from a successful conclusion to the DDA, particularly on market access." Pursuant to the Hong Kong Ministerial Declaration, member states invited the Director-General to create a task force that shall provide recommendations on how to operationalize the AfT. If properly conceived, structured, and managed, the AfT can become one of the most important vehicles to deliver development to SSA countries.[107] Strategic issues of interest to SSA countries in the AfT are many. These include the coverage, the scope, and the types of needs to be supported by the AfT, governance and operational modalities of the AfT, and how financial needs of countries are to be appraised. At an informal African WTO Trade Ministerial Meeting in Cairo in 2009, African Ministers of Trade underscored the importance of the AfT in addressing the supply-side capacity and trade-related infrastructure and they stressed "the need to maintain the momentum in securing additional, predictable and sustainable resources."[108] They also reiterated "the importance of ensuring that the offer matches the demand, and the need for improving the aid supply mechanism, while strengthening its monitoring and assessment in

[104] Ibid., paragraph 12.1(ii).

[105] Ibid., paragraph 12.1(iii).

[106] Hong Kong Ministerial Declaration, *supra* note 3, paragraph 57: "Aid for Trade should aim to help developing countries, particularly LDCs, to build the supply-side capacity and trade-related infrastructure that they need to assist them to implement and benefit from WTO Agreements and more broadly to expand their trade."

[107] Two documents guide discussions on AfT: the OECD Paris Declaration on Aids Effectiveness (2005) and the Recommendations of the WTO Task Force on Aid for Trade (2006).

[108] Informal African WTO Trade Ministerial Meeting, "Consolidating the Development Dimension" (October 28, 2009), Cairo, Egypt.

order to maximize AFT effectiveness and impact."[109] SSA countries also worry that the AfT could create debt burden for beneficiary countries. For AfT to be effective in Africa, some factors must be present: (a) strong and purposeful country leadership; (b) renewed and stronger emphasis on regional integration and projects; (c) the need for each country and subregion to identify key priorities; (d) the need to mobilize and involve the private sector and harness public–private partnerships; (e) the need to scale up financing in line with Gleneagles and Hong Kong commitments; and (f) cooperation and coordination among all AfT actors.[110]

The AfT is essentially a new wine in an old wine skin; although the term is new, the idea of financial transfers to poor countries is not new in the history of the multilateral trading system. Unless carefully structured, the AfT could easily become a mere financial compensation for poor countries – payment for their continued marginalization in the multilateral trading system and for losses they will predictably suffer in the Doha Round.[111] The AfT must be constantly reviewed to determine its effectiveness in Africa.[112] The 2008 Aid-for-Trade Roadmap appears to provide a basis for monitoring the initiative.[113] There are additional questions that must be asked. Will funding under the AfT be at the expense of traditional development aid, especially given the global economic crisis and the resulting decline in aid flows? What direct and indirect conditionalities are attached to the AfT now or may be attached in the future? What mechanisms are in place to ensure wide stakeholder and bottom-up approaches in the design and implementation of programs under the AfT at the national and regional levels? What lessons might the designers of the AfT initiative learn from past development programs in Africa such as the Integrated Framework and the Joint Integrated Technical Assistance Program? How can the AfT support regional integration initiatives in Africa? What mechanisms will be established to minimize abuse of funds on the ground and promote transparency, accountability, and efficiency in the management of funds? How can SSA countries ensure that the AfT does not become a

[109] Ibid.

[110] United Nations Economic Commission for Africa, the African Development Bank, and the World Trade Organization, *Mobilizing Aid for Trade: Focus on Africa* (November 2007).

[111] Joseph E. Stiglitz and Andrew Charlton, "Aid for Trade" (March 2006), Report for the Commonwealth Secretariate, available at http://works.bepress.com/cgi/viewcontent.cgi?article=1008&context=joseph_stiglitz.

[112] The First Global Review was held on November 19–20, 2007. The Second Global Review of Aid for Trade was held in Geneva on July 6–7, 2009. In the lead up to the Global Review, a high level AfT meeting was held in Lusaka, Zambia on April 6–7, 2009.

[113] World Trade Organization, "2008 Aid-for-Trade Roadmap," WT/COMTD/AFT/W/6 (June 16, 2008).

substitute for the development promise of the DDA? Given that the AfT is not part of the Doha Round negotiations, how can SSA countries that suffer adjustment cost from the negotiations be assured of continued funding once the agreements are concluded?[114]

5. THE DOHA ROUND: OBSTACLES TO A PRO-DEVELOPMENT OUTCOME FOR AFRICA

African countries have cause to question the commitment of industrialized countries to a true development-oriented multilateral trading system. The relationship between Africa and the ADCs also poses real challenges for the continent and deserves a closer analysis. Furthermore, disagreements among scholars over the possible gains from trade liberalization for developing countries in general and LDCs in particular also cast a bad shadow over Doha Round negotiations. Overall, regarding efforts to improve their trade performance and foster economic growth, SSA countries face a host of external challenges.

A. *North–South Issues*

African leaders must continue to question the avowed commitment of industrialized countries to Africa's development and must continue to advance the continent's vision of development. In a 2004 ministerial declaration, African Ministers of Finance, Planning and Economic Development noted with alarm the fact that Africa's OECD partners "have been increasing domestic support to their farmers in recent years"[115] even while negotiations were going on and that market access "remains constrained also by high tariffs and tariff peaks on strategic agricultural products." With respect to tariff peaks, some as high as 900 percent, it is hard to imagine how countries in Africa can ever hope to diversify their exports. A review of the use of technical barriers to trade and sanitary and phytosanitary measures in developing countries with a view of curtailing their destructive impact on African economies is equally important.

African policymakers and scholars must continue to interrogate the claim that the dominant free-trade model can and does indeed promote development in the poorest countries. Projections of the likely outcome of the Doha Round for Africa are sobering. Frank Ackerman has argued that the dominant

[114] See generally, Sam Laird, "Aid for Trade: Cool Aid or Kool-Aid?," G-24 Discussion Paper Series No. 48 (November 2007).

[115] See Kampala Ministerial Declaration, at paragraph 6.

interpretation of the leading trade models – an interpretation that suggests that the economic effects of trade liberalization on the world as a whole are positive – is mistaken. Contrary to previous estimates, Ackerman argues that estimated benefits of trade liberalization are not only small in the aggregate but also skewed toward developed countries. Overall, he argues that the expected contribution of trade liberalization to economic development and poverty alleviation is extremely limited.[116] Reviewing the potential impact of the Doha Round in developing countries, Sandra Polaski, Director of the Trade, Equity, and Development project at the Carnegie Endowment, reaches the same troubling conclusions in a 2006 report.[117] First, the report concludes that any of the plausible trade scenarios will produce only modest gains, of the order of a one-time increase in world income of U.S. $40 to U.S. $60 billion.[118] Second, according to the report, even the modest gains that would accrue from trade liberalization would have different economic effects on different countries and regions, with the poorest countries emerging as the net losers under all likely Doha scenarios. The biggest losers "are some Sub-Saharan African countries, which see a reduction in income of just under one percent."[119] Third, although some developing countries will benefit, the report finds that "about 90 percent of the gains from Doha scenarios would come from liberalization of trade in agriculture" and that most of the gains go to China and Asian countries as opposed to Latin America and African countries.[120] Fourth, regarding agricultural liberalization, the report concludes that the benefits of liberalization "flow overwhelmingly to rich countries, while developing countries actually suffer slight losses as a group."[121] Finally, the report raises the possibility that "the poorest countries may lose from any agreement unless additional special measures are taken on their behalf," noting that "[t]he result shows that Bangladesh, East Africa, and the rest of Sub-Saharan Africa are adversely affected in almost every scenario."

SSA countries have cause to take findings that suggest marginal gains from trade for developing countries and possible losses for LDCs seriously. To proceed with any future negotiations, they will have to insist on additional special protective measures, including protection for special products and sensitive sectors, trade adjustment assistance, and enhanced aid for trade capacity

[116] Frank Ackerman, "The Shrinking Gains from Trade: A Critical Assessment of Doha Round Projections," GDAW Working Paper No. 05–01 (2005).

[117] Sandra Polaski. *Winners and Losers: Impact of the Doha Round on Developing Countries* (Carnegie Endowment for International Peace, 2006).

[118] Ibid., at viii.

[119] Ibid.

[120] Ibid.

[121] Ibid.

building. Additionally, the continent must guard against making liberalization commitments in exchange for SDT provisions of questionable utility.

B. *South–South Issues*

SSA countries rarely draw attention to tension in their South–South relations. Perhaps as a result of shared history of colonialism or oppressions or both, African leaders are reluctant to criticize the trade policies of other developing countries, particularly the ADCs. An examination of the proposals that SSA countries submitted as part of the Doha Round negotiations suggest that African leaders are neither expecting nor demanding much from ADCs. The DFQF Initiative under the Hong Kong Ministerial Declaration is an example. Paragraph 47 of the declaration committed all developed countries, and only "*developing-country Members declaring themselves in a position to do so,*" to implement DFQF market access for products originating from LDCs.[122] However, limiting the geographic coverage of the initiative is not in Africa's interest and erodes the potential benefit from the initiative. A report by the International Food Policy Research Institute (IFPRI) calls for a redesign of the DFQF Initiative extending the number and geographic coverage of granting countries, to include in particular dynamic economies such as Brazil, China, and India.[123]

Although alliances with their, southern neighbors are important in ongoing negotiations, African leaders must be willing to address perceived problems in the trade policies of the ADCs that are detrimental to the continent's economic interests. They must also be willing to criticize the negotiation tactics of these countries when they undermine the continent's own bargaining positions and proposals. Although new alliances with the ADCs are welcomed, African leaders must not hesitate to probe the short-term and long-term benefits of these alliances for the continent. South–South alliances are proliferating and deepening. Initiatives such as the New Strategic Partnership for Promoting South–South Cooperation, the 2000 Beijing Declaration of the

[122] Paragraph 47, emphasis added; the sentence reads as follows: "Building upon the commitment in the Doha Ministerial Declaration, developed-country Members, and developing-country Members declaring themselves in a position to do so, agree to implement duty-free and quota-free market access for products originating from LDC." Hong Kong Declaration, *supra* note 3.

[123] Berisha-Krasniqi et al., *supra* notes 7, 14, arguing that to be effective, the DFQF Initiative "must be supported by both OECD and BrIC countries."

Forum on China–Africa Cooperation, the Marrakech Declaration on South–South Cooperation (2003), the Marrakech Framework of Implementation of South–South Cooperation (2003), the Declaration on the Asia–African New Strategic Partnership (2005), the Declaration of the Beijing Summit of the Forum on China–Africa Cooperation (2006), and the more exclusive India–Brazil–South Africa (IBSA) Trilateral Dialogue Forum[124] all speak to renewed attempts to strengthen ties between Africa and Asia. Indeed, South–South trade and investment holds much potential for Africa's growth.[125] There are many benefits associated with increasing South–South relations.[126] Nevertheless, South–South trade and investment relations are not always mutually supporting, nor do they automatically result in win–win situations. Regarding ongoing negotiations, three issues are troubling: the possible negative impact on Africa of the outcome of the Lamy Triangle negotiations, the problem of preference erosion, and the apparent unwillingness of ADCs to make market access commitment to countries in Africa.

1. Africa and the Lamy Triangle Negotiations

Presently, African countries are caught in a battle between industrialized countries, principally the EU and United States, on the one hand, and ADCs, principally, India, Brazil, and China, on the other. The fate of Africa when triangular differences are not promptly resolved, or are resolved without keen attention to their potentially adverse impact on LDCs, is a concern. Thus far, states that make up the triangle have sought convergence points in the

[124] IBSA is a trilateral initiative between India, Brazil, and South Africa established in 2003 with the goal of promoting South–South cooperation and exchange. The IBSA Dialogue Forum was formalized with the adoption of the "Brasilia Declaration" in June 2003. See http://www.ibsa-trilateral.org/.

[125] Developing countries are trading and investing more, and doing so increasingly among themselves. Indeed, outward FDI from developing and transition economies is expanding fast – reaching U.S. $133 billion in 2005, the highest level ever – and is increasingly going into other developing countries. See "New Dynamics of South–South Development," Keynote address by Supachai Panitchpakdi, Secretary-General of the U.N. Conference on Trade and Development (UNCTAD), on United Nations Day for South–South Cooperation, December 19, 2006. Available from http://www.unctad.org/Templates/webflyer.asp?docid=7991&intItemID=3549&lang=1.

[126] According to Supachai Panitchpakdi, Secretary-General of UNCTAD, for developing countries, increasing South–South relations have many benefits, based largely on complementary environmental, climatic, cultural, economic, and social conditions. In the investment arena, for example, South–South FDI brings technology, skills, know-how, and business models that are often more suitable for developing-country needs than those from the developed world. See ibid.

market access and domestic pillars of the agricultural negotiation, with little success. Inadequate representation of the interest of African countries in the Lamy Triangle negotiations is a concern. Regarding the special safeguard mechanisms debacle, although special safeguard mechanisms are of serious importance to countries in Africa, the position of all developing countries and LDCs was primarily argued by Mr. Kamal Nath, Indian Minister for Commerce and Industry. Did India adequately and successfully represent the interests of some 100 developing nations that had an interest in the issue? This less-than-transparent and-democratic process occurred despite repeated pleas by many SSA countries for inclusion in the negotiations. In a 2007 declaration issued by the African, Caribbean, and Pacific Group of States, participants gave this statement:

> We have been concerned that the recent negotiating process has been less than transparent and participatory. *Although it is widely known that important negotiations are taking place in the G4 process, the vast majority of members have little or no knowledge of the progress and content of different stages of the negotiations. Although two developing countries are part of the G4, we cannot expect them to carry the responsibility of representing the views and positions of all developing countries.* We have been told that the Geneva multilateral process is central, but without knowledge of the political or technical aspects of the G4 negotiations, it is not possible for the majority of members to prepare themselves or provide inputs.[127]

Concern about transparency and inclusion in trade negotiations is heightened by recent suggestions about how to jump-start the Doha trade talks and reach a pro-liberalization outcome. Believing that one factor that constrains the Doha Round bargaining program is the large number of negotiating members, some authors have suggested limiting negotiations to OECD countries and a few middle-income countries. Razeen Sally comes to this conclusion:

> Stated baldly: only a minority of the WTO members have the bargaining power and capacity to advance negotiations. These are the OECD countries and about a score or so of advanced developing countries (most of them in the G20). Hence the key liberalizing and rule-making deals in the WTO must be done by the 30-plus countries (counting the EU as one) that account

[127] The Secretariat of the African, Caribbean and Pacific Group of States, "Declaration on Development Concerns and Issues in the Current WTO Negotiations" (June 21, 2007); emphasis added. See http://www.acpsec.org/geneva/declaration_development_e.htm.

> for over 80% of international trade and an even bigger share of foreign direct investment.[128]

It would be wrong to exclude SSA countries from negotiations. Excluding poor countries from negotiations will undermine the credibility of the WTO and reinforce the view that the multilateral trading system is for rich countries. Second, it is not even clear which middle-income countries would be excluded. Will China, India, and Brazil be in or out? Third, excluding poor countries goes against the development objectives of the Doha Round.[129] Fourth, limiting future negotiations to rich countries violates the letter and spirit of the Doha Ministerial Declaration, particularly Paragraph 48, which states that negotiations shall be open to "*all* members of the WTO," and Paragraph 49, which promises that negotiations "shall be conducted with a view to ensuring benefits to *all* participants and to achieving an overall balance in the outcome of the negotiations."

Overall, transparency in trade talks is very important for the credibility of the WTO. SSA countries must reject any effort to buy their agreement. The negotiating process must be multilateral, transparent, and adopt a bottom-up approach. In 2009, African trade ministers gave this statement:

> We strongly reemphasize that the negotiating process must remain multilateral and fully transparent, with a bottom-up approach. We consider that informal bilateral and plurilateral consultations may be useful in enhancing mutual understanding. However, such consultations cannot be a substitute for a genuine multilateral process, nor should they affect the consensus reached within the multilateral context. We also stress the need for Africa's full participation in all negotiating processes based on balanced and consensually agreed agendas. In this respect, we underline that issues pertaining to the African Group should be adequately addressed and not sidelined nor relegated.[130]

[128] Razeen Sally, "The End of the Road for the WTO?," 5(1) *World Economics* (2004), 1. Several factors appear to support this position: the fact that many developing countries lack the resources needed to effectively participate in trade negotiations and the fact that LDCs are not required to liberalize under current negotiations and, hence, are functionally if not formally excluded from negotiation, and the fact that given their negligible share in world trade, including poor countries in negotiations is inefficient and practically useless. See Bouët and Laborde, *supra* note 72, at 17.

[129] Ibid., at 18 (finding that the exclusion of WTO members is efficient but quite opposite to the essence of multilateralism).

[130] In 2007, the ACP Council of Ministers, in its meeting in Brussels on May 22–24, 2007, adopted a decision that reaffirmed that the WTO negotiating processes "should be transparent, inclusive and with a bottom-up approach" and furthermore underlined that "ACP members should be accorded adequate time to examine in detail the proposals submitted by other WTO Members

2. Preference Erosion

Preference erosion is a major concern of African countries in ongoing negotiations.[131] African countries are also grappling with preference erosions resulting from unilateral liberalization by industrialized and newly industrializing countries and from new preferential trade arrangements that exclude them. Experts already note that "it is difficult for African countries to seek greater market access while trying to retain preferences, because any most-favored-nation (MFN) reduction in trade barriers tends to level the playing field."[132] Is preference erosion a huge problem? Experts disagree.[133] Africa's less-than-optimal utilization of existing preferences means that countries in the region will not be drastically affected by the impact of preference erosion, some have argued.[134] If deeper tariff cuts and attendant preference erosion is inevitable, then African countries may need to rethink any future liberalization commitments on their part that are prompted by promises of preferential treatments. They must adopt policies that can help the continent cushion the effects of these erosions as they occur and must also factor potential erosions into their present strategies.

3. Market Access in Emerging Economies

Trade opportunities for Africa's primary export are still dominated by developed country markets. However, Africa must increasingly look beyond

and Chairs of the negotiating bodies with a view to consulting their respective authorities and taking informed decision on these proposals."

[131] Preference erosion, Yang explains, refers to the "reduction in the tariff advantage enjoyed by a preference beneficiary vis-à-vis its competitions." Preference erosion is a problem because it "reduces the export competitiveness of the beneficiary by making its competitors' exports less expensive in the preference-giving market." See Yang, *supra* note 57, at 2. See Bouët and Laborde, *supra* note 72, at 5, concluding that, under the DDA, LDCs would improve their access to foreign markets "but would also suffer an erosion of preferences, especially in agriculture."

[132] Ibid., at 11.

[133] Yang, *supra* note 57. Here he is citing a 2003 IMF report suggesting that, for LDCs as a whole, losses from preference erosion as a result of MFN tariff cuts by the Quad – Canada, Japan, EU, and the United States – will "probably amount to less than 2 percent of exports" and that for the few countries that may experience significant losses, such losses are manageable because unlike other trade shocks, the impact of preference erosion can be anticipated. Yang, however, cautions against drawing conclusions about the impact of preference erosion on African countries based on the few studies that are available.

[134] Ibid., at 13, observing that there is "considerable empirical evidence to suggest that preference beneficiaries often fail to take advantage of preference offered, either because they are unable to meet the rules of origin associated with preferential market access, or because domestic industries fail to respond to increased export opportunities."

industrialized countries' markets to markets in Asia and Latin America. The Doha Round package must also be evaluated for their effect on South–South trade. Judging from the December 2008 Chairs' proposal, will a resulting Doha Agreement improve or discourage South–South trade?[135] In a recent report, Boutë and Laborde conclude that South–South trade improvements "will be limited in the Doha Agreement due to generous flexibilities for developing countries and will not lead to significant reorientation of developing countries' exports." To encourage more South–South trade, they suggest (a) reducing flexibilities that affect South–South trade; (b) expanding regional agreements among developing countries; and (c) increasing investment in trade-related infrastructure adapted to South–South trade.[136]

The ADCs could become Africa's most dynamic export market because of rapid income growth and rising standards of living. In 2000–2001, trade between India and Africa stood at about U.S. $3 million; the number jumped to about U.S. $36 million in 2007–2008. In March 2009, the Indian External Affairs Minister, Pranab Mukherjee, forecasted that "[g]iven the concrete opportunities that exist between the two sides, India–Africa trade could easily be doubled to $70 billion over the next five years."[137] Given the potential that exist in ADC markets, policymakers in Africa must begin to identify, highlight, and condemn destructive tariff and nontariff barriers to African goods in ADC markets.[138] What at-the-border and behind-the-border rules, regulations, and standards in China, India, Brazil, and other emerging economies operate as barriers to African export? What tariff and nontariff barriers do African exporters face in these markets? According to a World Bank report, African exports face relatively high tariffs in Asia.[139] Specifically, "[a]mong Asian countries, the tariff levels of China and India on African products remain high."[140] The report further notes that the overall tariff effectiveness on African imports in Asian countries "is in part a reflection of the lack or limited scope of Asian

[135] Ibid., at 8.

[136] Ibid.

[137] Ashok B. Sharma, "India Calls to Boost Trade with Africa to $70 bn," *The Financial Express*, March 23, 2009. Available at http://www.financialexpress.com/news/india-calls-to-boost-trade-with-africa-to-70-bn/437998.

[138] In the Forum on China–Africa Cooperation – Beijing Action Plan 2007–2009, China pledged to increase the number of export items to China eligible for zero-tariff treatment from the LDCs in Africa from 190 to over 440.

[139] Harry G. Broadman, *Africa's Silk Road: China and India's New Economic Frontier* (2006), 120. He observed that "[a]lthough Asian tariffs for Africa are gradually declining, the trend is very weak, especially for exports from African least developed countries (LDCs)." See Yang, *supra* note 35, at 8, observing that in the industrial sector, Africa faces much higher tariffs in developing-country markets.

[140] Ibid.

preferences granted to Africa compared to those granted by the United States and EU."[141] Tariff peaks and escalations in the Asian market are another cause of concern.[142] According to the World Bank, tariff escalation "is quite visible in Asian markets on some of the leading exports from Africa."[143] Nontariff barriers in key Asian and Latin American markets pose serious problems for Africa as well. The increase of technical measures and sanitary and phytosanitary measures in many countries, the fact that most technical measures are applied to agricultural products, the primary export from Africa,[144] and the fact that developed countries and Asia have doubled their technical measures up to 50 percent[145] mean that, for Africa, the promised gains from trade may not materialize any time soon. Overall, African countries carry a higher nontariff barrier burden than any other continent because "the majority of LDCs are in Africa," the World Bank has noted.[146]

Thus far, African countries have sought greater market access in industrialized countries. However, the continent has an ever-increasing interest in trade reforms in other developing countries and should push for these reforms in the course of ongoing negotiations and in the context of bilateral trade and investment negotiations. Using the continent's most attractive assets – natural resources – as bargaining chips, African leaders can open up ADC markets in ways that can significantly benefit ordinary men and women in Africa. In dealings with the ADCs, African leaders must pay attention to the *composition* of trade as well as the *terms* of trade. Troubling is the evidence that "African exports to China and India have consisted mostly of raw materials, corresponding with the investment focus," whereas "African imports from Asia consist mainly of manufactured products."[147] African countries must increasingly press the ADCs on these issues. Preferential schemes for African goods by ADCs must also be seriously evaluated for their effectiveness. In 2007, China announced the elimination of tariffs on 440 products exported by African

[141] Ibid.

[142] Ibid., at 126, specifically "Asia's tariff structure consists of many peaks and escalations." Tariff peaks arise when a government maintains excessively high tariffs on products that it considers sensitive in order to protect domestic producers. "Tariff escalation" is a term used to describe a situation in which an importing country, with a goal of protecting its processing or manufacturing industry, sets low tariffs on imported raw materials used by the industry but sets higher tariffs on finished products to protect the goods produced by the industry.

[143] Ibid., at 126.

[144] Ibid., at 133, noting that LDCs carry a higher than average burden of nontariff barriers because they export mainly agricultural products.

[145] Ibid.

[146] Ibid. The World Bank also notes that nontariff barriers are "present in African industries where protection of domestic businesses from import surges is sought." Ibid., at 134.

[147] Economic Report on Africa 2008, *supra* note 19, at 33.

LDCs that have diplomatic relations with it. In 2008, India announced a duty-free tariff preferential scheme for forty-nine LDCs. How these preferential schemes are working in practice must be constantly monitored and fully evaluated.[148] It is also not clear how nontariff barriers such as rules of origin, costs of documentation, and sanitary and phytosanitary measures undermine or nullify what, at first glance, appear to be generous preference schemes for African LDCs by China and India. Regarding China's preference scheme, although many important primary products or simply transformed manufactures qualify for duty-free treatment, important products such as cotton are excluded from the list. Cotton, a very vital export for LDCs in Africa, faces a 40 percent tariff in China and costs the affected LDCs an implicit transfer of $68.6 million per year.[149]

In sum, countries in SSA must go beyond their commitment to South–South solidarity and increasingly press the ADCs for meaningful and effective trade and investment arrangements.[150] Emerging South–South initiatives such as the IBSA Dialogue Forum and the Forum on China–Africa Cooperation can be useful platforms for addressing serious trade and investment issues and a mechanism for strengthening cooperation in key sectoral areas of interest to Africa. Although unilateral trade preferences can be valuable, it is important to carefully scrutinize each preference scheme and assess the difference, if any, such scheme is likely to have on the economies of recipient countries. To ensure that countries use the temporary price advantage that preference schemes offer to expand their existing export industries and create or develop new ones, SSA countries must address major supply-side constraints to their export.[151]

148 In evaluating the value of these preferences, several questions must be asked. Are the preferences well tailored to the export capacity of African LDCs? What is the average margin of preference for qualifying products? What is the overall economic value of each preference? What products are excluded from the duty-free list? See Adam Minson, "China's Preferential Trade Policy for Africa," 1 *China in Africa* (February 2008), estimating, using a simplistic "implicit transfer" calculation, that the overall economic value of China's preference scheme for African LDCs to be of the order of $10 million per year and suggesting that the most valuable Chinese preferences are either primary products or simply transformed manufactures.

149 Ibid.

150 In 2008, Ghana and Brazil signed a memorandum of understanding on cooperation in the energy sector during Brazilian President Lula da Silva's visit to Ghana. Although the Brazilian President told reporters that Brazil had made Africa a priority in its international relations and although he called for more flexibility to give market access to agricultural products from poor countries and removal of agricultural subsidies by rich countries, he was less clear on how African export can enjoy greater market access in the Brazilian market.

151 Minson, *supra* note 148, at 3, observing that, barring unexpected strong supply response from Africa, China's unilateral preference scheme "will not alter trade flows to China much, and

6. BEYOND DOHA: STRATEGIES FOR ACTION FOR SSA COUNTRIES

"[T]he greatest challenge facing Africa at the dawn of this millennium," the African Union's Commissioner for Trade and Industry, Mrs. E. Tankeu, recently noted, "is to achieve rapid and sustainable development, eradicate poverty . . . and integrate [the] continent into the global community as an effective and respectable partner."[152] The present impasse in trade talks provides an opportunity for African leaders to reassess the costs and benefits of participation within the multilateral framework, rethink their negotiating strategies and tactics, reevaluate their relationship with key industrialized countries and the ADCs, and look inward for solutions to the continent's development challenges. Regarding the later, meaningful and committed domestic reform as well as renewed focus on intraregional trade is urgently needed.

A. *Regional Integration*

Perhaps the most beneficial frameworks for Africa are interregional and intraregional trade arrangements.[153] Unfortunately, in Africa, intraregional trade agreements have not always been accompanied by significant intraregional trade.[154] Intra-African trade currently accounts for a miserly 10 percent of Africa's total export and has remained largely unchanged between 1970 and 2004.[155] Between 1996 and 2005, African export to the world grew faster than trade within the continent.[156] This is unfortunate because regional integration can "drive intra-African trade and stimulate export diversification."[157] As Omar Kabbaj, President of the African Development Bank Group, rightly notes, the policies of open regionalism "have the added advantage of enabling

certainly will not reduce the bilateral trade deficits run by those of Africa's economies that do not export oil."

[152] Statement by Mrs. E. Tankeu, AU Commissioner for Trade and Industry, Conference of African Ministers of Finance, Planning and Economic Development, Kampala, Uganda, May 21, 2004.

[153] UNCTAD, *Economic Development in Africa: Strengthening Regional Economic Integration for Africa's Development* (June 25, 2009).

[154] UNCTAD, *Trade and Development Report 2007* (2007), 100, observing that "the relatively small weight of intraregional trade in Africa, despite the existence of several (and frequently overlapping) RTAs, is due largely to their structure of production and the composition of their exports. As many countries are still specialized in a small number of primary products, while most of their imports consist of manufactures, the potential for intraregional trade is limited."

[155] Yang, *supra* note 56, at 4.

[156] Economic Report on Africa 2008, *supra* note 19, at 85.

[157] "Africa Needs to Remove Obstacles to Trade, Says Amoako," Economic Commission for Africa Press Release No. 11/2004.

African producers to develop the know-how and the capacity to compete in the global market." Regional integration can make for regional stability, enterprise development, product diversification, and overall economic growth. U.S. Secretary of State Hillary Clinton recently noted, "if African countries began to trade with one another, they would quickly have more increase in GDP than they could ever imagine by just bilateral agreements with Europe and the United States."[158] A serious, concerted, and sustained effort directed at improving intraregional trade is called for in a number of areas, including the elimination of tariff and nontariff barriers to intraregional trade, improvement of deficient physical infrastructure, and reform of institutional infrastructure in the continent.

Constraints to intraregional trade are legion and generally include inadequate physical infrastructure, relatively small markets, lack of current market information and trading skills, uncertain policy environment, and unstable market opportunities.[159] A recent report from the U.N. Conference on Trade and Development (UNCTAD) suggests measures that African countries could take in order to unlock the opportunities offered by regional economic integration. The report suggests the following: developing a regional cooperation strategy centered on infrastructure development, undertaking FDI projects on a regional basis, deepening the regulatory measures to encourage intra-African FDI, encouraging regional rather than bilateral investment agreements, further developing a strong financial sector, implementing and enforcing provisions contained in relevant treaties, promoting the creation of large service firms, addressing trade facilitation and regional integration in a mutually supported manner, and ensuring that migration brings net gains for both the home and host countries.[160]

Policymakers on the continent recognize the need to speed up the economic integration of the continent. In the February 3, 2009 declaration on the international financial crisis, African heads of state invited the African Union Commission to finalize the Minimum Integration Programme and diligently carry out its concerted implementation with the aim of integrating the continent politically and economically.[161] The heads of state also invited the African

[158] Hillary Rodham Clinton, Secretary of State, "Remarks at the Corporate Council on Africa's Seventh Biennial U.S.-Africa Business Summit," available at http://www.state.gov/secretary/rm/2009a/10/130182.htm.

[159] CAADP, *supra* note 49, paragraph 1.8.2.

[160] See UNCTAD, *Economic Development in Africa Report 2009: Strengthening Regional Economic Integration for Africa's Development* (2009). See also "Strengthening Regional Integration in Africa: Some Policy Recommendations," available at http://www.unctad.org/Templates/WebFlyer.asp?intItemID=4920&lang=1.

[161] See "Addis Ababa Declaration on the International Financial Crisis," *supra* note 5, paragraph 15.

Union Commission "to fast track and quickly finalise the preparatory work for the establishment of the African Investment Bank, the African Monetary Fund and the African Central Bank."[162]

B. *Domestic Reform*

Because the benefits of multilateral trade reform and liberalization are neither automatic nor autonomous, African leaders must take steps to facilitate economic growth and maximize possible benefits from a post-Doha multilateral trading system. The institutional and physical prerequisites for strong, vibrant, and competitive private-sector-led growth must be strengthened. Corruption remains a major enemy of progress and sustainable development in the continent. A healthy and educated workforce is also a vital to the continent's competitiveness because it helps to attract foreign investment and is important for moving up in the value chain.[163] Although there are notable country exceptions and wide variation in the performance of individual countries, by and large Africa lags behind other regions on most of the twelve pillars in the Global Competitiveness Index: institutions (public and private), infrastructure, macroeconomic stability, health and primary education, higher education and training, goods market efficiency, labor market efficiency, financial market sophistication, technological readiness, market size, business sophistication, and innovation.[164] The challenge for policymakers in Africa is to curb official corruption, invest in education and health, genuinely promote the rule of law and ensure political stability, build credible and transparent institutions, reduce external debt, mobilize domestic and external resources to meet the millennium development goals, integrate trade into broader development policies, and adopt policies that stimulate economic growth while shielding the poor and vulnerable groups.

Of all developing regions, Africa's exports are the least diversified. Export and production diversification is important if SSA countries are to improve their trade performance and reduce risk to future economic crisis. Although this calls for a reform of domestic policies and significant infrastructure improvement, there is also a role for the international community. The result of Doha Round negotiations for nonagricultural products will undoubtedly affect efforts of countries at diversification, particularly efforts to promote manufacturing and move away from overreliance on primary commodity exports. How to conduct

[162] Ibid., at paragraph 16.

[163] World Economic Forum, *The Africa Competitiveness Report 2009* (2009), vxi.

[164] Ibid., at 4. The World Economic Forum defines competitiveness as "the set of institutions, policies, and factors that determine the level of productivity of a country."

tariff-cutting exercises and what to do with tariff peaks and tariff escalations are issues that have implications for SSA countries.

Perhaps in realization of the need to integrate trade reform and liberalization into the process of domestic economic reforms, the 2004 Ministerial Conference of the Economic Commission for Africa set its theme as "Mainstreaming Trade Policy in National Development Strategies." Mainstreaming trade policy into national development strategies would require a reexamination of a host of issues, including investment climate and regulations, rural infrastructure, export promotion, competition law and policy, trade capacity building, and tariff harmonization. Effective mainstreaming would also require that African governments adopt measures to provide assistance for adjustment costs, which are attendant with trade reform and liberalization.[165]

7. CONCLUSION

Several conclusions can be made. First, SSA countries must continue to insist that the DDA negotiating process must be transparent and inclusive, adopt a bottom-up approach, and take into account resource constraints that may limit the participation of developing countries, particularly LDCs. They must be bold to expose less-than-transparent negotiation processes when they occur. Second, preferential market access such as that agreed to by the WTO Members for LDCs and defined in the Hong Kong Ministerial Declaration is a welcome start but is not enough; structural distortions in agricultural markets must also be removed. Third, SSA countries in general and African LDCs in particular are seriously affected by rules of origin, sanitary and phytosanitary regulations, and technical regulations; effective market access requires that these issues be addressed as well. Fourth, in the agricultural negotiations, SSA countries must not lose sight of nontrade concerns of interest to the continent: (a) rural development (production, jobs, and income); (b) poverty reduction; (c) food security; (d) environmental protection; (e) adoption of a sectoral development policy; and (f) farming diversity and flexibility in the formulation of national policies.[166] Fifth, effective market access must also be supported by effective, sustained, and sustainable technical assistance and capacity-building initiatives, given evidence that trade-related infrastructure is a significant determinant of trade flows.[167] The WTO's AfT agenda must be

[165] Ibid.

[166] WTO, "Negotiating Proposals by the Democratic Republic of the Congo," G/AG/NG/W/135 (March 12, 2001).

[167] Bouët, Mishra, and Roy, *supra* note 46, suggesting that even if preferences help raise the levels of Africa's export, the continent will likely continue to trade less than it should, given the low quality of trade-related infrastructure in the continent.

constantly subjected to serious scrutiny. The premise, packaging, and delivery must be vigorously interrogated. Is the AfT package merely a "bribe" to buy the agreement of developing countries to a Doha Round agreement that is not in their interest and bound to result in net losses for them? Finally, SSA countries must increasingly seek concessions from developing countries such as Brazil, Russia, India, and China (the BRIC countries), whose growth in the past few years has driven the growth of the global economy and who are increasingly seen as critical for ensuring continued global economic prosperity.

Despite assurances by the WTO Director-General to the contrary, to many observers the Doha Round is all but dead.[168] Predictably, trade negotiations have followed country-strategic interests. The sheer number of countries formally involved in the negotiation, the fact that talks have thus far focused on the agricultural sector (a highly sensitive sector), the diversity in the economic size and situation of participants, and the emergence of countries such as Brazil, India, and China as key players in global trade are some of the factors that complicate the Doha negotiations. Even if the Round could be revived, few believe that the development dimension remains central to the outcome of the Round despite claims to the contrary by the WTO Director-General.[169] There has been no significant progress on issues of interest to Africa despite conclusion by bodies such as the Group of Eight (G-8) that "[a]n ambitious and balanced conclusion to the Doha Round is the best way to make trade work for Africa and increase African countries' integration into the global economy."[170] It is increasingly doubtful that the expectations for the Doha

[168] On March 26, 2010, WTO's Director-General told the Trade Negotiations Committee that, judged by his informal discussions with delegations during the WTO's stock-taking week, "nobody is contemplating dropping the ball" and that "[e]veryone is still very much committed to the mandate of the Round and to its successful conclusion." See Trade Negotiation Committee, "Stocktaking Ends with Collective Determination to Start Building Global Doha Package" (March 26, 2010), available at http://www.wto.org/english/news_e/news10_e/tnc_dg_stat_26mar10_e.htm.

[169] Director-General Pascal Lamy told the Trade Negotiations Committee on March 26, 2010 that, in discussions with delegations during the stock-taking week, delegations emphasized a number of principles that should guide the next steps of trade negotiation: the centrality of the multilateral dimension of the negotiations, the need to build on what is already on the table in the shape of Chairs' texts, and the centrality of the development dimension to the outcome of the Round. See Trade Negotiation Committee, "Stocktaking Ends with Collective Determination to Start Building Global Doha Package" (March 26, 2010), available at http://www.wto.org/english/news_e/news10_e/tnc_dg_stat_26mar10_e.htm. In comparison, see Raj Bhala, "Resurrecting the Doha Round: Devilish Details, Grand Themes, and China Too," 45 *Tex. Int'l L. J.* 1 (2009), observing that even if the Doha Round can be resurrected and completed, that resurrection is quite unlikely to alleviate the suffering of the poor or strengthen moderate Muslim countries.

[170] See the G-8 Gleneagles Declaration, available at http://data.unaids.org/Topics/Universal Access/PostG8_Gleneagles_Africa_en.pdf.

Round will be realized. There does not appear to be enough political will at the WTO to address core impediments to African export. Even if a deal on agriculture is realized, negotiations on other issues including sanitary and phytosanitary measures, rules, technical barriers to trade, trade-related investment measures, antidumping, rules of origin, subsidies and countervailing measures, trade-related aspects of intellectual property, and the dispute settlement understanding all have serious implications for developing countries and may erode any gains realized from successful negotiation on agriculture. The lack of progress in the work mandated on the modalities for agriculture and development dimension raises serious concerns that Africa will remain on the losing side of the globalization process.

The failure of the Doha Round will be particularly troubling to SSA countries given the present global economic crisis and the attendant contraction in international trade. As a result of the crisis, trade flows in Africa has been seriously constrained by three external factors: the falling price for export commodities, the growing decline in overall trade volumes, and the shortage of trade finances. External trade and a successful development-oriented Doha Round is a critical element in the efforts of SSA countries to mitigate the impact of the crisis, cope with the effects of the crisis, and reduce future risks by adopting trade policies that limit their vulnerability to future crisis and build their resilience over the longer term.[171] In the wake of the crisis, experts identify expanding trade and expanding trade finance as necessary mitigation measures that are needed in SSA; this requires meaningful commitment from the international community.[172] At the recently concluded Sixth Ordinary Session of the African Union Conference of Ministers of Trade in Kigali, Rwanda, 1–2 November 2010, African Ministers of Trade emphasized that "successful conclusion of the Doha Round, with the development component at its core, remains an imperative for African countries . . . as it will further support their integration into the multilateral trading system, and contribute to restoring

[171] At an informal African WTO Trade Ministerial Meeting, the Ministers of Trade from African countries underscored "that the early and successful conclusion of the Doha Development Round, with the developmental component at its core, has become imperative as a stimulus for the growth of African economies, and represent their means towards further integration in a more strengthened and development friendly multilateral trading system, in addition to contributing to restoring the confidence in world markets." See "Informal African WTO Trade Ministerial Meeting, Consolidating the Development Dimension," Cairo (October 28, 2009), available at http://www.iatp.org/tradeobservatory/library.cfm?refID=106957.

[172] Augustin Kwasi Fosu and Wim Naudé, "Policy Response to the Global Crisis in Africa," 3 *United Nation University* (2009), p. 2. The international community's role in mitigation measures is, inter alia, to facilitate the demand for Africa's exports, provide sustainable technical assistance that can help countries address the supply-side constraints to the effective participation in the multilateral trading system.

confidence in the current profile world markets." Also very troubling to SSA countries is the fact that despite the avowed commitment to trade liberalization, protectionist measures are on the rise in the G-20.[173] In the wake of the global financial crisis, protectionist forces have emerged in many countries and are expected to strengthen as the recession gets worse.[174] In many industrialized and newly industrializing countries, "[g]overnments' crisis-fighting measures have spawned new, murkier forms of protection."[175]

Absent a successful conclusion of the Doha Round, a patchwork of bilateral and regional trade deals may be the way for the foreseeable future. Consequently, Africa's trade ministers must either press to resume multilateral negotiations or shift their focus toward creating and strengthening fair bilateral and regional trade arrangements and instituting serious economic, political, and social reforms at the domestic level; they must resist pressures to accept side payments as prize for a failed Doha Round.[176] International financial transfers, such as aid for development or adjustment packages, are okay provided they are not a substitute for reforming the multilateral trading system and rebalancing decades of unfair trade rules in agriculture. Although such side payments may be the only tangible gain some poor countries can hope to make from the Doha Round,[177] there are several problems with such side payments.

The Doha Round cannot address all the development challenges facing Africa. Greater coherence in international monetary, financial, and trade policy making and better coordination in the activities of the key global institution are needed. The trade policies of the United States, the European Union, and

[173] G-20 leaders pledged to avoid protectionist policies and revive Doha Round talks at their November 2008 summit in Washington, DC, their April 2009 summit in London, and their September summit in Pittsburgh. At the April 2009 summit in London, G-20 leaders "underscore[ed] the critical importance of rejecting protectionism and not turning inward in times of financial uncertainty," and pledged, within the next twelve months, to "refrain from raising new barriers to investment or to trade in goods and services, imposing new export restrictions, or implementing [WTO] inconsistent measures to stimulate exports." They also pledged to "strive to reach agreement this year on modalities that leads to a successful conclusion to the WTO's Doha Development Agenda with an ambitious and balanced outcome." See London Declaration Summit on Financial Market and the Global Economy, November 15, 2008. At Pittsburgh, G-20 leaders pledged to fight protectionism and made a commitment to "bring... the Doha Round to a successful conclusion in 2010." See Leaders' Statement adopted at the Pittsburgh Summit, September 24–29, 2009.

[174] Richard Baldwin and Simon J. Eveneth, "Introduction and Recommendations for the G-20," in Richard Baldwin and Simon Eveneth, eds., *The Collapse of Global Trade, Murky Protectionism, and the Crisis: Recommendations for the G20* (2009), p. 1.

[175] Ibid.

[176] Bouët and Laborde, *supra* note 72, at 19.

[177] Ibid., at 20, noting that "[f]or LDCs, the obtained side payments are the only source of gain (e.g., Bangladesh and SSA) and are quite significant (about 2.5 of SSA countries)."

China will have a significant impact on the trade performance of SSA countries and must be constantly scrutinized; cumulatively, the three countries account for nearly 70 percent of African trade.[178] Countries in SSA must also seek to build new South–South alliances and to strengthen and scrutinize existing ones; this will establish new markets for the continent's export and help reduce their export exposure to advanced economies.[179] Although trade relations with China have improved over the past couple of years (China now accounts for roughly 13 percent of African export), the terms of trade with China are troubling. Overall, SSA countries must approach trade and investment negotiation from a position of strength rather than a position of timidity and powerlessness. After all, "Africa is key to the United States and to global energy security,"[180] the U.S. Secretary of State recently noted. Nonetheless, in trade talks, Africa is often treated and allows itself to be treated as a charity case. With principled, dedicated, and visionary leadership committed to a people-centered development strategy and respect for the rule of law, and using its best assets as strong bargaining chips, Africa can approach bilateral and multilateral trade talks from a position of strength.

[178] It is significant that under AGOA and despite pledges by successive U.S. administrations to help Africa diversify the continent's export base, oil and mineral fuels still account for roughly 80 percent of all U.S. imports from Africa and 92 percent of all U.S. imports under AGOA. See Arieff, Weiss and Jones, *supra* note 35, at 7.

[179] Ibid., at 7, observing that "African countries' exposure to advanced economies – the degree to which economic shifts in developed countries may impact African economies through decreased demand for African export – has increased in recent years."

[180] Hillary Rodham Clinton, Secretary of State, "Remarks at the Corporate Council on Africa's Seventh Biennial U.S.–Africa Business Summit," available at http://www.state.gov/secretary/rm/2009a/10/130182.htm.

5

The Politics of Legitimacy in the UNCITRAL Working Methods

Claire R. Kelly

The process of international law-making is, in part, a function of politics. States, and society, assert their interests and values and strive to have them reflected in the resulting substantive law. The ability to control the process of international norm generation – who participates, how decisions are made, and when agendas move forward – is the power to control the substance of international law making. States also use process to generate legitimate norms. Good procedures enable representative, transparent, and effective rules. Whether process serves politics or legitimacy (or both) is not always easy to determine.

This chapter considers a controversy over the methods of work (working methods) at the United Nations Commission on International Trade Law (UNCITRAL) and whether it represents a political struggle or a debate over the best means to achieve more legitimate rules. UNCITRAL develops international norms that affect a variety of trade issues.[1] It has had considerable success. As an organ of the United Nations (UN), it operates under the procedures set forth by the General Assembly.[2] Although it has not adopted its own

[1] The issues addressed "include dispute resolution, international contract practices, transport, insolvency, electronic commerce, international payments, secured transactions, procurement and sale of goods." United Nations Commission on International Trade Law, *The UNCITRAL Guide: Basic Facts About the United Nations Commission on International Trade Law* at 1, U.N. Sales No. E.07.V.12 (2007); hereafter "UNCITRAL, *Guide*."

[2] Rule 161 of the Rules of Procedure of the General Assembly states that any procedural rules applicable to General Assembly committees, as well as Rules 45 and 60, will apply to subsidiary bodies unless otherwise specified. See United Nations, "Rules of Procedure of the General Assembly," at 44, U.N. Doc. A/520/Rev.17 (2008); hereafter "U.N., 'Rules of Procedure.'"

Note: I am grateful to Dean Joan Wexler and the Summer Research Stipend Program at Brooklyn Law School for their generous support. I appreciate the comments of Neil B. Cohen and Dana Brakman Reiser and I am also thankful for the helpful research assistance of John Patitucci, Carrie Allynn Ross, and Victoria J. Siesta.

rules of procedure as have some other UN organs,[3] it has, in practice, developed working methods that are customarily followed[4] and that are currently under debate.

I examine the controversy over UNCITRAL's working methods by using a legitimacy analysis to assess the substantive and political attributes of the proposals under consideration. I assess whether the proposals strengthen UNCITRAL's legitimacy claims or are more likely the function of particular political interests aimed at influencing the content of the substantive law, or both.

Part 2 explains UNCITRAL's work, as well as its working methods and proposals to clarify or change these working methods. Part 3 describes the political challenges to international law-making and various paradigms for assessing the legitimacy claims of standard-setting bodies, such as UNCITRAL. Part 3 then applies these paradigms to the current controversy. Part 4 concludes by exploring what this analysis can tell us about international law-making efforts more generally.

1. UNCITRAL AND ITS WORKING METHODS

A. *The Work of UNCITRAL*

UNCITRAL is an organ of the UN, formed in 1967 with twenty-nine member states.[5] It derives its authority from the UN,[6] and its membership now includes sixty states. Its mandate is to harmonize and modernize the law of international trade.[7] It pursues these goals by preparing both legislative and nonlegislative instruments for use in commercial law, including, inter alia, bankruptcy, transport law, sales, and securitization.[8] As its documents proclaim,

[3] United Nations Commission on International Trade Law, "UNCITRAL Rules of Procedure and Methods of Work," paragraph 10, U.N. Doc. A/CN.9/638 (October 17, 2007); hereafter "UNCITRAL, 'Fortieth Session Secretariat's Note.'"

[4] See UNCITRAL, "Fortieth Session Secretariat's Note," *supra* note 3, paragraphs 13–17, 27, and 32.

[5] G.A. Res. 2205 (XXI), U.N. Doc. A/6396 (December 17, 1966).

[6] Ibid.

[7] UNCITRAL, *Guide supra* note 1, at 1. UNCITRAL focuses on the international trade law that governs the relationships between private parties, i.e., commercial law. It has no power to impose rules; it can only draft instruments that states may choose to adopt in some fashion. The World Trade Organization, in contrast, regulates the trade laws of its member states.

[8] See the full list of original topics, including international sale of goods; international commercial arbitration; transportation; insurance; international payments; intellectual property; elimination of discrimination in laws affecting international trade; agency; and legalization of documents. "Report of the United Nations Commission on International Trade Law on the

> These instruments are negotiated through an international process involving a variety of participants, including member States of UNCITRAL, which represent different legal traditions and levels of economic development; non-member States; intergovernmental organizations; and non-governmental organizations. Thus, these texts are widely acceptable as offering solutions appropriate to different legal traditions and to countries at different stages of economic development.[9]

UNCITRAL conducts its work through (a) the commission, (b) working groups, and (c) the secretariat. The commission, at its annual plenary sessions, sets the agenda, including future work topics; monitors the work of the working groups; reviews technical assistance efforts; and finalizes texts prepared by working groups. Working groups draft the substantive instruments for specific issue areas.[10] UNCITRAL constitutes these groups with official state delegations from a worldwide geographic and economic cross-section of its sixty member states.[11] UNCITRAL also invites nonmember states to attend (and, to some degree, participate in) the working groups.[12] The secretariat, with the help of experts, performs preparatory work prior to the establishment of the working groups.[13] In addition, the secretariat assists both the commission

Work of Its First Session," 23 U.N. GAOR Supp. (No. 16), paragraphs 40, 48, U.N. Doc. A/7216 (1968); reprinted in 1 *U.N. Comm'n on Int'l Trade L. Y.B.* (1968–1970) 77, 78–81.

[9] UNCITRAL, *Guide supra* note 1, at 1.

[10] Id., at 39–41 (listing working groups); id., at 45–48 (listing UNCITRAL texts).

[11] Id., at 2–4 (describing the composition of both UNCITRAL's membership and other commission participants). UNCITRAL began with twenty-nine members, increased to thirty-six in 1973, and then to sixty in 2004. The members are elected by the General Assembly for staggered six-year terms. Members are supposed to be representative of different regions and economic and legal systems. See "Origin, Mandate, and Composition of UNCITRAL," available at http://www.uncitral.org/uncitral/en/about/origin_faq.html (accessed November 1, 2008).

[12] UNCITRAL, "Fortieth Session Secretariat's Note: Addendum 5," paragraphs 13–19 (October 22, 2007), noting that nonmember states are invited to observe working group sessions and may be allowed to participate.

[13] See UNCITRAL, "Fortieth Session Secretariat's Note: Addendum 1," paragraph 33 (October 17, 2007), stating that work done by UNCITRAL's working groups "should, as a general rule, be preceded by the Secretariat's preparatory work". At the Commission's eleventh session, it created an ad hoc working group specifically to recommend working methods to be followed whenever new subject matters are given to working groups. UNCITRAL, "Fortieth Session Secretariat's Note," *supra* note 3, paragraph 20. The recommended methods, which were all adopted, provide that the Secretariat should only give a new issue to a working group where it has done sufficient preparatory work indicating that the matter is "suitable" and would allow the "working group to commence work in a profitable manner." Furthermore, the Secretariat's preparatory work should include consultations with international organizations (IOs). See also UNCITRAL, "UNCITRAL Rules of Procedure and Methods of Work: Observations by the United States," paragraph 24, U.N. Doc. A/CN.9/639 (November 22, 2007); hereafter "UNCITRAL, 'U.S. Observations'" (discussing preparatory work and experts).

and the working groups. UNCITRAL's substantive work happens at the working-group level.

B. *The Working Methods*

UNCITRAL's working methods have evolved in part out of the flexible and adaptive approach that UNCITRAL has taken to its procedures. UNCITRAL has no official rules of procedure.[14] It operates, to some extent, under the Rules of Procedure of the General Assembly (RPGA).[15] The RPGA have general provisions addressing a variety of matters including, inter alia, delegations,[16] adoption of agendas,[17] official and working languages,[18] discussion of reports,[19] and voting rights.[20] In particular, Chapter XIII of the RPGA generally addresses the functioning of UN committees and commissions such as UNCITRAL,[21] although it does not provide for substantive business conducted by UNCITRAL.[22] UNCITRAL has proclaimed that the principles of the RPGA shall apply where appropriate, unless UNCITRAL makes a specific change.[23] This flexibility in procedure has led to the evolution of

[14] UNCITRAL, "France's Observations on UNCITRAL's Working Methods," paragraph 2, U.N. Doc. A/CN.9/635 (May 24, 2007); hereafter "UNCITRAL, 'France's Observations.'"

[15] UNCITRAL, "Fortieth Session Secretariat's Note," *supra* note 3, paragraph 4 (noting that the U.N. Charter provides that the General Assembly's Rules of Procedure apply to all "subsidiary organ[s] unless the Assembly or the subsidiary organ decides otherwise"); ibid., paragraph 10 (stating that UNCITRAL has not developed specific rules of procedure, but has applied those of the General Assembly).

[16] U.N., "Rules of Procedure," *supra* note 2, at 7.

[17] Rules 12 through 24 describe the procedures by which the Secretary-General develops and distributes agendas for both regular and special sessions, and they list required and supplemental criteria; ibid., at 4–7.

[18] According to Rule 51, there are six official and working languages used in the General Assembly and all committees: English, French, Spanish, Chinese, Arabic, and Russian; id. at 15.

[19] Rule 66 states that discussion of reports will only occur if deemed necessary by at least one-third of the present and voting members; id. at 18.

[20] Rule 82 simply states that "[e]ach member of the General Assembly shall have one vote." Id., at 22.

[21] See UNCITRAL, "France's Observations," *supra* note 14, paragraph 2.2.

[22] When establishing certain committees or commissions, the U.N. has specifically provided that each should adopt their own rules of procedure. Other times, as with the resolution establishing UNCITRAL, it has not mentioned rules of procedure at all. See UNCITRAL, "Fortieth Session Secretariat's Note," *supra* note 3, paragraph 7. When the General Assembly neither provides rules of procedure nor specifically instructs the individual committee or commission to adopt its own, the rules of the General Assembly apply to the subsidiary organ's functions unless the organ decides to formalize its own set of rules; id., paragraph 8.

[23] Initially, when UNCITRAL first considered whether to adopt rules of procedure, it "decided that the rules relating to the procedure of committee of the General Assembly as well as rule 45 and 60 [62] would apply to the procedure of the Commission, until such time as

UNCITRAL's working methods. In response to queries concerning these working methods, UNCITRAL compiled a Note by the Secretariat on UNCITRAL Rules of Procedure and Methods of Work.[24] Two of the particular subjects discussed in response to queries were (a) consensus and (b) participation by nonmembers.[25]

1. Consensus

The Secretariat's Note provides that working groups and the commission act by "consensus."[26] At issue, however, is the meaning of the word "consensus." The commission views consensus as a means of achieving "a larger cooperation."[27] Recalling prior UNCITRAL discussions, the secretariat notes the following:

> It was stated in that body that this would permit the Commission, whose members were States with different social-economic systems, different levels of development and different legal systems and historical traditions, to base its work on careful regard for proposals submitted and respect for mutual interests. In the opinion of these representatives, the consensus method was conducive to achieving a larger cooperation among countries having different legal, economic and social systems and would ensure that the uniform rules derived from the work of the Commission were generally acceptable.[28]

Still, the term "consensus" does not mean complete unanimity.[29] Indeed, those times when unanimity was achieved, the commission specifically used the term "unanimous" to refer to "a higher degree of agreement."[30] Thus, the commission viewed consensus as possible even where states articulated "explicit reservations" regarding the decision.[31] According to the secretariat, "[t]he basis of consensus is that efforts are made to address all of the concerns raised by participants so that the final text is acceptable to all. It should not

the Commission adopted its own rules of procedure." Where these rules do not address an issue, the General Assembly Rules would apply mutatis mutandis, as appropriate. UNCITRAL, "Fortieth Session Secretariat's Note," *supra* note 3, paragraph 9.

[24] Id.

[25] Other issues raised include the languages used by the working groups as well as the use of in camera proceedings. UNCITRAL, "France's Observations," *supra* note 14, paragraph 7.

[26] Id., paragraph 6. See also UNCITRAL, "Fortieth Session Secretariat's Note: Addendum 4," paragraphs 6–15 (October 18, 2007), discussing consensus in UNCITRAL.

[27] UNCITRAL, "Fortieth Session Secretariat's Note: Addendum 4," *supra* note 26, paragraph 7.

[28] Id., paragraph 7 (citation omitted).

[29] Id., paragraph 8, noting that "consensus . . . [does] not necessarily imply universal consensus."

[30] Id., paragraph 10.

[31] Id., paragraph 11. In its report, the Secretariat discusses instances in which, although consensus was reached, members maintained objections or reservations to specific paragraphs, or even to the document as a whole.

be understood as giving any State the power to veto what is otherwise the prevailing view of the meeting."[32] Nonetheless, a state may make a formal objection that would block consensus. However, UNCITRAL would not view such an objection as a veto; the proposal could still move forward and the members could then take a vote on it.[33] Under the General Assembly rules, votes only require a simple majority. The secretariat notes that, as a result, a practice has evolved in which "consensus [is] based upon what was sometimes described as 'substantially prevailing view.'"[34]

2. Participation

UNCITRAL also prides itself on its openness.[35] To some extent, its success relies on its ability to bring together not only states but experts and interest groups to solve difficult problems.[36] Naturally, delegations from each member nation attend the working-group meetings.[37] These delegations "include Government officials, academics, experts or private sector lawyers."[38] The commission has maintained a flexible and inclusive approach to the role of observers.[39] It has also developed a practice of inviting experts to attend meetings.[40] For example, despite objections raised by France (discussed in later text)

32 UNCITRAL, *Guide supra* note 1, at 6.

33 UNCITRAL, "UNCITRAL Rules of Procedure and Methods of Work," paragraph 17, U.N. Doc. A/CN.9/653 (March 19, 2008); hereafter "UNCITRAL, 'Forty-First Session Secretariat's Note.'"

34 Id., paragraph 17.

35 UNCITRAL, "Report of the United Nations Commission on International Trade Law," paragraph 378, U.N. Doc. A/63/17 (June 16–July 3, 2008), noting that UNCITRAL's practice of including observers, although possibly presenting its own set of problems, has helped the commission to achieve positive results and "universal acceptability of its standards."

36 Id., citing "broad openness" to observers "as a key element in maintaining the high quality and the practical relevance of the work of the Commission." See also UNCITRAL, *Guide supra* note 1, at 1 (noting that broad inclusion of states and nonstate organizations allows the commission to develop standards adaptable to the spectrum of international legal traditions, as well as varying levels of economic development).

37 UNCITRAL, *Guide supra* note 1, at 5.

38 Id., at 6.

39 As used by the commission and each of its working groups, the term "observer" refers both to nonmember states and to "non-State entities." UNCITRAL, "Report of the United Nations Commission on International Trade Law," *supra* note 35, paragraph 378. See also UNCITRAL, "Fortieth Session Secretariat's Note: Addendum 5," *supra* note 12, paragraph 2 (delineating the difference between "representative" states and "observer" states).

40 Each intergovernmental body has the authority to invite whichever nonstate organizations it wants to participate in its meetings or grant observer status. UNCITRAL, "Fortieth Session Secretariat's Note: Addendum 5," *supra* note 12, paragraph 3. The Secretariat compiles and maintains mailing lists of organizations whose expertise is relevant to issues addressed by the various working groups. Invitation letters are sent to each organization whose presence is

the commission sees no problem with letting observers circulate documents in working groups.[41] Observers have the same rights as member states to make statements and respond to proposals.[42] Thus, observers, whether they are nonmember states, intergovernmental organizations (IGOs), or nongovernmental organizations (NGOs), are acting as participants.[43] Not surprisingly, observer states applaud their inclusion in the consensus-building process.[44]

The participation of nonstate entities, whether experts, NGOs, IGOs, or private lawyers traveling as part of an official state delegation, depends on their ability to have their attendance funded by someone other than UNCITRAL. UNCITRAL does not pay participants' expenses.[45]

In responding to queries concerning participation, the secretariat notes that the commission may wish to compile a list of organizations, categorize them, and "authorize the Secretariat to issue a standing invitation to them."[46]

requested for either a particular working group meeting, or a general meeting of the commission. Although the Secretariat uses the same mailing lists for both types of meetings, it condenses them when inviting nonmembers to commission sessions so that only those organizations whose work is directly relevant to issues under consideration are invited. Id., paragraph 26. Nonstate organizations may request placement on the mailing lists, subject to the approval of the Secretariat and member states; id., paragraph 27. Observer organizations will continue to receive invitations to participate so long as their work remains relevant; id., paragraph 28.

[41] UNCITRAL, "Report of the United Nations Commission on International Trade Law," *supra* note 35, paragraph 378.

[42] UNCITRAL, "Fortieth Session Secretariat's Note: Addendum 5," *supra* note 12, paragraph 49, which notes that "observers have been given the right to make statements to the same extent as States members"; id., paragraph 55, referencing observers' rights to respond to proposals, and to occasionally make proposals.

[43] Id., paragraphs 13–19.

[44] As an observer, "Turkey strongly supports the Commission's practice of taking into account the view of the observer States" for purposes of consensus. UNCITRAL, "UNCITRAL Rules of Procedure and Methods of Work: Compilation of Comments by Governments (Australia and Turkey)," at 4, U.N. Doc. A/CN.9/660/Add.1 (June 3, 2008); hereafter "UNCITRAL, 'Comments by Australia and Turkey'"; accord. UNCITRAL, "UNCITRAL Rules of Procedure and Methods of Work: Compilation of Comments by Governments (Belgium)," at 2, U.N. Doc. A/CN.9/660/Add.5 (June 20, 2008), advocating for observer participation, but also noting that clear distinctions should be made between states and NGOs. Member states also find observer participation beneficial to determinations of consensus, as well as facilitation of debate on substantive issues. UNCITRAL, "UNCITRAL Rules of Procedure and Methods of Work: Compilation of Comments by Governments (Spain)," paragraph 7, U.N. Doc. A/CN.9/660/Add.2 (June 6, 2008), referencing consensus; UNCITRAL, "UNCITRAL Rules of Procedure and Methods of Work: Compilation of Comments by Governments (El Salvador)," at 4, U.N. Doc. A/CN.9/660/Add.3 (June 10, 2008), referencing substantive debate.

[45] UNCITRAL, "France's Observations," *supra* note 14, paragraph 3.1.

[46] UNCITRAL, "Forty-First Session Secretariat's Note," *supra* note 33, paragraph 32. With this suggestion, the Secretariat calls upon the opinion of the Secretary-General, as proposed at the first UNCITRAL session, which stated that the commission could create two lists of observer organizations. The first would consist of those organizations whose expertise is relevant to all

The commission might also identify other organizations that have special competence and develop criteria for their involvement in particular sessions.[47]

2. OBSERVATIONS ON UNCITRAL'S WORK METHODS

A. *France's Challenge*

France challenged UNCITRAL's working methods. France's concern arose in response to changes at UNCITRAL, including its growth in membership, the strengthening of the secretariat, and its growing prominence as the "core legal body of the United Nations system in the field of international trade law."[48] Given these developments, France felt it was time to review UNCITRAL's procedures,[49] including the meaning of consensus and the level of nonmember participation.

1. Consensus

France sought clarification of UNCITRAL's decision-making process. France recognized that UNCITRAL decisions may be adopted without a vote and, indeed, "[a]t UNCITRAL there has never been a vote."[50] France's observations suggested that the atmosphere of collegiality and consensus-driven decisions may no longer be able to persist as UNCITRAL's membership grows,[51] and thus it sought clarification on the meaning of consensus.[52] While acknowledging

of the commission's work, whereas the second would be limited to organizations with "special competence in topics that are of a particular concern." Id., paragraph 30: Organizations on the general list would have a standing invitation to participate at any commission meeting; id., paragraph 32: The commission would retain ultimate authority over the list and could include or exclude groups as necessary.

47 The names of these organizations would appear on a second list suggested by the Secretariat, and they could only attend those sessions to which they were specifically invited. Id., paragraphs 30 and 33: The Secretariat also suggests that the commission create requirements that organizations must fulfill for inclusion on this list. Generally, the Secretariat recommends that the work of these organizations be both "in conformity with the spirit, purposes and principles" of the U.N., and supportive of UNCITRAL's work. Id., paragraph 34. More specifically, the organizations should be "international, regional or subregional [in] nature," and should have both recognized expertise in a given field and the ability to meaningfully add to the work of the commission based on membership and sectorial or industrial representation; ibid., paragraph 35.

48 UNCITRAL, *Guide supra* note 1, at 1.

49 UNCITRAL, "France's Observations," *supra* note 14, paragraph 1.

50 Id., paragraph 5.1.

51 Id., paragraph 5.2.

52 Id.

that consensus does not require the absence of objection, it contended that "there cannot be a consensus without the consent of all delegates."[53] Specifically, consensus cannot exist in the following situations:

- a simple majority of delegates supports a proposal and more than one other expresses a divergent opinion;
- a proposal presented as a compromise by the chair of a working group has not received the approval of all its members; and
- a formal objection is presented by a delegation.[54]

France objected to consensus as "a 'substantially prevailing view' within a working group."[55] It contended that if UNCITRAL cannot operate by consensus (based on its understanding of consensus) despite persistent efforts, then resort should be had to General Assembly Rule 125, which permits a decision by a majority vote.[56] Australia echoed France's concerns, noting that "on occasion in certain Working Groups, consensus has been deemed to have been reached when the room was clearly divided on the decision in question."[57]

2. Participation

France also challenged the degree and nature of NGO participation in the UNCITRAL decision-making process. According to France, at UNCITRAL, "NGOs play a major role because of the expertise they possess in the areas under discussion."[58] The role of NGO experts permeates the entire process,[59] and NGOs "participate on a de facto equal basis with Member States in the sessions of the working group to produce the draft instrument."[60] UNCITRAL's funding constraints compound NGOs' influence. As France acknowledged,

[53] Id.

[54] Id.

[55] UNCITRAL, "UNCITRAL Rules of Procedure and Methods of Work: Compilation of Comments by Governments (France)," at 2–3, paragraph 2, U.N. Doc. A/CN.9/660 (May 28, 2008); hereafter "UNCITRAL, 'Comments by France.'"

[56] UNCITRAL, "France's Observations," *supra* note 14, paragraph 5.2.

[57] UNCITRAL, "Comments by Australia and Turkey," *supra* note 44, at 2.

[58] UNCITRAL, "France's Observations," *supra* note 14, paragraph 3.1.

[59] Of particular concern to France is the fact that when UNCITRAL undertakes to draft an instrument, it is experts, or the groups that they represent, who often initiate the process and provide most of the technical information considered by the respective working groups. However, these experts are neither representatives nor delegates of any member. Furthermore, the working groups generally operate without any guidelines and the draft instruments that they submit to the plenary session are only altered "if there is a strong current of opinion in favour of such changes." Id.

[60] Id.

which experts attend is a function of which ones the states want to bring and whether they can afford to bring them.[61]

France objected to national NGO participation, noting that "[i]n the past the [NGOs] active within UNCITRAL were the small number that had a stated interest in the field of international trade. More recently, UNCITRAL has opened up to a larger number of NGOs that are more obviously national in nature."[62] These groups influence UNCITRAL's work product.[63] That work product can have a national effect, even when it is not binding, such as for legislative guides. France contended that the reality is that the current participation of NGOs exceeds that permitted by Resolution 1996/31 of the UN Economic and Social Council, which provides "the general framework" for NGO activities.[64] France proposed that these entities are more properly called "nonstate entities" or "professional associations" rather than NGOs.[65] To limit the influence of these nonstate entities, France sought a process by which working groups can determine who can attend their meetings and also provide for "in camera" meetings where requested by a member state.[66]

France suggested that experts' sphere of influence in the process should be limited to informal events, colloquia, seminars, and meetings, and in no case should expert views at these events be considered binding on members.[67] Nor should any NGO or expert group be permitted to block a proposal that would

[61] Id.

[62] Id., paragraph 6.1 (footnote omitted).

[63] For example, UNCITRAL's *Legislative Guide on Insolvency Law* "implicitly blesses insolvency laws providing for the cramdown of classes of claims . . . [which is an] approach followed under American bankruptcy law but none other." See Susan Block-Lieb and Terence C. Halliday, *Legitimation and Global Lawmaking* (2006), at 38–39, Fordham L. Legal Studies Research Paper No. 952492 (2006), available at http://ssrn.com/abstract=952492. NGOs participating in the Working Group on Insolvency Law included both the American Bar Association and the American Bar Foundation; see, e.g., UNCITRAL, "Report of Working Group V (Insolvency Law) and Working Group VI (Security Interests) on the Work of Their Second Joint Session," at 3, paragraph 7, U.N. Doc. A/CN.9/550 (March 31, 2004). The preface to the *Legislative Guide* also acknowledges that "[NGOs] *participated actively* in the preparatory work." UNCITRAL, *Legislative Guide on Insolvency Law* at iii, U.N. Sales No. E.05.V.10 (2005); emphasis added.

[64] UNCITRAL, "France's Observations," *supra* note 14, paragraph 6.1. Resolution 1996/31 makes specific reference to provisions of the U.N. Charter distinguishing the roles of nonmembers and those of NGOs insofar as nonmembers may "participate" in deliberations whereas NGOs may only "consult." ECOSOC Res. 1996/31, paragraph 18, U.N. ESCOR, Substantive Sess., 49th plen. mtg., Supp. No. 1, at 53, U.N. Doc. E/1996/96 (July 25, 1996). The resolution further states that the consultative role of NGOs should not be expanded to the point where it "overburden[s] the Council or transform[s] it from a body for coordination of policy and action . . . into a general forum for discussion." Id., paragraph 19.

[65] UNCITRAL, "France's Observations," *supra* note 14, paragraph 6.2.

[66] Id.

[67] Id., paragraph 3.2.

otherwise have achieved a consensus of support from member states.[68] France proposed that the information provided by experts should not form the basis of drafts of documents.[69]

France also objected to the blurring of the distinction between commission members and observers, a blurring the secretariat readily admits has occurred.[70] This blurring, according to France, undermines member states because it dilutes the consensus-building process with the views of observers. France proposed that observers should not be permitted to circulate working documents on their own initiative and should be given the opportunity to speak either before or after the members have spoken.[71]

Ultimately, France made nine proposals, four of which are most relevant for this Chapter.[72] First, for decision-making processes, reassert that no consensus exists when a simple majority of delegates approves a proposal, that a working-group chair's compromise proposal must always be approved by the working group, and that a formal objection presented by one or more delegations blocks the consensus and must be reported in the minutes.

Second, establish an observer status for nongovernmental organizations, to be divided into two categories, namely those institutions with a general interest in international trade, which may be granted permanent status, and those organizations with expertise on a particular topic, which may be approved only for the duration of the work on that topic. Third, specify the rights of these nonstate entities: to be consulted and speak at the start of a session in

[68] Id., paragraph 5.1.

[69] Id., paragraph 3.2 (stating that NGOs should only be permitted to circulate information documents unless otherwise requested or authorized by members).

[70] UNCITRAL, "Comments by France," *supra* note 55, at 4, paragraph 4. See also UNCITRAL, "Forty-First Session Secretariat's Note," *supra* note 33, paragraphs 44–45 (concerning deliberative participation); id, paragraphs 48–49 (concerning circulation of documents and written proposals).

[71] Id., at 4, paragraph 4.

[72] The other five are as follows: First, give the working groups precise mandates and resubmit to the plenary session or consult member states in writing if any change is envisaged to those mandates. Second, the Secretariat is to inform member states in advance of the international colloquia it intends to convene on topics addressed by one or more working groups, and to provide member states with all necessary information. Third, hold formal consultation with states whenever necessary, in particular if controversial points have been raised at colloquia or seminars, and produce reports on the proceedings of these meetings. Fourth, for informal meetings of expert groups, seek the agreement of the plenary session when the annual timetable of sessions is established, taking care to achieve a balance between these meetings and working group sessions. Fifth, ensure simultaneous translation into English and French of the documents submitted to the expert groups, and apply the principle of parity between these two UN working languages in UNCITRAL's official activities. See UNCITRAL, "France's Observations," *supra* note 14, paragraph 7.

order to give their views on the topic under debate, but not to take part in the discussion or decision at the end of the debate; to circulate information documents but not working documents. Fourth, authorize a working-group meeting to be held in camera if one or more delegations belonging to the group request it.[73]

The secretariat had already proposed drawing a distinction among nonstate observers.[74] France supported this proposal, but it was apparently concerned with the influence that some states may have because of their ability to bring or fund experts, and it sought further clarification concerning the independence of these entities from states.[75]

B. *The U.S. Response*

In response to the French challenge, the United States has taken a pragmatic approach to negotiations at UNCITRAL,[76] and it appears to be satisfied with the process as it currently operates. As a threshold matter, the United States differed in its view regarding the applicability of the RPGA.[77] The United States pointed to the secretariat's explanation that, although some of the RPGA applies, the commission "[is] guided by the general principle that the rules of procedure of the GA [will] apply *mutatis mutandis* to the Commission,"[78] subject to the commission's discretion "to alter specific rules."[79] Thus, in the United States' view, UNCITRAL neither operates exclusively under the RPGA nor needs to draft a new set of rules.[80]

[73] Id., paragraph 7.

[74] UNCITRAL, "Forty-First Session Secretariat's Note," *supra* note 33, paragraph 32.

[75] UNCITRAL, "Comments by France," *supra* note 55, at 3, paragraph 3. Here, France references ECOSOC Resolution 1996/31, which requires that all NGOs seeking (or previously granted) observer status derive all of their funding from their individual members or from national affiliates. All such voluntary contributions must be reported to the Committee on Non-Governmental Organizations and, to the extent that NGOs receive funding from other sources, those contributions must be sufficiently explained to the Committee. ECOSOC. Res. 1996/31, *supra* note 64, paragraph 13.

[76] Mary Helen Carlson, "U.S. Participation in Private International Law Negotiations: The Treatment of Forum Selection Clauses and Contractual Freedom in the Draft UNCITRAL Convention on Contracts for the International Carriage of Goods Wholly or Partly by Sea." Presented to the Transport Law Committee of the ABA Section of International Law and Practice (April 4, 2008), available at http://www.abanet.org/intlaw/spring08/materials/ Carlson%20-%20U.S.%20Participation%20in%20Private %20International%20Law%20Negotiations.pdf

[77] UNCITRAL, "U.S. Observations," *supra* note 13, paragraph 4.

[78] Id.

[79] Id.

[80] Id., paragraph 5.

The United States steered away from France's attempt to have consensus defined:

> The opinions of the United Nations Office of Legal Affairs (quoted in the Secretariat paper) conclude that there is no definitive or authoritative interpretation of consensus and it is somewhat difficult to arrive at an exact definition of the term. The Office of Legal Affairs has concluded that a decision may be considered as having been made "by consensus" if the decision was "arrived at as a result of a collective effort to achieve a generally acceptable text and consequently the participating delegations are considered to be more closely associated with the decision."[81]

The United States also saw no problem with the use of experts in preparing materials for the working groups. The working groups request assistance from the secretariat, which determines what assistance it will provide to the working groups.[82]

> In light of the limited resources available to the Secretariat, the Commission and its working groups have vested the Secretariat with a measure of discretion in the implementation of its tasks. It is also common practice for the Commission and the working groups to authorize the Secretariat to have assistance of outside experts in the completion of its preparatory work, as in most other UN bodies. Such assistance may take various forms, most commonly as intersessional informal expert group meetings. This practice should continue.[83]

Nevertheless, the United States agreed that no state can have a consensus imposed upon it and any member can insist on a vote on any issue.[84]

With respect to the participation of NGOs, the United States emphasized the technical nature of UNCITRAL's work and the need for the participation of experts.[85] It felt that the secretariat ably manages the process of selecting and inviting experts.[86] It admitted that some clarifications are in order. First, it should have the relevant standards and expectations about participation of nonmember states, IGOs, specialized agencies, and NGOs restated in the letter

[81] Id., paragraph 9 (footnotes omitted).

[82] Id., paragraph 24.

[83] Id. (footnotes omitted).

[84] UNCITRAL, "U.S. Observations," *supra* note 13, paragraph 11.

[85] Id., paragraphs 12–13.

[86] Id., paragraph 13 (discussing that the Secretariat identifies relevant experts and invites them to working group sessions, but that it only does so when the NGOs have "specific expertise on the issues under consideration").

of invitation to the observer delegation or in the commission's report. Second, it should handle participation by nongovernmental observers according to two categories of nongovernmental observers, that is, those with a "general interest for international commerce," which can be granted a permanent status, and those with "special expertise" in one of the topics discussed, which should not be admitted beyond the duration of the particular subject in which they have expertise.

Third, it should continue to remind observer organizations of their role as contributors of technical information, information on practices of an affected economic or commercial sector, and other relevant information, and that they do not participate as decision makers.[87] The United States also rejected the view that there should be nonpublic meetings. First, the General Assembly Rules provide for public meetings,[88] and moreover the United States believes "transparency and openness are key to UNCITRAL's success."[89]

C. *Where the Tensions Lie*

France's concern stemmed from the combination of the role of nonstate members, and in particular nonstate entities, and confusion over the meaning of consensus.[90] In other words, it appears that France objected to the dilution of member state control over the decisions ultimately adopted by UNCITRAL. The United States appeared more open to retaining the flexibility it believed is inherent in the UNCITRAL process, even though the increase in UNCITRAL membership may make a high level of agreement more difficult than it has been in the past. It seemed to have a broader view of consensus as reflecting the support of the participating nations. It viewed the participation of experts as essential, and it seems unconcerned with who funds expert participation.

One may view these different positions through a political lens. Both the United States and France have a stake in the resulting norms, because those norms, if widely adopted, will affect their particular interests. French commercial law and U.S. commercial law differ. The French law retains the basic conceptions of the civil law tradition whereas U.S. commercial law reflects the United States' common law heritage. Some of the differences in the systems are foundational. Where model commercial law instruments are drafted with concepts foreign to either tradition, nations may perceive a disadvantage.

[87] Id., paragraph 14.
[88] Id., paragraph 19.
[89] Id., paragraph 20.
[90] UNCITRAL, "Comments by France," *supra* note 55, at 2, paragraph 1.

They may fear that they will have to transform their legal systems or that their lawyers or their businesses will be less able to adapt and benefit from the resulting harmonization. Thus, states may want UNCITRAL to adopt rules that look like their rules, or function like their rules, or at least function *with* their rules. Any alternative, other than one of these three, may be perceived as a political disadvantage.

In contrast, these tensions may be seen as a disagreement over the best means to achieve legitimacy for the norms espoused by the organization. Essentially, the tensions between these positions reflect two views concerning the efficacy of UNCITRAL's work. On the one hand, France casts the process as one connected to state sovereignty, centrality, and consent. Important to France's position is that UNCITRAL's legitimacy stems from the authority of its member states. Conversely, one can view the United States' position as reflecting a more pragmatic view of efficacy, one that stems from success. According to this view, UNCITRAL needs to actually develop norms that are useful and will be used, even if there is a diminished level of agreement, so long as there is enough agreement to achieve adoption and implementation. It needs this flexibility. Tying the organization to a strict version of state consent will only impede flexibility and thus efficacy. UNCITRAL also needs experts to do its work and their expertise should not be affected by who brings them. Under this view, UNCITRAL's legitimacy can be viewed as a function of its success.[91]

3. LEGITIMACY AND POLITICS IN INTERNATIONAL ORGANIZATIONS

To assess the various proposals, it is useful to evaluate whether they improve UNCITRAL's legitimacy criteria, those factors that affect the external perception of UNCITRAL norms as legitimate, in light of the alternative possibility that these proposals are aimed at states' political concerns. Legitimacy and politics go hand in hand, especially in international organizations (IOs).[92]

[91] See, e.g., Weiler, "The Rule of Lawyers and the Ethos of Diplomats: Reflections on the Internal and External Legitimacy of WTO Dispute Settlement," 13 *Am. Rev. Int'l Arb.* 177 (2002), reflecting upon the importance of internal organization and dynamics of international organizations.

[92] See Broude, "The Rule(s) of Trade and the Rhetos of Development: Reflections on the Functional and Aspirational Legitimacy of the WTO," 45 *Colum. J. Transnat'l L.* 221, 225 (2007), discussing the WTO and referring to legitimacy as "the elixir of political governance." See also Claude, "Collective Legitimation as a Political Function of the United Nations," 20 *Int'l Org.* 367, 368 (1966), noting that although international politics is a struggle for power, it is also one over legitimacy.

Authority is derived from both politics and legitimacy. IOs are empowered by the states that wish them to act on their behalf.[93] They are further empowered if they are perceived as legitimate. However, states also compete for power within the IO.[94] Thus, it is not always clear whether state proposals are aimed at improving the legitimacy of the organization or at increasing the relative power of the individual state. Global governance institutions need legitimacy because it enables effectiveness. In turn, legitimacy will enhance the power of the organization and therefore the power of the influential states within that organization. Legitimacy claims can be assessed in a variety of ways. Ultimately, IOs require a mix of legitimating criteria.

A. *Politics and Legitimacy Analysis for Global Governance Institutions*

Politics involves the struggle for authority or power.[95] In IOs, the role of politics can be as stark as a state pushing for a particular subject to be governed by international norms. It might involve a push for legal harmonization or even legal transplantation. In contrast, it may reflect a policy preference for one method of accomplishing an objective rather than another. IOs that develop norms have choices: What situations need norms? Which or whose norms? How should norms be implemented? Those choices may privilege one state over another. Thus, where states push various processes in international law-making organizations, there is always the possibility that they are doing so because the processes will affect the policy choices available to the organization. These same quests can be seen as (and can in fact be) tools to achieve greater legitimacy for the organization and the rules it develops.

Global governance institutions must have legitimacy.[96] Some global governance institutions, such as the WTO, develop rules that they impose on states with some measure of success.[97] Because these rules are not completely self-enforcing (although they may have some self-enforcement power),[98] these

93 Keohane, "The Contingent Legitimacy of Multilateralism 2," GARNET Working Paper No. 09/06 (2006), available at http://www.garnet-eu.org/fileadmin/documents/working_papers/0906.pdf ("Multilateral institutions by no means supersede States as the most important actors in world politics. On the contrary, they are created by States, and States dominate their decision-making.").

94 Id., at 5–6 (discussing power politics in IOs).

95 Morgenthau, *Politics Among Nations: The Struggle for Power and Peace* (1967), at 25.

96 Buchanan and Keohane, "The Legitimacy of Global Governance Institutions," 20 *Ethics & Int'l Aff.* (2006) 405, 407.

97 Id., at 406.

98 See Kelly, "Realist Theory and Real Constraints," 44 *Va. J. Int'l L.* (2004), 545, 575–576 (discussing "self-enforcing" regimes).

institutions need legitimacy to aid their effectiveness.[99] IOs have always faced a compliance challenge.[100] Without the traditional power of a sovereign, IOs must secure compliance by other means.[101] States may follow rules because of instrumental reasons – they are rationally motivated to obey rules that are in their self-interest[102] – or because of legitimacy – they feel that the rules ought to be obeyed.[103]

Legitimacy is equally as important for global norm-generating institutions.[104] Institutions such as UNCITRAL, the International Institute for the Unification of Private Law, or the Hague Conference on Private International Law generate norms that may or may not be adopted by states.[105] One might conclude that because the norms generated in these institutions must ultimately be adopted by states to have any force, legitimacy is less relevant or adequately supplied by the consenting states. However, as others have pointed out, in a world of undemocratic or weakly democratic states, consent is a poor measure of legitimacy.[106] Moreover, these norm-generating institutions develop norms, in part, to aid states that have not developed norms in a particular area of law.[107]

99 Buchanan and Keohane, *supra* note 96, at 407.

100 See Hurd, "Legitimacy, Power, and the Symbolic Life of the UN Security Council," 8 *Global Governance* (2002), 35, 35 (noting that IOs seek legitimacy in part because they have difficulties securing compliance); Kelly, "Legitimacy and Law-Making Alliances," 29 *Mich. J. Int'l L.* (2008), 605, 606–607, stating that one reason for which IOs seek legitimacy through law-making alliances is to secure greater compliance with their norms; hereafter "Kelly, *Legitimacy*."

101 Hurd, "Legitimacy and Authority in International Politics," 53 *Int'l Org.* 379, 379 (discussing that "the international social system does not possess an overarching center of political power to enforce rules," so there must be other explanations for compliance with international norms).

102 Hurd, *After Anarchy: Legitimacy and Power in the United Nations Security Council* (2007), 37–40.

103 Franck, *The Power of Legitimacy among Nations* (1990), 24–26 (describing the "compliance pull").

104 See, e.g., Karmel and Kelly, "The Hardening of Soft Law in Securities Regulation," 34 *Brook. J. Int'l L.* (2009) 583, for a discussion on the importance of legitimacy in international securities regulation.

105 G.A. Res. 2205 (XXI), *supra* note 5, paragraph II.8(b)–(d); Statute of the International Institute for the Unification of Private Law, Art. 1 (March 15, 1940), available at www.unidroit.org/mm/statute-e.pdf (as amended March 26, 1993) Art. 14; Statute of the Hague Conference on Private International Law, Art. 1 (July 15, 1955), available at http://www.hcch.net/index_en.php?act=conventions.text&cid=29 (as amended January 1, 2007) Art. 8.

106 Buchanan and Keohane, *supra* note 96, at 413 (stating that the "Pedigree View" of legitimacy fails to account for nondemocratic States); id. at 414 (discussing weak democratic states).

107 See, e.g., G.A. Res. 2205 (XXI), *supra* note 5, pmbl. (reasoning that a U.N. organ specifically dealing with the unification of international trade is necessary because discordant norms serve as barriers to trade, and NGOs and IGOs alone cannot effectively promote broader participation partly as a result of their limited authority and membership); id., paragraph II.8(b)–(c) (stating that UNCITRAL's harmonization of international trade law should include both the promotion of participation in existing laws and the development of new ones); id.,

Therefore, certain states will have no real choice but to either adopt the law developed by these institutions or have inadequate norms for a particular issue area.[108] Thus, state preferences are shaped by the norms developed in these institutions.[109]

Assessing an IO's legitimacy claims implicates, as others have explained, "an actor's normative belief that a rule or institution ought to be obeyed."[110] One cannot attempt to truly assess a subjective belief, but one can attempt to assess the objective criteria upon which that belief is based.[111] Thus, organizations may claim that their rules are legitimate from a normative standpoint because they are good rules, or are representative of the constituents affected by them, or result from good process.[112] Whether states believe these claims are warranted is a sociological and subjective matter.[113]

Although the actual perception of legitimacy is a sociological and subjective matter, the claim to legitimacy is one that can be assessed objectively. An IO's legitimacy claims can be assessed by what Professor Fritz Scharpf, and later Robert Keohane and Joseph Nye, describe as input criteria ("the means by which constituents participate in IOs, e.g., representation, inclusiveness, or process")[114] and output criteria[115] ("substantive outcomes, e.g., trade

paragraph II.9 (instructing UNCITRAL to consider the interests of all parties, "particularly those of developing countries, in the extensive development of international trade").

108 Because UNCITRAL is concerned not only with unifying international trade norms but also with formulating them, developing countries or other states without established trade norms should adopt those promoted by UNCITRAL if they wish to participate effectively in the international market. See id. pmbl. (noting that UNCITRAL's work is necessary to fulfilling UNCTAD's interest in "promoting the establishment of rules furthering international trade as one of the most important factors in economic development").

109 Buchanan and Keohane, *supra* note 96, at 408 note 5. See also Kelly, "The Value Vacuum: Self-Enforcing Regimes and the Dilution of the Normative Feedback Loop," 22 *Mich. J. Int'l L.* (2001) 673, 687–688, introducing a modified constructivist theory of international relations.

110 Hurd, *supra* note 102, at 7.

111 Id., at 7–8.

112 Kelly, *Legitimacy*, *supra* note 100, at 613–614 (discussing legitimacy claims in terms of institutional functioning and accomplishments, and input and output criteria).

113 Buchanan and Keohane, *supra* note 96, at 405.

114 Kelly, *Legitimacy*, *supra* note 100, at 613. See also Keohane and Nye, "Between Centralization and Fragmentation: The Club Model of Multilateral Cooperation and Problems of Democratic Legitimacy," Kennedy School of Government Working Paper Series, RWP01–004 (2001), 12–15, available at http://ksgnotes1.harvard.edu/Research/wpaper.nsf/rwp/RWP01–004/$File/rwp01_004_nye_rev1.pdf (discussing input legitimacy criteria and noting that inputs can be either electoral and nonelectoral).

115 Fritz W. Scharpf, *Governing in Europe: Effective and Democratic?* (1999), 2 (discussing input and output legitimacy); Keohane and Nye, *supra* note 114, at 3 (noting that both inputs and outputs can affect legitimacy).

liberalization, or fairness, and whether goals set by the IOs themselves are reached, i.e., is the IO effective").[116]

To improve input legitimacy criteria, IOs will try to improve both the representative nature of their rule making as well as the process by which they make rules. IOs that allow for the participation of those affected by their rules are representative.[117] It would be difficult, if not impossible, in the international realm for an IO to be democratic. Nonetheless, IOs can attempt to structure their norms to reflect the will of the entities on whose behalf they act.[118] IOs can improve process, such as fair procedures, deliberations, transparency, and rules, against abuse. IOs can utilize traditional administrative law devices, such as notice, comment, and power sharing.[119]

Alternatively, output legitimacy focuses on good outcomes: whether a law, standard, or rule is fair, just, well ordered, universally accepted, or supportive of a particular goal such as trade liberalization. Effectiveness depends on developing useful norms.[120] It results from expertise, sometimes combined with a limited constituency or limited focus and mandate.[121] Process and inclusion may also foster effectiveness and engender better rules that will be more readily accepted by those affected by them.[122] Focusing on good outcomes requires a normative assumption of what is a good outcome.

The very nature of legitimacy – its normative and sociological aspects, as well as the value judgments required for any normative framework – reveals that legitimacy is an ongoing dynamic balancing act. As a result, procedural criteria are helpful to ensure that an institution remains accountable and

[116] Esty, "Good Governance at the Supranational Scale: Globalizing Administrative Law," *115 Yale L.J.* (2006), 1490, 1517, discussing legitimacy in terms of outcomes.

[117] See Keohane and Nye, *supra* note 114, at 14 (discussing the legitimacy of domestic democracies).

[118] See Esty, *supra* note 116, at 1504–1505 (noting that claims to legitimacy are strongest where there is a sense of community, but that it is increasingly harder for constituents to identify with policymakers on a global scale).

[119] Id., at 1534–1537 (discussing that horizontal and vertical power-sharing mechanisms can increase the legitimacy of international rulemaking); Nico Krisch and Benedict Kingsbury, "Introduction: Global Governance and Global Administrative Law in the International Legal Order," 17 *Eur. J. Int'l L.* (2006), 1, 4 (noting the tendency of IOs to improve participation and accountability by incorporating various administrative law mechanisms into their decision making, including procedures for notice and comment).

[120] Keohane and Nye, *supra* note 114, at 15. *See also* Keohane, *supra* note 93, at 15 (noting the need for epistemic legitimacy whereby IOs properly utilize both existing and new information to develop standards that remain open to improvement).

[121] See, e.g., Coicaud, "Conclusion: International Organizations, the Evolution of International Politics and Legitimacy," in *Legitimacy of International Organizations* (2001), 521 (discussing limited focus and mandate).

[122] Keohane, *supra* note 93, at 5 (noting that where effectiveness depends on legitimate processes, output legitimacy is thus reliant upon input legitimacy).

flexible. I believe that as both input and output criteria have their weaknesses and the process of international law making must necessarily be a dynamic one, a model that attempts to balance these criteria, such as the one put forth by Alan Buchanan and Robert Keohane, is most helpful. They propose a normative standard for institutional legitimacy that captures both output and input criteria. Buchanan and Keohane seek to construct a model that provides for the "ongoing critical revision of [an institution's] goals, through interaction with agents and organizations outside the institution."[123] Their model seeks to strike the right balance of public support on moral grounds, a minimum level of justice, democratic consent as well as democratic values, and flexibility and accountability.[124]

An assessment of an institution's claim to legitimacy should therefore consider the following: whether the institution's level of effectiveness justifies its role; whether there is some level of participation by those affected by its rules; and whether some processes exist to protect both its normative mission and its representative credentials. The exact calibration of this model for any specific endeavor is a larger project. Here I briefly discuss the challenges of applying a dynamic model of legitimacy by using the UNCITRAL working-methods controversy.

B. *Considering the Legitimacy Value of the Proposals to UNCITRAL's Work Methods*

The French proposals suggested that reaching consensus on any given matter requires a greater degree of agreement than sometimes exists.[125] France also rejected the dilution of working documents that serve as the basis for consensus by nonmembers. France's proposals would restrict the influence of nonstates and nonmembers in drafting these working instruments.[126]

One could view these objections as political, as a means for France to achieve a substantive outcome more akin to its own interests, or as an attempt to secure more legitimate norms. First, concerning consensus, the secretariat's position, as well as that of the United States, seems to be that when a decision is the result of a substantially prevailing view, one can say that it has been achieved by consensus.[127] However, from a power perspective, France has its influence diminished if the level of agreement needed for consensus is lessened

[123] Buchanan and Keohane, *supra* note 96, at 406.
[124] Ibid., at 417–418.
[125] See *supra* notes 53 and 54 and accompanying text.
[126] See *supra* notes 69 and 71 and accompanying text.
[127] See *supra* notes 34 and 81 and accompanying text.

when France objects to the action at hand. France's prefatory comments to its proposals suggest that it is concerned with UNCITRAL's procedures in light of the increase in membership and the growing importance of the organization,[128] suggesting that it may be concerned with the dilution of its influence. The dilution of its power could be considerable. This concern would, theoretically, apply to other states with whom France competes for power, but the power dynamics would necessarily be affected by the relative power of each state.

However, the meaning of consensus affects a variety of issues. Before the parties reach agreement, the level of agreement needed for consensus serves as leverage for those holding a minority opinion. In those instances in which consensus requires a high level of agreement, those in the majority position will need to compromise to achieve their goals. In those in which the meaning is diluted, less will be sacrificed. Viewed from this perspective, the meaning of consensus seems like a political bargaining tool. This characterization seems especially appropriate when one understands that if the matter were put to a simple majority vote, as it may be in UNCITRAL,[129] the majority position would likely pass and the minority position would fail. The level of consensus needed will not affect whether the majority position ultimately prevails, but it might affect the compromises that the majority is willing to make to have its position adopted by consensus.

Interestingly, this negotiation effect not only impacts the political positions of the individual states, but it implicates a political issue for the institution as well. The ability of the institution to operate by consensus affects its power within the international community. As IOs compete with each other for relevance, the states within the institution, and the institution itself, have an interest in maintaining the institution's power. France may feel that a weakened level of agreement necessary for consensus enables other parties to misrepresent the level of agreement actually achieved, thus empowering a decision with more legitimacy than it deserves. Thus, the proposal could be defended on the basis of an input legitimacy framework.

The meaning of consensus matters more from an input legitimacy perspective than from an output legitimacy perspective. Input legitimacy focuses on, inter alia, participation. Output legitimacy focuses on effective norms. One could suppose that the level of agreement correlates with the efficacy of the norm, but it is not hard to imagine a situation in which that would not be the case. Admittedly, the level of agreement may affect the acceptance of the norm by states, which may impact its effectiveness and output legitimacy.

[128] UNCITRAL, "France's Observations," *supra* note 14, paragraph 1.

[129] See *supra* note 33 and accompanying text.

Likewise, one can view the concern over participation from a political perspective. The participation of nonstates (or nonmember states) dilutes the representation of member states. Again, though, this influence would presumably dilute the interest of all member states. Nevertheless, the effect of that dilution depends on the relative power positions of each state within UNCITRAL. Moreover, France, or other countries, may feel that the influence of nonstates benefits another state in particular, or that one state, perhaps because of the influence of nonmembers, is able to dominate the document-drafting process. France may see the influence of nonmembers as favoring the views of another state, perhaps the United States. Thus, the concern over participation may be motivated by political concerns.

Indeed, it would seem that the proposal is necessarily political because more participation would almost always improve an organization's input legitimacy credentials, and thus any objection would likely be a political one. Expert participation seems particularly helpful, when, as is the case at UNCITRAL, there is some vetting process to discern who should be allowed to participate as an expert.[130] One challenge to IOs is that they fail to represent those affected by them.[131] Because the democratic analogy fails to translate well in the international sphere for a variety of reasons,[132] it would seem that representation from various groups would be welcomed from a legitimacy perspective, especially if those groups are experts.

France may claim that the participation of nonmembers actually undermines representative legitimacy by giving some states more representation than others. France and the United States do not disagree over the suggestion that experts be categorized according to their level of expertise.[133] Rather, France seems troubled by who is funding the experts, implying that some states are given undue representation because of expert participation.[134] If input credentials, such as representation, are important, then the nature and scope of that representation should matter. Just because states are present in an organization does not mean that they share the same level of influence. Now, it may be that we do not want them to do so. Some states have stronger interests, more at stake, or better expertise. Perhaps it is normatively desirable that they exert greater influence.

[130] *See supra* notes 40, 46, 47, 86.

[131] Keohane and Nye, *supra* note 114, at 14–15.

[132] Buchanan and Keohane, *supra* note 96, at 416; Kelly, *Legitimacy*, *supra* note 100, at 617; Keohane and Nye, *supra* note 114, at 11–15.

[133] See *supra* note 73 and accompanying text; see *supra* note 87 and accompanying text.

[134] See *supra* notes 61 and 75 and accompanying text.

Nevertheless, I believe that if one uses the broad notion of input legitimacy as the proper yardstick, participation by nonmembers will strengthen a legitimacy claim. UNCITRAL's legitimacy thrives in part on its claim to expertise both because it is seen as welcoming wide participation by experts as well as states (input), and because its documents are viewed as effective (output). Although experts might give greater support to one state's position, as long as the contributor is an expert and other experts are also permitted to participate, it would seem to serve the organization's interests, and input legitimacy.

This last point, that other experts are also permitted to participate, is an important one. Simply because an entity is an expert does not mean that it holds the only view of what would be an effective standard or rule. The very existence of IOs like UNCITRAL demonstrates that there are a variety of ways to approach difficult problems and that no one view of how the law should operate is correct for all circumstances. Experts can tell us how things will work (or not work) and, in doing so, they may make policy recommendations about how best to fashion rules. However, there may be larger policy questions at stake that would privilege the views of another set of experts. Simply put, a common law expert will not be helpful in addressing the value of a civil law approach to a particular problem. Understanding that we live in a world where there are fundamentally different approaches to legal problems reveals that the term "expert" has its limitations. Ideally, legitimacy is fostered by hearing from all the experts and, to the extent that France's proposals suggest there are experts whose voices are silenced, it would trigger legitimacy concerns as well.

4. CONCLUSION

Thinking about process in terms of legitimacy is important. Organizations compete for relevance in part by competing for legitimacy. Law making that is seen as legitimate is more likely to be implemented and obeyed. States within those organizations compete for influence by competing for control over the law-making process. What seems like a political struggle can also have legitimacy implications, and vice versa. Here are some points to keep in mind when trying to evaluate proposals.

1. Input and output legitimacy both matter; organizations strive for, and need, both.
2. The right balance of input and output criteria depends on the organization and may be dynamic within the organization.

3. Proposals to alter the processes of organizations serve both politics and legitimacy.
4. The same proposal may affect both politics and legitimacy at the same time.
5. When one is considering proposals, it is helpful to think of how those proposals affect input and output legitimacy criteria separately.
6. Legitimacy affects the power (politics) of the organization itself.
7. To the extent that states have (or lack) relative power in an organization, their positions are affected by the legitimacy (power) of the organization.

Ultimately, it is difficult to speculate about the true motivation of any state when making proposals. Also, any proposal may be the result of mixed motivations. Furthermore, any proposal may serve (or disserve) legitimacy criteria, regardless of motivation. Nevertheless, assessing the legitimacy impact of proposals seems worthwhile to facilitate useful IOs.

PART II

THE POLITICS OF INTERNATIONAL INVESTMENT TREATY MAKING

6

The Politics of the European Union's Investment Treaty Making

Marc Bungenberg

1. INTRODUCTION

The 2006 European Union (EU) Commission Communication, "Global Europe, Competing in the World,"[1] focuses on securing the EU's place in multipolar international economic relations. The Treaty of Lisbon[2] is one of the instruments through which the EU is seeking to enhance its role as a major player in the global economy, particularly in the area of investment policy. In this area, the legal competences of the European Community[3] (EC) before the entry into force of the Treaty of Lisbon were very limited,[4] in contrast to the largely exclusive EC competences in trade policy.[5] The Lisbon "project"

[1] Commission Communication, "Global Europe: Competing in the World," COM (2006) 567 final.

[2] OJ 2007 C 306/1 et seq.

[3] Before the entry into force, the European Community (EC) alone – and not the EU – acted in trade and investment matters, because at this stage it alone possessed legal personality. The legal basis for this is the EC Treaty; therefore European trade and investment law are part of European "community law." With the entry into force of the Treaty of Lisbon (OJ 2007 C 306; for a consolidated version see OJ 2008 C 115), the Union's two main treaties are named "Treaty on European Union" (TEU, revised) and "Treaty on the Functioning of the European Union" (TFEU). As acting entity, the EU now replaced the EC; see Article 1 TEU, revised: "The Union shall be founded on the present Treaty and on the Treaty on the Functioning of the European Union (hereinafter referred to as 'the Treaties'). Those two Treaties shall have the same legal value. The Union shall replace and succeed the European Community."

[4] L. Mola, "Which Role for the EU in the Development of International Investment Law?," SIEL Online Proceedings Working Paper 26 (2008), available at http://www.ssrn.com/link/SIEL-Innaugural-Conference.html, point 1. For a comprehensive analysis of EU investment powers before Lisbon, see N. Maydell, "The European Community's Competence to Conclude International Agreements on Investment" (2008), PhD dissertation, Vienna University.

[5] On this, see J. Chaisse, "Adapting the European Community Legal Structures to the International Trade," 17 *EBLR* (2006) 1615 seq.; H.-G. Krenzler and C. Pitschas, "Die Gemeinsame Handelspolitik im Verfassungsvertrag – ein Schritt in die richtige Richtung," in C. Herrmann, H.-G. Krenzler, and R. Streinz (eds.), *Die Aussenhandelspolitik im Vertrag über eine Verfassung*

of consolidating the competence of bilateral investment treaty (BIT) making at the European level presents an interesting junction between economic law and politics, at both the international and European levels.

This chapter seeks to explain the interaction of law and politics of BIT making in the EU. Part 2 outlines the functions of investment protection law as an important economic factor in the competition of legal orders, after the failure of multilateralization in the area of investment.[6] Before this background, it shows the weakness of the current European system of investment protection in comparison to the standard achieved by the United States in its approach to investment protection. A coherent external EU investment policy does not exist at the time of this writing. Rather, foreign investment policy and protection are divided between the EU and its member states. Before Lisbon, the EU was facing major constitutional deficits in this area, as shown in Part 3. Even though the EC competences for investment treaty making "before Lisbon" were limited, the EU Commission was nevertheless already heading toward a broad and proactive approach on this issue. The EU was also making efforts to develop its own foreign investment promotion and protection policy by including investment (protection) law in preferential trade agreements (PTAs) and by setting up its own EU Minimum Platform on Investment (MPoI).[7] As we shall see, this is of interest not only because of its implications for investment law, but because of the constellation of political interests at the global, European, and member state levels, which are limited by legal structures but at the same time bearing on the development of international economic law.

The interesting changes and consequences that are expected to arise from the Lisbon Treaty for the investment policy of the EU and its member states are discussed in Part 4, along with the necessity of a new EU Model BIT. With the Lisbon Treaty the EU has gained competences in the area of foreign direct investment, which are now part of the EU Common Commercial Policy and

für Europa (2005), 5 et seq.; M. Cremona, "The External Dimension of the Single Market," in Bernard and Scott (eds.), *The Law of the Single European Market – Unpacking the Premises* (2002), 351 et seq.

[6] See on this in general B. Ferrarini, "A Multilateral Framework for Investment?," in S. Evenett (ed.), *The Singapore Issues and the World Trading System: The Road to Cancun and Beyond* (2003); On the MAI see P. Muchlinski, "The Rise and Fall of the Multilateral Agreement on Investment: Where Now?," 34 *Int'l Lawyer* (2000) 1033.

[7] See the "Minimum Platform on Investment for the EU FTAs," revised version (March 6, 2009); on this in general, see N. Maydell, "The European Community's Minimum Platform on Investment or the Trojan Horse of Investment Competence," in: A. Reinisch and C. Knahr (eds.), *International Investment Law in Context* (2008), 73–92; M. Burgstaller, "European Law and Investment Treaties," 26 *J. Int'l Arbit.* (2009) 181, at 204 et seq. The MPoI serves as a standardized negotiation proposal for ongoing and future PTA negotiations with third states.

thereby have become an "exclusive EU competence."[8] The legal implications of such an assertion of authority are unclear with respect to some 1,300 BITs concluded independently by EU member states (approximately 50 percent of all BITs worldwide). Will all of these BITs have to be renegotiated and "replaced" by EU BITs with sovereign states and PTAs? Even after the Lisbon modifications, the EU's investment policy and its legal fundaments do not deliver a sufficient legal basis for acting efficiently in the global arena of the twenty-first century. Because of insufficient exclusive competences in the area of portfolio investments, the post-Lisbon EU will still have to conclude mixed agreements, complicating the political process of the negotiation and conclusion of BITs, because the EU as well as all of its member states will have to ratify those agreements.[9]

Finally, Part 5 summarizes the ways politics and law interact in the development of the new EU policy on investment treaty making. To put the EU in a position to compete with the other superpowers, the competences of the Common Commercial Policy *de lege ferenda* will have to be extended further to every conceivable aspect of foreign investment.

2. INTERNATIONAL INVESTMENT LAW AND BITS AS PART OF THE REGULATORY COMPETITION OF SYSTEMS

Superpowers challenge each other, and every additional emerging power challenges the current system, adding its own interests and further complicating matters. In international trade, political realism has led both the United States and the EU to act independently from each other and favor PTAs[10] over bipolar EU–United States cooperation. At the same time, the emergence of China as a new economic superpower is challenging the existing economic order. Competition between the United States, China, and the EU for their positions in the new economic order of the twenty-first century – not only in trade, but

[8] See Article 2 TEU, revised. According to the definition given to "exclusive competence" there, "only the Union may legislate and adopt legally binding acts, the Member States being able to do so themselves only if so empowered by the Union or for the implementation of Union acts."

[9] Only in policy areas where the EU has exclusive external competences for all matters dealt with in the international treaty in question can the European institutions can act alone; if international treaties cover areas of joint competences of the EU and the EU member states then the EU together with the EU member states has to conclude a "mixed agreement." The latter leads to an obligatory ratification by the EU as well as the 27 EU member states. On this see, e.g., P. Eeckhout, *External Relations of the EU – Legal and Constitutional Foundations* (2004), Chapter 7.

[10] On the general usage of the term PTA instead of FTA (free trade agreement) and RTA (regional trade agreement), see J. Bhagwati, *Termites in the Trading System* (2008), p. XI.

in investment as well – is therefore a fact to which all actors in the global arena must adapt. The offers that existing global players can make individually to the states of the emerging economies and developing countries will be a relevant factor for the future economic world order.[11] Thus, the struggle for agreements with emerging markets, especially on market access, resources, and investments, as well as the competition between the EU, the United States, Japan, and more recently the "BRIC" countries (Brazil, Russia, India, and China), will reach a new definition of importance.

Furthermore, new models for a future economic world order are being discussed. Bergsten, for example, has proposed that China and the United States should work together as leaders responsible for the new world order, as a new "G2"[12] – thereby setting the EU aside. According to him, the EU is also an economic superpower, but, except in trade, it does not speak with a single voice.[13] Thus, it will be difficult to work with the EU. This can be explained by the complicated vertical allocation of competences between the EU and its member states and the lack of a continuous presidency as well as an EU foreign minister.

In general, the globalization of markets leads to regulatory competition in the field of economic law. Investments seek locations for production, distribution, research, and development on the basis of efficiency criteria only. Almost global market access for business affects governments, who present investors with legal systems offering stability, freedom, and protection of inward and outward investments. Governments have always had the role of system providers in order to attract investment. In 1956, Tiebout[14] presented an influential model publication precisely explaining some of the regulatory factors likely to channel economic activities to certain locations.[15] Today's globalization of the markets for goods and capital imposes a merciless "competition of systems."[16]

[11] On this see P. Khanna, *The Second World, Empires and Influence of the New Global Order* (2008).

[12] F. Bergsten, "A Partnership of Equals," 87 *Foreign Affairs* (2008) 57 et seq.

[13] F. Bergsten, "How to Manage China's Challenge to the Global Economy" (transcript of June 19, 2008), available at http://www.cfr.org/publication/16601.

[14] C. Tiebout, "A Pure Theory of Local Expenditures," 64 J. *Pol. Econ.* (1956) 416 et seq.; for an overview on the economic theory on interjurisdictional competition and legal federalism, see S. Sinn, *Competition for Capital, on the Role of Governments in an Integrated World Economy* (1993); H. Siebert (ed.), *Locational Competition in the World Economy* (1995); L. Gerken, *Der Wettbewerb der Staaten* (1999); V. Vanberg and W. Kerber, "Institutional Competition Among Jurisdictions," 10 *Const. Pol. Econ.* (1994) 219 et seq.

[15] K. M. Meessen, "Economic Law as an Economic Good," in K. M. Meessen, M. Bungenberg, and A. Puttler (eds.), *Economic Law as an Economic Good: The Rule and the Tool Function in the Competition of Systems* (2009), at 5.

[16] K. M. Meessen, *Economic Law in Globalizing Markets* (2004), at 9.

In the areas of trade and investment, that leads to a "competitive liberalization" with a liberal trade and investment regime.[17]

An escape from competition of economic law systems is possible by harmonizing certain areas of economic law on the international level. A precondition for regulatory competition – also in the area of investment protection law – is that the system is not entirely centralized or harmonized.[18] Even though the growth rates of international investment have stimulated attempts to "internationalize" investment law by means of international investor protection regulations, setting up a multilateral framework for investments has failed. The Havana Charter of 1947–1948 already included some provisions on investment, but only the General Agreement on Tariffs and Trade provisions on trade entered into force. The Multilateral Agreement on Investment (MAI), an ambitious project by the Organization for Economic Cooperation and Development (OECD) that was mainly aimed at adding a general right to invest to the protection of existing investment, failed in 1998.[19]

The 1996 World Trade Organization (WTO) Ministerial Conference in Singapore adopted a mandate for the WTO Working Group on Trade and Investment, which was specified and renewed in Doha in 2001,[20] but the September 2003 Ministerial Conference in Cancun did not grant a mandate to negotiate a MAI.[21] "Trade and Investment" was finally removed from the Doha Agenda.[22] Ever since, the main actors in the global arena have given priority to bilateral and regional trade negotiations.[23] The EU, China, and the United States are building separate networks of free trade relations and PTAs as "superhubs,"[24] being aware of the importance of an internationalized

[17] F. Bergsten, "Competitive Liberalization and Global Free Trade: A Vision for the Early 21st Century," Institute for International Economics Working Paper 1996–15.

[18] W. Kerber, "The Theory of Regulatory Competition and Competition Law," in K. Meessen et al., *supra* note 15, at 28.

[19] On the OECD approach, see "Chapter III Art. 1 MAI Negotiating Text," available at http://www1.oecd.org/daf/mai/pdf/ng/ng987r1e.pdf; see on this P. Muchlinski, *supra* note 6, at 1033 et seq.

[20] For the WTO approach see WT/MIN(01)/DEC/1 (November 20, 2001), point 20.

[21] See, e.g., P. Sauvé, "Multilateral Rules on Investment: Is Forward Movement Possible," 9 *J Int'l Econ. L.* (2006) 325 et seq.; on the Cancun ministerial summit in general see, e.g., J. Bhagwati, "Don't Cry for Cancún," 83 *Foreign Affairs* (2004) 52 et seq.; R. Sally, "The End of the Road for the WTO?," 5 *World Econ.* (2004) 1 et seq.

[22] See "Decision Adopted by the General Council on 1 August 2004," Doc. WT/L/579.

[23] For the position of the EU see *Commission, Global Europe: Competing in the World, COM* (2006) 567 final; see also S. Woolcock, "European Union Policy Towards Free Trade Agreements," ECIPE Working Paper 3 (2007).

[24] On the United States and the EU as superhubs see P. J. Lloyd and D. MacLaren, "The EU's New Trade Strategy and Regionalisation in the World Economy," *Aussenwirtschaft* (2006) 423.

legal investment setting.[25] Instead of multilaterally binding rules on foreign investment, a patchwork of bilateral and regional treaties has developed.

The increasing importance of investment policy in international economic negotiations is obvious. Rules on investment promotion and protection can stimulate trade relations and have an influence on the quality of investments.[26] The synergic effect of the expansion of trade and investment is supposed to lead the way to further economic growth.[27] Limits on the ability of governments to interfere with the operation of foreign investors reduce the political risks associated with an investment, which should result in greater levels of investment in a given economy.[28] Rules on investment promotion as well as protection are therefore part of an improved body of economic law in the context of regulatory competition, and, because of the interrelation with trade rules and chapters on investment, they more and more often form an integral part of new PTAs. At the same time, the number of so-called pure BITs continues to rise.[29]

Key issues to tackle in investment agreements are the degree of liberalization governing the entry of foreign investment, the treatment accorded to investments in the postestablishment phase, the level of investment protection, and modes of dispute settlement. Further relevant issues are environmental concerns and the protection of social and human rights. Those are some of the parameters that one must take into account when discussing EU investment politics in a comparative approach.[30]

Concerning the admission and protection of foreign investments, the United States is using "pure" BITs parallel to including investment promotion and protection chapters in broader free trade agreements (FTAs).[31] Until recently, the United States had not negotiated the inclusion of investment rules in

[25] For this awareness see, e.g., the press release, "Preliminary Analysis of Korea–EU Free Trade Agreement," which states that "there is no investment chapter or investor–state dispute settlement provisions in the Korea-EU FTA (competency for investment matters rests with the individual EU Member States), whereas KORUS features investor protections." USTR (October 2010), available at http://www.ustr.gov/about-us/press-office/press-releases/2009/october.

[26] M. Lesher and S. Miroudot, "The Economic Impact of Investment Provisions in Regional Trade Agreements," OECD Trade Policy Working Paper 36 (2006).

[27] P. Gugler and J. Chaisse, "Foreign Investment Issues and WTO Law – Dealing with Fragmentation while Waiting for a Multilateral Agreement," in J. Chaisse and T. Balmelli (eds.), *Essays on the Future of the World Trade Organization* (2008), Vol. I, 135.

[28] S. McGuire and M. Smith, *The European Union and the United States – Competition and Convergence in the Global Arena* (2008), 142.

[29] See UNCTAD, "Recent Developments in International Investment Agreements (2008 – June 2009)," IIA Monitor 3 (2009), 2 Figure 1; in 2008, 59 new BITs were concluded; the total number of BITs rose to 2,676 at the end of 2008.

[30] P. Gugler and V. Tomsik, "The North American and European Approaches in the International Investment Agreements," NCCR Working Paper 4 (2006), at 4 and 15.

[31] S. McGuire and M. Smith, *supra* note 28, at 142.

PTAs, but this has changed significantly.[32] Investment chapters have become an important element of U.S. PTAs.[33] After 2002 the U.S. government concluded PTAs containing investment chapters with Australia,[34] various central American states and the Dominican Republic,[35] Chile,[36] Morocco,[37] Oman,[38] Peru,[39] and Singapore.[40] In addition, PTAs with Colombia,[41] Korea,[42] and Panama[43] have been signed but as of this writing are still awaiting Congressional approval and implementing legislation. Furthermore, the United States has signed 40 BITs,[44] mostly with developing countries. Both BITs and investment chapters in PTAs follow the U.S. Model BIT (2004), which was created under the 2002 Bipartisan Trade Promotion Authority.[45] The objective of the U.S. Model BIT is to provide a consistent approach between the investment chapters of the PTAs and future U.S. BITs.[46] This treaty, generally "concerning the encouragement and reciprocal protection of investment," uses a broad definition of investment. The scope of application of the new U.S. PTAs extends to all "investments." The treatment provisions of the U.S. Model BIT apply to the preestablishment phase as well: In its Articles 4 and 5, the 2004 U.S. Model BIT[47] explicitly stipulates the national treatment and most favored nation treatment also for the "establishment, acquisition, and expansion" of investments.[48]

[32] G. Gagné and J.-F. Morin, "The Evolving American Policy on Investment Protection," 9 *J. Int'l Econ. L.* (2006), 357.

[33] See on this A. Capling and K. M. Nossal, "Investor–State Dispute Mechanisms in International Trade Agreements," *Governance* 19/2 (2006), 57; G. Gagné and J.-F. Morin, *supra* note 32, at 357.

[34] United States–Australia Free Trade Agreement (May 18, 2004).

[35] United States–Dominican Republic–Central America Free Trade Agreement (August 5, 2004). In addition to the Dominican Republic and the United States, the parties are Costa Rica, El Salvador, Guatemala, Honduras, and Nicaragua.

[36] United States–Chile Free Trade Agreement (June 6, 2003).

[37] United States–Morocco Free Trade Agreement (June 14, 2004).

[38] United States–Oman Free Trade Agreement (January 19, 2006).

[39] United States–Peru Trade Promotion Agreement (April 12, 2006).

[40] United States–Singapore Free Trade Agreement (May 6, 2003).

[41] United States–Colombia Trade Promotion Agreement (November 22, 2006).

[42] United States–Republic of Korea Free Trade Agreement (June 30, 2007).

[43] United States–Panama Trade Promotion Agreement (July 11, 2007).

[44] See the listing at http://tcc.export.gov/Trade_Agreements/Bilateral_ Investment_Treaties/index.asp.

[45] See 19 U.S.C.S. § 3801.

[46] On this see M. Kantor, "The New Draft Model U.S. BIT: Noteworthy Developments'," 21 *J. Int'l Arbit.* (2004) 383 et seq.

[47] See http://www.ustr.gov/assets/Trade_Sectors/Investment/Model_BIT/asset_upload_file847_6897.pdf.

[48] P. Gugler and V. Tomsik, *supra* note 30, at 5.

In contrast to the coherent and flexible international investment treaty policy of the United States, the EU until recently has not shown much interest in investment promotion and protection. Nevertheless, the EU is fully aware that it needs to improve its legal policy for establishing an effective and competitive environment for international business operations of its enterprises and investment practices. It has to react to the changes in order to make use of upcoming opportunities.[49] However, as the EU Commission observed in 2006, "in comparison to NAFTA countries' agreements, EU agreements and achievements in the area of investment lag behind because of their narrow content. As a result, European Investors are discriminated vis-à-vis their foreign competitors and the EU is losing market shares."[50] Therefore, the EU Commission is taking a new approach to the establishment of its own investment policy. This had already started with the EU–Chile Agreement,[51] and it continued with EU ambitions to set up an EU investment platform (EU MPoI)[52] and the inclusion of investment chapters in currently negotiated EU PTAs.[53]

3. THE EU AND MEMBER STATE SITUATION IN FOREIGN DIRECT INVESTMENT PROTECTION: BEFORE LISBON

Europe's existing system of investment protection is complex. The first part of this examination focuses on intracommunity investment regulation and the issue of concluding and enforcing BITs between EU member states. The second part scrutinizes the external investment dimension.

A. *EU Internal Investment Protection and the Relationship between EU Member States*

Investments within the EU – meaning with an investor from Member State A investing in Member State B – are subject to a system of multilevel protection, comprising the European Convention on Human Rights (ECHR),[54]

[49] See Commission Communication, *supra* note 1.

[50] EU Commission, "Upgrading the EU Investment Policy," Note for the attention of the 133 Committee, Brussels (May 30, 2006).

[51] OJ 2002 L-352, signed on November 18, 2002.

[52] See later text at Section 3.B.

[53] See later text at Section 3.B.

[54] On this see C. Pfaff, "Investitionsschutz durch regionalen menschenrechtlichen Eigentumsschutz am Beispiel der Europäischen Menschenrechtskonvention (EMRK)," in C. Knahr and A. Reinisch (eds.), *Aktuelle Probleme und Entwicklungen im Internationalen Investitionsrecht*

the freedom of establishment and movement of capital,[55] and EU fundamental rights.[56] Furthermore, customary international law,[57] national fundamental rights, and in certain cases even BITs concluded between EU member states[58] – might be of relevance. Most of these BITs were concluded before both states acceded to the EU. Only 2 of approximately 190 intra-EU BITs in force[59] have been concluded between "old Member States," namely Germany on one hand and Greece and Portugal on the other hand; no claims are known to be registered under these 2 BITs.[60]

The guarantees included in intra-EU BITs partly overlap with the basic freedoms of the internal market, the protection of fundamental rights in community law, and the ECHR,[61] but there are important differences as well. The EC Treaty guaranteed – just as the TFEU does today – market access and the right to invest, and as long as the freedom of capital movement is applicable, this guarantee also applies to non-EU enterprises – even if they are not established in an EU member state.[62] Protection against expropriation and the "right to property" was introduced into European law by the European Court of Justice (ECJ)[63] as a fundamental right and is regarded as a necessary element of an "open market economy with free competition" (see Article 4 of the Treaty Establishing the European Community). The dimension of enforcement is one of the main differences between protection under EU law and under a BIT. The latter usually provides investors with direct access to international arbitral bodies,[64] whereas under EU law investors have to deal with the courts of the member states.

In cases of nonconformity between BITs and the aforementioned guarantees, this question arises: Which source of law prevails? The European

(2007), 163–192; M. Ruffert, "The Protection of Foreign Direct Investment by the ECHR," 43 *Ger. Yearbook Int'l L.* (2000) 116 et seq.

55 See S. Hindelang, *The Free Movement of Capital and Foreign Direct Investment: The Scope of Protection in EU Law* (2009).

56 Case 44/79, *Hauer* [1979] ECR 3727; C. Calliess, "The Protection of Property," in D. Ehlers (ed.), *European Fundamental Rights and Freedoms* (2007), 448 et seq.

57 See R. Dolzer and C. Schreuer, *Principles of International Investment Law* (2008), 11 et seq.

58 See M. Burgstaller, *supra* note 7.

59 H. Wehland, "Intra-EU Investment Agreements and Arbitration: Is European Community Law an Obstacle?," 58 *Int'l Comp. L. Q.* (2009) 297, at 298.

60 A. van Aaken, "Fragmentation of International Law: The Case of International Investment Protection," 17 *Finn. Yearbook Int'l L.* (2008) 93, at 121.

61 C. Söderlund, "Intra-EU-Investment Protection and the EC Treaty," 24 *J. Int'l Arbit.* (2007) 455.

62 On the scope of application in these cases see Case C-524/04, *Test Claimants*, [2007] ECR I-2107; Case C-196/04, *Cadbury Schweppes* [2006] ECR I-7995.

63 Case 4/73, *Nold* [1974] ECR 491; Case C-84/95, *Bosphorus* [1996] ECR I-3953.

64 A. van Aaken, *supra* note 60, at 123.

Commission is of the opinion that EC–EU law prevails over the nonconforming BIT norms from the date of accession of new states.[65] However, arbitral tribunals may hold a different view on the question of jurisdiction as well as the applicable law in cases of conflicts[66] and in the literature it is argued that in no way may the EC restrict the possibility of investor–state arbitration.[67] In *Eastern Sugar v. Czech Republic*, a case brought against a member state under an intra-EU member state's BIT, the Czech Republic argued that the BIT in force between the Netherlands and the Czech Republic would not be applicable after the accession of the Czech Republic to the EU. However, the arbitral tribunal established its jurisdiction on the basis of the following arguments: (a) the relevant BIT had not been terminated, (b) the acts in question had been undertaken before accession, (c) the BIT protection did not conflict with the EC and therefore supremacy was not an issue, (d) there was no policy formulation by the EU on intra-EU BITs, and (e) availability of investor–state arbitration between some members states is not a discrimination of relevance under the EC Treaty.[68]

Because even effective prevalence of EC law does not entail at the same moment the automatic invalidity of a BIT,[69] the Economic and Financial Committee (EFC) and the EU Commission have requested that member states terminate the BITs of intra-EU member states;[70] up until now, the EU member states have been very reluctant to do so.[71] In addition, almost all BITs contain post-termination protection periods. If further intra-EU BIT-based investment disputes arise before the termination of those BITs, then

[65] See "Letter of 13 January 2006," from A. Schaub, Internal Market and Services, to Zelinka, Czech Deputy Minister of Finance; excerpts of this letter appear in *Eastern Sugar v. Czech Republic* (Partial Award of 27 March 27, 2007), 24 et seq.

[66] *Eastern Sugar v. Czech Republic, supra* note 65.

[67] C. Söderlund, *supra* note 61, at 456 et seq.

[68] *Eastern Sugar v. Czech Republic, supra* note 65, paragraphs 155–180.

[69] Report of the ILA 2008 Committee on Foreign Investment; for ECJ jurisdiction on state-to-state dispute settlement, see Case C-459/03, *MOX Plant Decision (Commission v. Ireland)* [2006] ECR I-4635.

[70] See "Annual EFC Report to the Commission and the Council on the Movement of Capital and the Freedom of Payments" (November 15, 2006), 7; the EFC invited the member states "to review the need for such BITs agreements and inform the Commission about the actions taken in this context so that progress can be reviewed by the EFC by the end of 2007."

[71] The BIT between Italy and Hungary was terminated in April 2009; the Czech Republic initiated the termination process for twenty-three Czech BITs, which the country had concluded with individual EU member states before its accession to the EU. See UNCTAD, "Recent Developments in International Investment Agreements (2008 – June 2009)," IIA Monitor 3 (2009), 5.

it is unlikely that arbitral tribunals will defer the case to the ECJ,[72] even if deciding a dispute contrary to EU law might cause difficulties regarding the enforceability of the arbitral award within the EU under the New York Convention.[73]

B. *The External Dimension of EU Investment Policy*

EU member states have a long practice of concluding BITs with third countries: In total there are approximately 1,300 of them. Already before the entry into force of the Lisbon Treaty there was some discussion about the extent to which the member states still possessed the competence to conclude international investment agreements with non-EU member states.[74] Although the EC Treaty (before the Lisbon Treaty) did not furnish the EC with any explicit competence in the field of investment, the ECJ had developed the doctrine of parallel internal and external competences (the ERTA Doctrine[75]) in its case law. Under this doctrine, wherever the EC–EU has acquired an exclusive internal competence having widely enacted secondary law in a certain field, an EC responsibility for external relations in the specific area follows automatically (*in foro interno, in foro externo*). However, neither in the field of capital movement nor in matters related to establishment had the internal EC competences been exercised widely enough to achieve harmonization of an entire policy field, and thereby create an exclusive external EC competence for investment matters in general.[76] Nonetheless, certain policy areas including regulation on treatment standards of third-country investment, such as for instance EU financial services regulation, have been sufficiently harmonized

[72] See ILA, "Committee on Foreign Investment, Conference Report" (2008). An arbitral tribunal is not a "court or tribunal of a Member State" that can request the ECJ for a preliminary ruling; the reason put forward by the ECJ is that the parties are under no obligation, in law or in fact, to refer their dispute to arbitration. See on this Case 102/81, *Nordsee* [1982] ECR 1095, paragraphs 10–12; Case C-126/97, *Eco Swiss* [1999] ECR I-3055, paragraph 34. On this see M. Burgstaller, *supra* note 7, at 189 et seq.; H. Wehland, *supra* note 59, at 301.

[73] For non-ICSID awards, enforcement will usually be governed by the New York Convention; in these cases, national courts may justify the refusal of enforcement of an award deemed incompatible with EC law with the public policy exception contained in Article V(2)(b); see H. Wehland, *supra* note 59, at 308.

[74] N. Maydell, *supra* note 7, at 73 et seq. See on this J. Ceyssens, *Towards a Common Foreign Investment Policy?, Legal Issues of Economic Integration* (2005) 259 seq.; J. Karl, "The Competence for Foreign Direct Investment," 5 *J. World Inv. & Trade* (2006) 413 et seq.; L. Mola, *supra* note 4.

[75] Case 22/70, *Commission v. Council (ERTA)* [1971] ECR 263.

[76] See ILA *supra* note 69, at 8; for further details see P. Eeckhout, *External Relations of the European Union* (2004), 58 et seq.

on the internal level to trigger exclusivity in the external area. Such exclusivity thus bars member states from concluding BITs or other international agreements that contain a general, unspecified scope, because such treaties would infringe on implied exclusive EC competence.[77]

In addition, the ECJ had found investment policy to be excluded from the scope of the Common Commercial Policy.[78] Thus, until the entry into force of the Lisbon Treaty, the Common Commercial Policy and the fundamental freedoms did not provide for exclusive EU competence in these areas. However, since the ECJ's Lugano Opinion, the EU also enjoyed implied nonexclusive external competences.[79] In this respect, the fundamental freedoms of the EC Treaty did lead to community competences permitting the conclusion of international agreements on market access and postmarket access standards.[80]

Therefore, on the one hand, EU member states no longer have the right to conclude BITs on the establishment of foreign investments. For this reason, national BITs are limited in their scope to postestablishment treatment only, whereas EC agreements did have to cover market access and the preestablishment phase.[81] As Karl[82] pointed out, the EC alone had the competence to conclude trade agreements with third countries; these treaties often include provisions on capital movements related to investment. As far as protection of established investors ("postestablishment") was concerned, it was the competence of the EU member states to regulate protection and dispute resolution by means of the conclusion of BITs with third countries. Thus, two layers of investment rules coexist.[83] Furthermore, even before the adoption of the Treaty of Lisbon, the EU's implied nonexclusive competences already empowered the union to conclude BIT types of investment agreements with third

[77] N. Maydell, *supra* note 4 at 169 et seq.

[78] ECJ, Opinion 2/92, *OECD-National Treatment Instrument* [1994] ECR I-5267; see on this J. Ceyssens, *supra* note 74, at 260.

[79] Opinion 1/03, Lugano Convention, [2006] ECR I-1145, paragraphs 114–115. On nonexclusive, implied external competences in general, see M. Klamert and N. Maydell, "Lost in Exclusivity: Implied Non-exclusive External Competences in Community Law," 13 Eur. *Foreign Affairs Rev.* (2008) 494 et seq.

[80] For the application of the ECJ's implied powers doctrine after Lugano on the EU's external investment competences, see M. Klamert and N. Maydell, *supra* note 79, at 511 et seq.; N. Maydell, *supra* note 7, at 81 et seq.

[81] See on this also N. Maydell, *supra* note 7, at 81 et seq.; P. Gugler and V. Tomsik, *supra* note 30, point 4.

[82] J. Karl, *supra* note 74.

[83] EU Commission, "Upgrading the EU Investment Policy," Note for the Attention of the 133 Committee, Brussels (May 30, 2006), at point 2.

countries, albeit without conferring exclusivity.[84] Such implied competence remains of great value to the EU even after the adoption of the Treaty of Lisbon in order to enable the EU to conclude investment agreements also encompassing portfolio investments.[85] This is necessary because it is commonly believed that the Lisbon Treaty's investment competence in Article 207 of the TFEU does not cover the latter category of investments.[86]

Given the slow progress in the Doha Round negotiations, the EU announced in 2006 that it would seek to conclude new PTAs.[87] As of this writing, the EU is negotiating PTAs with the Gulf Cooperation Council,[88] the Association of Southeast Asian Nations,[89] India,[90] Mercosur,[91] and Canada.[92] The EU partnership agreements with Russia[93] and China[94] have expired, but successor agreements are being sought. Negotiations on a "Club Med" are anticipated in the near future.[95] Obviously, the EU has given up its moratorium on negotiating new PTAs with emerging economies, playing a catch-up game, after China, Japan, Korea, Australia, New Zealand, and the United States started (re-)enforcing their PTA relationships.[96] As a novelty compared to older PTAs, the scope of these agreements is supposed to extend to "investment,"[97] comparable to the U.S. approach discussed in earlier text. Even if there was no

84 M. Klamert and N. Maydell, "Rechtsfragen der impliziten Aussenkompetenzen der EG illustriert am Beispiel der Dienstleistungsrichtlinie und der Minimum Platform on Investment," 4 *Eur. Rev.* (2008) 601 et seq.

85 N. Maydell, *supra* note 4, at 238 et seq.

86 See later text, Section 4.B, on the treaty of Lisbon.

87 See R. Abbott, "EU Trade Policy – Approaching at Crossroads," Chatham House Briefing Paper (June 2008).

88 Negotiations started in 1991; see OJ 1990 C 231/216.

89 The European Commission adopted negotiating mandates for new FTAs with trade partners in the ten-nation Association of Southeast Asian Nations bloc on May 2, 2007.

90 Negotiations started on June 28, 2007.

91 Negotiating directive for an association agreement of September 13, 1999; negotiations ongoing.

92 At the Canada–EU Summit on May 6, 2009 in Prague, Czech Republic, the launch of negotiations toward a comprehensive economic and trade agreement was announced.

93 See the joint statement of the EU–Russia summit on the launch of negotiations for a new EU–Russia Agreement from June 27, 2008.

94 Negotiations for a partnership and cooperation agreement were launched in January 2007 and should, when completed, result in an upgrade of the original 1985 Trade and Cooperation Agreement.

95 See the Joint Declaration of the Paris Summit for the Mediterranean, July 13, 2008.

96 See, e.g., J. Bhagwati, *Termites in the Trading System* (2008); R. Sally, *Trade Policy, New Century: The WTO, FTAs and Asia Rising* (2008).

97 See EU Commission Communication, "Global Europe: Competing in the World," COM (2006) 567 final; nevertheless, the E–South Korea FTA does not contain any provisions on investment.

exclusive EU external competence in this policy area, an analysis of current EU PTAs showed a new concern about investment policy within the European Commission. The EU–Chile Agreement[98] provides for a general right of establishment and full national treatment at the preestablishment and postestablishment phases for both natural and legal persons, as well as a consent to state-to-state dispute-settlement arbitration. The European Commission pushed ahead with these ambitions, setting up an EU investment platform and including investment chapters in new EU PTAs. In the EU–India FTA negotiations, the commission is negotiating rules on improved market access and national treatment for investors that will foster transparency by clarifying the regulatory framework, aimed at freeing the flow of payments and investment-related capital movement and seeking to facilitate the movement of investment-related natural persons.[99]

The EU's position[100] before the entry into force of the Treaty of Lisbon was such that the EU PTAs including investment provisions would not be designed to replace the BITs of member states. The European Commission's ambition to become a new actor in this increasingly important area of international economic law is obvious, but, crucially, the pre-Lisbon vertical allocation of competences between member states and the European level limited a coherent EU investment policy.

In addition to its efforts as made evident in its bilateral negotiations, the European Commission has sent a strong signal that it wishes to acquire all the competences needed to negotiate investment deals. In November 2006, following the Commission's proposal, the Council of the European Union adopted the Minimum Platform on Investment (MPoI) for EU PTAs with third countries.[101] The MPoI serves – like national Model BITs – as a standardized negotiation proposal for ongoing and future FTA negotiations with third countries that include an investment protection element. The MPoI's purpose is to facilitate agreement between the EU Commission and EU member states every time a potential PTA is under negotiation as an agreed platform.[102] Moreover, the MPoI clearly strengthens the role of the Commission in relation to

98 OJ 2002 L-352, signed on November 18, 2002.

99 On the EU–India FTA, see EU Commission (September 2007), available at http://www.euindiachambers.com/Events/euindiafta.pdf.

100 This is emphasized by an article in the MPoI: "Article [. . .] Other agreements: Nothing in this Title shall be taken to limit the rights of investors of the Parties to benefit from any more favourable treatment provided for in any existing or future international agreement relating to investment to which a Member State of the Community and [COUNTRY] [A "REGION" COUNTRY] are Parties."

101 Council of the European Union, Doc. 15375/06 (November 27, 2006).

102 N. Maydell, *supra* note 7, at 75.

the member states in the process of external negotiations. The agreement with CARIFORUM (the Caribbean Forum)[103] is the first agreement that adopted the new approach. The negotiations on a Comprehensive Economic Partnership Agreement between Canada and the EU seem to be founded on the MPoI as well.[104]

Will the implementation of this approach (which has also been called an EU "power-grab"[105]) play the trump card of making existing BITs illegal?[106] Article 307 of the EC Treaty required member states to eliminate inconsistencies between their BITs and EU law.[107] This might lead to an obligation to terminate those BITs, should they be found to be inconsistent with primary or secondary European law. In decisions of March and November 2009 in infringement proceedings against Austria,[108] Sweden,[109] and Finland[110] before the ECJ, the court declared that certain provisions on the transfer of capital in the BITs of these EU member states with third countries violate EU law, obviously relying on the principle of effectiveness (*effet utile*).[111] In doing so the ECJ sought to minimize as far as possible the breach to the integrity of the European Community's legal order caused by preexisting international obligations.

[103] Economic Partnership Agreement between the CARIFORUM States, of the one part, and the European Community and Its Member States, of the other part (signed October 15, 2008); OJ 2008 L 289/I/3.

[104] See the Joint Report on the EU–Canada Scoping Exercise (March 5, 2009), point 3.7, on investment: "Whilst bilateral investment flows already represent a notable share of both parties' total foreign direct investment (FDI), the Group agreed that there were opportunities for increasing bilateral investment flows. The scope of the negotiations on investment should cover pre- and post-establishment in all sectors in order to improve market access and provide for the non-discriminatory treatment of investors and investments, and to improve transparency. The scope should include substantive and procedural obligations at both the central and sub-central government levels." Available at http://trade.ec.europa.eu/doclib/docs/2009/march/tradoc_142470.pdf.

[105] F. Eriksson, *Financial Times*, March 12, 2008.

[106] See J. Ceyssens, *supra* note 74, at 259 seq.

[107] Article 307 of the EC Treaty states that the treaty does not affect international obligations entered into by the member states before its entry into force. To the extent that such agreements are not compatible with the EC Treaty, the member state or states concerned shall take all appropriate steps to eliminate the incompatibilities established.

[108] Case C-205/06, *Commission vs. Austria* [2009], decision of March 3, 2009, [2009] ECRI, 1301.

[109] Case C-249/06, *Commission vs. Sweden* [2009], decision of March 3, 2009, [2009] ECRI, 1335.

[110] Case C-118/07, *Commission vs. Finland* [2009], decision of November 19, 2009, not yet published in the ECR.

[111] See the Opinion of Advocate General Maduro in Case C-205/06, delivered on July 10, 2008, *Commission vs. Austria* and Case C-249/06, *Commission vs. Sweden*.

In these decisions, the ECU, neither left member states any room to maneuver nor allowed exemptions from the treaty obligations. It held that Article 307 of the EC Treaty is of general scope and applies to any international agreement that is capable of affecting the EC Treaty.[112] The obligation under Article 307 of the EC Treaty is an expression of the duty of loyal cooperation formulated in Article 10 of the EC Treaty.[113] It is this duty that obliges member states to amend agreements incompatible with the treaty,[114] even though such agreements are recognized as fully valid from an international as well as European law perspective.[115] The ECJ has stressed that incompatibilities with the EC Treaty are not limited to the decided cases and that all member states are obliged to take all appropriate measures to eliminate incompatibilities with the EC Treaty.[116] Before the ECJ decisions against Sweden and Austria were delivered, the European Commission had already announced that it would consider its options in the light of these rulings.[117] It is most likely that the commission will institute additional infringement proceedings against EU member states.

4. EU INVESTMENT POLICY AFTER LISBON

As already pointed out, the EU in pre-Lisbon times had limited and qualified external competences in the field of investment, and therefore international investment agreements as well as investment promotion and protection chapters as part of PTAs could only be concluded as mixed agreements by the EU and its member states, acting together. This made it difficult not only for the EU itself but also for (potential) contracting partners because the ratification process is burdensome – any of the twenty-seven member states can veto the entry into force of the agreement. In contrast to this situation, the Treaty of Lisbon provides for an explicit and exclusive competence of the union in matters concerning "foreign direct investment" as part of the Common Commercial Policy. However, do the Lisbon amendments and modifications bring about

[112] Case C-205/06, *Commission vs. Austria* [2009], ECRI, 1301, paragraph 34; Case 812/79, *Attorney General vs. Burgoa* [1980] ECR 2787, paragraph 6.

[113] See the Opinion of Advocate General Tizzano in Case C-216/01, *Budvar* [2003] ECR I-13617, point 150; Opinion of Advocate General Maduro, Case C-402/05, *Kadi*, point 32; Opinion of Advocate General Maduro in Case C-205/06, delivered on July 10, 2008, *Commission vs. Austria* and Case C-249/06, *Commission vs. Sweden*, point 33.

[114] Case C-249/06, decision of March 3, 2009, *Commission vs. Sweden* [2009], ECRI, 1335, point 45.

[115] See t he Opinion of Advocate General Maduro, *supra* note 111, point 33.

[116] Case C-205/06, *Commission vs. Austria* [2009], ECRI, 1301, paragraph 43.

[117] See "Annual EFC Report" (2007), point 18.

enough progress to enable the EU to position itself as a global actor in the global economy of the future?

A. *Reasons for Introducing Explicit Competences on Investment*

The intention of this far-reaching transfer of competences in aspects of foreign direct investment is to strengthen the EU as an actor in bilateral and multilateral negotiations on investment policy.[118] As noted, chapters on investment are increasingly often a part of PTAs[119] and the EU's bargaining power with third countries is stronger than those of individual member states, in particular the smaller ones, and therefore there might be a better chance to obtain more favorable conditions for EU investors.[120] The European Commission has stressed that "[f]uture FTAs should also include new provisions for investment. . . . A new, ambitious model EU investment agreement should be developed in close coordination with Member States. It could be usefully complemented by a dialogue on investment promotion and facilitation."[121] The EU will then be able to negotiate investment treaties with market access provisions as well as preestablishment treatment more forcefully and will be able to narrow down the existing differences between the BITs of the EU and the BITs of the countries taking part in the North American Free Trade Agreement.[122]

B. *Scope of the Post-Lisbon Investment Policy Competences*

After the entry into force of the Lisbon Treaty, the EU possessed the exclusive competence in the field of "foreign direct investment" (Article 207 of the TFEU).[123] Nevertheless, the scope of application of the EU foreign investment policy is not yet clear. Most BITs in force use the much broader term "investment" or the narrower terms "establishment" and "enterprise."[124] Neither the International Monetary Fund (IMF) interpretation given to the term "foreign direct investment" (reflecting the objective of obtaining a lasting interest by a resident entity in one economy in an enterprise resident in another

[118] European Commission, Draft Articles Concerning External Action, CONV 685/03 (April 23, 2003).

[119] See earlier text in Section 2.

[120] J. Karl, *supra* note 74, at 425.

[121] European Commission, Staff Working Document SEC 1230 (2006), 18.

[122] See Report of the ILA 2008 Committee, *supra* note 69.

[123] See, on the definition of exclusive competence, *supra* notes 8 and 9.

[124] J. Karl, *supra* note 74, at 420.

economy)[125] nor community law in the capital directive[126] provides any guidance with respect to the kind of policy instruments the EU would have at its disposal.[127]

To assess the future scope of foreign direct investment in the Common Commercial Policy, some commentators have very restrictively argued that the Lisbon Treaty only includes investment liberalization.[128] This would cover a competence for internal and external regulation of market access, providing preestablishment and national treatment. Investment protection, in contrast, would remain entirely within the scope of the member states' BITs. In favor of this narrow approach, Tietje points out that Article 345 of the TFEU states that "the treaties shall in no way prejudice the rules in Member States governing the system of property ownership."[129]

Some commentators[130] argue in the opposite direction: The EU shall in the future be able to conclude agreements that include comprehensive investment rules similar to those included in U.S. FTAs. This competence would cover not only market access, preestablishment and postestablishment standards of treatment, and performance requirements, but also investor–state dispute-settlement provisions and even the question of protection in terms of the conditions under which expropriation takes place. So far, the European Commission has not given any official statements on this matter

Obviously, the wording of Article 207 of the TFEU does not contain any explicit limitation, and for reasons of efficiency and practicability (*effet utile*), the EU should possess the competence for every conceivable aspect of (foreign direct) investment promotion and protection.[131] Therefore, only the extension of the scope of application of the Common Commercial Policy to portfolio investments[132] and other forms of investment (e.g., intellectual property rights) will not be covered by the scope of application of the term "foreign direct investment." On the contrary, investments of sovereign wealth funds from abroad would be covered by the Common Commercial Policy if they are to be determined as foreign direct investments and thus fall within the exclusive

[125] IMF Balance of Payments Manual (1993).

[126] Council Directive 88/361/EEC (1988), OJ L-187/5.

[127] J. Karl, *supra* note 74, at 421.

[128] See, e.g., M. Krajewski, "External Trade Law and the Constitution Treaty?," 42 *Common Market L. Rev.* (2005) 91, at 112.

[129] C. Tietje, "Die Aussenwirtschaftsverfassung der EU nach dem Vertrag von Lissabon," 83 *Beiträge zum Transnationalen Wirtschaftsrecht* (2009) 14.

[130] See also J. Karl, *supra* note 74, at 422.

[131] See also J. Karl, *supra* note 74, at 422.

[132] See later text at Section 4.E.

sphere of the EU – not even Sarkozy would be allowed then (from a legal point of view) to set up a protectionist regime.[133]

C. *The Future of Existing Member State BITs and the Question of Their Termination*

As already mentioned, Germany has, to date, concluded almost 140 BITs, Great Britain more than 120, France almost 100, and Austria 50.[134] Under the Lisbon Treaty, the exclusive power in regard to foreign direct investments will be transferred to the EU level. As a direct consequence, EU member states are actually not permitted to conclude new BITs any more.[135] Nevertheless, on December 1, 2009 – the day of the entry into force of the Lisbon Treaty – Germany signed a new BIT with Pakistan, and Austria followed with a new BIT with Kazakhstan in January 2010. Before signing the BIT, Germany had at least consulted the EU Commission. Still, before this agreement can enter into force, permission by the EU to proceed in this way is necessary. This permission can be given only in an ordinary legislative procedure.[136]

The discussion on the legal status of the existing member states' BITs "after Lisbon" has already started.[137] Existing BITs with non-EU countries will generally remain in force.[138] Nevertheless, it is the member states' obligation to amend, modify, or even terminate agreements that are incompatible with the treaty. The question to be answered by the ECJ will be whether or not this new exclusive competence might lead to an obligation to terminate those existing BITs, especially taking into account the strict recent jurisprudence relating to Article 307 of the EC Treaty and member states' BITs.[139] However, a transition

[133] See *The Economist*, October 25, 2008, p. 16 ("The State as Owner – Re Bonjour, Monsieur Colbert"), p. 33 ("Nicolas Sarkozy – The President Who Loved Summits"), and p. 34 ("France Tests a Different Type of National Champion").

[134] See the overview under www.worldbank.org/icsid.

[135] J. Ceyssens, *supra* note 74, at 287; C. Pitschas and H.-G. Krenzler, "Die Gemeinsame Handelspolitik im Verfassungvertrag – ein Schritt in die richtige Richtung," in Herrmann, Krenzler, and Streinz (eds.), *Die Aussenwirtschaftspolitik der Europäischen Union nach dem Verfassungsvertrag* (2005) 11, at 31; C. Tietje, *supra* note 129, at 19 on this and furthermore pointing out a standstill obligation even before the entry into force of the Lisbon Treaty.

[136] See Article 207 paragraph 2 and Article 289 TFEU.

[137] See J. Ceyssens, *supra* note 74, at 259 seq.

[138] Report of the ILA 2008 Committee on Foreign Investment, *supra* note 69.

[139] The member states would be obliged to adapt their BITs to EU law as a result of Article 351 of the TFEU (the former Article 307 of the EC Treaty) analog and Article 4 paragraph 3 TEU revised. See on the strict application of Article 307 paragraph 2 EC Treaty Case C-205/06, *Commission vs. Austria* and Case C-249/06, *Commission vs. Sweden* [2009] ECRI, 1335, Opinion of Advocate General Maduro in Case C-205/06, delivered on July 10, 2008, *Commission vs. Austria* and Case C-249/06, *Commission vs. Sweden*, point 33.

period is not provided for by the treaty, and there is no provision recognizing the right of member states to keep in place their existing agreements.

Another approach that is both legitimate and practical would be permission granted by the EU[140] for the member states to keep their BITs in force until the conclusion of EU international investment agreements to avoid a vacuum – a situation of no treaty protection. In the long term, of course, member states' BITs will have to be replaced by new agreements concluded at the EU level that include investment, if the wording of Article 207 of the TFEU, with a transfer of powers to the EU level, is taken seriously. Nevertheless, member states may be allowed to continue to pursue their own investment insurance schemes and other financial support to foreign investments.[141]

D. *Negotiation and Conclusion of New Agreements Relating to Portfolio Investments*

The crucial question (after the entry into force of the Lisbon Treaty) besides the extent of competences in the field of foreign direct investments is the question of competences for portfolio investments. It might be necessary to include the regulation of portfolio investments in international investment agreement negotiations, but an external EU competence in this area can only result out of competences beyond the Common Commercial Policy, such as the provisions on the free movement of capital,[142] association agreements,[143] and development.[144] It could therefore only cover provisions of market access and "post establishment treatment," and it would generally not cover aspects of investment protection.[145] Article 63 of the TFEU cannot cover BITs on investment protection or expropriation, and it would also be questionable to derive an external competence for setting up a dispute-resolution mechanism based on the freedom of capital movements.[146] Concerning these points, no secondary legislation has been adopted and, as the ECJ clearly pointed out in Opinion 2/00, if harmonization at the community level has been achieved

[140] See on this possibility Case 41/76, *Donckerwolcke* [1976] ECR 1921, 1937; see on this practice also Vedder and Lorenzmeier, in Grabitz and Hilf (eds.), *EG-/EU-Vertrag Kommentar*, Art. 133 EG, pt. 23; C. Tietje, *supra* note 129, at 18.

[141] See on this J. Ceyssens, *supra* note 74, at 259 seq.; also see the proposal by the commission for Regulation Establishing Transition of Arrangements for Bilateral Investment Agreements, COM (2010) 344 final.

[142] Article 63 TFEU.

[143] Article 217 TFEU.

[144] Article 211 TFEU.

[145] J. Karl *supra* note 74, at 425.

[146] See J. Ceyssens *supra* note 74, at 282.

in only a small part of such a field, the EC and its member states share the competence to conclude international agreements.[147]

Therefore, even after the Lisbon Treaty enters into force, future agreements that cover all forms of investments and their protection, including a procedure on dispute resolution, would not in their entirety fall under an exclusive EU competence,[148] and the Common Commercial Policy, together with competences resulting out of the freedom of capital movement and the application of the ERTA Doctrine, would not be a sufficient basis for an all-inclusive EU agreement. It thus depends on the definition of "direct investments" and the EU's intention, to what extent "portfolio investments" should be protected, whether international investment agreements will have to be concluded as mixed or as agreements by the EU.[149]

The conclusion of "pure BITs" without having the member states be able to veto, in contrast, would only be possible if these agreements with regard to portfolio investments solely cover preestablishment and postestablishment regulation but do not include provisions on protection and expropriation. Therefore, the demands of EU investors as well as those of its negotiating partners might not be met. EU BITs comparable to the U.S. Model BIT covering portfolio and direct investment, preestablishment and postestablishment rules, protection of investment in cases of direct and indirect expropriation, as well as investor–state arbitration rules would need joint action of the EU with its member states.

At this point it must be asked if the protection of portfolio investments accompanied by a dispute-resolution mechanism is a necessary tool in the competition of systems "game." It has to be remembered that portfolio investments remain protected under the rules of international customary law.[150] Additionally, domestic and international investment insurance schemes give guarantees for EU investors abroad.[151] Diplomatic protection of EU portfolio investments could be granted by the investor's home country or by the EU, depending on a case-by-case analysis. A binding link to OECD codices on

[147] ECJ, Opinion 2/00, *Cartagena Protocol*, paragraphs 43–47.

[148] M. Krajewski, *supra* note 128, at 112.

[149] See the fairly similar C. Tietje, *supra* note 129, at 17.

[150] See, e.g., P. E. Comeaux and N. S. Kinsella, *Protecting Foreign Investment Under International Law* (1997); M. Sornarajah, *The International Law of Foreign Investment* (1994).

[151] See information regarding the Multilateral Investment Guarantee Agency, 24 *Int'l Legal Mater.* (1985) 1598; in Germany the government appointed a consortium formed by Pricewaterhouse-Coopers Aktiengesellschaft Wirtschaftsprüfungsgesellschaft (PwC AG), as lead partner, and Euler Hermes Kreditversicherungs-AG (Euler Hermes) to manage the investment guarantee scheme; see http://www.agaportal.de/en/dia/index.html.

foreign investments[152] within the concluded BITs could give further guarantees to those investments as well. Where there is a sufficient link to trade, even the Trade Barrier Regulation (TBR)[153] could be applied and investors might under certain circumstances be able to force the commission to intervene on their behalf. Furthermore, the TBR – as secondary law – could be modified and extended in its scope of application from trade barriers to questions related to foreign investments. However, even with these second-best protection possibilities for portfolio investments, the protection standard of future EU BITs will remain limited in comparison to the U.S. Model BIT. Customary international law never has proven to be an effective means to protect investments on a wider scale. The same is true regarding the TBR; this instrument does not give undertakings the necessary possibilities to protect their trade interests, either.

E. *Politicization of the Common Commercial (and Investment) Policy*

Under the Lisbon Treaty, the entire Common Commercial Policy, including the conclusion of investment agreements and investment clauses in PTAs, is "politicized": Trade policy is used as an instrument in the pursuit of other external policy objectives. EU trade and investment policy is brought under the same external action heading as other elements of EU external policy and is therefore to be conducted within the context of the framework of the general principles and objectives of the union's external action.[154] This binding linkage points out not only that the EU has a liberalization agenda, but that other objectives must be taken into account in the negotiation of bilateral trade and investment agreements as well.[155] At the same time, the Lisbon Treaty strengthens the role of the European Parliament in this field significantly and puts it into play in the area of investment policy. In general, the Parliament has to be consulted before an agreement

[152] OECD, Decision of the Council on National Treatment, available at http://www.oecd.org/dataoecd/32/21/1954854.pdf.

[153] Council Regulation 3286/94, OJ 1994 L-349/71.

[154] See Articles 205 and 207 TFEU with explicit reference to Article 21 EU; Article 21 EU includes general aims such as the support for democracy, the rule of law and human rights, sustainable economic, social, and environmental development, improvement of the environment, and sustainable development of global resources and good global governance.

[155] M. Cremona, "A Constitutional Basis for Effective External Action? An Assessment of the Provisions on EU External Action in the Constitutional Treaty?," EUI Working Papers Law 30 (2006), paragraph 52; C. Tietje *supra* note 129 at 19 et seq.

is concluded,[156] and parliamentary consent is required in almost all cases of new agreements.[157]

Taken together, it is this strengthened role of the European Parliament connected with the politicization of the entire Common Commercial Policy that constitutes the greatest potential impact of the Lisbon Treaty on EU external trade policy. The European Parliament is fully aware of its new "superpowers" resulting from these institutional changes. In 2006, it announced it would give its consent to only those agreements containing a human rights clause.[158] Recently the European Parliament announced – before the Lisbon Treaty has even gone into force – that it would give its consent to the conclusion of a FTA between the EC and the Gulf Cooperation Council, as required under the Lisbon Treaty, only if those objectives laid down in Article 21 of the TEU (Lisbon version) were sufficiently taken into account.[159]

F. *EU Model Law on Investment*

The EU is eager to develop its own EU Model Investment Protection Agreement as the basis for future agreements to be concluded by the EU after the entry into force of the Lisbon Treaty. This model agreement will face multiple challenges – dispute resolution, standards of protection including the most favored nation clause, the scope of investments included, taking into account the "investment and . . . " topics, and so on. The high quality of such an EU Model Investment Protection Agreement and the conclusion of EU BITs comparable to the standard reached today by German BITs, for example, could prevent EU companies from engaging in treaty shopping[160] and establishing outside the EU in order to secure a better procedural standing in investment disputes and make them leave their establishments within the EU.

[156] M. Cremona, "The Draft Constitutional Treaty: External Relations and External Actions," 40 *Common Market L. Rev.* (2003) 1347, at 1364.

[157] See Article 218 paragraph 6. On this see, e.g., J. Monar, "Die Gemeinsame Handelspolitik der Europäischen Union im EU-Verfassungsentwurf," *Aussenwirtschaft* (2005) 99, at 111; European Policy Analysis 3 (2008), 4.

[158] See the Resolution of the European Parliament of December 14, 2006, EP-Doc. A 6 – 4/2006. On this topic in general, see L. Bartels, *Human Rights Conditionality in the EU's International Agreements* (2005).

[159] See the Resolution of April 24, 2008.

[160] On the extent of this see M. Burgstaller, "Nationality of Corporate Investors and International Claims against the Investor's Own State," 7 *J. World Inv. & Trade* (2006) 857 et seq.; M. Krajewski and J. Ceyssens, "Internationaler Investitionsschutz und innerstaatliche Regulierung," 45 *Archiv. des Voelkerrechts.* (2007) 180, at 190.

The effectiveness of international investment protection depends on an accepted and effective forum for dispute resolution. The most popular forum in this regard is arbitration according to the rules of the International Centre for Settlement of Investment Disputes (ICSID) Convention – but the EU is not a member of ICSID. Being an international organization, the EU is at least for the moment not qualified to become a member of the ICSID system. Unless the IMF Agreement, the World Bank Agreement, or the ICSID Convention – all of which are relevant for ICSID membership,[161] which is only open to states[162] – are amended, ICSID dispute resolution will not be an option for an EU Model BIT, if it is not supposed to be a mixed agreement. According to the ICSID Convention, each amendment to the convention requires that all contracting states have ratified, accepted, or approved the amendment. Therefore, in the real competition of systems in practice, such an amendment is very unlikely.[163] Working on the idea of a future mixed agreement, the question is still open as to whether the EU would – as is the case in the WTO system – represent the member states regarding judicial proceedings or – as in the Energy Charter Treaty system – leave it to the member states to participate themselves in investment arbitration. There are in fact reasons to follow the latter approach, considering that the failures of one of the members should not harm the reputation of all the others.[164] Furthermore, the option of ICSID proceedings would then still be possible, contrary to a situation in which the EU would take over the place of a respondent in proceedings.

Thus, at present, ICSID arbitration is excluded from EU investment protection, and investors protected under an EU investment treaty would not institute ICSID proceedings. As an alternative, a parallel dispute-settlement system could be set up. Furthermore, with respect to EU investor protection, an amended system of diplomatic protection should be established. The scope of the TBR could easily be extended to matters of investment leading to a future Regulation on Trade Barriers and Investment Protection. Proceedings could be launched by the European Commission on behalf of EU investors,

[161] Article 67, ICSID Convention.

[162] See Article II, Agreement on the International Monetary Fund together with Article II, Agreement on the International Bank for Reconstruction and Development.

[163] M. Burgstaller, *supra* note 7, at 206; on the position of the EU in International Organizations see F. Hoffmeister, "Outsider or Frontrunner?," 44 *Common Market L. Rev.* (2007) 41 et seq.; I. Govaere, J. Capiau, and A. Vermeersch, "In-Between Seats: The Participation of the European Union in International Organizations," 9 *Eur. Foreign Affairs Rev.* (2004) 155 et seq.

[164] See J. Griebel, "Überlegungen zur Wahrnehmung der neuen EU-Kompetenz für ausländische Direktinvestitionen nach Inkrafttreten des Vertrags von Lissabon," 55 *Recht der Int'l Wirtschaft* (2009) 473 et seq.

if investor–state arbitration on the basis of an EU international investment agreement is not feasible for whatever reason.

Furthermore, obligations on promoting social standards, sustainable development, human rights, good governance, and the like have to be included in such an EU Model BIT because of the binding link of the Common Commercial Policy to the general principles and objectives enumerated in Article 21 of the TEU.[165] In negotiations of international investment agreements, it might be counterproductive to ask for more than a requirement to "take into account" those listed principles; otherwise, the EU investment platform will lose attractiveness for potential contracting partners from emerging markets.[166] Investment protection for EU investors abroad is needed whether or not these countries fulfill these standards. EU investors can independently be bound to comply with EU standards through secondary law, even when engaging and establishing abroad. An obligation on respecting the OECD Guidelines for Multinational Enterprises[167] as well as on the ideas of the Global Compact[168] might be an alternative to having provisions on public goods be part of the agreement.

Today's BITs concluded by the EU member states contain numerous most favored nation (MFN) clauses. A future EU Model BIT will have to deal with the scope of application of those MFN clauses and make sure that those clauses that are part of old member states' BITs cannot be invoked against the EU. In addition, it is necessary to exclude from the benefit of an MFN clause the most advanced integration agreements concluded by the EU that could lead to a later accession to the EU.[169]

5. EXTENDING EU COMPETENCES AND CONCLUDING REMARKS

The discussion of the politics of EU investment treaty making takes place on both an internal level and an external level. At the intra-EU level, the EU is trying to generate competences in investment treaty making, while the EU member states at the same time are eager to further extend their BITs

[165] See earlier text in Section 4.E.

[166] See, e.g., *Financial Times*, March 4, 2007, "Rights Obstacle to EU–India Trade Pact" (by J. Johnson). For a critical position on this development of the Common Commercial Policy, see C. Tietje, *supra* note 129, at 20.

[167] *OECD Working Papers Vol. V: The OECD Declaration and Decisions on International Investment and Multinational Enterprises Basic Texts* (1997).

[168] For more information, see http://www.unglobalcompact.org.

[169] EU Commission, Note for the Attention of the 133 Committee (May 30, 2006), at 2.

networks. On the external level, the EU is interested in becoming a global actor in the politics of investment liberalization and protection. However, the EU is limited in its capacity to strengthen this role in the global political economy. Before Lisbon, the EU was limited in its legal competence to act on its own; after Lisbon, the EU extended external competences, but at the same time it had to pursue and observe additional noninvestment objectives in all of its international treaty making. The European Parliament will have the power to make sure that the European Commission follows these constitutional obligations.

The current perception of the European Commission is that, in comparison with the investment agreements of the United States and other states, EU agreements and achievements in the area of investment before Lisbon lag behind because of their narrow content. The EU cannot negotiate and conclude full-range investment agreements or PTAs containing investment chapters without having the member states participate in the negotiations as well as in the ratification process, because of the vertical allocation of competences between the European level and the member states' level. European investors might be in a competitive disadvantage in regard to their foreign competitors, consequently losing market share.[170] Thus, the EU will be putting itself at a disadvantage if it did not seek to improve investment conditions, because this topic is becoming more relevant in the negotiation process of the new generation of FTAs, as highlighted earlier in this text.

Even after the entry into force of the Lisbon Treaty, still no EU BIT could be concluded that would be comparable either in its quality and extent with the U.S. Model BIT or in protection standards with today's EU member states' BITs, but the centralization of competences for foreign direct investments is at least a first step toward the creation of a comprehensive EU investment policy reflecting the nature of the international economy, in which trade and investment are inextricably linked.[171]

Even after Lisbon, future agreements on investment will be difficult to negotiate. If the EU is to have a coherent position on globalization, then it cannot leave aside investment policy.[172] To be able to react to the needs of its external policy requirements in general and to be able to compete, for example, with the U.S. investment agreements, the EU needs – just as the current U.S. practice is today – to be able to conclude pure BITs just as well

[170] EU Commission, "Upgrading the EU Investment Policy," Note for the attention of the 133 Committee (May 30, 2006).

[171] See S. Woolcock, "The Potential Impact of the Lisbon Treaty on European External Policy," SIEPS European Policy Analysis 8 (2008), 5.

[172] S. Woolcock, *supra* note 171, at 4.

as it might have to incorporate investment chapters into broad PTAs. In the latter case, though, the aforementioned limited competence in investment is of no importance; because of the inclusion of other topics, which are not in the exclusive competence of the EU, such agreements will in most cases have to be mixed agreements anyway, so that both the EU and its twenty-seven member states will have to sign and ratify them. Furthermore, it has to be remembered that noneconomic principles laid down in Article 21 of the EU Treaty (Lisbon version) have to be included in future agreements, which might hinder the negotiation of new PTAs as well as EU BITs with emerging markets and thereby put the EU at a competitive disadvantage in regard to other global players. Here, from the point of view of efficiency, this linkage might also have drawbacks for the EU's bargaining power.

It is obvious that certain modifications of the constitutional conditions for international investment agreements in a post-Lisbon environment would offer the chance to formulate a more efficient EU Model BIT. If the EU wants to become a global player in investment politics, then it will need the capacity to conclude general international investment agreements of a high quality – not having to differentiate between foreign direct and portfolio investments and by that also being able to conclude pure EU BITs without having its member states be able to veto. However, even without any further primary law reforms, the post-Lisbon situation might enable the EU to negotiate and conclude international investment agreements covering investment law from market access to protection of portfolio as well as foreign direct investments. To become an effective negotiator in investment matters, the European Commission obviously will have to expand nonexplicit competences in the area of regulation of portfolio investments. At first sight, the EU might therefore find itself in a situation in which it is unable to meet the demands of its negotiating partners to extend the scope of the agreement beyond foreign direct investments, unless the EU participates in such negotiations jointly with its member states,[173] where the EU and its member states might have diverging views concerning the envisaged agreements. As pointed out, investment protection relies on a network of bilateral agreements of investment regulation of nation states. Up until this point, this regime has been controlled by the state, but the EU plans to take over the leading role from its member states and finally being in a position to formulate a coherent Common Commercial Policy – including all relevant aspects of trade and investment.

In other policy areas the European Commission has found ways to force member states to accept the conclusion of Community agreements rather

[173] See J. Karl, *supra* note 74, at 425.

than mixed agreements. In the case of aviation policy, a central outcome of the above-mentioned ERTA jurisprudence was a strong negotiation mandate for the commission for a new "Open Skies Agreement" with the U.S.[174] Beforehand the ECJ hat ruled that several areas covered by open skies agreements concluded by the EU member states were issues of exclusive EC competence and therefore violated EC law.[175] The Commission then called upon the member states to denounce existing operations under the agreements in question.[176] At the same time, member states were blocked from negotiating new agreements on their own. Finally, a European solution was considered an advantage.[177] Here the Commission made use of the opportunity to increase the cost of no agreement for the member states in a politically sensitive domain by exploiting the advantages of internal allies; this was due mainly to the ECJ ruling, but also to member states with Commission-like preferences.[178] This case study might serve as an example for the European Commission and the member states of how an effective EU investment policy can possibly be set up.

According to the ERTA Doctrine, member states are no longer competent to conclude treaties to the extent that the underlying subject matter has been made part of EU legislation. The potential EU competence could become exclusive if the scope of internal legislation were altered by an international agreement pertaining to that legislation to be concluded by a member state.[179] Applying the ERTA Doctrine to the new EC agreements with the CARIFORUM (the Caribbean Forum) and with respect to the MPoI, member states even before the entry into force of the Lisbon Treaty were no longer competent to conclude any treaties that contained provisions on market access, national treatment, and MFN in the field of foreign direct investments. The member states' BIT practice then might already have violated EC law because of lack of competence.[180]

[174] OJ 2007 L 134/4 et seq.

[175] Cases 466 – 476/98 [2002], ECR I 9518 et seq.

[176] EU Commission, Communication from the Commission on the Consequences of the Court Judgment for European Air Transport Policy (November 5, 2002), COM (2002) 649 final; on this see C. Woll, "The Road to External Representation: The European Commission's Activism in International Air Transport," 13 *J. Eur. Pub. Policy* (2006) 52–69.

[177] C. Woll, *supra* note 176, at 64.

[178] T. Delreux, "Commission and Member States in EU–U.S. Open Skies Negotiations: Opportunities and Constraints in the Internal Decision-Making Process," IIEB Working Paper 35 (April 2009), at 21.

[179] Case 22/70, *Commission v. Council (ERTA)* [1971] ECR 263, paragraph 17.

[180] M. Burgstaller, *supra* note 7, at 206; N. Maydell, *supra* note 7, at 91.

Transferring the aviation approach to investment policy would mean that the European Commission could argue that numerous BITs violate European law, and furthermore that EU member states are no longer competent to negotiate the modification of existing member states' BITs. Thus, because of the jurisprudence of the ECJ, especially in the aforementioned cases,[181] the EU possesses the means for implementing an investment policy after the entry into force of the Lisbon Treaty.

The discussion on EU investment regulation is just starting. To make it work efficiently, it still has a long way to go. This chapter has attempted to present the complex interaction of legal, constitutional, economic, and indeed political factors that will inform this process, as a case study of the politics of international economic law making.

[181] Case C-205/06, *Commission vs. Austria* [2009], ECRI, 1301, Case C-249/06, *Commission vs. Sweden* [2009], ECRI, 1335, Case C-118/07, *Commission vs. Finland* [2009], not yet published in the ECR. See on these cases the earlier text in Section C.2.

7

The Politics of China's Investment Treaty-Making Program

Axel Berger

1. INTRODUCTION

China's rise as an economic player is causing significant power shifts in the world economy.[1] Its strength as a low-cost manufacturer helps to supply global markets with cheap products and simultaneously increases the global demand for commodities. This growing economic presence – in accordance with the classical argument by Paul Kennedy on *The Rise and Fall of the Great Powers*[2] – consequentially augments China's political influence in international relations.

A phenomenon demonstrating China's economic rise is its growing outward foreign direct investments (FDIs).[3] They have recently been widely discussed in the literature as part of a larger trend of developing countries' emergence as sources of investments.[4] Less visible in the literature is a second trend,

[1] See, e.g., Kaplinsky and Messner, "The Impact of Asian Drivers on the Developing World," 36 *World Development* (2008) 2.

[2] P. Kennedy, *The Rise and Fall of the Great Powers: Economic Change and Military Conflict from 1500 to 2000* (1987).

[3] Hanemann and Rosen, "China's Changing Outbound Foreign Direct Investment Profile: Drivers and Policy Implications," *Peterson Institute for International Economics* (2009).

[4] See, e.g., Sauvant, "New Sources of FDI: The BRICs," 6 *Journal of World Investment and Trade* (2005) 5; United Nations Conference for Trade and Development (UNCTAD), *World Investment Report 2006. FDI from Developing and Transition Economies: Implications for Development* (2006); Aykut and Goldstein, "Developing Country Multinationals: South–South Investment Comes of Age," OECD Development Centre Working Paper 257 (2006); H. G. Broadman, *Africa's Silk Road* (2007); Pamlin and Baijin, *Rethink China's Outward Investment Flows* (2007); UNCTAD and the United Nations Development Programme, *Asian*

The author thanks the editors of this volume and its anonymous reviewers. For comments on previous versions of this chapter, I am grateful to Katharina Berger, Thilo Hanemann, Julia Kubny, Erik Lundsgaarde, and Don Wallace, as well as Steffen Stürznickel, who provided excellent research assistance. These individuals bear no responsibility for the argumentation of this paper, which is entirely my own.

namely Beijing's growing acceptance of international investment agreements as legal instruments for the protection of FDIs.[5] Most notably, China has been negotiating bilateral investment treaties (BITs) since the end of the 1990s that include far-reaching substantive and procedural investment protection. This new policy was a turning away from China's traditional stance toward international investment law that accentuated the host country's sovereign right to regulate foreign investments – a policy typical for FDI-importing countries. Nowadays China is demonstrating new confidence as an actor of importance in the global governance system for FDI, shown by its willingness to engage in BIT negotiations with the United States.

Against this background, this chapter empirically investigates the evolution of China's BIT policy since the early 1980s. On the basis of this analysis, it asks whether the change in China's BIT policy is substantial enough to make a deal with the United States a realistic aim. Section 2 gives an overview of the development and substance of today's global BIT system, introducing main concepts that will be used in the chapter's argumentation. Section 3 describes the rise of China as a home country for outward FDIs and their strategic determinants. Section 4 outlines China's traditional restrictive BIT approach. Section 5 argues that China has been negotiating legalized BITs

Foreign Direct Investment in Africa (2007); P. Gammeltoft, "Emerging Multinationals: Outward FDI from the BRICS countries," Paper presented at the IV Globelics Conference, Mexico City, September 22–24, 2008.

5 See, e.g., Kong, "Bilateral Investment Treaties: The Chinese Approach and Practice," 8 *Asian Yearbook of International Law* (2003); Cai, "Outward Foreign Direct Investment Protection and the Effectiveness of Chinese BIT Practice," 7 *Journal of World Investment and Trade* (2006) 5; Cai, "Change of the Structure of International Investment and the Development of Developing Countries' BIT Practice," 8 *Journal of World Investment and Trade* (2007) 6; Cai, "China–US BIT Negotiations and the Future of Investment Treaty Regime: A Grand Bargain with Multilateral Implications," 12 *Journal of International Economic Law* (2009) 2; Chen, "Should the Four Great Safeguards in Sino–Foreign BITs Be Hastily Dismantled? Comments on Provisions Concerning Dispute Settlement in Model U.S. and Canadian BITs," 7 *Journal of World Investment and Trade* (2006) 6; Chen, "Distinguishing Two Types of Countries and Properly Granting Differential Reciprocity Treatment. Re-comments on the Four Safeguards in Sino–Foreign BITs Not to Be Hastily and Completely Dismantled," 8 *Journal of World Investment and Trade* (2007) 6; Braun and Schonard, "The New Germany–China Bilateral Investment Treaty – A Commentary and Evaluation in Light of the Development of Investment Protection under Public International Law," *ICSID Review* (2007); Rooney, "ICSID and BIT Arbitration and China," 24 *Journal of International Arbitration* (2007) 6; Schill, "Tearing Down the Great Wall. The New Generation Investment Treaties of the People's Republic of China," 15 *Cardozo Journal of Internal & Comparative Law* (2007) 73; Berger, "China and the Global Governance of Foreign Direct Investment. The Emerging Liberal Bilateral Investment Treaty Approach," Deutsches Institut für Entwicklungspolitik Discussion Paper 10 (2008); Heymann, "International Law and the Settlement of Investment Disputes Relating to China," 11 *Journal of International Economic Law* (2008) 3; N. Gallagher and W. Shan, *Chinese Investment Treaties. Policies and Practice* (2009).

with developing as well as developed countries since the late 1990s that are comparable to the European Model BIT. Section 6 assesses the prospects of the ongoing BIT negotiations between China and the United States. Finally, Section 7 summarizes the chapter's main findings.

2. PROTECTION OF FDIS THROUGH BILATERAL INVESTMENT TREATIES

The global governance system for FDI is made up of a dense and complex network of international investment agreements that are usually concluded on a bilateral basis. BITs form the most important legal institution for the governance of FDI.[6] They are defined as agreements that "protect investments by investors of one state in the territory of another state by articulating substantive rules governing the host state's treatment of the investment and by establishing dispute resolution mechanisms applicable to alleged violations of those rules."[7] The aim of BIT contracting parties is to promote economic cooperation, believing that enhanced legal protection will ultimately result in increasing FDI flows that foster economic development processes in host as well as home countries. BITs, however, generally do not allow for direct regulatory measures by host states, potentially diminishing the developmental impact of FDI. Furthermore, the results of quantitative econometric studies on the effectiveness of BITs in increasing FDI flows are mixed and lead to an inconclusive picture.[8]

6 See, e.g., R. Dolzer and M. Stevens, *Bilateral Investment Treaties* (1995); UNCTAD, *Bilateral Investment Treaties in the Mid-1990s* (1998); UNCTAD, *Bilateral Investment Treaties 1995–2006: Trends in Investment Rulemaking* (2007). Beyond BITs, investment rules are increasingly being incorporated into double taxation treaties and economic integration agreements such as FTAs; see, e.g., UNCTAD, *Taxation. UNCTAD Series on Issues of International Investment Agreements* (2000); UNCTAD, *Investment Provisions in Economic Integration Agreements* (2006). On the multilateral level, investment-related rules are mainly integrated into single World Trade Organization agreements such as the General Agreement on Trade in Services, the Agreement on Trade-Related Investment Measures, and the Agreement on Trade-Related Aspects of Intellectual Property Rights. Among member countries of the OECD, the whole spectrum of international investment relations is governed in the Code of Liberalization of Capital Movements and the Declaration on International Investment and Multinational Enterprises.

7 Vandevelde, "The Economics of Bilateral Investment Treaties," 41 *Harvard International Law Journal* (2000) 2, at 469–470.

8 See, e.g., Hallward-Driemeier, "Do Bilateral Treaties Attract Foreign Direct Investment? Only a Bit . . . and They Could Bite," World Bank Policy Research Working Paper 3121 (2003) and Tobin and Rose-Ackermann, "Foreign Direct Investment and the Business Environment in Developing Countries: The Impact of Bilateral Investment Treaties," Yale University Working Paper (2005) that find no or only little evidence for the effectiveness of BITs. Banga, "Impact of

The concept of legalization, as developed by Abbott et al., will be used to describe the characteristics of the global BIT system.[9] Legalization is a special form of institutionalization – understood as the expansion of rules, norms, and decision-making procedures that influence expectations, interests, and behavior of actors – and "represents the decision . . . to impose international legal constraints on governments."[10] The degree of legalization varies substantially from one issue area to another and within issue areas over time. Along three main criteria – *obligation*, *precision*, and *delegation* – the degree of legalization can be described as a continuum ranging from soft to hard law. In this respect, "[h]ighly legalized institutions are those in which rules are obligatory on parties through links to the established rules and principles of international law, in which rules are precise (or can be made precise through the exercise of delegated authority), and in which authority to interpret and apply the rules has been delegated to third parties acting under the constraints of rules."[11]

The current institutional structure in the area of international investment protection is highly legalized according to the aforementioned characteristics. With respect to the first criterion, modern BITs entail rules that impose binding obligations on the parties that can be enforced through investor–state dispute settlement. Although BIT texts are often drafted in an open and imprecise manner – usually encompassing no more than ten pages – they can be described as hard law because they delegate the authority of interpretation and implementation to transnational arbitration bodies.[12] BITs notably grant

Government Policies and Investment Agreements on FDI Inflows," Council for Research on International Economic Relations Working Paper No. 116 (2003); Neumayer and Spess, "Do Bilateral Investment Treaties Increase Foreign Direct Investment to Developing Countries?," 33 *World Development* (2005) 10; Salacuse and Sullivan, "Do BITs Really Work? An Evaluation of Bilateral Investment Treaties and Their Grand Bargain," 46 *Harvard International Law Journal* (2005); and Busse et al., "FDI Promotion through Bilateral Investment Treaties: More Than a Bit?," 146 *Review of World Economics* (2010) 1, instead arrive at a positive relationship between BITs and FDI flows. Berger et al. (2010), "More Stringent BITs, Less Ambiguous Effects on FDI? Not a Bit!," Kiel Working Papers (2010) show that the impact of strong investor–state dispute settlement provisions on FDI flows remains elusive. UNCTAD, *The Role of International Investment Agreements in Attracting Foreign Direct Investment to Developing Countries* (2009) concludes that BITs are only one determinant of FDI flows. Policy and institutional determinants at the level of the host country for protecting and liberalizing foreign investments significantly impact FDI flows.

9 Abbott et al., "The Concept of Legalization," 54 *International Organization* (200) 3.

10 Goldstein et al., "Introduction: Legalization and World Politics," 54 *International Organization* (2000) 3, at 386.

11 Abbott et al., *supra* note 10, at 418.

12 Keohane et al., "Legalized Dispute Resolution: Interstate and Transnational," 54 *International Organization* (200) 3, at 485 state that in "transnational dispute resolution, . . . access to courts and tribunals and the subsequent enforcement of their decisions are legally insulated from the

foreign investors direct legal personality under international law. Without being obliged to submit a claim to domestic courts, foreign investors may sue host countries directly before a transnational tribunal and thus limit national legal sovereignty: "[O]nce in force, the role played by non-state actors in the regime's enforcement mechanisms can be of greater significance than the role played by states."[13] Modern BITs usually provide foreign investors with high levels of substantive and procedural protection. They follow a legalized approach to international investment protection.[14] *Legalized BITs* include broad definitions of investment, comprehensive absolute and relative standards of treatment, provisions on the compensation for expropriation, and the free transfer of funds as well as unrestricted investor–state dispute settlement mechanisms. While providing high levels of legal protection for foreign investors, legalized BITs limit host countries' regulatory discretion to impose restrictions on the entry and operation of multinational enterprises. The utilization of legalized investment agreements tends to lead to a more open and less regulated global investment regime. The *restrictive approach*, in contrast, includes several regulations limiting the substantive and procedural protection of foreign investments and thereby preserves the sovereign right of host states to maintain national laws and regulations on the entry and operation of foreign investors in accordance with national development strategies.

The first BIT was signed between Germany and Pakistan in 1959; in 2008 the total number of BITs amounted to 2,676 treaties worldwide.[15] Throughout the 1970s and 1980s BITs slowly spread, with roughly 20 treaties being signed annually, mainly between European and developing countries. With the decision of the United States to adopt BITs as a foreign investment protection device, their number started to increase. When developing countries decided to give up their struggle for a new international economic order, the number of BITs rose even further because developing countries started to compete in capturing a share of global FDI flows. They faced the dilemma of either

will of individual national governments. These tribunals are therefore more open to individuals and groups in civil society."

[13] Schneiderman, "Globalization, Governance, and Investment Rules," in J. Clarke and G. R. Edwards (eds.), *Global Governance in the Twenty-First Century* (2004), at 68.

[14] Both the legalized and the restrictive BIT approaches are understood as ideal types. In the Weberian sense, ideal types are "formed by the one-sided accentuation of one or more points of view and by the synthesis of a great many diffuse, discrete, more or less present and occasionally absent concrete individual phenomena, which are arranged according to those one-sidedly emphasized viewpoints into a unified analytical construct." See M. Weber, *The Methodology of the Social Sciences* (1997), at 88.

[15] See UNCTAD, *World Investment Report 2009. Transnational Corporations, Agricultural Production and Development* (2009), at 32.

signing BITs that privileged the contracting party exporting FDI, or possibly losing FDI to other countries and thus increasing their competitive advantage.[16]

Although BITs are generally negotiated on a reciprocal basis, providing the same level of legal protection for both signatories, they are in fact agreements between a FDI-exporting and a FDI-importing country. The actual level of investment protection found in BIT provisions is therefore a function of the expectations of both parties and their respective bargaining power. Because developing countries depend on FDI inflows as a source of external financing, they usually agree to the model agreements put forward by FDI-exporting countries. The level of legalization in international investment law has grown over time. Only large developing countries such as China, India, and Brazil have been able to refrain from signing (legalized) BITs.[17] With rising outward FDIs from these countries, though, their international investment policies are changing, as will be argued in subsequent text in the case of China. With the transformation of these emerging countries from being mere importers of FDI to being exporters of FDI too, the traditional pattern of BIT negotiations taking place between rich industrialized countries and poor developing countries is being complemented by negotiations now taking place among FDI exporters. The negotiations toward a Sino–United States BIT are just the most prominent example of this trend.

BIT contents today show a considerable uniformity with regard to general provisions on substantive and procedural protection of foreign investments. From a political economy perspective, the main difference found in BITs is the degree to which they protect investments already in the preestablishment phase – that is, before the FDI project has been admitted through the host country's authorities in accordance with national laws and regulations:

> This approach consists in providing foreign investors with national treatment and MFN treatment not only once the investment has been established, but also with respect to the establishment. This means that investors of one party will receive treatment not less favourable with regard to investing in the territory of the other party than domestic investors and investors of any other third country.[18]

16 See, e.g., Guzmàn, "Explaining the Popularity of Bilateral Investment Treaties: Why LDCs Sign Treaties that Hurt Them," Harvard Jean Monnet Working Paper 12/97 (1998); Elkins et al., "Competing for Capital: The Diffusion of Bilateral Investment Treaties, 1960–2000," 60 *International Organization* (2006) 4.

17 China's traditional restrictive BIT approach is described in more detail in Section 4.

18 UNCTAD, *Trends in Investment Rulemaking, supra* note 7, at 22.

The *admission model* BIT, which has been adopted by European countries and developing countries such as China alike, provides investment protection only after the admission of the FDI project. The *preestablishment model*, applied by the United States from the 1980s onward, by Canada from the mid-1990s onward, and by Japan from the beginning of this century, entails provisions on the protection of FDI even before their admission. By granting foreign investors market access, these treaties restrict the screening powers of host states in the preestablishment phase and their sovereignty in regulating the entry of foreign investors, leading to a liberalization of host countries' regulatory systems.[19] To assess the prospects that a China–United States BIT will be successful negotiated, Section 6 describes the United States' preestablishment model in more detail. In the following section, however, it is argued that China applies the widespread admission model in its BITs.

3. CHINA'S EMERGING OUTWARD FOREIGN INVESTMENTS

The growth of Chinese outward FDIs is the latest stage of an economic development process that started in the late 1970s with the Chinese leadership's decision to gradually open up the economy. During the past three decades, China has been mostly perceived as the workbench of the global economy, receiving high inflows of foreign investment in export-oriented industries. China is traditionally seen as the largest developing host country of global FDI. It accounted for a total inward FDI stock of U.S. $378.1 billion in 2008 and attracted FDI flows amounting to U.S. $108.3 billion in 2008. While still being a net FDI-importing country, China has become an important source country for foreign investments.[20] Especially noteworthy is the sharp increase of outward FDI flows from U.S. $12.3 billion in 2005 to U.S. $52.1 billion.

[19] See Gugler and Tomsik, "The North American and European Approaches in the International Investment Agreements," 4 *Transnational Dispute Management Review* 5 and UNCTAD, *Trends in Investment Rulemaking*, *supra* note 7, at 22–25.

[20] Outward FDI statistics are prone to inaccuracies, which potentially limits their explanatory power. Inaccuracies problems can be assumed to increase with disaggregation of the data; therefore, the geographical distribution of Chinese outward FDI is not presented here. There are reasons to expect both underestimation as well as overestimation of actual Chinese outward FDI. For a discussion of statistical problems with regard to Chinese outward FDI see, e.g., Frost, "Chinese Outward Direct Investment in Southeast Asia: How Much and What Are the Regional Implications?," Southeast Asian Research Centre Working Paper Series 67 (2004); Aykut and Ratha, "South–South FDI Flows: How Big Are They?," 13 *Transnational Corporations* (2004) 1, at 160–162; Hanemann and Rosen, *supra* note 4, at 3–6; Schüler-Zhou and Schüller, "The Internationalization of Chinese Companies. What Do Official Statistics Tell Us about Chinese Outward Foreign Direct Investment?," 3 *Chinese Management Studies* 1 (2009). Especially the problem of round-tripping, which leads to an inflation of outward FDI statistics, has to be taken into account in order to assess Chinese outward FDI data. See Xiao,

Accumulated outward FDIs, having been marginal during the first half of the 1980s, have since grown strongly and reached U.S. $147.9 billion in 2008. China is currently the fourth-largest foreign investor among developing countries in terms of flows and the sixth-largest investor in terms of stocks.[21]

Although it has high expansion rates of outward FDIs, China remains a minor player in terms of global FDI transactions; it accounts for less than 1 percent of the global outward FDI stock only. With the outward FDIs of China being comparable with that of Austria and the Netherlands, China is to date far off from "buying up the world."[22] Notwithstanding China's small global investment position, outward FDIs are growing rapidly relative to inward FDIs. Outflows from China grew more rapidly than inflows during the past several years, demonstrating that China's overall importance as an FDI-exporting economy is evolving. Chinese outward FDIs accounted for 17 percent of inflows in 2005 and 48 percent of inflows in 2008.[23]

Chinese outward FDIs are bound to increase further in the future. Reasons for this dynamic can mainly be attributed to business-sector drivers, with increasing foreign investments being the result of push factors at the domestic level and pull factors at the global level. On one hand, Chinese companies are confronted with a growing competitive pressure on the domestic market. In the wake of the opening up of the Chinese economy that culminated in the accession to the World Trade Organization (WTO) in 2001, they are pushed to relocate mature industries to lower wage economies, especially to neighbouring Asian countries. Furthermore, at least since the global financial and economic crisis that resulted in a considerable drop of Chinese exports, it has become evident that it is imperative for China to refocus its growth model. The needed turn from a growth model that relied mainly on low-cost manufacturing and a large trade surplus to one that requires increased domestic consumption and higher value-added manufacturing will push outward FDIs even further.[24] On the other hand, Chinese companies are increasingly taking advantage of the global business environment's opportunities. In contrast to the traditional perspective that attributes (Western) multinationals' internationalization to a previous accumulation of competitive advantages (asset exploitation), recent studies suggest that multinationals from emerging economies tend to internationalize in order to build up competitive advantages

"People's Republic of China's Round-Tripping FDI: Scale, Causes and Implications," Asian Development Bank Institute Discussion Paper 7 (2004).

21 UNCTAD, *supra* note 16, at Annex B.

22 Hanemann and Rosen, *supra* note 4, at 6.

23 UNCTAD, *supra* note 16, at Annex B.

24 Hanemann and Rosen, *supra* note 4, at 9.

(asset augmentation).[25] Recent large mergers and acquisitions emphasize that this development applies especially to Chinese multinationals. They invest abroad to acquire scarce advanced technologies, brand names, distribution networks, and managerial know-how.[26]

In addition to business-level drivers, the Chinese government has a vital interest in promoting outward FDIs. The Going Global strategy of the Chinese government aims at encouraging its national companies' foreign investments abroad. This strategy, which was first announced in 1998 and was embedded in the Tenth Five-Year Plan for National Economy and Social Development in 2001, marked the transition of Beijing's outward FDI policy from regulation to encouragement.[27] The buildup of a number of global champions capable of competing on the global market has since been an explicit industrial policy goal. The main motivations are economic security considerations giving priority to foreign resource exploration projects as well as the aim of enhancing the international competitiveness of Chinese enterprises, accelerating their foreign market presence, and acquiring design, innovation, and managerial skills.[28] Besides the introduction of selective policy measures at the national level – such as tax incentives, special loans and credits, and the relaxation of foreign exchange requirements – the conclusion of legalized BITs has been another measure aimed at promoting outward FDIs by Chinese companies.[29]

In sum, the growth of Chinese outward FDIs in recent years emphasizes the need to comprehend China not only as an FDI-importing country, but increasingly as an FDI-exporting economy, too. The reconfiguration of Chinese FDI flows has led to a significant change in Beijing's stance toward the protection of foreign investments. Section 5 investigates China's new BIT policy; first, though, Section 4 describes the main features of China's previous restrictive approach.

4. CHINA'S TRADITIONAL APPROACH TOWARD INTERNATIONAL INVESTMENT LAW

The overall economic reform process that started in 1978 led to significant changes in China's stance on international investment law. During the first

[25] See, e.g., J. A. Mathews, *Dragon Multinational. A New Model for Global Growth* (2002) and J. A. Mathews, "Dragon Multinationals: New Players in 21st Century Globalization," 23 *Asia Pacific Journal of Management* (2006) 5.

[26] See Lunding, "Global Champions in Waiting. Perspectives on China's Overseas Direct Investment," *Deutsche Bank Research Current Issues* (August 4, 2006), at 4.

[27] See Cai, "Effectiveness," *supra* note 6, at 626.

[28] See UNCTAD, *supra* note 5, at 210.

[29] See UNCTAD and United Nations Development Programme, *supra* note 5, at 55.

three decades of self-imposed isolation from the world market, Beijing adopted a hostile approach toward international investment law. One major rationale for this policy can be found in China's adherence to the Marxist doctrine of rejection of private property. Another rationale for China's hostile stance on international investment protection lay in China's experience of colonial rule and foreign intervention. International (investment) law had hence been viewed by Chinese politicians and scholars as a means "used by the imperialists and hegemonists . . . to carry out aggression, oppression and exploitation."[30] Its validity had therefore been rejected. China's policy accentuated the sovereign right to control the entry of FDI, regulate foreign investors, and nationalize foreign property without being obliged to compensation. Consequently, China signed no BIT until 1982, when it concluded a first treaty with Sweden.[31]

At the end of 2009, China had already signed 126 BITs,[32] making it the second largest contracting party to BITs worldwide.[33] This increase in the sheer number of agreements since the early 1980s reveals Beijing's growing acceptance of international investment law. With regard to actual treaty provisions and their effectiveness in protecting foreign investments, however, one must examine two different but important stages in order to gain a clear understanding of the historical evolution of China's BIT approach. In 1998, Beijing changed its international investment policy from a *restrictive model* accentuating the regulation of inward FDIs to a *legalized approach* emphasizing the encouragement of outward Chinese FDIs.[34] This remarkable change in China's international investment policy making has been ascribed by a number of scholars to China's evolution from a mere FDI-importing country to an economy that – while still receiving large amounts of foreign investments – is increasingly investing abroad.[35] As the preceding section has shown, China is becoming an FDI-exporting economy.

The remaining part of this section investigates the main first-generation BIT provisions that characterize the restrictive approach, whereas the next section examines the peculiarities of China's second generation of BITs.

30 Kong, *supra* note 5, at 108.

31 *Ibid*, at 109.

32 Quantitative figures on Chinese BITs included in this chapter are drawn from the Investment Treaties Online database provided by UNCTAD. This database is generally acknowledged to represent the most comprehensive, yet not exhaustive, full-text compilation of BIT texts. Where possible, the data provided by UNCTAD are complemented by data found in other sources, especially secondary literature. UNCTAD's Investment Treaties Online database is made available at http://www.unctadxi.org/templates/DocSearch____779.aspx, accessed February 10, 2010.

33 Germany has signed 135 BITs as of the end of 2008.

34 See, e.g., Cai, *supra* note 6, at 626.

35 See, e.g., Ibid. and Schill, *supra* note 6.

Chinese BITs contain all the standard provisions found in global BIT practice. They usually start with a preamble that states the intention of creating "favourable conditions for investments of investors of one Contracting Party in the territory of the other Contracting Party," aiming at promoting mutual investments. The BIT is meant to "intensify the economic cooperation of both States on the basis of equality and mutual benefit."[36] Both BITs in place before 1998, as well as those after 1998, adopt the widespread admission model. Accordingly, absolute and relative standards of treatment of FDI in Chinese BITs are only in force once the investment has been admitted by the host country's government. Furthermore, Chinese BITs entail provisions on the definition of investment and the investor, their treatment, expropriation, the transfer of funds, compensation for losses as a result of war, civil strife, and the settlement of disputes. In the following text, the main emphasis is laid on relative and procedural investment protection provisions. They are for the most part generally acknowledged to represent the most important elements of BITs and they are furthermore central to the understanding of the evolution of China's approach.

Throughout the 1980s and 1990s China adopted an international investment policy approach that was characteristic of any given FDI-importing developing country. China's restrictive policy adopted the so-called three guiding principles of international economic cooperation and exchange. China's authorities upheld their sovereignty to screen and regulate FDI, insisted on the equality and mutual benefit of host and home states, and referred to the international practice.[37] Kong observes that it "is obvious that utilitarianism or even mercantilism has been the driving force behind the investment legislation" and that "China's attitude towards FDI in this period was rooted in mixed feelings of attraction and aversion."[38] While negotiating BITs in great numbers, the Chinese international investment policy until the late 1990s remained marked by a reluctance to imply strong legal protection to foreign investments.

Until 1998, China signed BITs containing serious reservations toward strong substantive as well as procedural protection of foreign investments. With regard to relative standards of treatment of foreign investors, China appeared reluctant to grant national treatment, that is, not to discriminate between domestic and international investors. The aim of protecting infant industries and especially state-owned enterprises from foreign companies' competition may serve as an explanation in this regard. A number of BITs with developed countries

36 See, e.g., the China–Egypt BIT (1994).
37 Kong, *supra* note 6, at 110.
38 Ibid.

made an exception and included provisions on national treatment; however, they contained far-reaching qualifications limiting the effective protection of foreign investments. Article 3(3) of the Sino–UK BIT concluded in 1986 states that "either Contracting Party shall to the extent possible, accord treatment in accordance with the stipulations of its laws and regulations to the investments of national or companies of the other Contracting Party the same as that accorded to its own nationals or companies."

Similar provisions can be found in the BITs with Slovenia (1993) and Iceland (1994). The best-effort character and the requirement to comply with national laws and regulations substantially reduced the effectiveness of these national treatment provisions. The wording of Article 3(1) of the Sino–Japan BIT from 1988 implies a rather strong national treatment provision in comparison: "The treatment accorded by either Contracting Party within its territory to nationals and companies of the other Contracting Party with respect to investments, returns and business activities in connection with the investment shall not be less favourable than that accorded to nationals and companies of the former Contracting Party."

This provision, however, is qualified by further explanations of the term "less favourable" in paragraph 3 of the Sino–Japan BIT's protocol:

> For the purpose of the provision of paragraph 2 of Article 3 of the Agreement, it shall not be deemed "treatment less favourable" for either Contracting Party to accord discriminatory treatment, in accordance with its applicable laws and regulations, to nationals and companies of the other Contracting Party, in case it is really necessary for the reason of public order, national security or sound development of national economy.

These examples show that national treatment provisions were very rarely included in the first generation of Chinese BITs. In the case that they formed part of the treaties, they were qualified to the extent that they enabled the Chinese authorities to discriminate against foreign investors in favor of domestic industries. Most Chinese BITs throughout the 1980s and the 1990s guaranteed most favored nation (MFN) treatment only.

As for national treatment, China rather warily granted foreign investors the right to transnational arbitration as a means to settle disputes over breaches of substantive BIT provisions. Earlier BITs at times did not even contain investor–state dispute settlement provisions at all.[39] China had started in 1985 to concede investor–state dispute settlement even before it signed the convention of the International Centre for Settlement of Investment Disputes

39 See, e.g., the China–Sweden BIT (1982), the China–Norway BIT (1984), the China–Thailand BIT (1985), and the China–Austria BIT (1985).

(ICSID) on February 9, 1990. The respective provisions on investor–state arbitration mentioned various forms of tribunals that a case could be filed at, such as ad hoc tribunals established under the common agreements of the disputing parties under the arbitration rules of the United Nations Commission on International Trade Law (UNCITRAL) or by a tribunal established under the ICSID convention.[40] First-generation BITs including investor–state dispute resolution provisions usually limited them to disputes concerning the amount of compensation due in case of expropriation and nationalization. Foreign investors' possibilities to appeal to transnational arbitration were restricted through various "safeguards."[41] Investors were required to exhaust local remedies first before being allowed to seek resort to transnational arbitration. Further restrictions found in China's first-generation BITs require the consent of both parties for a dispute's submission to a transnational arbitration tribunal and the application of the host country's laws. In essence, such restrictions reduce the effectiveness of investor–state dispute settlement provisions found in China's first-generation BITs, granting them a mere symbolic nature. They comply with the "Chinese tradition of avoiding litigation"[42] and were meant to preserve the sovereign rights of host states' authorities in regulating FDI.[43]

China's refusal to include unrestricted national treatment and legalized investor–state dispute settlement provisions in Sino–foreign BITs can be traced back to China's history as an FDI-importing country. The Chinese development model depended heavily on the positive discrimination of domestic companies through the imposition of local content and performance requirement on foreign investing companies.

5. CHINA'S NEW INTERNATIONAL INVESTMENT POLICY

In the second phase of its BIT policy, which started in 1998, China proactively began to negotiate legalized investment treaties. China initiated a gradual shift toward stronger provisions for substantive and procedural investment protection. Chinese BITs today entail almost all standard provisions found in mainstream European-country BITs.

The China–Barbados BIT, signed in July 1998, can be described as a watershed because it was the first treaty to offer foreign investors unrestricted access

40 See Rooney, *supra* note 6, at 704.
41 See Chen, "Safeguards," *supra* note 6.
42 Kong, *supra* note 6.
43 Chen, "Safeguards," *supra* note 6, at 900.

to international arbitration.[44] This pioneering provision on investor–state dispute settlement, which was adopted in forty-five later BITs,[45] marked a turning away from the first-generation BIT approach of restricted investment dispute settlement. This change is all the more remarkable because safeguards against full-fledged investor–state arbitration were at the heart of the first-generation BIT approach. This innovation has been described by Cai "as the most significant measure in Chinese BIT practice in recent years."[46] Not surprisingly, this acceptance of transnational arbitration has been criticized by some Chinese scholars of international law. Chen, for instance, calls for a reconsideration of China's current policy to better protect domestic companies from the increasing competition of foreign investors' operations in China. He argues that, with the Chinese economy still being in a transition phase enjoying high investment inflows, such unrestricted investor–state dispute settlement provisions would leave developing China worse off.[47]

The incorporation of transnational arbitration provisions into the China–Barbados treaty broke with the tradition of including safeguards against investor–state dispute settlement. The treaty's Article 10 on the Settlement of Investment Disputes, exemplary for later BITs, writes down the investor's right to transnational arbitration with regard to all aspects of the treaty.[48] After an initial period of six months, in which both parties have the opportunity to settle their dispute amicably, the investor is given the right to submit the dispute for resolution by international arbitration. Abstaining from putting down all procedural aspects of arbitration, Article 2 (a, b) is referring to ICSID and UNCITRAL rules. The only restriction demanded by China is the refusal to grant the right for transnational arbitration once the investor has chosen to access the host country's domestic judiciary. Another restriction, namely the requirement to exhaust an administrative review procedure that has been introduced in later BITs,[49] is supposed to determine the proper and legal conduct

44 There is no particular reason that the new model BIT text was applied in the negotiations with Barbados in the first place. Gallagher and Shan, *supra* note 6, at 40–41, argue that the decision of the Chinese government to adopt the legalized approach can be ascribed to the initiation of BIT negotiations with Canada in 1997.

45 It is important to note that not all post-1998 BITs entailed liberal investment dispute settlement provisions. The Sino–Quatar BIT (1999), the Sino–Bahrain BIT (1999), and Iran (2000) inter alia adopted the traditional restrictive approach described in Section 4.

46 Cai, *supra* note 6, at 646.

47 Chen, "Safeguards" and Chen, "Distinguishing," both *supra* note 6.

48 The China–Barbados BIT refrained from restricting the validity of the investor–state dispute settlement to the amount of compensation, as pre-1998 BITs had done. Later BITs like the China–Botswana BIT (2000) in Article 9 (1) explicitly allow for transnational arbitration for "any dispute between an investor of one Contracting Party and the other Contracting Party."

49 See, e.g., Article 6 (a) of the Protocol of the China–German BIT (2003).

of administrative agencies under Chinese law. This provision, however, does not involve court proceedings and has, therefore, only a very limited restrictive capacity.[50] Recent treaties, such as the Chinese BIT with Mexico and the free trade agreement (FTA) with New Zealand, both signed in 2008, include more elaborate investor–state dispute settlement provisions, describing in greater detail the arbitration procedure.

The noteworthy fact of Beijing's turn toward comprehensive investor–state arbitration is that it has been a proactive undertaking aimed at protecting Chinese outward FDIs. Some recent studies analyze investor–state dispute settlement provisions mainly from the angle of Sino–developed country BITs.[51] The essence of China's new BIT policy, however, is that comprehensive investor–state dispute settlement procedures have been introduced first and foremost in treaties signed with developing countries, which, as a group, are the main destination of Chinese outward FDIs. It shows China behaving like an FDI-exporting country, trying to increase the legal protection of its own foreign investments. Against this background, (re-)negotiations of older BITs with, among others, the Netherlands, Finland, and Germany are regarded as a mere consequence of this change.[52] A large majority of second-generation Sino–foreign BITs that included comprehensive investor–state arbitration procedures has been signed with developing countries. Less then one-fourth of second-generation BITs with comprehensive investor–state dispute settlement provisions have been signed with developed countries.

Apart from legalized investor–state dispute settlement provisions, China gradually introduced a number of other treaty innovations. The Chinese BIT with Botswana, signed in June 2000, includes a stronger provision for compensation for losses that are due to war and civil strife. In addition to the regular MFN clause, Article 5 of this BIT grants foreign investors the same treatment as domestic investors in the case of war and civil strife:

> Investors of one Contracting Party whose investments in the territory of the other Contracting Party suffer losses owing to war, a state of national emergency, insurrection, riot or other similar events in the territory of the latter Contracting Party, shall be accorded by the latter Contracting Party treatment, as regards restitution, indemnification, compensation and other settlements not less favourable that that accorded to the investors of its own or any third State.

[50] See Schill, *supra* note 6, at 17.

[51] See, e.g., Rooney, *supra* note 6 and Heymann, *supra* note 6.

[52] See Berger, *supra* note 6, at 26.

Apart from the treaty signed in 1988 with Australia, the first BIT to include up-to-date absolute standards of treatment of foreign investors was the Chinese BIT with Brunei signed in November 2000. It covered the general principles of fair and equitable treatment, full protection and security, and nondiscrimination, without qualifying these provisions as older treaties had done before.

In recent times, the Chinese government started to include references to the concept of the minimum standard of treatment, implicitly accepting the validity of a customary international law. The China–New Zealand FTA signed in 2008 is a landmark in this respect. Whereas treaties signed after the year 2000 stated that "Contracting Parties shall at any time be accorded fair and equitable treatment and shall enjoy full protection and security in the territory of the other Contracting Party,"[53] the China–New Zealand FTA, for the first time, defines this standard in greater detail, insisting that it shall be interpreted in "accordance with commonly accepted rules of international law."[54] The Chinese BIT concluded with Mexico in 2008 goes even further. The absolute treatment standards found in this treaty reflect "the international law minimum standard of treatment of aliens." Although China avoids any mention of customary international law, it refers to "[s]tate practice and opinio juris," two accepted concepts constituting international custom.[55] Eventually, in the most recent FTA concluded with Peru in 2009, the fair and equitable treatment standard is consistent with customary international law. Article 132 of this agreement reads as follows:

> 1. Each Party shall accord fair and equitable treatment and full protection and security in accordance with customary international law in its territory to investment of investors of the other Party.
> 2. For greater certainty,
>   (a) the concepts of "fair and equitable treatment" and "full protection and security" do not require additional treatment to that required under the minimum standard of treatment of aliens in accordance with the standard of customary international law.[56]

Although this clarification could be read as a safeguard against excessive interpretation of absolute treatment standards, it is, at the same time, a remarkable step because China traditionally rejected customary international law

53 See, e.g., China–Czech Republic BIT (2005), Article 2 (2).
54 China–New Zealand FTA (2008), Article 143 (1).
55 China–Mexico BIT (2008), Article 5 (2).
56 China–Peru FTA (2009), Article 132 (1, 2).

as a Western concept, potentially disregarding the interests of developing countries.[57]

The previous section stated that a limited number of first-generation Sino–foreign BITs with developed countries included national treatment provision. They, however, contained far-reaching qualifications of their applicability. Three different approaches toward national treatment can be assessed in the second generation of China's BIT practice. First, until the year 2000, Chinese BITs with developing countries continued the traditional practice of not including national treatment provisions at all.[58] Second, from the year 2000 onward, China included qualified national treatment in its BITs with developing countries.[59] These treaties adopt the national treatment provisions found in first-generation BITs with the United Kingdom, Slovenia, and Iceland. For example, Article 3 (2) of the Chinese BIT with Botswana signed in 2000 reads as follows: "Without prejudice to its laws and regulations, each Contracting Party accord[s] to investments and activities associated with such investments by the investor of the other Contracting Party treatment not less favourable than that accorded to the investment and associated activities by its own investors."

The legal reservation "without prejudice to its laws and regulations" limits the effectiveness of the national treatment provision to a best-effort clause. In essence, these BITs do not provide for national treatment unless the host countries' laws and regulations grant foreign investors treatment not less favorable than that accorded to domestic investors. Most developing partner countries, however, have already agreed to grant national treatment in BITs with industrialized countries. Through the multiplying effect of the MFN clause that is an integral part of every Sino–foreign BIT, Chinese investors could thus import stronger national treatment provisions from other BITs. Against this background, Chinese outward FDIs toward developing countries, de facto, is protected by such a national treatment standard.

Third, Chinese BITs concluded with developed countries entail national treatment provisions that are less restrictive.[60] The first treaty to include the new

[57] See Cai, "Negotiations," *supra* note 6, at 468.

[58] See China–Barbados (1998); China–Quatar (1999); China–Bahrain (1999); China–Brunei (2000).

[59] See China–Botswana (2000), China–Iran (2000), China–Jordan (2001), China–Trinidad (2002), China–Côte d'Ivoire (2002), China–Guyana (2003), China–Djibouti (2003), China–Benin (2004), China–Uganda (2004), China–Russia (2006), and China–Mexico (2008). The treaty with France, signed in 2007, is an exception because it maintains this practice.

[60] See China–the Netherlands (2001), China–Germany (2003), China–Finland (2004), China–Czech Republic (2005), and China–Korea BIT (2007). The up-to-date national treatment provision has also been adopted in BITs signed with some developing and transition countries, e.g., the China–Bosnia BIT (2002) and the China–India BIT (2006). This national treatment

national treatment provision was the BIT concluded in 2001 between China and The Netherlands. Article 3 (3) reads as follows: "Each Contracting Party shall accord to investments and activities associated with such investments by the investors of the other Contracting Party treatment no less favourable than that accorded to investments and activities by its own investors or investors of any third State."

The restrictions toward national treatment are included in the protocol to these treaties:

> In respect of the People's Republic of China, Paragraphs 2 and 3 of Article 3 do not apply to: any existing non-conforming measures maintained within its territory; the continuation of any non-conforming measure referred to in subparagraph a); an amendment to any non-conforming measure referred to in subparagraph a) to the extent that the amendment does not increase the non-conformity of the measure, as it existed immediately before the amendment, with those obligations.
>
> It will be endeavoured to progressively remove the non-conforming measures.

This amendment permits China to maintain laws and regulations toward foreign investors that are incompatible with national treatment. China, however, agrees in the protocol to include a standstill commitment toward so-called nonconforming measures; in other words, it agrees not to increase discriminatory treatment toward foreign investors, and it promises to gradually remove such measures. As a result of these two obligations, national treatment provisions included in recent BITs between China and developed countries are stronger than the best-effort provision found in Chinese BITs with developing countries. Remarkably, China is able to make developed partner countries bear more obligations than it is willing to do. Whereas Chinese authorities are still allowed to discriminate against foreign investors, Chinese investors can rely on national treatment in the respective partner country. The declaration of intent to reduce discriminatory rules and regulations is a weak legal obligation. In other words, China is able to secure a special and differential treatment, a provision common to trade law but rarely adopted in international investment agreements, which are reciprocal in nature. This expansion, however, of national treatment provisions in Chinese BITs, notwithstanding their limited applicability, can be explained by the growing acceptance of national

provision has also been included in the China–New Zealand FTA signed in 2008, as well as the China–Peru FTA signed in 2009.

treatment in Chinese law, especially with respect to China's accession to the WTO.[61]

What are the consequences of China's turn toward a legalized international investment policy? Some Western commentators expect Chinese investors to increasingly make use of BIT provisions through transnational arbitration.[62] So far, there is only one publicly known case in which a Chinese investor is involved.[63] This limited utilization of transnational arbitration by Chinese companies is somewhat surprising against the background of legalized investor–state dispute settlement provisions being adopted in Sino–foreign BITs already in 1998 and Chinese outward FDIs facing considerable political risks in developing countries and national sentiments in developed countries. One possible explanation for this puzzle is the "Chinese lack of affinity for international arbitration"[64] and the country's preference for settling disputes informally through diplomatic consultations. It would, therefore, be too rash to apply the behavior of multinational enterprises from industrialized countries that are responsible for the substantial increase of transnational arbitration to Chinese companies, of which a considerable number are still state owned.

Another, yet more relevant, explanation is the limited coverage of legalized investor–state dispute settlement provisions in terms of the volume of outward FDIs. In other words, the partner countries of the forty-five Sino–foreign BITs that entail liberal investor–state dispute settlement provisions are only of minor importance as outward FDI destinations. Within this group, only Germany is among the top host countries of Chinese investments. Cai hence argues "that the actual effect of the investment protection offered by these . . . Sino-foreign BITs is wholly negligible" and "that, at least in the near future, Chinese outward FDI can't significantly benefit from" legalized BITs.[65] This situation, however, is likely to change. The legal protection of Chinese outward FDIs is expected to grow as Beijing gradually expands the coverage of its BIT program. China recently concluded BITs with large emerging countries such as India and Mexico. The investment chapters of China's FTAs with New Zealand and Peru, as well as the China–Association of Southeast Asian Nations investment agreement, indicate that legalized BIT provision will also be adopted in future trade and broader economic cooperation treaties. Finally, China is negotiating

[61] See Wang, "Historical Evolution of National Treatment in China," 39 *The International Lawyer* (2005) 3, at 778.

[62] See, e.g., Rooney, *supra* note 6, at 711 and Heymann, *supra* note 6, at 526.

[63] See Diaz, "Chinese Investor Launches BIT Claim against Peru at ICSID," *Investment Treaty News* (March 2, 2007).

[64] Kong, *supra* note 6, at 130.

[65] Cai, "Effectiveness," *supra* note 6, at 647.

investment treaties with important FDI destinations such as Canada and the United States.

6. SINO–UNITED STATES BIT NEGOTIATIONS

It has been argued that China's BIT policy has changed significantly during the past ten years. The new Chinese approach to international investment policy making is comparable to the admission model applied by European countries. To what extent, however, is China's new legalized BIT policy compatible with the preestablishment model applied by the United States? This question is crucial for any assessment of the prospects of success of the ongoing negotiations between China and the United States toward a BIT.

Initiated by the Bush Administration, investment negotiations are part of the Strategic Economic Dialogue that was launched in September 2006, which aimed at easing economic tensions between both countries. The launch of BIT negotiations was announced in June 2008 after seventeen months of preliminary talks. The Obama Administration is continuing with this process on a technical level, discussing the respective approaches toward international investment protection.[66] In December 2009, both sides agreed to expedite the negotiations.[67] The rationale for a treaty is high, because both parties have interests in negotiating a BIT. From the U.S. point of view, a BIT would help to increase the enforcement of intellectual property rights and investment protection in general, especially vis-à-vis state-owned companies. From a Chinese perspective, the main rationale for a BIT is found in mitigating protectionist sentiments against Chinese investments that are due to national security fears in the United States. Despite mutual interests in increased protection of investment flows, though, the prospects of a Sino-United States BIT are rather bleak. This is mainly due to fundamental differences in the respective international investment policy approaches, especially with regard to market access of foreign investors.

The United States made clear from the outset that it is aiming at a comprehensive agreement. Backed by the business community, the administration is seeking a strong agreement that, broadly speaking, aims at achieving three fundamental goals: A BIT with China should (1) provide for high levels of

66 See, e.g., the remarks of USTR Ronald Kirk in front of the United States Senate's Committee on Finance during his confirmation hearing on March 9, 2009 made available at http://finance.senate.gov/hearings/testimony/2009test/031109QFRs%20for%20SubmissionRK.pdf, accessed February 10, 2010.

67 See U.S.–China Joint Statement, November 2009, Beijing, China, available at http://www.whitehouse.gov/the-press-office/us-china-joint-statement, accessed February 10, 2010.

substantive investment protection, (2) include a comprehensive investment dispute settlement clause, and (3) note that the United States is pursuing a preestablishment approach that features substantive provisions granting market access for foreign investors.[68] Article 3 (1) of the 2004 model agreements reads as follows: "Each Party shall accord to investors of the other Party treatment no less favorable than that it accords, in like circumstances, to its own investors with respect to the establishment, acquisition, expansion, management, conduct, operation, and sale or other disposition of investments in its territory."

U.S. BITs apply a negative list approach with regard to exceptions from this provision. Accordingly, market access in all sectors would have to be granted except to those explicitly stated in the agreement. This approach potentially limits the number of sectoral exceptions included in the preestablishment provision, because host countries would first have to argue their case if they wanted a certain sector to be excluded. The positive list approach as applied in the General Agreement on Trade in Services (GATS), in contrast, allows more exceptions, because consensus on the question of which sectors would have to be liberalized is even more difficult to reach. Whereas the positive list approach secures small developing host countries some form of institutionalized veto option, the negative list approach enables home countries to utilize their bargaining power. Thus, only host countries with high economic power will be able to limit the degree of market access enshrined in U.S. BITs.

It has been argued in this chapter that China did accept national treatment of foreign investors in BITs with developed partner countries, but only regarding the postestablishment phase and with exceptions allowing grandfathering of national industries. As a member of the WTO and a signatory of the GATS, China agreed to market access for investments in the service sector in connection with a positive list approach, a position that clearly goes beyond its policy in bilateral investment negotiations so far. The acceptance of market access for foreign investments in the service sector nevertheless has to be judged against the fact that multilateral trade negotiations follow a single undertaking approach, which allows compensation in other issue areas. China's potential acceptance of the U.S. Model treaty would amount to a further revolution of its BIT practice and its national regulatory system, because the

[68] The new U.S. Model BIT includes further provisions differing from the global mainstream BIT approach, such as comprehensive investor–state dispute settlement provisions, transparency requirements, and environmental and labor issues. See, e.g., Kantor, "The New Draft Model U.S. BIT: Noteworthy Developments," 21 *Journal of International Arbitration* (2004) 4 and Gagné and Morin, "The Evolving American Policy on Investment Protection: Evidence from Recent FTAs and the 2004 Model BIT," 9 *Journal of International Economic Law* (2006) 2.

preestablishment provision would trigger a number of behind-the-border regulatory changes.

Seen against the background of China's current international investment policy and especially the latest international investment agreements signed with Mexico and Peru, it becomes obvious that the Chinese approach is moving closer to the U.S. approach with regard to the first and second fundamental goals of the United States' negotiators, namely substantive and procedural investment protection. It would, however, be a stretch too far to argue that the Chinese approach has been "Americanized," as scholars of international investment law on either side of the pacific have recently argued.[69] In view of the track record of China international investment policy making, however, it is doubtful that China would agree to the third strategic demand, market access, which is at the center of the U.S. BIT policy.[70] From a political economy perspective bilateral investment negotiations are, therefore, not the appropriate instrument to initiate such a far-reaching shift in China's regulatory system. In sum, the strong emphasis of the United States on its model BIT, especially protection of FDI in the preestablishment phase, makes a compromise unlikely as a result of China's need for a considerable degree of discretion for the protection of its (state-owned) business sector.

Apart from these fundamentally different approaches toward the liberalization and protection of FDI, the current political situation in the United States potentially increases the obstacles to a Sino–United States BIT. At the center of attention are looming national security concerns. Especially the highly publicized, yet aborted, takeover of the American oil company Unocal by the state-owned Chinese China National Offshore Oil Corporation in 2005 and the failed bid by the United Arab Emirates–based ports-management business, Dubai Ports World, for six major seaports in the United States makes clear that national security concerns are an increasing threat to foreign investments from emerging markets. With regard to Chinese investments in the United States,

69 See, e.g., Cai, "Negotiations," *supra* note 6 and Alvarez, "The Evolving BIT," *Transnational Dispute Management* (2009).

70 In this respect it is important to note that the European Union and China are currently engaged in discussions on a Partnership and Cooperation Agreement that should replace the 1985 EU–China Trade and Cooperation Agreement. The envisaged agreement should incorporate, among other things, an investment chapter. The European Commission is pushing for preestablishment investment protection that should complement member country BITs signed with China. Furthermore, the negotiation history of the recently concluded investment agreement signed between China and the Association of Southeast Asian Nations shows that China is not willing to grant market access for foreign investors. So far, China has rejected to agree to preestablishment investment protection. Against this background it is unlikely that China would concede market access rights to U.S. investors while, at the same time, denying European and Asian investors such treatment.

Beijing is therefore expected to demand inclusion of legal safeguards against political reviews of its investments by the Committee on Foreign Investment in the United States – a request the United States is likely to refuse.

A variable that has not been touched on so far is the impact of the financial and economic crisis on the prospects of Sino–United States BIT negotiations. There are good reasons to suspect either aggravating or facilitating effects. With the financial crisis having severe impacts on the real economy, rising protectionism becomes more likely. This would apparently affect Transpacific relations, because the United States is running a high trade deficit with China. With the increasing influence of protectionism in the U.S. Congress, ratification of a BIT would become increasingly unlikely. The financial crisis, however, could also have positive effects on a bilateral investment deal. One indication for this positive outlook is the recent welcoming of sovereign wealth funds' investments in troubled financial institutes in the United States. As a result of the mere necessity created by the financial crisis, the attitude toward investments from emerging markets, in particular China, has already changed during the past few months. Furthermore, although BIT negotiations are usually seen as rather technical and arcane in the context of talks between two major actors in the global FDI system, they potentially could become a highly politicized instrument. If, therefore, the financial and economic crisis is perceived by both the United States and China as a window of opportunity to tackle some crucial issues like trade and financial imbalances, the investment talks that are embedded in the high-level Strategic Economic Dialogue are likely to profit from the increasingly cooperative atmosphere. Although both the negative and the positive scenario are partially convincing, it will depend on the positions taken by the Chinese government and the Obama Administration in the time to follow to prove their likelihood.

7. CONCLUSIONS

This article argues that China has proactively initiated a remarkable change of its formerly restrictive BIT policy toward a legalized approach. China increasingly adheres to international standards of the legal protection of FDI. The analysis of individual provisions of Chinese BITs reveals a gradual yet decisive policy shift towards stronger and more comprehensive substantive and procedural investment protection. Since 1998, Beijing has been negotiating treaties that contain comprehensive investor–state dispute settlement provisions. China even abandoned its hostile stance on national treatment of foreign investors, a policy that was characteristic of its development strategy during the transitional process that started in the late 1970s. National treatment provisions are a common feature of China's current BIT policy. In its new BITs with developing countries China uses the respective provision of its new model agreement that restrictively grants national treatment without prejudice to the host countries' laws and regulations. In BITs with developed countries, China agrees only to grant national treatment of foreign investors unless the continuation of existing "non-conforming measures" is guaranteed. This exception notably applies only for the Chinese market. Chinese investments in the respective developed partner country have to be treated not less favorable than domestic investors. China, therefore, is able to maintain a special and differential treatment with respect to national treatment.

The growth of outward FDIs has led the Chinese government to abandon its traditional restrictive approach that aimed at regulating inward FDIs and to adopt a new legalized policy that – in line with its Going Global strategy – provides Chinese investors with strong substantial and procedural investment protection. Notwithstanding the reservations toward unrestricted national treatment, the current Chinese model text is comparable to the admission model BIT adopted by European countries. Is it also compatible with the U.S. Model BIT that includes preestablishment national treatment provisions? The analysis of the prospects of the ongoing negotiations toward a Sino–United States BIT concludes that a compromise toward a potential treaty may be hard to achieve on the basis of existing differences in international investment policy making and the shape of the new international environment in times of a global financial and economic crisis, and because its impact on bilateral investment negotiations is still unclear. Nonetheless, China's mere acceptance of the United States' initiative and the seriousness of Chinese negotiators are strong signs of the transition in China's BIT policy that has been taking place since the late 1990s.

8

The Politics of South–South Bilateral Investment Treaties

Lauge Skovgaard Poulsen

1. INTRODUCTION

Bilateral investment treaties (BITs) were originally intended as legal instruments to promote and protect investments by rich capital-exporting states in the developing world. Although BITs signed between developing countries (hereinafter South–South BITs) did begin to emerge from the mid-1960s with the 1964 Kuwait–Iraq BIT, the typical BIT was, until recently, negotiated between a developed and a developing country (hereinafter North–South BITs). Accompanied by rising outward foreign direct investment (FDI) stocks from developing countries, however, this pattern has begun to change, as many developing countries have increasingly entered into BITs among themselves.[1] South–South BITs today account for around 40 percent of the global network of BITs, and more than 100 developing countries have entered into BITs with other developing countries. Most have been signed within the same region, and many recent South–South BITs have been facilitated at minilateral conferences organized by the United Nations Conference on Trade and Development (UNCTAD), often sponsored by capital-exporting countries, such as Germany, Switzerland, or France.[2]

[1] UNCTAD, "South–South Cooperation in International Investment Agreements," *Series on Issues in International Investment Policies for Development* (2005).

[2] UNCTAD, *Progress Report: Work Undertaken within UNCTAD's Work Programme on International Investment Agreements between the 10th Conference of UNCTAD, Bangkok, February*

Note: An extended version of this chapter was first published in 2009 in the *Northwestern Journal of International Law and Business*. It was previously presented in November 2008 at the Politics of International Economic Law: The Next Four Years meeting in Washington, D.C., organized by the American Society for International Law's International Economic Law Interest Group, and in January 2009 at the 50th Annual Convention of the International Studies Association: Exploring the Past, Anticipating the Future meeting in New York, organized by the International Studies Association. Thanks to Marc Busch for useful suggestions.

Given the initial purpose of BITs, this development in the international investment regime is notable and raises a number of questions. Does the popularity of South–South BITs imply that after decades of resistance, developing countries have finally converged completely to the norms of the developed world with respect to foreign investment treatment and protection standards?[3] If true, that could give proponents of a multilateral investment treaty a strong political argument, for if developing countries consistently incorporate "traditional" North–South BIT standards even into South–South BITs, there is no apparent reason that they should refuse to incorporate similar standards in a multilateral framework. Alternatively, however, South–South BITs might espouse a different vision of international investment rules compared with their North–South counterparts. If so, what – if any – implications would that have for the global investment protection regime? Does it mean, for instance, that investment flows between developing countries are increasingly covered by BIT standards systematically different from those for investments made between developed and developing countries?

To examine these questions, we need to investigate whether there are systematic differences in investment rule making between South–South and North–South BITs. As noted by UNCTAD in its cursory review of South–South BITs, such an analysis has to be comprehensive and detailed enough to credibly identify whether or not South–South BITs in fact incorporate specific features.[4] This chapter outlines and discusses the results of such an analysis based on an investigation of 303 BITs signed by 100 countries from 1994 to 2006, which were analyzed according to a set of quantitative indicators of investment provisions, which in turn allow large-*n* statistical analyses. The

2000 and July 2002 (New York: United Nations, 2002); Olof Karsegard, Pedro Bravo, and Hubert Blom, *UNCTAD Work Programme on Capacity Building in Developing Countries on Issues in International Investment Agreements: Final In-Depth Evaluation Report* (New York: United Nations, 2006).

3 From the 1929 Draft Convention on the Treatment of Foreigners to the recent Doha Round of WTO negotiations, many developing countries have time and again objected to Western proposals for multilateral investment rules based on legally binding minimum standards. See, e.g., Dattu, "A Journey from Havana to Paris: The Fifty-Year Quest for the Elusive Multilateral Agreement on Investment," 24 *Fordham International Law Journal* (2000) 275; G. Van Harten, *Investment Treaty Arbitration and Public Law* (2007), Chapter 2; C. Wilcox, *A Charter for World Trade* (1949), 145–148; Abs and Shawcross, "The Proposed Convention to Protect Private Foreign Investment," 9 *Journal of Public Law* (1960) 115; Fatouros, "An International Code to Protect Private Investment – Proposals and Perspectives," 14 *University of Toronto Law Journal* (1961) 77; D. Henderson, *The MAI Affair: A Story and Its Lessons* (2000); Sauvé, "Multilateral Rules on International Investment: Is Forward Movement Possible?," 9 *Journal of International Economic Law* (2006) 325.

4 UNCTAD, *supra* note 12, at 47.

sampling and methodology is briefly outlined in the Annex, along with the definition of what constitutes a South–South BIT.[5]

Space constraints naturally preclude investigating all substantive and procedural BIT provisions. Focus is therefore on two standards that have been in dispute between developing countries and developed countries in multilateral discussions on investment rules in the past, namely (postentry) national treatment provisions and provisions on repatriation of investment-related funds. The analysis finds that South–South BITs *do* in fact vary systematically from North–South BITs with respect to these two provisions, because South–South BITs are typically less comprehensive in scope. South–South BITs have been more likely to restrict, or exclude, national treatment from their substantive provisions, as well as to include certain carve-outs to the transfer provisions to allow exceptional measures taken under balance-of-payments difficulties, for instance. The implications for the international investment protection regime are unclear, however, because South–South BITs have typically failed to ensure that their more narrow scope is not potentially "leveled out" by the treaties' most favored nation (MFN) provisions. This is somewhat perplexing, and using interview feedback from BIT negotiators, I conclude by speculating whether this de facto coherence in developing countries' BIT networks might be unintended.

The chapter is structured as follows. The first section briefly discusses the methodology applied in the analysis, because it departs substantially from the traditional legal literature investigating BITs. The second section introduces the national treatment standard and reviews whether South–South BITs have been more likely to restrict or completely exclude the standard compared with North–South BITs. The third section introduces BITs' transfer clauses and reviews whether South–South BITs have been more likely to allow restrictions to foreign investors' repatriation of funds. The fourth section reviews whether the differences are leveled out by the treaties' MFN provisions and discusses the implications of the results. The final section concludes.

2. METHODOLOGY

The literature investigating the content of BITs can generally be divided into two categories.[6] Whereas one set of studies compares and contrasts several

[5] Further details can be found in the full paper.

[6] Haslam, "A Flexibility for Development Index: Can International Investment Agreements Be Compared Quantitatively?," 19 *European Journal of Development Research* (2007) 251.

treaty obligations across a few treaties,[7] another takes the issue-based approach, which investigates one particular aspect of BITs with ad hoc references to a large stock of treaties as illustrations.[8] Both of these approaches have their obvious advantages and drawbacks. None of them, however, can credibly identify and/or correlate variation in the content of BITs across countries or time. This can be done only by comparing a large and representative sample of BITs, which in turn is practically possible only if based on a quantification of the treaties' content relying on a set of transparent underlying criteria.

One thing is necessity; however, another is feasibility. For although the exercise of quantifying legal documents is not new within the social sciences,[9] many would undoubtedly consider it pointless to even try to capture the content of complex legal documents, such as BITs, with numeric values. A comprehensive evaluation of a treaty's terms and conditions is bound to be a qualitative exercise, which has to carefully consider the ordinary meaning of its terms in their context and in light of their object and purpose.[10] An in-depth analysis of a given BIT is therefore not well suited for quantitative analysts trying to observe the world through binary codes of 1s and 0s. But although this scepticism is perhaps well founded, most would probably nevertheless agree that it is possible to code certain aspects of BITs in a meaningful and informative manner. For instance, irrespective of discipline, most scholars group BITs into two distinct groups: one that grants investors a right of admission (typically, Northern American BITs), and one that does not (typically, European BITs). This is of course a simplified distinction; admission clauses can, and do, vary substantially. But however imperfect, it is nevertheless generally accepted as a legitimate "binary coding" of BITs that can identify general features of different treaties.[11] The following analysis simply takes this exercise one step further by grouping BITs according to an additional set of criteria useful to investigate my empirical question, namely whether systematic variation in BITs is codetermined by having both parties be developing

7 See, e.g., Kantor, "The New Draft Model US BIT: Noteworthy Developments," 21 *Journal of International Arbitration* (2004) 383.

8 See, e.g., UNCTAD's Series on Issues on Issues in International Investment Agreements, available at www.unctad.org/Templates/Page.asp?intItemID=2322&lang=1.

9 See, e.g., the publications based on the "Comparative Constitutions Project," available at: www.comparativeconstitutionsproject.org/publications.htm; and the contributions on the interaction between investor protection and financial development by Porta et al., such as "Legal Determinants of External Finance," 52 *Journal of Finance* (1997) 1131; and "Law and Finance," 106 *Journal of Political Economy* (1998) 1113.

10 Cf. Article 31 of the 1969 Vienna Convention on the Law of Treaties.

11 See, e.g., R. Dolzer and C. Schreuer, *Principles of International Investment Law* (2008), at 81.

countries. Note, however, that the analysis does *not* intend to compare the BITs according to an aggregate quantitative score based on some underlying concept such as the treaties' strength or flexibility for development. This has been tried elsewhere.[12] But although not necessarily an illegitimate exercise, it involves major and ultimately subjective assumptions on the role of different provisions that is more than problematic for most purposes, including this analysis.

3. NATIONAL TREATMENT

The first standard included in the analysis is that of national treatment (NT). The purpose of an NT clause in investment treaties is to oblige host states not to discriminate, de jure or de facto, between foreign investors and similarly situated national investors.[13] In BITs, the clauses typically stipulate that foreign investors and their investments shall be "accorded treatment no less favourable than that which the host state accords to its own investors,"[14] and some, such as American BITs, specify that the clause applies only in "like situations"[15] or "like circumstances."[16] Being a relative or contingent standard, NT will of course be of little use if domestic investors have limited rights. However, the purpose of NT provisions in BITs differs fundamentally from the NT concept that was part of the New International Economic Order of the 1970s. Whereas the latter was intended to limit the rights that foreign investors could rely on through international law, BITs do not preclude that standards more favorable than those granted to national investors should be applied to foreign investors (on the contrary).[17]

Not surprisingly, developed countries have been strong proponents of including NT in their BITs in order to "level the playing field" among their investors abroad and host states' domestic companies.[18] Developing countries, on the other hand, have at times sought to exclude,

[12] See Hicks, "Dissecting the Black-Box: Bilateral Investment Treaties and Global Investments," presented at the Annual Meeting of the International Studies Association, San Francisco, March 27, 2008; and Haslam, *supra* note 6.

[13] Dolzer and Schreuer, *supra* note 11; A. Newcombe and L. Paradell, *Law and Practice of Investment Treaties Standards of Treatment*, chapter 4 (2009).

[14] See, e.g., Danish Model BIT 2008, Art. 3.1 (on file with author).

[15] See, e.g., U.S. Department of State, U.S. Model Bilateral Investment Treaty, Art. 2.1 (1994).

[16] See, e.g., U.S. Department of State, U.S. Model Bilateral Investment Treaty, Art. 3.1 (2004).

[17] Dolzer and Schreuer, *supra* note 11, at 178; UNCTAD, *National Treatment* (New York: United Nations, 1999), at 37.

[18] It is typically only in North American BITs that we find legally binding preentry NT provisions; see T. Pollan, *Legal Framework for the Admission of FDI* (2006), at 70–82.

or substantially limit, the standard in order to favor their own nationals.[19] On occasion this agenda has been pursued on the basis of infant-industry protection arguments, which (in theory) provide developing countries an economic justification for a certain level of discrimination against foreign competition.[20] In multilateral discussions, such arguments have been made by developing countries for decades. During the discussions on the UN Draft Code on Transnational Corporations in the 1980s, for instance, developing countries thus proposed to limit the NT standard by allowing measures specified in legislation relating to developing countries' development objectives.[21] Similarly, even though large-scale protectionist experiments have gone out of fashion in most of the developing world, several developing countries were cautious about granting foreign investors unlimited NT in the recent discussions on investment issues in the Doha Round, as that would prevent them from subsidizing or providing other benefits to national investments, thereby potentially undermining national development strategies.[22]

The question is therefore whether there are systematic differences between North–South and South–South BITs with respect to NT standards. Is some developing countries' scepticism toward wide-ranging NT provisions in multilateral discussions reflected in BITs signed among themselves? To investigate this, I compare the share of BITs that exclude or limit NT provisions across the two BIT dyads. Limitations are here understood as clauses, where the NT standard is either not legally binding or subject to domestic laws (and thus substantially restricted). It suffices to say that this simple distinction will result in grouping BITs, where NT provisions would potentially be applied somewhat differently on case-by-case basis. However, certain simplifications are necessary if we want to identify general but still meaningful patterns across a large number of treaties. For my purposes, certain sector-specific reservations therefore do not count as major limitations.[23] In addition, I do not distinguish

19 Salacuse, "BIT by BIT: The Growth of Bilateral Investment Treaties and Their Impact on Foreign Investment in Developing Countries," 24 *International Lawyer* (1990) 655, at 668.

20 P. Krugman and M. Obstfeld, *International Economics: Theory and Policy* (2008), 8th ed., Chapter 10.

21 United Nations Center on Transnational Corporations (UNCTC), *Bilateral Investment Treaties* (1988), at 33; see further UNCTC, "Report on Outstanding Issues in the Draft Code on Transnational Corporations," paragraphs 55–61, U.N. Doc E/C.10/1984/S/5 (1984), reprinted in 23 *ILM* 602.

22 WTO, "Report of the Working Group on the Relationship between Trade and Investment to the General Council," WT/WGTI/6 (2002), paragraph 93, available at: www.wto.org/english/docs_e/docs_e.htm.

23 Although a formal distinction can be made between "reservations" and "exceptions," I use these terms interchangeably, along with the term "limitations." See generally Newcombe and Paradell, *supra* note 13, Chapter 10.

TABLE 8.1. *National treatment (postestablishment)*

Treatment	Share of BITs: Total	North–South	South–South
I: No NT	0.20 (0.15–0.24)	0.08 (0.04–0.12)	0.36 (0.28–0.45)
II: Parties shall strive to provide NT or NT is subject to domestic laws	0.07 (0.04–0.09)	0.05 (0.01–0.08)	0.10 (0.04–0.15)
III: Specific exceptions	0.11 (0.07–0.14)	0.16 (0.10–0.21)	0.03 (0.00–0.06)
IV: No exceptions	0.63 (0.58–0.69)	0.72 (0.65–0.79)	0.51 (0.42–0.60)
V: No NT or major limitations to NT (I or II)	0.26 (0.21–0.31)	0.12 (0.07–0.17)	0.46 (0.37–0.55)
N	303	179	124

Note: The 95% confidence intervals are shown in parentheses. Percentages do not necessarily add up to 100 due to rounding.

between BITs specifying that NT shall be provided in the "same" or "identical" circumstances[24] and BITs where this basis of comparison is not included. Neither do I distinguish between BITs using the term "no less favourable" treatment and those using terms such as "same" treatment or "as favourable" treatment. Finally, for my purposes the general taxation exception to NT found in most BITs is not considered to substantially restrict the NT provisions, nor is the exception to NT based on prudential measures in financial services[25] or intellectual property rights guaranteed under international intellectual property conventions.[26]

A breakdown of the sample is provided in Table 8.1. Purely aspirational NT clauses are few and distributed more or less equally across the two BIT dyads. A greater share of North–South BITs have NT clauses with specific exceptions, but this is almost solely driven by U.S. and Canadian treaties that include exceptions to their NT provisions for the preestablishment and postestablishment phases. The major difference, however, is that more than one-third of South–South BITs do not include an NT provision at all, compared with only 8 percent of North–South BITs. This means that only 12 percent of North–South BITs exclude or limit their NT provisions as defined herein, whereas the share is 46 percent for South–South BITs. The confidence intervals for the two groups do not overlap, and the difference is therefore unlikely to be

24 See, e.g., Belize–United Kingdom BIT 1982, Art. 3.

25 See, e.g., Barbados–Canada BIT 1996, Art. 11.

26 See, e.g., Nicaragua–United States BIT 1995, Art. 2.

TABLE 8.2. *National treatment (postestablishment)*

	Logistic regressions	
	Maximum likelihood (I)/(II) Odds ratio	Maximum penalized likelihood (III) Odds ratio
South–South BIT	2.34/**	2.46**
	(2.01/4.31)	(5.64)
N	218	290

Notes: The dependent variable is coded as 1 if the NT clause is absent, nonlegally binding, or subject to domestic laws. (I) Standard errors adjusted for correlation among home country BITs; (II) standard errors adjusted for correlation among host country BITs. Constants and coefficients on other included regressors are not reported. Chi-square values after Wald tests are shown in parentheses for (I) and (II); chi-square value after a likelihood ratio test is shown in brackets for (III).
* Significant at 10%; ** significant at 5%; *** significant at 1%.

due to random variation in the sample. It thus seems that South–South BITs have indeed been much less likely than North–South BITs to incorporate wide-ranging NT clauses. This conclusion is interesting and relevant in and by itself. By basing the analysis on a large and representative sample of treaties, Table 8.1 gives a much clearer picture of rule-making patterns in the international investment regime than do the traditional cursory and nonsystematic reviews.

An additional question, however, is whether the pattern is due to the differences in BIT partners, or instead reflects some other underlying factors. Apart from whether the home state is a developing or developed country, there are of course many other reasons that a host state might, or might not, wish to grant foreign investors NT in its BITs. I therefore test whether the systematic difference between North–South and South–South BITs is due to some omitted variable bias. The results of this analysis are outlined in Table 8.2 (see the Annex for further information on the covariates and regression techniques). The difference between South–South and North–South BITs is substantial in all estimations, and it is significant in two out of three. After conditioning on the included covariates, South–South BITs are still between two and three times more likely to limit or exclude NT provisions. Thus, although the econometric analysis is admittedly somewhat simplistic and limited in scope, I am nevertheless confident that developing countries have been more likely to exclude or limit NT in their BITs when the other contracting party has been a developing country. As we shall see in the following text, this is not the only systematic difference between South–South and North–South BITs.

4. TRANSFER CLAUSES

Another BIT provision that has been associated with a divergence of views between developing and developed countries is the free transfer of investment-related funds out of the host state. Although such clauses can and do differ from treaty to treaty, most BITs stipulate that a wide range of payments and other investment-related funds shall have a right to be transferred out of the host state without delay and, typically, in a freely convertible currency.[27] From foreign investors' point of view, these clauses are key in investment treaties, because the ability to freely repatriate funds can be an important factor in their investment-decision process. Developing countries, in contrast, often have an interest in not restraining their ability to adopt a certain restrictive exchange rate or other measures, for instance, as a means to prevent or confront economic and financial crises. Particularly, the numerous investment claims brought against Argentina in the wake of its 2001 financial crisis have sparked a debate on the risks in not subjecting such guarantees to certain exceptions.[28] However, although this particular crisis might have brought attention to this issue, it has always been controversial. Jeswald Salacuse thus stated in 1990 that "the negotiation of BIT provisions on monetary transfer is often one of the most difficult negotiations to conclude. Capital-exporting countries seek broad, unrestricted guarantees on monetary transfers, while developing countries press for limited guarantees, subject to a variety of exceptions."[29]

As with the NT standard, this difference in preferences was also clear in the discussions on the UN Draft Code on Transnational Corporations, where rules on currency transfer were one of the key issues that developed and developing countries could not agree on.[30] Similarly, during the recent investment negotiations in the Doha Round, many developing countries argued that a host state should be able to prevent foreign investors from freely transferring revenues and capital out of its country if under economic difficulties.[31] Although such

[27] R. Dolzer and M. Stevens, *Bilateral Investment Treaties* (1995), at 85–96.

[28] See Viterbo, "Dispute Settlement over Exchange Measures Affecting Trade and Investments: The Overlapping Jurisdictions of the IMF, the WTO, and the ICSID," presented at the Society for International Economic Law's Inaugural Conference, Geneva, July 2008.

[29] Salacuse, *supra* note 19, at 669. See also Kole and Wälde, "Economic Crises, Capital Transfer Restrictions, and Investor Protection under Modern Investment Treaties," 3 *Capital Markets Law Journal* (2008) 154.

[30] UNCTC (1984), *supra* note 21, at 179.

[31] This suggestion was strongly opposed, for instance, by the U.S. delegation; see WTO's Working Group on the Relationship between Trade and Investment, "Report on the Meeting Held on 16–18 September 2002 – Note by the Secretariat," WT/WGTI/M/19 (2002).

an exception is included in some North–South BITs, it is far from the norm (see the following text).

I therefore compare the two groups of BITs again, this time to see whether South–South BITs have been more likely to include certain safeguards against exceptional measures taken under balance-of-payments difficulties.[32] Such safeguards come in several forms. One option is to subject the transfer clause to domestic laws, in which case the host state is free to limit the flow of capital out of its economy during economic crises as long as it is done through law.[33] Another option is to allow exceptions to the free transfer of funds, but only during balance-of-payments difficulties and typically with a requirement that such restrictions should be necessary, nondiscriminatory, and on a temporary basis.[34] Finally, some treaties include other major restrictions, such as certain Chilean BITs attempting to restrict short-term capital inflows and outflows.[35] For my purposes, provisions safeguarding the powers of financial services regulators,[36] or national laws concerning bankruptcy, trading or dealing in securities, criminal or administrative violations, or compliance with resolution of tribunals[37] are not considered to specifically safeguard measures taken during economic crises. Similarly, I do not find the "lumpy transfers" exception to be as restrictive as those already mentioned, and BITs including these are therefore grouped with BITs without direct safeguards.[38]

Table 8.3 provides a breakdown of the sample. Whereas the share of BITs that include balance-of-payments exceptions is low, and practically the same in North–South and South–South BITs, a much larger share of South–South BITs include other major restrictions to the transfer clause and/or subject it to domestic laws. From the confidence interval we see that between 31 and 48 percent of all South–South BITs incorporate such restrictions, whereas only 5 to 14 percent of North–South BITs do. As with NT provisions, this difference is therefore not only substantial in absolute terms, but

[32] For a discussion as to whether international law makes it illegal for a contracting party to a BIT to restrict such transfers during balance-of-payments crises without such exceptions, see Kole and Wälde, *supra* note 29.

[33] See, e.g., Portugal–Bulgaria BIT 1993, Art. 5.

[34] See, e.g., Argentina–UK BIT 1990, Art. 6.

[35] See, e.g., Chile–Austria BIT 1999, protocol.

[36] See, e.g., Peru–Canada BIT 2006, Art. 14.

[37] See, e.g., Mozambique–United States BIT 1998, Art. 5.

[38] Kole and Wälde define the lumpy transfer exception as permitting "the parties to limit transfers of proceeds of liquidation to a certain percentage of an investment's value per year, so long as the investor is permitted to maintain the value of the investment domestically" (*supra* note 29, at 163). It is typically American BITs that include such exceptions (e.g., United States–Egypt BIT 1986, Art. 5). To test whether BITs with these exceptions were biasing the estimations, I ran all the regressions also without U.S. BITs. This did not substantially change the results.

TABLE 8.3. *Repatriation of investment-related funds*

Repatriation	Share of BITs: Total	North–South	South–South
I: Transfers subject to domestic laws or other major restrictions	0.22 (0.17–0.27)	0.10 (0.05–0.14)	0.40 (0.31–0.48)
II: Free transfers guaranteed except under balance-of-payments difficulties	0.05 (0.03–0.08)	0.06 (0.02–0.09)	0.05 (0.01–0.09)
III: No balance-of-payments or other major restrictions to transfer clause	0.73 (0.68–0.78)	0.85 (0.80–0.90)	0.56 (0.47–0.65)
N	303	179	124

Note: The 95% confidence intervals are shown in parentheses. Percentages do not necessarily add up to 100 due to rounding.

also statistically significant, and the regressions analyses in Table 8.4 confirm that it persists after conditioning on several important covariates. South–South BITs are here between three and four times more likely to include restrictions to their transfer clauses with estimates significant across all model specifications.

It could be, however, that my narrow focus only on transfer clauses is not entirely justified here, because developed countries might have included safeguards against restrictions imposed during balance-of-payments crises elsewhere in their BITs. Arguably, this can be done by including a general

TABLE 8.4. *Transfer of investment-related funds*

	Logistic regressions: Maximum likelihood (I)/(II) Odds ratio	Maximum penalized likelihood (III) Odds ratio
South–South BIT	3.67***/*** (8.49/13.11)	3.49*** (11.07)
N	290	290

Notes: The dependent variable is coded as 1 if the transfer clause includes balance-of-payments restrictions or other major restrictions such as subjecting the clause to domestic laws. (I) Standard errors adjusted for correlation among home country BITs; (II) standard errors adjusted for correlation among host country BITs. Constants and coefficients on other included regressors are not reported. Chi-square values after Wald tests are shown in parentheses for (I) and (II); chi-square value after a likelihood ratio test is shown in parentheses for (III).
* Significant at 10%; ** significant at 5%; *** significant at 1%.

TABLE 8.5. *Security exceptions*

	Share of BITs		
Exception	Total	North–South	South–South
I: No security exceptions	0.79 (0.75–0.84)	0.74 (0.67–0.80)	0.86 (0.80–0.92)
II: Security exceptions for certain provisions, but not transfer provision	0.10 (0.06–0.13)	0.15 (0.09–0.20)	0.03 (0.00–0.06)
III: Security exception covers transfer provision (typically when it covers the whole treaty)	0.11 (0.07–0.14)	0.12 (0.07–0.17)	0.11 (0.05–0.16)
IV: Security exception for entire BIT or restrictions to transfer clause	0.37 (0.31–0.42)	0.26 (0.19–0.32)	0.52 (0.44–0.61)
N	303	179	124

Notes: The 95% confidence intervals are shown in parentheses. For item IV, the restrictions include balance-of-payment restrictions as well as other major restrictions such as subjecting the clause to domestic laws. Percentages do not necessarily add up to 100 due to rounding.

exception based on national security concerns. In World Trade Organization (WTO) jurisprudence, at least, the exception based on "essential security interests" in Article XXI(b) of the General Agreement on Tariffs and Trade has been constructed to include exchange control measures to protect economic interests.[39] In BITs such exceptions can cover the whole treaty[40] or only parts of it such as their NT and MFN standards,[41] general nondiscrimination provisions,[42] full protection and security provisions,[43] or with respect to performance requirements.[44] Although all of these provisions can be relevant when establishing whether measures taken to prevent or confront an economic crisis constitute a breach of a BIT *as a whole*,[45] a narrower question is whether the security exception covers the transfer provision in particular. I therefore repeat the aforementioned analysis but this time group BITs with direct restrictions in their transfer clauses with BITs that allow exceptions to national security interests.

Table 8.5 shows that North–South BITs have in fact been more likely to include security exceptions, but the share of BITs with a security exception

39 Kole and Wälde, *supra* note 29, at 160.
40 See, e.g., India–Australia BIT 1999, Art. 15.
41 See, e.g., Albania–Spain BIT 2003, Art. 4.
42 See, e.g., Guatemala–BLEU BIT 2005, Art. 3.
43 See, e.g., Turkey–Morocco BIT 1997, Art. 2.
44 See, e.g., Kuwait–Croatia BIT 1997, Art. 3.
45 Kole and Wälde, *supra* note 29.

TABLE 8.6. *Limitations on transfer clauses (including security exception)*

	Logistic regressions	
	Maximum likelihood (I)/(II) Odds ratio	Maximum penalized likelihood (III) Odds ratio
South–South BIT	1.82/** (2.83/4.30)	1.77* (3.03)
N	290	290

Notes: The dependent variable is coded as 1 if the transfer clause includes balance-of-payments restrictions or other major restrictions such as subjecting the clause to domestic laws. It is also coded as 1 if the BIT includes a security exception covering the transfer provision. (I) Standard errors adjusted for correlation among home country BITs; (II) standard errors adjusted for correlation among host country BITs. Constants and coefficients on other included regressors not reported. Chi-square values after Wald tests are shown in parentheses for (I) and (II); chi-square value after a likelihood ratio test is shown in parentheses for (III).
* Significant at 10%; ** significant at 5%; *** significant at 1%.

that covers the transfer provision is more or less similar between the two types of BIT dyads (and the difference is not statistically significant). The overall conclusion therefore remains the same: Even though a little more than half the sample's South–South BITs incorporate a security exception that covers the transfer provision and/or include restrictions to the transfer clause, only around one-fourth of North–South BITs do so. Accordingly, it is not surprising that although the estimates did become lower in the logistic regressions after security exceptions were also considered, the differences are still substantial across all three specifications and statistically significant in two out of three (Table 8.6). I therefore remain confident that South–South BITs have been more likely to allow exceptions to the free transfer of funds, for instance as a means of insulating the contracting parties from capital flight in times of economic crises.

5. IMPLICATIONS

Thus far I have shown that NT provisions have been more likely to be restricted or excluded altogether in South–South BITs and transfer clauses have similarly been more likely to be restricted. Although this pattern is interesting in and of itself, the differences also hold after multiple possible covariates are controlled for.[46] With respect to these two provisions, at least, it is therefore

[46] Moreover, in a separate set of regressions not reported here, I controlled for whether these results still hold after taking into account the extent to which the BITs incorporate a legally

not entirely correct when textbooks on international investment treaties state that a review of BITs signed among developing countries "does not reveal significant differences with agreements concluded with developed states,"[47] or the "treaties concluded between developing countries have in substance remained very similar to those concluded by capital exporting countries."[48] Rather, a systematic (as opposed to ad hoc) review of the treaties does in fact reveal that developing countries have been more likely to agree to a different set of rules in South–South agreements, which potentially allows them flexibility to pursue developmental concerns to a greater extent than North–South BITs.

Where does this leave us? On the one hand, the conclusion may imply that although many past differences with respect to foreign investment protection between developed and developing countries have been overcome, one should perhaps not overstate the degree of consensus purely based on the fact that South–South BITs are proliferating. If so, then the popularity of South–South BITs cannot, in and of itself, be used as an argument that a multilateral treaty on investment is more feasible today than it was ten years ago. On the other hand, the systematic differences should perhaps not be taken as an indicator of developing countries' collective interests in the international investment regime. Instead, it could simply be that demands in BIT negotiations between developing countries have been more easily accommodated, not because they are necessarily thought to be prudent by both the contracting parties but simply because negotiators may not consider the BIT particularly relevant in practice. For instance, a senior developing-country official involved in negotiating BITs mentioned in an interview that: "things were much more flexible when negotiating with developing countries."[49] Another BIT negotiator gave this recollection: "Our negotiations with developing countries were generally much quicker and much easier. When demands were made we didn't object, as most understood that these treaties were basically just signals, rather than hard and serious legal agreements."[50] By contrast, it would probably be rare for developed countries to accept major limitations to their model BITs and they may therefore simply have walked away from negotiations if such

binding consent to international investor–state arbitration. This did not change the results or conclusions. For a useful analysis on systematic patterns in rule making concerning dispute settlement clauses, with a methodological approach closely related to the analysis presented here, see Jason Webb Yackee, "Conceptual Difficulties in the Empirical Study of Bilateral Investment Treaties," 33 *Brooklyn Journal of International Law* 405 (2007–2008).

47 Dolzer and Schreuer, *supra* note 11, at 21.

48 Dolzer and Stevens, *supra* note 27, at 9–10.

49 Not-for-attribution interview, January 2009.

50 Not-for-attribution interview, April 2009.

demands were made. A third BIT negotiator further explained, "We never actually had a position in our BIT-negotiations, whether with developed or developing countries. So we just signed off when drafts were presented to us, and that's why we have different obligations in different treaties."[51] Accordingly, further investigation could examine whether the specific characteristics of South–South BITs have in fact been intended by developing countries to espouse a different vision of international investment rules, or they merely are because developing-country negotiators have not felt the need to insist on a particular set of provisions when demands were made. The quotation given here would suggest the latter.

Apart from symbolic and political implications, though, does the systematic difference found imply that investors seeking protections under BITs should expect a different set of standards, when covered under South–South BITs, than when they are covered by a North–South BIT? Are investors more likely to be met with restrictions to NT and repatriation of investment-related funds when covered by South–South BITs? The statistical review given here seems to imply this to be the case. In practical terms, however, the content of BIT provisions cannot be investigated in isolation.

The analysis has thus far been based on the treaty texts alone and therefore has not taken into account MFN provisions. As a general rule, MFN provisions operate in BITs according to all matters falling within the scope of the treaty.[52] Whether the *ejusdem generis* principle implies that the clause only covers substantive provisions is unclear from existing awards.[53] Neither is it clear whether the clause allows an investor to invoke only those provisions from other investment treaties that are "compatible in principle," and if so what that means in terms of limiting its application.[54] What is clear, however, is that cases decided so far have generally allowed a contracting party to "import" substantive provisions from other BITs entered into by the other contracting party. In *Bayindir v. Pakistan*, for instance, the tribunal held that the MFN provision allowed the investor to invoke a fair and equitable treatment clause from another BIT.[55] Similarly, in *CME v. Czech Republic*, the tribunal argued

[51] Not-for-attribution interview, July 2009.

[52] OECD, "Most-Favored-Nation Treatment in International Investment Law," OECD Working Paper (2004); Dolzer and Schreuer, *supra* note 11, at 186.

[53] See, e.g., *Emilio Augustin Maffezini v. Spain*, ICSID Case No. ARB/97/7, Decision on Jurisdiction, January 25, 2005; and *Vladimir & Moise Berschader v. Russian Federation*, SCC Case No V(080/2004). See generally Hsu, "MFN and Dispute Settlement: When the Twain Meet," 7 *Journal of World Investment & Trade* (2006) 25.

[54] Dolzer and Schreuer, *supra* note 11, at 191.

[55] *Bayindir v. Islamic Republic of Pakistan*, ICSID Case No. ARB/03/29, Decision on Jurisdiction, November 14, 2005, paragraphs 231–232. See also *MTD Equity Sdn. Bhd. and MTD Chile S.A. v. Republic of Chile*, ICSID Case No. ARB/01/7, Award, May 25, 2004, paragraphs 103–104.

that the investor could rely on an expropriation provision from another BIT to determine the standard of compensation.[56] Arguably, this implies that even if a South–South BIT does not include an NT provision, for instance, the MFN clause may oblige the parties to extend NT nevertheless, as long as they have included NT in at least one other BIT.[57]

It is therefore notable that *all* BITs in the sample include a MFN provision and none of them exempt NT or transfer clauses from the clause's coverage. Because few countries have consistently limited NT or transfer clauses in all their BITs, this means that, as a general rule, differences in substantive rules between South–South and North–South BITs are leveled out by the treaties' MFN provisions. As a result, the more restricted standards in South–South BITs will rarely become relevant for investors in practice, who can often continue to rely on BITs with more favorable provisions. This, of course, leaves us with a considerable puzzle: Why have developing countries often allowed more flexibility to host states in BITs signed with each other but then failed to make sure that this "policy space' is not canceled out by the treaties' MFN clauses? If the more limited substantive provisions in South–South BITs have little, if any, relevance for the legal rights granted to foreign investors in practice, why limit them in the first place?

At a first glance, one possible explanation could be that the exceptions have been intended as signals of a distinct South–South BIT agenda more in tune with the one that developing countries have expressed in multilateral investment negotiations as a group. If so, the negotiating parties may not have been too concerned with whether the limitations actually have implications for foreign investors in practice. The contracting parties may thus have tried to *appear* as though they sign "development friendly" BITs while at the same time appeasing investors that they are granted "normal" BIT protections. However, such clever intentions are unlikely to have driven the pattern. It is important to note that the overwhelming majority of BITs have been signed largely under the radar of public opinion. Except for BITs with the United States, the vast majority of BIT negotiations seem to have caught (surprisingly) limited attention,[58] and it is therefore difficult to see how the aspects of

56 *CME v. Czech Republic*, UNCITRAL Case, Final Award, March 14 2003, 9 *ICSID Reports* 264 (2003).

57 UNCTAD, *Bilateral Investment Treaties 1995–2006: Trends in Investment Rule-Making* (New York: United Nations, 2007), at 33.

58 See, e.g., Lauge Skovgaard Poulsen and Damon Vis-Dunbar, "Reflections on Pakistan's Investment – Treaty Program after 50 Years: An Interview with the Former Attorney General of Pakistan, Makhdoom Ali Khan," *Investment Treaty News*, March 16, 2009; Department of Trade and Industry, Republic of South Africa, "Government Position Paper on Bilateral Investment Treaty Policy Framework Review" (June 2009), available at http://www.pmg.org.za/files/docs/090626trade-bi-lateralpolicy.pdf.

South–South BITs investigated here could be intended as symbolic political statements.

So perhaps a more plausible explanation could be that many developing countries may have simply failed to realize the full implications of MFN provisions. Indeed, there are indications that developing countries have often failed to understand the true nature and scope of BITs when signing up for them.[59] It suffices to say that this suggestion may appear paternalistic to some[60] or perhaps even disingenuous,[61] and naturally several developing countries have undoubtedly been well informed when entering into BITs. Others, however, probably have not. When asked about why the MFN provision had not been adjusted to accommodate the different standards in the country's BIT network, one former BIT negotiator for instance mentioned this: "We didn't have a consistent approach because there wasn't an understanding that consistency was required. . . . No-one seemed to realise the implications of the MFN provision."[62] BIT negotiators from other countries have similarly mentioned that their predecessors did not know how MFN provisions – or other key provisions for that matter – worked, because they often had no background or training in international law,[63] and one recalled that the speed with which many South–South BITs were signed exacerbated this capacity problem: "In all these mini-conferences, UNCTAD would actively promote BITs to be signed amongst the participants – often within as little as a few hours – and I couldn't see that any serious considerations were given by the countries what-so-ever."[64] In addition, though officials from developing countries might have a better understanding today of the effect of different BIT provisions than they did ten years ago, it is probably still very incomplete in many cases. One negotiator puts it like this: "While workshops held by various international organisations might help somewhat in upgrading developing countries' negotiating capacity, they haven't solved the problem. There is still not a very good understanding of what is implied by the different provisions, so even if negotiators from the developing world take their job seriously, they are often not entirely aware of what they are doing."[65] Accordingly, even if developing countries aim to restrict certain provisions in their South–South BITs, these

[59] Dolzer and Schreuer, *supra* note 11, at 8; Poulsen and Vis-Dunbar, *supra* note 58; South Africa Department of Trade and Industry, *supra* note 58.

[60] Francisco Orrego Vicuna, "Regulatory Expropriations in International Law: Carlos Calvo, Honorary NAFTA Citizen," 11 *New York University Environmental Law Journal* 19, 31 (2002).

[61] Not-for-attribution interview with former Eastern European BIT negotiator, April 2010.

[62] Not-for-attribution interview, May 2009.

[63] Not-for-attribution interviews, February 2009, August 2009, and April 2010.

[64] Not-for-attribution interview, August 2009.

[65] Not-for-attribution interview, January 2009.

statements suggest that they might not have the proper legal expertise to make sure such restrictions actually matter in practice. If this is in fact the case, then that would naturally raise a more general question pertaining to the level of understanding within developing countries when entering into BITs and, as such, the level of rationality we as observers should assume about the BIT-making process. Although I am currently undertaking such a research project, these explanations remain provisional and somewhat speculative for now and must therefore be subject to further investigation.

6. CONCLUSION

This chapter analyzed two substantive BIT provisions across a large sample of treaties from the mid-1990s to 2006. It showed that treaties signed by two developing countries vary systematically from more normal North–South BITs. In South–South BITs, NT provisions have tended to be more restricted (or completely absent), and transfer clauses more likely to allow restrictions to foreign investors' repatriation of funds. Given the methodology of the analysis, much more precise inferences were made about the share of treaties including certain clauses than traditional nonsystematic reviews of investment rule making. Also in contrast to the vast majority of other studies investigating the *content* of BITs, I used regression techniques to control for possible omitted variable biases and showed that the systematic pattern persisted even after adjustment for a number of important covariates.

The last section of the chapter noted, however, that none of the South–South BITs made sure that such restrictions were not potentially leveled out by the treaties' MFN provisions, and the chapter concluded by speculating whether this de facto coherence in developing countries' BIT networks might be unintended. If true, this would be problematic. As stated by UNCTAD, "[i]f countries are unable to properly understand and assess the content of the agreements to which they have agreed because of their complexity, the risk arises that they will enter into agreements that they are unprepared to honour fully."[66] Ultimately, however, the intent of developing countries when entering into South–South BITs is left open for further research to investigate. In the absence of detailed survey data, this would arguably require the application of qualitative methodologies such as interviews or detailed case studies, as the objectives of developing countries can only truly be inferred by investigating the ideas and strategies of key actors involved in the politics and

[66] UNCTAD, "International Investment Rule-Making: Stocktaking, Challenges and the Way Forward," *UNCTAD Series on International Investment Policies for Development* (2008), at 51.

negotiations of investment treaty rule making. So it is unfortunate that few – if any – studies assessing why, and how, developing countries have signed BITs include systematic inputs from officials involved in the process themselves. To understand the behavior of developing countries in the international investment regime, future research should therefore triangulate quantitative studies investigating systematic patterns in rule making (like this chapter) with qualitative studies investigating the actual intent of the contracting parties. This might also allow a further clarification of differences *among* developing countries, such as whether those with large outward FDI flows have systematically different strategies and intentions than do developing countries with only few investments abroad. This question and related questions would require not treating developing countries as a monolith with one fixed set of interests, as done in so many studies, including, to some extent, this one.

7. ANNEX

A. *Sample and Coding*

The sample used comprises 303 BITs signed by 100 countries from 1994 to 2006, available in English or French from UNCTAD's online BIT database.[67] Out of these, 191 were signed between 1994 and 1999, and the rest were signed between 2000 and 2006 (many recent BITs have not yet been made available on UNCTAD's database). Although the sampling process was random, it nevertheless resulted in a slight oversampling of countries with large BIT programs. I addressed this by means of a resampling to allow the majority of countries included in the data set to have a sampling rate of between 20 and 30 percent. The language criteria created a substantial undersampling of Italian treaties, but I am nevertheless rather confident that the sample is sufficiently representative of the total population of BITs.[68]

How to distinguish between developing and developed countries is always tricky, particularly in studies over time. For my purposes, I define a developed country as one that the World Bank has classified as a "high-income" country for the majority of the period in focus. Apart from Western countries, this includes countries such as South Korea and Kuwait. Although these countries

[67] UNCTAD's online BIT database can be found at http://www.unctadxi.org/templates/DocSearch____779.aspx.

[68] See generally UNCTAD, *World Investment Report: Transnational Corporations, Extractive Industries and Development* (New York: United Nations, 2007), describing the spatial and temporal distribution of BITs; UNCTAD, *Bilateral Investment Treaties 1959–1999* (New York: United Nations, 2000).

have signed numerous treaties with Western countries, their role in South–South BIT negotiations is arguably often that of capital exporters; I thus expect their interests to be similar to those of Western capital exporters seeking as favorable terms for their investors abroad as possible.[69] Among the sampled treaties, a North–South BIT therefore has one of the following countries as its home state: the 15 "old" members of the European Union, members of the European Free Trade Association, Australia, New Zealand, the United States, Canada, Japan, Korea, Hong Kong, Singapore, Israel, Kuwait, or the United Arab Emirates. This classification leaves 124 South–South BITs, which corresponds to 41 percent of the total sample. Because BITs often include different obligations for the contracting parties, all indicators are coded on the basis of the obligations of host states vis-à-vis home state investors. North–South BITs always have the developed country as the "home state," whereas the home state in South–South BITs is distributed randomly across the sample between large and small developing countries.

B. *Explanatory Variables*

My explanatory variable of interest is a dummy variable indicating whether the BIT dyad is between two developing countries or not. I controlled for a host state's level of development by including the natural log of its gross domestic product (GDP) per capita income, and its level of incoming investment by the natural log of its inward FDI stock. I controlled for its political environment by including a dummy variable for whether it has a socialist legal tradition (typically former or current Communist countries) and two variables indicating whether it had a left-wing and/or a nationalist government in the year it signed the BIT.[70] I moreover include a dummy variable for whether the host state is from Latin America (the "home region" of the Calvo Doctrine) and similarly include dummy variables to capture systematic tendencies in the BIT networks of the ten countries with the largest number of BITs signed at the end of the period.[71] As a measure of the economic integration between the BIT partners, I included a variable measuring their bilateral trade flows as a share of the host state's GDP, and finally I included a dummy for whether the BIT had been signed after the year 2000 to capture possible time effects.

69 *See* Salacuse, *supra* note 19, at 658–659.

70 In the sensitivity analysis, various indexes attempting to measure the investment climate of the host state were included as well. This reduced the observations by almost one-third, and because the indexes were generally not significant in any of the estimations.

71 As a result of the undersampling of Italian BITs, Italy is not included as a dummy.

TABLE 8.7. *Variable description*

Independent variables	N	Mean	S.D.	Min.	Max.	Sources
Dyadic variables						
South-South BIT	303	0.41	0.49	0	1	1
Bilateral trade (% of host GDP)	291	1.05	2.87	0	34.74	1, 2
Host variables						
Log of GDP per capita (U.S. $)	292	7.31	1.03	4.76	9.16	1
Ln inward FDI stock (million U.S. $)	292	8.28	1.89	3.26	12.51	3
Left-wing executive	303	0.25	0.44	0	1	4
Nationalist executive	302	0.14	0.35	0	1	4
Socialist legal tradition	303	0.32	0.47	0	1	5
Latin American country	303	0.20	0.40	0	1	–

Sources: 1, World Bank, World Development Indicators; 2, International Monetary Fund, Direction of Trade Statistics; 3, UNCTAD, FDI statistics; 4, T. Beck, G. Clarke, A. Groff, P. Keefer, and P. Walsh, "New Tools in Comparative Political Economy: The Database of Political Institutions," 15 *World Bank Economic Review* 165 (2001); 5, R. La Porta, F. Lopez-De-Silanes, and A. Shleifer, "The Economic Consequences of Legal Origins," 46 *Journal of Economic Literature* 285 (2008).

A summary of the covariates (excluding the country and period dummies) is given in Table 8.7.

C. *Logistic Regression Techniques*

As both provisions are coded as binary variables, the estimations use logistic regression techniques. However, because the content of a specific BIT is likely to be dependent on the content of other BITs signed by the same host or home state, the assumption of unit independence necessary for normal logit models is not upheld in this case. Although some country-specific dummies are included as controls, this is not sufficient, and in two separate sets of regressions I therefore adjust standard errors for correlations between individual home or host countries' BITs, respectively. To confront issues of "separation" when the country-specific controls predicted the outcome perfectly (or almost perfectly), I left these controls out in my initial logit estimations.[72] However, because this risks underspecifying the model, a second set of regressions are run with the likelihood function penalized in order to produce consistent parameter

[72] Following the advice of R. Davidson and J. G. MacKinnon, *Estimation and Inference in Econometrics* (1993), at 521. See a further explanation in the full version of the paper.

estimates in the presence of separation.[73] This estimation technique does not allow adjustment of the standard errors, however, and I am therefore left with three regressions on each dependent variable confronting different, but ultimately related, estimation challenges.[74] If the different specifications all lead to the same conclusions, then this would naturally increase our trust in the robustness of the results (and vice versa).

73 Details of this technique are described in Zorn, "A Solution to Separation in Binary Response Models," 13 *Political Analysis* (2005) 157; Firth, "Bias Reduction in Maximum Likelihood Estimates," 80 *Biometrika* (1993) 27.

74 An alternative specification strategy would have been hierarchical modeling. This is clearly not suitable here, however, as we cannot regard country-specific effects as a random variable, as required in the random effects model, and a fixed effect estimation is impossible as a result of the separation problem.

PART III

THE POLITICS OF SOVEREIGN WEALTH AND INTERNATIONAL FINANCIAL LAW

9

The Politics of Sovereign Wealth Funds

Benign Investors or Smoking Guns?

Yvonne C. L. Lee

1. INTRODUCTION

The U.S subprime financial crisis of mid-2007 and a further deceleration of the U.S. economy, largely driven by the housing market correction, created unprecedented opportunities for several sovereign wealth funds (SWFs)[1] to acquire, at distressed prices, portfolio investments and assets in North America and Western Europe. This chapter focuses upon the politicization of recent investments by SWFs from "non-Western" countries[2] such as the acquisitions of the Chrysler Building and portfolio stake holdings in Barclays, Credit Suisse, Citigroup, Merrill Lynch, Morgan Stanley, and UBS AG.[3] In Section 2, the chapter takes note of the initial hostile reactions of certain Western countries, placing them in historical context. SWF investments have been perceived as potential threats to the national security and economic interests of Western recipient states. Such politically driven perceptions are reminiscent of the arguments raised in earlier times by developing countries in the discourse with

[1] Sovereign wealth investments in their respective constitutive forms are collectively and singularly referred to as "SWFs" or "SWF."

[2] For convenience, this chapter adopts general references: The term "non-Western countries" refers to the newly developed, developing, and less developed countries, particularly countries that are geographically situated east of North America and Western Europe, such as China, Russia, Middle Eastern countries such as Kuwait, Saudi Arabia, and the United Arab Emirates, and Singapore. The term "Western countries" refers to North America and Western Europe.

[3] For specific details, see the Sovereign Wealth Funds Institute, an independent research source, available at http://www.swfinstitute.org/.

Note: This chapter is an adapted version of a paper presented in November 2008 at the Politics of International Economic Law: The Next Four Years meeting in Washington, D.C., organized by the American Society for International Law's International Economic Law Interest Group, and in March 2009 at the Sovereign Wealth Funds Symposium, held by the Georgetown Journal of International Law. The author acknowledges the support of the Ministry of Education, Singapore (Academic Research Fund R-241–000-067–112).

capital-exporting, developed countries concerning the New International Economic Order. The political rhetoric of "national security" and "sovereignty" has been raised as a shield or sword, depending on the disparate national interests of states at the relevant times. The use of such archaic and elusive rhetoric obfuscates real issues by accepting and treating national security and interests as a paramount concern. This chapter therefore proposes an alternative, holistic perspective for the analysis of any SWF investment.

In Section 3, the chapter outlines the divergent and similar concerns of interested actors and examines the existing regimes of domestic and international governance and regulations that apply to the much-debated non-Western SWF investments. Section 4 considers key initiatives by two primary interest groups, the SWFs as investors and the recipient states: the Generally Agreed Principles and Practices[4] (the "Santiago Principles") embodying guidelines for SWFs' internal management and investment objectives, and the OECD Declaration on Sovereign Wealth Funds and Recipient Country Policies[5] ("OECD Declaration on SWFs"). Because the diversity of national and regional interests coupled with the politicization of issues renders consensus on any international finance norm almost impossible, this chapter explores the potential of "good practices" to shape international and national law and practice. It then recommends, in Section 5, a regime of good practices that would serve as an effective model of governance for SWFs, mitigating the unwelcome effects of politicization.

2. THE ELUSIVE RHETORIC OF "NATIONAL INTERESTS" AND "SOVEREIGNTY"

International law is regularly employed to advance the national interests of states.[6] Moreover, the manner in which countries use international law corresponds to the rise or fall of their fortunes. This section briefly traces the political arguments utilized by developed countries and newly independent states in the development of international law relating to SWFs during decolonization and postcolonization.[7] The reversal of arguments by countries in relation to

[4] See the International Working Group of Sovereign Wealth Funds, International Monetary Fund, "Sovereign Wealth Funds Generally Accepted Principles and Practices" (October 2008) at http://www.iwg-swf.org/pubs/santiagoprinciples.pdf.

[5] See the OECD Investment Committee (October 2008), available at http://www.oecd.org/dataoecd/0/23/41456730.pdf.

[6] See, e.g., John Donaldson, *International Economic Relations: A Treatise on World Economy and World Politics* (New York: Longmans, Green and Co, 1928).

[7] See e.g., Antony Anghie, *Imperialism, Sovereignty and the Making of International Law* (Cambridge: Cambridge University Press, 2005) and M. Sornarajah, "Power and Justice: Third

SWF investments is noteworthy. For Western countries, international law was first brandished as a sword in the colonial subjugation of territories and thereafter in the neocolonial expansion of economic influence. It was then lifted as a shield against the increasing economic influence of SWFs of certain non-Western countries in the name of sovereignty. In response, such non-Western countries have adopted the arguments then raised by the Western countries seeking to advance their economic influence.

A. *Brandishing International Law as a Shield and a Sword*

Although international law recognizes that all states are "equal sovereigns," this equality exists primarily in a formal sense.[8] Political and economic power and interests impact on a state's arguments and on legal outcomes. Both developed countries and developing countries, as former colonial powers and colonies, respectively, have utilized international law to advance their respective national interests – and vice versa.[9]

Former colonial powers exercised their economic, political, and military powers over the rest of the world, under a putative civilizing mission. Principles of international law, such as the doctrine of terra nullius[10] and the mandate system of the League of Nations,[11] were employed by former colonial powers.[12] Following the wave of decolonialization in the 1960s and 1970s, several commentators have observed that the former colonial powers, as developed countries, engaged in "neocolonialism" by perpetuating their economic and political control over former colonies through lop-sided economic practices and political relations. They achieved this by internationalizing norms such as liberalization and privatization, which entailed, inter alia, the removal of protectionist trade and investment barriers and tariffs, and equal

World Resistance in International Law," 19 *Singapore Year Book of International Law* (2006) 19.

8 See Article 2(1) of the United Nations Charter; c.f. the economic and military disparity between nation-states. See, e.g., Antony Anghie, "Finding the Peripheries: Sovereignty and Colonialism in Nineteenth-Century International Law," 40(1) *Harv. Int'l L. J.* (1999), particularly at 52–54, 66–78 for a reconception of sovereignty.

9 See, generally, Behrooz Morvaridi, *Social Justice and Development* (New York: Palgrave Macmillan, 2008).

10 A specific application of the concept of res nullius to land, terra nullius allowed the occupation of land that was unclaimed by a sovereign state recognized by European powers: *Clipperton Island Case, France v. Mexico* (1931) ICJ Rep. 1951 at 184.

11 See Article 22, *The Covenant of the League of Nations* (1919).

12 See, e.g., Anghie, *supra* note 8 at 52–54; and Eric Carlton, *Occupation: The Policies and Practices of Military Conquerors* (London: Routledge, 1992).

treatment of foreign and domestic investment, in developing countries as recipient countries.[13]

In response, non-Western countries resorted to international law by sponsoring the New International Economic Order[14] to redress the historical injustices and economic disparity caused by colonial exploitation and unequal postcolonial treaties.[15] However, the developing countries' attempt failed, largely as a result of the imbalance of political power.[16] Developed countries claimed that the principle of laissez faire and minimal regulation of such investment resulted in market accountability, participation, and transparency, thus promoting democracy and the rule of law.[17] Seeking to achieve global competitiveness by attracting foreign capital and trade, starkly poorer postcolonial states granted significant financial and trade concessions to the developed states.[18] Treaty regimes such as the General Agreement on Tariffs and Trade (GATT) and international financial institutions such as the World Bank and International Monetary Fund (IMF), dominated by developed countries,[19] rigorously promoted economic national laws and policies such as free markets and trade, removal of trade barriers, and a "prompt, adequate and effective"[20] minimum standard of compensation for takings of foreign property, and restricted social spending.[21] Such arguments and initiatives are arguably veiled attempts to

[13] See, e.g., Jean Paul Sartre, *Colonialism and Neo-Colonialism*, translated by Bewers et al. (New York: Routledge, 2001).

[14] See "Declaration on the Establishment of a New International Economic Order," UN A/RES/S-6/3201 (May 1, 1974) ["NIEO"], paragraph 4g; Article 2 of "Charter of Economic Rights and Duties of States," UN A/RES/29/3281 (December 12, 1974).

[15] See Morvaridi, *supra* note 9, particularly at pp. 47–53: The developing countries' concerns were reinforced by the dependency theory, which sought to prove that economic growth or capital accumulation would fail as long as there were unequal relations between the nations, development, and poverty elimination based on capitalist market economy. See also A. G. Frank, *Capitalism and Underdevelopment in Latin America* (London: Penguin, 1971). However, dependency theory has been criticized for the lack of empirical support and theoretical failings; see, e.g., P. T. Bauer, *Dissent on Development; Studies and Debates in Development Economics* (London: Weidenfeld and Nicolson, 1971).

[16] See, e.g., Pradip K. Ghosh, *New International Economic Order: A Third World Perspective* (London: Greenwood Press, 1984).

[17] For a discussion on the Third World's tussle with the powerful states, see, e.g., Sornarajah, *supra* note 7.

[18] See, e.g., Kwame Nkrumah, "The Mechanisms of Neo-Colonialism," in his *Neo-Colonialism, the Last Stage of Imperialism* (London: Thomas Nelson & Sons, 1965).

[19] See, e.g., Anghie, *supra* note 7 and World Bank, *Development and Human Rights, the Role of the World Bank* at 259–260, available at http://www.worldbank.org/html/extdr/rights/.

[20] A formula first used by Cordell Hull, then U.S. Secretary of State, during the Mexican expropriations of 1938.

[21] For a discussion of the structural adjustment policies of the World Bank and the IMF, see David P. Fidler, "A Kinder, Gentler System of Capitulations? International Law, Structural Adjustment Policies, and the Standard of Liberal Globalised Civilization," 35 *Tex. Int'l. J. F.*

impose "neoliberalism," a social and moral philosophy beyond economic liberalism, thereby preserving the status quo of economic elites.[22]

B. *SWFs – An Old Phenomenon*

SWFs, as investment arms of sovereign states, first emerged in the early 1950s.[23] As a broad but convenient term, "SWFs" embodies a diverse group of entities of different constitutive characteristics and investment objectives such as funds, pension schemes, state enterprises in home countries, and investment vehicles constituted under foreign laws.[24] According to the Santiago Principles, SWFs are "special purpose investment funds or arrangements" created out of "balance of payments surpluses, official foreign currency operations, the proceeds of privatizations, fiscal surpluses, and/or receipts resulting from commodity exports" and owned by the central government for "macroeconomic purposes."[25]

C. *A Reversal of Capital Flows and Rhetoric*

Non-Western SWFs as rich sources of capital[26] are, however, a recent phenomenon.[27] In the past, the developed countries were the primary net capital exporters. The economic divide between capital exporters and importers

(2000) 387. See also Antony Anghie, "Time Present and Time Past: Globalization, International Financial Institutions and the Third World," 32 *NYU Journal of Int'l Law And Pol.* (2000) 243 at 255–263.

[22] See, e.g., David Harvey, *A Brief History of Neoliberalism* (Oxford: Oxford University Press, 2005) for his view that neoliberalism has been successful in restoring economic elites. See also, Susanne Soederberg, *The Politics of the New International Financial Architecture: Reimposing Neoliberal Dominational in the Global South* (New York: Zed Books, 2004).

[23] Kuwait Investment Authority is the first known SWF, created in 1953 to reduce the country's reliance on oil because it is a nonrenewable resource.

[24] See IMF, "Sovereign Wealth Funds – A Work Agenda" (February 29, 2008), Annex II, available at http://www.imf.org/external/np/pp/eng/2008/022908.pdf.

[25] Appendix 1 of the Santiago Principles. See also, IMF, "Global Financial Stability Report: (September 2007), available at http://www.imf.org/External/Pubs/FT/GFSR/2007/02/pdf/text.pdf, particularly Chapter 1; Commonwealth Secretariat, "Sovereign Wealth Funds – Issue Note" (September 2008), available at http://www.thecommonwealth.org/files/183308/FileName/FMM_08__INF_2.pdf; Sovereign Wealth Fund Institute, available at http://www.swfinstitute.org/swf.php.

[26] See Sovereign Wealth Funds, "Largest Funds by Assets under Management," available at http://www.swfinstitute.org/funds.php, for an estimated total fund size of U.S. $3,652.7 billion.

[27] See, e.g., Swaminathan S. Anklesaria Aiyar, "Strange Rise of Eastern Neo-Colonialism," *The Times Of India* (February 25, 2009) for an observation of the change in global financial power with the rise of non-Western SWFs and the corresponding increased flow of funds to Western countries.

was paralleled by the sociopolitical divide between two groups of countries, formerly and collectively known as the First World and Third World.

A reversal of economic fortunes and the direction of capital flows has recently occurred. Developed Western countries such as the United States, the United Kingdom, and France have chalked up worrisome budget deficits. In contrast, several non-Western countries with economies ranging from advanced to developing, such as China, India, Kuwait, Russia, Singapore, and the United Arab Emirates, were beneficiaries of escalated oil prices and the exponential growth of emerging markets between 2006 and 2008.[28] Their enhanced economic stature is underscored by the non-Western SWFs' intensive shopping spree, particularly from mid-2007 to the third quarter of 2008.[29] An increase in capital flows from several non-Western countries to developed countries resulted.[30] The situation of wealth is thus no longer geographically confined to countries traditionally referred to as the West, the First World, or the North – in other words, "the North is in the South, and the South is in the North."[31]

Many of the non-Western SWFs' portfolio investments do not exceed the usual regulatory limits on foreign share holdings in recipient countries. Nonetheless, such investments, given the lack of transparency and political strategies by such SWFs, have been perceived as potential threats to the

[28] See, e.g., the estimates provided by McKinsey Global Institute, *The New Power Brokers: How Oil, Asia, Hedge Funds and Private Equity Are Shaping Global Capital Markets* (October 2007), Exhibit 1.2, p. 22.

[29] For example, in 2007, China Investment Corporation acquired a U.S. $3 billion stake in Blackstone Group; Dubai's Istihmar won the bid for Barneys New York; Mubadala Development Company, owned by the Abu Dhabi government, purchased a 7.5 percent stake in Carlyle Group for U.S. $1.35 billion; Dubai International Capital purchased a U.S. $1.26 billion stake in hedge fund Och-Ziff Capital Management Group; Citic Securities, China's state-controlled investment bank, invested U.S. $1 billion in Bear Stearns; Abu Dhabi Investment Authority purchased a 4.9 percent stake in Citigroup for U.S. $7.5 billion; Dubai International Capital, owned by the ruler of Dubai, acquired a minority stake in Sony; and Singapore's GIC invested 11 billion Swiss francs in Swiss private bank UBS.

[30] *See* UNCTAD, *World Investment Report* 2008, at Table 1 – FDI flows, by region and selected countries, 1995–2007 and p.10, available at http://www.unctad.org/en/docs/wir2008overview_en.pdf in relation to the inflows and outflows of foreign direct investments among developed economies and developing economies such as Asia. Foreign direct investment outflows from South, East, and Southeast Asia reached a new high amounting to U.S. $150 billion, reflecting the growing importance of developing countries as outward investors. Foreign direct investment outflows from West Asia increased for the fourth consecutive year to U.S. $44 billion in 2007 – nearly six times its level in 2004.

[31] See IMF, Interview published in *Le Monde* (October 30, 2008), available at http://www.imf.org/external/np/vc/2008/103008.htm, for the observation by IMF chief Dominique Strauss-Kahn that although the projection for global growth was 3 percent, emerging economies would enjoy a 6 to 7 percent growth compared to 0 percent for the advanced economies.

national security and interests of Western recipient states.[32] These weighty concerns were not allayed by the absence of management control. For example, prior to the third quarter of 2008, notwithstanding the fact that Singapore SWFs were invited by Citigroup and Merrill Lynch to participate in capital-raising exercises without rights of control or governance, various voices warned that the investments would undermine the economic and national security interests of the United States, and they called for heightened scrutiny and restriction of certain non-Western SWF investments.[33]

Although some cautioned against unwarranted nationalistic and protectionist reactions against SWFs, others called for a defense of national interests against a perceived loss of sovereignty and economic subjugation to non-Western Asian countries.[34] A few politicians further identified specific SWFs such as China, Middle Eastern countries, and Russia, whose objectives may be aligned with long-standing military or terrorism concerns.[35] In contrast, Norway's SWF, Government Pension Fund–Global,[36] has frequently been showcased as an exemplary SWF with its best practices model.[37] "National interests" is, however, an elusive term[38] that includes concerns against economic market competition, domestic sectarian politics, and xenophobia or

[32] Senate Banking, Housing and Urban Affairs Committee Hearing on Foreign Government Investment in the United States (November 14, 2007), as cited by Martin A. Weiss, "Sovereign Wealth Funds: Background and Policy Issues for Congress," CRS Report for Congress (January 15, 2009), RL34336.

[33] See, e.g., Matthew R. Byrne, "Protecting National Security and Promoting Foreign Investment: Maintaining the Exon–Florio Balance," 67 *Ohio St. L. J.* (2006) 849.

[34] See, e.g., Helene Fouquet and James G Neuger, "Sarkozy Calls for EU Funds to Buy Cut-Price Shares," *Bloomberg.Com* (October 21, 2008); and Ben Hall, "Sarkozy Puts €20bn Barrier around Industry," *Financial Times* (November 20, 2008).

[35] See e.g., Guy Dinmore, "Italy Set to Curb Sovereign Wealth Funds," Financial Times (October 21, 2008); and Alistair Thompson, "China Marches on in Africa Despite Downturn," *Reuters* (January 27, 2009).

[36] See http://www.norges-bank.no/default____25991.aspx.

[37] See, e.g., Delia Velculescu, "Norway's Oil Fund Shows the Way for Wealth Funds," *IMF Survey Magazine* (July 9, 2008), available at http://www.imf.org/external/pubs/ft/survey/so/2008/POL070908A.htm.

[38] The shield of "national security" raised against SWF investments is broader than the exceptions of "essential security interests" under Article XXI of the General Agreement on Tariffs and Trade (GATT) and Article XIV of the General Agreement on Trade in Services (GATS), respectively. Although the exceptions of essential security interests have been critiqued as overreaching, they are textually qualified by "necessary" and subject to relatively more established precedents such as the ICSID decisions, *CMS Case Transmission Company v. the Argentina Republic*, ICSID Case ARB/01/08 (2003), *Sempra Energy Internationa v. the Argentine Republic*, ICSID Case ARB/02/16 (2007), *Enron Corporation and Ponderosa Assets, L.P. v the Argentine Republic*, ICSID Case ARB/01/03 (2007), *LG&E Corp., LG&E Capital Corp. and LG&E International Inc. v. the Argentine Republic*, ICSID Case ARB/02/1 (2007), and *Continental Casualty Co. v Argentina*, ICSID Case ARB/03/9 (2008).

nationalism, as differentiated from intentional economic espionage and covert military intelligence and surveillance. In the absence of any concrete negative evidence, there is little to substantiate these beyond abstract concerns.

The calls by Western countries for increased scrutiny and regulation are reminiscent of claims raised in the past by non-Western developing countries regarding their right to regulate foreign investment and transnational corporations in accordance with their national laws and objectives.[39] Their abandonment of previously advocated norms of the free market and the "Invisible Hand"[40] in favor of protectionist management reflects a desire to preserve their economic advantage. Their change in rhetoric suggests that the international law relating to trade and investment is neither a general nor an equitable law. If the international norms of free market and trade are inherently fair and objectively desirable for all, then developed countries should have no reason to abandon such previously advocated and celebrated norms. The politics of self-interest[41] is evident when developed states assert sovereignty rights in the face of non-Western countries' positive performance based on terms formulated by developed states from a position of dominance in international financial institutions, and non-Western SWF states adopt arguments of free markets that are most frequently associated with developed countries.

Increasingly, instead of the long-standing classifications such as First World or Third World, developed or developing countries, a country's ideological and practical position toward market liberalization and foreign investment is shaped by its economic health, the robustness of its gross domestic product, and foreign reserves. Any genuine attempt to evaluate the merits of an SWF investment should, instead of adopting the politicized rhetoric of national security as a starting point of discussion, consider a wide range of divergent and overlapping concerns and interests, as discussed in the following section.

3. NON-WESTERN SWFS – SMOKING GUNS OR BENIGN INVESTMENTS?

The concerns surrounding contemporary SWF investments repeat many old questions about the relationship between the ownership of large enterprises and state power. Although most relevant states, corporations, and individuals

[39] UN General Assembly, "Permanent Sovereignty over Natural Resources," UN Doc. Res. 1803 (XVII) (December 14, 1962).

[40] See Adam Smith, *Wealth of Nations* (1776) (London: Methuen & Co., 1904).

[41] Morgenthau, *Politics among Nations* (1973) 5th ed., at 290–291; John M. Rothgeb Jr., *Foreign Investment and Political Conflict in Developing* Countries (London: Praeger, 1996).

may not call for an outright ban or restriction on the inflows and outflows of capital per se, they have succeeded in establishing greater restrictions on investment inflows to sectors sensitive for national security or financial market systems vulnerable to being reshaped by foreign government intervention.[42]

The theory that non-Western SWFs are "smoking guns"[43] evidencing malign political intentions, given their sovereign characteristics, perpetuates a "politics of fear." It assumes a starting point that is based on inherent suspicion, and it skews any rational cost–benefit analysis of SWF capitalization by requiring non-Western SWFs to rebut the presumption of being a threat to national interests of recipient countries. Given the amorphous nature of national interests, rebutting such a presumption is an unreasonable if not impossible task. Some have alleged that SWFs, though similar to hedge funds without long-term investment objectives, are less transparent than hedge funds and therefore more ominous. However, a closer analysis shows that this is a myth, because different SWFs have different levels of transparency.[44] Moreover, such generalizations conveniently gloss over the levels of secrecy and accountability enjoyed by so-called private investors such as private equity funds, hedge funds, and investment banks.[45]

Instead of a broad discriminatory approach limiting SWF investments, the starting point of analysis should be context-specific, embodying consideration of a wide range of both political and economic interests such as the popular or democratic will in recipient and home countries, political ideologies, the international economic norms of laissez faire, the protective and public welfare functions of governments, and the sovereignty of recipient countries. Home and recipient countries impose different governance regimes pursuant to their applicable laws, which comprise a range of public and private forms of accountability. The emerging international norms of corporate social

[42] See, e.g., Kathryn C. Lavelle, "The Business of Governments: Nationalism in the Context of Sovereign Wealth Funds and State-Owned Enterprises," 62 *J. Int'l Affairs* (2008)131–147.

[43] See, e.g., Jenik Radon, "Sovereign Wealth Funds: Samaritans or Trojan Horses," paper presented at The Politics of International Economic Law: The Next Four Years, American Society of International Law, International Economic Law Interest Group, Washington, D.C., November 13–15, 2008.

[44] See, e.g., Edwin M Truman, "Four Myths about Sovereign Wealth Funds," *Voxeu.Org* (August 14, 2008), available at http://www.voxeu.org/index.php?q=node/1539.

[45] See, e.g., David Cho, "Hedge Funds Mystify Markets, Regulators – Deeply Powerful, Largely Unchecked," *Washington Post* (July 4, 2007): This concerns the largely unregulated and understood hedge funds, which are responsible for more than one-third of stock trades and control more than U.S. $2 trillion worth of assets. See also, Kavaljit Singh, "SWFs Mark Structural Shift in World Financial Order," *The Economic Times (India Times)*, (November 11, 2008).

responsibility, governance, and sustainability add another layer of interests to be addressed apart from more straightforward notions of profitability.[46]

A. *Restrictions on SWFs in Recipient Countries*

To start with, the right of a state to control the entry and regulation of foreign investments that flows from sovereignty is unlimited. A state may therefore significantly affect foreign interests, subject only to prohibited expropriation under customary international law or bilateral or regional treaty agreements. Under customary international law, host states may directly or indirectly expropriate foreign investments only subject to certain conditions such as the nondiscriminatory taking of the investment for a public purpose as provided by law and with compensation.[47] Foreign assets and use thereof may be subject to taxation or trade restrictions. Such measures are not unlawful in the absence of special facts.[48] Nondiscriminatory measures relating to antitrust, consumer protection, securities regulation, environmental protection, and zoning and planning that are essential to the efficient functioning of the state are typically noncompensable takings.[49] It is, however, possible that many SWFs do not factor the likelihood of a sovereign exercise of control or regulation affecting SWF investments as a significant "hurdle rate" to investment. This is because most SWFs categorize their investments, particularly portfolio investments, as private, with profit maximization as their main objective, without any proven intention to exercise political or military influence.

1. Regulatory Restrictions[50]

Several Western countries have sought to establish entry barriers against the seeming threat of non-Western countries. For example, in October 2008, a national interests committee was constituted in Italy to establish SWF

[46] See e.g., Bryan W. Husted, "Risk Management, Real Options, Corporate Social Responsibility," 60 *J. Bus. Ethics* 175 (2005) and C. R. Sunstein, *Free Markets and Social Justice* (Oxford: Oxford University Press, 1997). Cf. Milton Friedman, "The Social Responsibility of Business Is to Increase its Profits," *N.Y. Times* (September 13, 1970) at 122.

[47] For a broad overview of regulatory restrictions on foreign investments in host states, see generally M. Sornarajah, "Controls by the Host State," in *The International Law on Foreign Investment* (Cambridge: Cambridge University Press, 2004).

[48] Ian Brownlie, *Public International Law* (Oxford: Oxford University Press, 2003) at 509.

[49] See, e.g., OECD, "Indirect Expropriation" and the "Right To Regulate" in *International Investment Law* (No. 2004/4) pp. 3–5, 16, available at http://www.oecd.org/dataoecd/22/54/33776546.pdf.

[50] These restrictions are different from those on the business and operations of companies having SWF stake holding, which are likely to be subject to multilateral agreements such as GATT, GATS, and Trade Related Investment Measures.

investment rules: SWFs were prohibited from buying more than 5 percent of individual Italian companies.[51] These types of entry barriers, which preserve financial status quo and interests other than national security, chill free market competition and arguably violate relevant provisions in free trade agreements that protect foreign investments in recipient countries under "national treatment" and "most-favored-nation treatment" principles.[52] First, unlike the usual existing laws that limit foreign ownership in sensitive sectors such as aviation, banking, telecommunications, media, and military industries in numerous states, the percentage restriction applies to all sectors. Second, the percentage restriction is preemptive in nature, as opposed to existing laws requiring regulatory review of foreign investment with a broad objective of protecting "national economic security," "public order," "public safety," and "national defense."[53]

Although most bilateral investment treaties (BITs) provide some assurances against direct and indirect expropriation, there are critical exceptions or qualifications.[54] Pursuant to the relevant provisions of BITs or domestic law, host or recipient states may, under specific circumstances, carve out restrictions or limitations falling within "legitimate public welfare objectives" such as "public health, safety and the environment" from the provisions relating to "indirect expropriation" of rights in investments.[55]

Regulators in recipient countries are also likely to require SWFs to undertake not to acquire rights of control or management, or any role in governance, in the relevant corporations, contrary to allegations that there is "little accountability to regulators."[56] Indeed, specific undertakings that relate to the suspension of voting or participation rights may be required under the recipient countries' securities laws or laws governing foreign investments.[57]

51 See, e.g., Dinmore, *supra* note 35.

52 See, e.g., in relation to financial investments, the free trade agreement between the U.S. and Singapore, available at http://www.ustr.gov/assets/Trade_Agreements/Bilateral/Singapore_FTA/Final_Texts/asset_upload_file708_4036.pdf (last accessed June 17, 2009), particularly Articles 10.2 (National Treatment) and 10.3 (Most-Favored-Nation Treatment).

53 U.S. Government Accountability Office, "Laws and Policies Regulating Foreign Investment in 10 Countries," Foreign Investment GAO-08–320 (February 2008).

54 See, e.g., OECD, *supra* note 49 at pp. 16–21 for observations on bilateral investment treaties' provisions and state practice.

55 See, e.g., the 2004 Model BIT issued by the U.S. Department of State, Annex B, paragraph 4(b), available at http://www.state.gov/documents/organization/38710.pdf, as reflected in one BIT, Exchange of Letters on Expropriation (July 6, 2003) in relation to U.S.–Singapore Free Trade Agreement.

56 See "The Invasion of the Sovereign-Wealth Funds," *Economist* (January 17, 2008).

57 For example, Singapore SWF, Temasek Holdings, which invested in Merrill Lynch, had no rights of control. See Merrill Lynch & Co., "Merrill Lynch Enhances Its Capital

2. "Takings" of SWF Investments[58]

Apart from direct expropriation such as seizure of the SWF investments by the recipient country, certain acts of the recipient country, such as restrictions on financial transfers and impositions of specific terms affecting the usual rights of commercial stakeholders, can adversely and significantly devalue SWF investments, thereby resulting in an indirect taking by the recipient country. In the absence of specific provisions of treaty or domestic law of the recipient country, the question whether the home state or SWF can claim compensation under customary international law depends on several factors.[59]

First, customary international law protects the physical property of foreign investors and foreign direct investment. Foreign direct investment is distinguished from portfolio investment by a lasting interest that "implies the existence of a long-term relationship between the direct investor and the enterprise and a significant degree of influence on the management of the enterprise."[60] The default criterion for determining the existence of such a direct investment relationship is the ownership of 10 percent of ordinary shares or voting power, though several countries have categorized investments that give rise to effective management control as foreign direct investment.[61] Portfolio investments such as stocks in listed corporations are subject to ordinary commercial risks and regulatory changes under the domestic laws of the recipient countries. However, as already discussed, numerous BITs include direct and portfolio

Position by Raising Up to $6.2 Billion From Investors, Temasek Holdings and Davis Selected Advisors" (December 24, 2008), available at http://www.ml.com/index.asp?id=7695_7696_8149_74412_86378_87784 (last accessed February 25, 2009); and Merrill Lynch & Co., "Term Sheet" (December 24, 2008), available at http://www.ml.com/media/92240.pdf (last accessed February 25, 2009).

58 See generally, Sornarajah, *supra* note 47; and C. F. Amerasinghe, "Issues of Compensation for the Taking of Alien Property in the Light of Recent Cases and Practice," 41 *Int'l Comp. L. Q.* 22 (1992).

59 *See* Sornarajah, *supra* note 47.

60 *See* IMF/OECD, *Foreign Direct Investment Statistics: How Countries Measure FDI* (2003) at p. 23, available at http://www.imf.org/external/pubs/ft/fdis/2003/fdistat.pdf; and OECD, *Benchmark Definition of Foreign Direct Investment* (Paris, 1996) at pp. 7–8, available at http://www.oecd.org/dataoecd/10/16/2090148.pdf.

61 See, e.g., OECD, *Benchmark Definition of Foreign Direct Investment* (1999) p. 5, available at http://www.oecd.org/dataoecd/10/16/2090148.pdf: "Foreign direct investment reflects the objective of obtaining a lasting interest by a resident entity in one economy ('direct investor') in an entity resident in an economy other than that of the investor ('direct investment enterprise'). The lasting interest implies the existence of a long-term relationship between the direct investor and the enterprise and a significant degree of influence on the management of the enterprise."

investments in the definition of foreign investment,[62] thereby affording some degree of protection from discriminatory takings or expropriation.

Second, the rights of a stakeholder of a corporation could not be protected by the diplomatic intervention of its home state under customary international law; only the state in which the corporation was incorporated could intervene on behalf of the corporation.[63] Unless provided for in treaties, governments that are stakeholders of SWFs constituted as a corporation under laws other than those of the recipient country do not have any recourse under international law.

Third, although customary international law allows a taking of foreign investment subject to three main conditions – the taking should be for a public purpose, on a nondiscriminatory basis, and compensation should be paid – there is no consensus concerning the manner of assessment of the compensation for nationalization of investments.[64] The national treatment principle stipulated in the OECD General Investment Policy Principles – "[f]oreign investors are to be treated not less favorably than domestic investors in like situations"[65] – does not address the issue of the standard of compensation. Given that several developed Western countries are now recipients of foreign investments, there might be a greater impetus for formulating a single standard for both aliens and nationals that is acceptable to both host and recipient states of foreign investments.

[62] See, e.g., Canada's Foreign Investment Promotion and Protection Agreements (FIPAs), available at http://www.international.gc.ca/trade-agreements-accords-commerciaux/agr-acc/fipa-apie/fipa-purpose.aspx?lang=en; and the communication of the United States to WTO, "Covering FDI and Portfolio Investment in a WTO Investment Agreement," WT/WGTI/W/142 (September 16, 2002), available at http://www.international.gc.ca/assets/trade-agreements-accords-commerciaux/pdfs/W142-e.pdf. See also the definition of "investment," Article 1, 2004 U.S. Model BIT, available at http://www.state.gov/documents/organization/117601.pdf. For a similar and arguably broader definition, see the German model treaty, available at http://www.fes-globalization.org/dog_publications/Appendix%201%20German %20Model %20Treaty.pdf.

[63] *See Barcelona Traction Case* [1970] ICJ Report 1. Subsequent treaties have, however, provided for the protection of foreign stakeholders.

[64] In relation to the taking of physical property, capital-exporting countries (typically, the developed countries) have claimed that such a standard is higher than that afforded to nationals of the host states, e.g., the Hull formula of "prompt, adequate and effective compensation," whereas developing countries assert the Calvo Doctrine, in which the same standard applies to both aliens and nationals. See, e.g., United Nations, *Conference on Trade and Development* (2000), at pp. 12–18, available at http://www.unctad.org/en/docs/psiteiitd15.en.pdf; and M. Sornarajah, *The International Law on Foreign Investment* (Cambridge: Cambridge University Press, 2004).

[65] See http://www.oecd.org/dataoecd/0/23/41456730.pdf.

B. *Accountability in Home Countries*

Generally, SWFs are able to resist adjustments to their respective asset allocations, time horizon, and risk levels, thereby maintaining their asset allocations even in the face of portfolio losses. SWFs are, however, subject to legal regimes of accountability, transparency, and disclosure in their home countries,[66] albeit to varying degrees.[67] Given the currently worsening financial crisis, non-Western SWFs face heightened scrutiny of their foreign investments, which have decreased significantly in value. Consequently, the varied responses of SWFs include the postponement of investments, the sale of investments with materially diminished expected returns, and a new focus in emerging markets or nonfinancial industries that afford higher dividend returns.[68]

For example, concerning Singapore's SWFs, a fair degree of accountability in the form of presidential and parliamentary oversight exists under domestic law.[69] The SWF scoreboards drawn up by Edwin Truman[70] may have motivated certain governments to boost existing levels of accountability and transparency for their SWFs' operations and investments. In relation to the then low ranking of Singapore's SWFs by Truman, the Singapore Government assured the parliamentarians that it was engaged "in talks with the US authorities" and Truman had sought its "inputs."[71] The continued economic crisis and the consequent depressed values of Singapore's SWF investments and significant losses, particularly U.S. portfolios such as Barclays,[72] Citigroup, Inc.,[73] and Merrill Lynch (recently taken over by Bank of America),[74] have led

66 See, e.g., Anna Gelpern, "Sovereign Wealth Turn," Rutgers School of Law–Newark Research Papers 025 (September 22, 2008), available at http://papers.ssrn.com/sol3/papers.cfm?abstract_id=1272395.

67 For an overview of the challenges of managing sovereign wealth, see generally Jennifer Johnson-Calari and Malan Rietveld (eds.), *Sovereign Wealth Management* (Central Banking Publications, 2007).

68 See, e.g., "Qatar Fund Puts Off Investments," *Gulf Daily News* (March 13, 2009).

69 See, e.g., Yvonne CL Lee, "Under Lock and Key: The Evolving Role of the Elected President as a Fiscal Guardian," 290 *Singapore J. Legal Studies* (2007).

70 See Edwin M. Truman, "A Scoreboard for Sovereign Wealth Funds" (October 19, 2007), available at http://www.iie.com/publications/papers/truman1007swf.pdf; and Edwin M. Truman, "A Blueprint for Sovereign Wealth Fund Best Practices," Policy Brief 08–3 (April 2008), available at http://www.petersoninstitute. org/publications/pb/pb08–3.pdf.

71 See speech by Second Minister of Finance Lim Hwee Hua in *Singapore Parliamentary Debates* (March 3, 2008).

72 See, e.g., Alvin Foo, "Temasek's Barclays stake 'sold'," *The Straits Times (Singapore)* (June 5, 2009).

73 See, e.g., Grace Ng, "GIC Pumps $9.8b into Troubled Citigroup," *The Straits Times (Singapore)* (January 15, 2008).

74 See e.g., Saskia Scholtes and Greg Farrell, "Singapore State Fund Counts Merrill Losses," *Financial Times*: "The state agency's unrealised losses could amount to more than US$2

to repeated calls for a substantive review of their global and regional investment strategies.[75]

In addition to the bottom-line accountability, certain SWFs are required by their respective domestic laws and internal regulations to ensure that their investments comply with environmental and human rights laws. For example, Norway's SWF, Government Pension Fund–Global, must ensure that its investments comply with ethical guidelines.[76] The business activities, operations, and management of investee corporations are closely monitored by a Council of Ethics. Any breach of the ethical guidelines is likely to result in a divestment.[77]

C. *Renewed Courtship of Non-Western SWFs*

The worsening global economy during the first half of 2009, without any sustained "bottoming out" of financial markets and return of market confidence, has witnessed the massive cutback in SWF investments and renewed courtship by the governments of and corporations in recipient states.[78] For example, Citigroup, Inc. had approached institutional holders of its preferred shares, the U.S. government and Singapore's SWF, the Group Insurance Commission (GIC), Saudi Arabia's Prince Alwaleed Talal, Capital Research Global Investors, and Capital World Investors, to increase direct stakes by converting their preferred shares.[79]

billion, excluding any hedges." Temasek's stake holding has recently been sold as a result of its investment focus shift from developed countries to emerging markets: See, "Temasek Holdings (Sale of Bank of America Shares)," *Singapore Parliamentary Debates* (May 28, 2009), Vol. 86.

75 See, e.g., "Debate on Annual Budget," *Singapore Parliamentary Debates* (February 10, 2009), Vol. 85, where it was observed that the collective losses incurred by the GIC and Temasek were estimated to be S$50 billion.

76 See the Web site of Norges Bank Investment Management (NBIM) at http://www.norges-bank.no/templates/article____41206.aspx. For a detailed discussion on ethical divestment of NBIM, see Simon Chesterman, "The Turn to Ethics: Divestment from Multinational Corporations for Human Rights Violations – The Case of Norway's Sovereign Wealth Fund," 23 *Am. U. Int'l L. Rev.* 577 (2008).

77 See, e.g., Terry Macalister, "Ethical Business: Norway Ejects Mining Giant Rio from its Pension Portfolio," *Guardian* (September 9, 2008).

78 See, e.g., Sundeep Tucker, "Sovereign Wealth Funds Set to Revive Investing," *Financial Times* (February 16, 2009).

79 See e.g., Eric Dash, "3rd Rescue Would Give U.S. 40% of Citigroup," *NY Times* (February 24, 2009); Fiona Chan, "Citi Asking US Govt, GIC To Up Direct Stakes," *The Straits Times (Singapore)* (February 24, 2009); U.S. Treasury, "Treasury Announces Participation in Citigroup's Exchange Offering" (February 27, 2009), available at http://www.treasury.gov/press/releases/tg41.htm; Citigroup Inc., "Citi to Exchange Preferred Securities for Common,

In early 2009, some European states courted China's SWFs, in what appears to be a reversal of their concerns about these SWFs' transparency and motives.[80] Indeed, it has been observed that in the wake of financial investors' rush to liquidity and safety, SWFs constitute the few remaining attractive sources of capital with risk tolerance.[81] A possible exception is the collapse of a proposed acquisition of a U.S. $19.5 billion stake in the Rio Tinto Group by China's state-owned Aluminum Corporation of China.[82] Although the collapse can be justified on commercial grounds,[83] the deal, which would have been the Chinese government's largest investment in a Western corporation, drew intense political opposition in Australia.[84]

One can therefore surmise from these developments – the widespread renewed pursuit and occasional rejection of SWF investments – that governments and corporations in recipient states are primarily driven by economic benefits as the paramount motivation instead of real concerns of national security. Similar to private institutional investors such as hedge funds, SWF investment decisions are heavily influenced by margins of risks and returns.[85] Nonetheless, the governments of potential and existing SWF investment recipients remain wary. A 2009 U.S. Congressional research report differentiates SWFs on two scales, that is, transparency and investment approaches, and generally categorizes the Western SWFs of Norway, Alaska, and Alberta, Canada as the most transparent with a conventional investment approach, the non-Western SWFs of Malaysia and Singapore as highly transparent but with a more strategic investment approach, and the non-Western SWFs of United Arab Emirates – Dubai, Qatar, and China as least transparent with the most strategic investment approach.[86]

Increasing Tangible Common Equity to as Much as $81 Billion" (February 27, 2009), available at http://www.citigroup.com/citi/press/2009/090227a.htm.

80 See, e.g., "China Set to Invest again in Europe," *Financial Times* (April 19, 2009): The head of China's flagship SWF, China Investment Corp, expressed relief that European snubs saved China from embarrassing investment losses.

81 See "From Vultures to White Knights," *Financial Times* (April 20, 2009).

82 See, e.g., Jamil Anderlini and Sundeep Tucker, "Outmanoeuvred," *Financial Times* (June 11, 2009).

83 See, e.g., "Chinese Ambassador: Chinalco Deal 'Win–Win' for Australia–China," *Xinhua News* (May 26, 2009).

84 The political campaigns against the deal coincided with the Australian Senate inquiry into foreign investments by state-owned entities: See the Senate Standing Committee on Economics, available at http://www.aph.gov.au/Senate/committee/economics_ctte/firb_09/index.htm.

85 Peter Thal Larsen and Kate Burgess, "Investor's Move Is the Envy of Other Funds," *Financial Times* (June 3, 2009): Abu Dhabi's SWF, International Petroleum Investment Corp., sold its entire Barclays stake holdings for a profit of U.S. $5.8 billion Cf. Temasek's losses from its Barclays sale, *supra* note 72.

86 Weiss, *supra* note 32.

4. A MODEL OF GOOD PRACTICES FOR SWFS

A. *The Absent Architecture for International Financial Markets*

Notwithstanding the increasing interlinkage between national capital markets and the interflow of capital among states, an architecture for international financial markets remains starkly absent. The question whether there is any meaningful potential in the regulation of international financial relations and global capital markets at the level of public international law remains uncertain.[87] The current matrix of actors – the Bretton Woods institutions, the Bank of International Settlements, and international financial organizations such as the Basel Committee and the International Organization of Securities Commissions – has evolved in response to different financial crises and market needs.[88] There is thus no coherent overarching economic, institutional, or legal framework.[89] The rules and enforcement mechanisms of such actors depend on the agreement and submission of states and corporations.

The area of international investment law is littered by a series of unsuccessful or marginalized attempts to create multilateral treaties by international organizations. States are unable to agree on the rules governing foreign investment.[90] As academics have astutely observed, the dominant trend is to "think globally [but] act locally"[91] – an approach still predominantly shaped by the national concerns. Regulatory power exercised at the level of the nation-state, being economically, politically, and legally endowed with sovereignty, is accepted as the primary standard setting and enforcement agency.

SWF investments taking the form of portfolio investments in recipient countries are primarily regulated by the national laws of the recipient countries, such as financial and securities laws. The fusion of diverging public–private, international, and foreign–domestic interests and laws poses a significant obstacle to any formation of an international norm regulating SWFs apart from loose

87 See, e.g., Peter Behrens, "The International Architecture of Global Financial Markets," 6(3) *Maastricht J. Eur. Comp. L.* (1999) 271–288.

88 See generally Rainer Grote and Thilo Marauhn (eds.), *The Regulation of International Financial Markets* (Cambridge: Cambridge University Press, 2006).

89 See Rolf H. Weber and Douglas W. Arner, "Toward a New Design for International Financial Regulation," 29 *U. Pa. J. Int'l. L.* 391 (2007) at 427.

90 In particular, the failed attempt by OECD to put forward a multilateral agreement on investment in the 1990s: See e.g., M. Sornarajah, "Multilateral Instruments on Foreign Investment," in *The International Law on Foreign Investment* (Cambridge: Cambridge University Press, 2004). In contrast, the North American Free Trade Agreement (NAFTA), a regional treaty, contains strong provisions on foreign investment and provides for a strong investor–state dispute resolution mechanism.

91 Grote and Marauhn, *supra* note 88 at 13.

cooperation frameworks,[92] and regional treaties[93] and BITs,[94] which may, as discussed in an earlier section, prohibit discriminatory measures affecting foreign direct and portfolio investments. Indeed, the lack of any real consensus among states, particularly in areas involving divergent national interests such as SWF investments, hinders the emergence of any international law governing SWFs and their investments.

B. *The Potential of SWF Principles*

In light of the different and overlapping national interests and the fluidity of financial markets, it is difficult to obtain the agreement or consensus necessary for the formation of treaties or customary international law governing the implementation, enforcement, and surveillance of international financial standards, particularly SWF investments.[95] The long-standing tension between market liberalism and nationalism prevails. Any regime of "hard" regulation modeled after the system of the World Trade Organization (WTO) will suffer the same disability of nonconsensus of its members.[96]

To avoid the crippling difficulty of obtaining consensus among the SWF and recipient countries, an alternative regime of international governance by good practices is preferred. The Santiago Principles and OECD Declaration on SWFs (collectively, "SWF Principles") issued by two interested groups of states,[97] that is, the International Working Group of Sovereign Wealth Funds

[92] See, e.g., International Accounting Standards of Basle, and the IMF Code of Good Practices on fiscal transparencies.

[93] See, e.g., NAFTA; ASEAN Treaty on the Protection and Promotion of Foreign Investment; Free Trade Agreement of the Americas; Dominican Republic–Central America–United States Free Trade Agreement (CAFTA–DR); Middle East Free Trade Area Initiative; and Asia-Pacific Economic Cooperation.

[94] See, e.g., the International Institute for Sustainable Development, available at http://www.iisd.org/investment/bits/: There are approximately, 2,500 BITs.

[95] See e.g., Neil Fligstein, *The Architecture of Markets: An Economic Sociology of Twenty-First-Century Capitalist Societies* (Princeton: Princeton University Press, 2001) and Mauro Guillen, "Corporate Governance and Globalisation: Is There a Convergence across Countries?," 13 *Adv. Int'l Comp. Man.* (2000), 175–204, both as cited by Peter Alexis Gourevitch and James J. Shinn, *Political Power and Corporate Control: The New Global Politics of Corporate Governance* (Princeton: Princeton University Press, 2005), particularly at 86–93.

[96] For example, since the 2001 Doha Ministerial Conference and 2004 Cancun Ministerial Conference, WTO members are still debating the pros and cons of negotiating a multilateral framework of investment rules. See "Trade and Investment from Bilaterals to A Multilateral Agreement?," WTO Briefing Note, Cancún WTO Ministerial Conference 2003, available at http://www.wto.org/english/thewto_e/minist_e/min03_e/brief_e/brief07_e.htm. See also Sornarajah, *supra* note 7.

[97] See *supra* notes 4 and 5.

(IWG)[98] and the OECD,[99] respectively, do not constitute "hard" law because they are not legally binding or enforceable. There is a reluctance to accord them "soft" law status. Indeed, SWFs and their home countries have intentionally used the labels of "principles" and "practices," which suggest an inherent flexibility and informality. The IWG, by not labeling its Santiago Principles as a code or soft law, avoids the dichotomy between hard and soft law; it "marginalizes strategies not framed in the soft v. hard law language."[100] The use of a code or soft law, for example, suggests an acceptance by parties that such a code may "harden" into binding law. This shifts the starting point of discussion from a focus on identifying and working toward common interests and objectives to a need to manage the prospect of specific norms being legally binding and potentially prejudicial in the future. Consequently, countries may not be free to engage in constructive debate to consider and examine the effectiveness of strategies toward achieving a specified goal. The SWF Principles should therefore be assessed on their own merits without the "garnish and frills of softness."[101] As a product of comity and cooperation between the SWF and recipient countries, the SWF Principles can form the integrative premise for specific agreements and arrangements in the future.

Notwithstanding the remarkable speed at which the SWF Principles were formulated shortly after the formation of IWG, they may be criticized on several grounds. First, they are illusory for their nonbinding nature. They are arguably soft law, akin to international agreements that are not legally binding, or lesser than soft law, amounting only to good practices. This criticism is, however, premised upon a particular Austinian conception of international law and its functions, and it unjustifiably discounts the growing influence of "nonlaw" on the laws, policies, and practices of states. It discounts the commercial feasibility in adhering to such nonlaw, given the incorporation of likely risks encountered in recipient countries as "hurdle rates" for SWFs. Second, the SWF Principles suffer from vague concepts such as "legal soundness" (Generally Accepted Privacy Principles or GAPP 1.1), "best interests of the SWFs" (GAPP 8), option to choose from either "recognized international or national auditing standards" (GAPP 12), carve-outs such that each principle is "subject to home country laws, regulations, requirements and obligations,"[102] an equivocal commitment to "explore the establishment of a standing group" for the facilitation of the

98 See http://www.iwg-swf.org/index.htm.

99 See the Organization for Economic Co-Operation and Development, available at http://www.oecd.org.

100 Anna Di Robilant, "Genealogies of Soft Law," 54 *Am. J. Comp. L.* 499 (2006) at 544.

101 Ibid.

102 See Santiago Principles, *supra* note 4 at 7.

understanding and implementation of the principles,[103] and the absence of a central regulator and enforcer.

However, although the SWF Principles do not create a mandatory framework of binding norms, adjudication, and enforcement bodies, the potential for recipient and home countries to reach a common understanding and practice should not be underestimated. Indeed, some shared elements between the two "interest" groups that recently issued the SWF Principles, that is, the SWF home countries and the recipient countries, may be observed: They are defined more by the health of their economies than the former political and social divide between North and South, First World and Third World. Both groups maintain their support for market liberalization, specifically the freedom of investment and benefits of free flows of capital. They also advocate the adherence to principles of accountability, independence, and transparency; protectionism and rogue investment strategies are distinguished from real national security concerns and fair commercial competition. A new "thin" financial rule of law has been fashioned.

Thus, the SWF Principles, as a product of comity and cooperation between recipient and home countries, can form the integrative premise for specific agreements and arrangement in future.[104] These countries are free to adopt specific aspects of good practices and to harden relevant national laws, policies, and practices. Good practices may be likened to a financial form of lex mercatoria, which is an "organic" set of self-creating and self-enforceable norms that can be "adopted" by international or domestic law and practice.[105]

Considerations of profitability, power, and politics have, however, pressurized certain recipient countries to adopt a nationalistic stance, in the face of the SWF Principles. For example, in late 2008, France established its own €20 billion strategic investment fund.[106] French President Sarkozy announced that, unlike the non-Western SWFs, the fund would not be "an international bargain-hunter" but rather a stabilizer of distressed companies that "might fall prey to predators."[107]

Nevertheless, the broad framework of the SWF Principles is likely to facilitate overall discourse, participation, and creation of good principles, policies,

[103] See Santiago Principles, *supra* note 4 at 6.

[104] See e.g., Oscar Schachter, "The Twilight Existence of Nonbinding International Agreements," 296 *Am. J. Int'l L.* (1977) at 304.

[105] See Robilant, *supra* note 114 at 519–520 and 544; and Celia Wasserstein Fassberg, "The Empirical and Theoretical Underpinnings of the Law Merchant: Lex Mercatoria–Hoist with Its Own Petard?," 5 *Chi. J. Int'l L.* (2004) 67.

[106] Katrin Bennhold, "French Fund to Help Shield Companies from Takeovers," *IHT* (November 20, 2008).

[107] Lionel Laurent, "Sarkozy's Sovereign Wealth Defense," *Forbes* (October 23, 2008).

and practices among recipient and home countries, and existing international and regional financial institutions and bodies. Within six months of the Santiago Principles' publication, the IWG reached a consensus to establish the International Forum of Sovereign Wealth Funds.[108] Although the forum is stipulated not to be a "formal supranational authority" and "its work shall not carry any legal force," it facilitates the continuation of the exhange of views and study of SWF activities among the SWF states, recipient countries, international organizations, and market functionaries. The forum serves as a foundational step toward the synchronization of differing domestic laws and practices, and the eventual adoption of uniform norms for SWF investments by each state.

The effectiveness of SWF Principles in relation to certain non-Western SWFs is already evident. For example, shortly after the IWG was formed to create the Santiago Principles, the Singapore SWF, the GIC, issued a report on its investment strategies and policies.[109] Although the GIC report has not attained the same standards of accountability, disclosure, and transparency as those relating to Western SWFs such as Norway, further changes are likely.[110] The other Singapore SWF, Temasek Holdings, recently adopted a more transparent stance, as evident from its press releases.[111] It currently ranks first on The Linaburg–Maduell Transparency Index,[112] ahead of Government Pension Fund–Global of Norway, compared to its tenth position out of forty-seven SWFs in the second quarter of 2008.[113] In another development, Mubadala, an Abu Dhabi SWF, released its annual report showing losses of Dh11.8 billion (U.S. $3.2 billion),[114] in a "first of its kind move" toward greater transparency by a Gulf state investment entity.[115]

C. A *Global "Coordinator"*?

In 2008, the IMF chief proposed a "new governance plan" or "global regulation strategy." He recommended that the IMF assume an enhanced role – as a

[108] See the "Kuwait Declaration" (April 6, 2009), available at http://www.iwg-swf.org/mis/kuwaitdec.htm.

[109] See http://www.gic.com.sg/PDF/GICreport0708_Full.pdf.

[110] Lim, *supra* note 70.

[111] See http://www.temasekholdings.com.sg/media_centre.htm.

[112] See http://www.swfinstitute.org/research/transparencyindex.php. The Linaburg–Maduell transparency index is a method of rating transparency of SWFs.

[113] See http://www.swfinstitute.org/news/augeight.php.

[114] See http://www.mubadala.ae/en/category/investor-relations-12/annual-report-1/.

[115] Andrew England, "Gulf Fund Reveals $3.2bn Loss as it Releases First Report," *Financial Times* (April 24, 2009).

"coordinator" or "architect," and a "mason" with a role in rebuilding economic growth for countries.[116] The success of the IMF's enhanced role depends on whether it is able to formulate policies that fairly represent and equally uphold the wide spectrum of interests of its diverse members.[117] In the past, the IMF provided monetary help to developing countries on very restrictive economic terms, which proved to be more harmful to their economies.[118] The ongoing financial crisis reveals the speed at which the IMF provides loan facilities to distressed Western countries[119] on relatively minimal terms.[120] A detailed comparison of the terms of respective facilities granted to distressed Western and non-Western countries during this "new" IMF season is warranted.[121]

Given the fluidity of the financial markets and diverse interests, it would not be feasible for the oversight of a regime of international governance for SWFs and their investments to be entrusted to any particular international or regional institution or group. Regional bodies represent the interests of their members, which may be weighted in favor of one group. For example, most of the 30 members of the OECD[122] are Western countries who have been the recipients of SWF investments. International organizations such as the IMF have structural flaws such as unequal quotas and voices. Although the IMF has broad jurisdiction over 185 members, and experience in the promotion of international monetary cooperation and growth of international trade, and the facilitation of exchange stability and equilibrium in the international

[116] See Dominique Strauss-Kahn, "Interview," *Le Monde* (October 30, 2008), available at http://www.imf.org/external/np/vc/2008/103008.htm (last accessed February 25, 2009).

[117] See e.g., Axel Peuker, "Strengthening the International Financial Architecture: Contribution by the IMF and World Bank," and Stefan Voigt, "Do We Need a New International Financial Architecture?," in Grote and Marauhn (eds.), *supra* note 87.

[118] See, e.g., "Indonesia Rejects IMF help," *BBC* (January 21, 2003).

[119] IMF, "IMF to Launch New Facility for Emerging Markets Hit by Crisis" (October 29, 2008), available at http://www.imf.org/external/pubs/ft/survey/so/2008/POL102908A.htm.

[120] See IMF, "IMF Set to Lend Ukraine $16.5 Billion, in Talks with Hungary (October 26, 2008), available at http://www.imf.org/external/np/sec/pr/2008/pr08259.htm; IMF, "IMF and Hungary Agree on Policies to be Supported by International Community," Press Release 08/260 (October 26, 2008), available at http://www.imf.org/external/np/sec/pr/2008/pr08260.htm; IMF, "IMF and Iceland Outline $2.1 Billion Loan Plan" (October 24, 2008), available at http://www.imf.org/external/pubs/ft/survey/so/2008/CAR102408A.htm.

[121] IMF approved U.S. $7.6 billion loan to Pakistan in November 2008: See, e.g., IMF, "Pakistan Gets US$7.6 Billion Loan from IMF" (November 24, 2008), available at http://www.imf.org/external/pubs/ft/survey/so/2008/CAR112408C.htm. However, there was some delay at the initial stages – see "IMF Concludes First Round of Talks to Bail out Pakistan," *The Economic Times* (October 31, 2008).

[122] Organization for Economic Cooperation and Development, available at http://www.oecd.org/pages/0,3417,en_36734052_36734103_1_1_1_1_1,00.html.

balances of payments of members,[123] it is dominated by Western countries such as the United States and major European Union countries.[124] The voting shares of non-Western countries do not correspond with the weight they carry in the global economy, in spite of the recent large-scale quota and voice reform to make quotas more responsive to economic realities and enhance the participation of low-income countries in the decision-making process.[125] For example, China has one director on IMF's executive board of 24 members, but only 3.66 percent of the total voting rights,[126] even though it accounts for almost 10 percent of the global economy. This is likely to change in light of the increasing shift of economic power to non-Western countries such as China and India,[127] and the broad consensus obtained at the G-20 London summit of 2009 to implement the package of the IMF quota and voice reforms by 2011.[128]

A plausible alternative to a global coordinator or regulator in the form of existing international organizations, such as the IMF, WTO, or World Bank, is having the G-20[129] as the global forum forging common ground for old and new economic powers. The G-20 London summit of 2009 purportedly marked the emergence of a new world order, with its proposed U.S. $1,100 billion package of measures to tackle the global downturn.[130] It is noteworthy that the G-20 and not the old economic powers such as the G-7 (Western powers with Japan) or the G-8 (G-7 plus Russia) is being used as a forum to redress the current economic problems.[131] The global financial and trade frameworks are clearly evolving with the rise of new economic powers – Brazil, Russia, India,

[123] See, e.g., Articles of Agreement of the International Monetary Fund, Article I – Purposes, available at http://www.imf.org/external/pubs/ft/aa/aa01.htm.

[124] See e.g., Nancy Birdsall, "Why it Matters Who Runs the IMF and the World Bank," in Gustav Ranis, James Raymond Vreeland, and Stephen Kosack (eds.), *Globalization and the Nation State: The Impact of the IMF and the World Bank* (Oxon, UK: Routledge, 2006).

[125] See IMF, "Reform of IMF Quotas and Voice: Responding to Changes in the Global Economy" (updated, March 2008), available at http://www.imf.org/external/np/exr/ib/2007/041307.htm; and "China Wants More Say in Global Financial Bodies," *IHT* (October 29, 2008).

[126] IMF Executive Directors and Voting Power, available at http://www.imf.org/external/np/sec/memdir/eds.htm.

[127] See "China Wants More Say," *supra* note 125.

[128] G-20 Communiqué from the London Summit, "The Global Plan for Recovery and Reform" (April 2, 2009), paragraph 20, available at http://www.g20.org/Documents/final-communique.pdf.

[129] The G-20 gathers the seven major industrialized countries (Britain, Canada, France, Italy, Japan, Germany, and the United States) and Argentina, Australia, Brazil, China, India, Indonesia, Mexico, Russia, Saudi Arabia, South Africa, South Korea, Turkey, and the European Union. See http://www.g20.org/.

[130] See, e.g., George Parker et al., "G20 Leaders Hail Crisis Fightback," *Financial Times* (April 2, 2009).

[131] Quentin Peel, "A Wider Order Comes into View," *Financial Times* (April 5, 2009).

and China (BRIC),[132] and the reversal of capital flow and economic power primarily from the geopolitical West to the East.[133]

5. AN EQUILIBRIUM BETWEEN MARKET LIBERALISM AND NATIONALISM

Contemporary SWF investments have attracted fears of "national security" and potential economic espionage. Although there has been no evidence justifying the fears of recipient states, the effect of having SWFs act as large stakeholders that buy and sell on the basis of their margins of risk and returns on domestic markets remains unclear. Both SWF and recipient states have utilized varying rhetoric such as "free market," "national interests," "sovereignty," and "protectionism" to either justify or challenge the desirability and legitimacy of SWF investments, depending on the size of their current and foreign reserves. Indeed, their articulated positions ironically amount to a reversal of their previously assumed positions, broadly categorized as market liberalism (free trade and markets) and nationalism (right to development).

The politicization of SWF investments is unavoidable, given the overlapping interests of various states and nonstate actors such as corporations, investors, and market intermediaries. A holistic approach should be adopted in any evaluation of SWFs and their investments. SWF investments are but one form of capital flows that is subject to existing restrictions under existing laws and bilateral and regional arrangements. The interlinkages of domestic and global financial markets expose each country's economy to externalities beyond its control. Although trade and capital liberalization has resulted in economic growth for several countries, governments are increasingly pressured by their respective constituencies to regulate with a view to alleviating domestic unemployment and poverty. It is critical that governments avoid taking protectionist measures based on nationalism and xenophobia to avoid a gridlock that will cripple many economies.[134]

[132] An acronym first coined by Jim O'Neill in "Building Better Global Economic BRICs," Goldman Sachs Global Economics Paper 66 (2001). The BRIC first summit was held in June 2009: See, e.g., Isabel Gorst, "Medvedev Urges 'Fairer Global Order'," *Financial Times* (June 16, 2009).

[133] See generally Jack Boorman, "Sixty Years after Bretton Woods: Developing a Vision for the Future," Michael Buchanan, "The BRIC Dream: An Update," and Gordon de Brouwer, "Institutions to Promote Financial Stability: Reflections on East Asia and an Asian Monetary Fund," in Richard Samans, Marc Uzan, and Augusto Lopez-Claros (eds.), *The International Monetary System, the IMF and the G-20 – A Great Transformation in the Making?*, World Economic Forum, the Reinventing Bretton Woods Committee (New York: Palgrave MacMillan, 2007).

[134] For proposed solutions to the current global economic crisis, see e.g., OECD, "Strategic Response to the Financial and Economic Crisis" (2009), available at http://www.oecd.org/

An equilibrium between market liberalism and nationalism must be forged. Presently, any attempt to seek a definite regime of governance or regulation will be futile. One should instead build on the common ground embodied in the SWF Principles, which constitute a realistic starting point for cooperation. The influences of actors with diverse objectives, ranging from profit maximization, to enhancement of public welfare and the upholding of global corporate social responsibility, to the need to take into account new financial "hurdle rates," continue to shape normative standards reflected in hard and soft laws. Large institutional investors such as SWFs and multinational corporations, given their financial ability to recapitalize key financial institutions and corporations, are vital crisis "stabilizers" for the interconnected economies of most countries.[135] Recipient and home countries should therefore achieve some if not optimal consensus in the form of good practices, and steer the course toward international governance of SWFs and their investments.

dataoecd/33/57/42061463.pdf; and OECD, "Financial Crises: Past Lessons and Policy Implications," 668 ECO/WKP(2009) (Februray 17, 2009), available at http://www.olis.oecd.org/olis/2009doc.nsf/LinkTo/NT00000BFA/$FILE/JT03259830.PDF.

135 See, e.g., Dr. Tony Tan Keng Yam, Deputy Chairman and Executive Director, GIC, Speech on "Scenarios for the Future of the Global Financial System" at the World Economic Forum (January 31, 2009), available at http://www.gic.com.sg/newsroom_speeches_310109.htm. Cf. Daniel W. Drezner, "Sovereign Wealth Funds and the (In)Security of Global Finance," 62 *J. Int'l Affairs* (2008) 115.

10

The Politics of International Financial Law and the Global Financial Crisis

Douglas W. Arner

In the postwar period, politics, finance, and law have been inextricably combined. If one thinks of international financial law from a traditional positivist standpoint in which it would be seen as formal state-to-state legal relationships, we have seen remarkably little, given the importance of finance for the stability and development of both individual domestic economies and the international economy. In this context, international financial law would essentially comprise monetary, liquidity, and surveillance arrangements through the International Monetary Fund (IMF) and the financial services provisions of the World Trade Organization (WTO) General Agreement on Trade in Services (GATS). Both of these can largely be seen to operate in the context of traditional realist hegemonic power contexts up to the global financial crisis of 2007–2009. Outside of these, financial law has generally been domestic in nature, though often operating in a cross-border context, with English and New York law being the dominant systems for financial activities. In general, the situation in which private actors structure their relationships under domestic law is the realm of private law and private international law ("private ordering"), along the lines of an anarchic vision of international political economy. However, in between these two extremes is an ever-growing range of nontraditional activities, bringing together politics, finance, and law, usually in the form of "soft law"[1] or "global administrative law."[2]

[1] For discussion, see G. Bertezzolo, "The European Union Facing the Global Arena: Standard-Setting Bodies and Financial Regulation," 34(2) *Eur. L. Rev.* 257 (2009); T. Meyer, "Soft Law as Delegation," 32 *Fordham Int'l L. J.* 888 (2009); P. Verdier, "Transnational Regulatory Networks and Their Limits," 34 *Yale J. Int'l L.* 113 (2009); A. Hamann and H. Fabri, "Transnational Networks and Constitutionalism," 6 *Int'l J. Constitutional L.* 481 (2008); S. Picciotto, "Constitutionalising Multilevel Governance?," 6 *Int'l J. Constitutional L.* 457 (2008).

[2] For discussion, see B. Kingsbury, "The Concept of 'Law' in Global Administrative Law," 20 *Eur. J. Int'l L.* 23 (2009); S. Cassese, "Administrative Law without the State? The Challenge of Global Regulation," 37 *NYU J. Int'l L. Politics* 663 (2005); B. Kingsbury, N. Krisch, and

In looking at the politics of international financial law, one sees that five aspects emerge from a survey of the postwar period. First, there is a clear need for some sort of mechanism to support economic dialogue, cooperation, and coordination, which was the role originally intended for the United Nations Economic and Social Council (UN EcoSoc) and now being filled by the Group of Twenty (G-20).[3] Second, trade arrangements are at the heart of the design, with special needs for financial liberalization and cross-border provision of services. Third, there is a need for some system of macroeconomic policy standard-setting and monitoring, including for monetary arrangements, which is to some extent the role that the IMF has come to play most of the time. Fourth, there is a clear necessity for appropriate financial stability and development arrangements to both prevent financial crises and resolve those crises that do occur, both at the sovereign level and at the level of global financial institutions and markets. Fifth, sustainable development is now no longer just a domestic issue but one with global implications – positive and negative. Investment relates to a number of these issues but has to date not been subject to the same sort of comprehensive approach as has been applied in other areas.

In looking at these issues, one can identify three major periods, in which differing regimes and dynamics dominated arrangements respecting international finance[4]: the Bretton Woods period (1944–1973); the period of internationalization (1974–1994); and the period of globalization (1994–present). Although it is possible that the global financial crisis of 2007–2009 will mark the end of the period of globalization, it appears that rather than a shift to a different regime, instead the existing regime will be reformed to some extent

R. Stewart, "The Emergence of Global Administrative Law," 68 *L. Contemporary Probs.* 15 (2005); see generally http://www.iilj.org/GAL/. For application of the global administrative law approach to international financial regulation, see D. Zaring, "Rulemaking and Adjudication in International Law," 46 *Columbia J. Trans'l L.* 563 (2008); M. Barr and G. Miller, "Global Administrative Law: The View from Basel," 17 *Eur. J. Int'l L.* 15 (2006); D. Zaring, "Informal Procedure, Hard and Soft, in International Administration," 5 *Chicago J. Int'l L.* 547 (2005).

3 The G-20, formed in 1999 in the wake of the Asian financial crisis, comprises Argentina, Australia, Brazil, Canada, China, France, Germany, India, Indonesia, Italy, Japan, Mexico, Russia, Saudi Arabia, South Africa, South Korea, Turkey, the United Kingdom, and the United States, as well as the European Union and the European Central Bank. In addition, the United Nations, World Bank, International Monetary Fund (IMF), and Financial Stability Board (FSB), among others, are also invited to attend.

4 At an international level, regimes may be defined as "sets of implicit or explicit principles, norms, rules, and decision-making procedures" structuring behavior. S. Krasner, "Structural Change and Regime Consequences: Regimes as Intervening Variables," 36(2) *Int'l Org.* (1982).

and reaffirmed through increased legalization.[5] At the same time, it remains possible that the current financial crisis will mark the beginning of a new period. Nonetheless, it does appear that the global financial crisis marks the end of hegemonic relations in the area of international financial law.

1. INTERNATIONAL FINANCIAL LAW UNDER BRETTON WOODS, 1944–1973

During the period of globalization (1870–1914) prior to World War I, the international economic regime operated in a largely hegemonic context, with the United Kingdom in the leading role at least from around 1870. The regime of the time was largely an informal one, based on principles of free trade and fixed exchange rates under the gold standard. The norms, rules, and decision-making procedures derived from these principles reflected the tradition of great power politics (the combination often expressed in neomercantilist economic competition), with little international formality, with Britain and other Western countries acting to impose the regime upon others through empire and coercion, if necessary. During this period, the only truly institutionalized framework was the gold standard – not an internationally legalized institution but rather a principle that imposed norms and rules on domestic behavior through domestic views of the necessity of maintaining the link between paper currencies and gold or silver. During this period of global finance prior to World War I, not only was there no international financial regulation, but in fact there was little domestic financial regulation either, and capital flows were generally unconstrained.

The interwar period (1914–1945) marked the end of the preceding international economic regime and great power balance. Although the period between the two World Wars was marked by various attempts to return to the previous regime of free trade and the gold standard, these were unsuccessful, with international economic relations fragmenting to support conflicting needs. At the same time, the United Kingdom's role at the center of the previous regime was eroded but without the United States being willing to take on Britain's former role. At the end of World War II, a new regime was designed to avoid the specific problems that had existed in both the pre-war and interwar periods.

[5] In the international relations context, "legalization" refers a set of characteristics defined as "obligation," "precision," and "delegation." K. Abbott, R. Keohane, A. Moravcsik, A. Slaughter, and D. Snidal, "The Concept of Legalization," 54(3) *Int'l Org.* (2000).

In August 1941, Franklin D. Roosevelt and Winston Churchill met near Nova Scotia in the Atlantic Ocean and laid down their vision of a peaceful world order after World War II in the Atlantic Charter.[6] This document was essentially based on three pillars: peace, financial stability, and trade between equal nations. The second and third pillars (discussed in 1944 under the auspices of the United States and the United Kingdom) focused on preventing international economic instability of the sort seen in the interwar period and supporting economic development through the reintegration of domestic economies. At Bretton Woods and Havana, countries agreed an overall design for the international economic system, with a new regime based on free trade, fixed exchange rates, domestic financial systems, and international cooperation and coordination of both macroeconomic affairs and reconstruction and development. Whereas in relation to trade and fixed exchange rates the Bretton Woods regime resembled the previous liberal economic order, in relation to finance and cooperation it took the opposite approach from the previous regime: rejection of global finance and support for international macroeconomic, reconstruction, and development cooperation and coordination.

Unlike the previous regime, the Bretton Woods system was to be highly institutionalized and legalized. Based fundamentally on open trade flows, fixed exchange rates, restricted capital flows, and international economic cooperation and coordination, it was to be embedded in a series of international treaty-based institutions and formal arrangements for interactions between sovereign nation-states in four main areas. Under the design, economic policy coordination was to take place through the United Nations (established in 1945), with the UN EcoSoc at the center.[7] Macroeconomic matters and monetary arrangements ("macroeconomic stability"), based on currencies fixed to the U.S. dollar, which was in turn fixed to gold, were to be maintained through the IMF (established in 1945).[8] Responsibility for finance for and coordination of reconstruction and development was placed with the International Bank for Reconstruction and Development (established in 1945).[9] Liberalization of

[6] See S. I. Rosenman (ed.), *The Public Papers and Addresses of Franklin D. Roosevelt, New York 1938–1950* (1941), Vol. 10, at 314.

[7] See UN Charter (1945), Chapters IX–X, esp. 57, 63; available at www.un.org/ecosoc/.

[8] The IMF Articles of Agreement were adopted at the United Nations Monetary and Financial Conference, Bretton Woods, New Hampshire on July 22, 1944 and entered into force December 27, 1945. They have subsequently been amended three times: (1) Board of Governors Resolution No. 23–5, adopted May 31, 1968 and effective July 28, 1969; (2) Board of Governors Resolution No. 31–4, adopted April 30, 1976 and amended effective November 11, 1992; and (3) Board of Governors Resolution No. 45–3, adopted June 28, 1990 and effective November 11, 1992. See www.imf.org.

[9] World Bank Agreement; see www.worldbank.org.

trade was the responsibility of the International Trade Organisation (ITO). Reflecting the view that although global trade was desirable, global finance was not, the Bretton Woods structure did not provide a specific hard law, international institution-based structure for finance because the design was based on the premise that finance would be domestic and subject therefore only to domestic regulation.[10] Financial stability was to be achieved through limiting the role of finance. As capital flows were to be restricted, there was no international treaty-based organization designed to address such issues and the existing organization, the Bank for International Settlements (BIS), was to be shut down.

The regime design encompassed three fundamental features. First, its structure was formal and institutional, based on an interlinked set of international treaties and institutions. Second, it assumed closed national financial markets, with limited capital flows, but open markets for trade in goods. Third, relationships among closed national systems were structured through an international institutional framework.[11] Institutionally, the Bretton Woods system was to include three new interlinked international organizations: the IMF, the World Bank, and the ITO. In each area, there was to be a high level of legalization, with treaty-based obligations, drafted with precision, with monitoring responsibility delegated to a specifically created international organization.

The design was based largely on the willingness of the United States to operate as economic and political hegemon, seeking to build a new order both beneficial for the rest of the world and at the same time structured to enhance the position of the United States in post-war international financial and economic affairs (and replacing Britain).

However, the Bretton Woods international economic architecture as designed never actually functioned: The ITO was stillborn[12] (though ultimately reincarnated as the WTO in 1994 after fifty years in the limbo of the General Agreement on Tariffs and Trade) and Cold War politics quickly rendered UN EcoSoc ineffective. Likewise, the role of the World Bank was quickly usurped in many ways first by the bilateral efforts of the United States through the Marshall Plan and related reconstruction initiatives, complemented later by the European Community with its aid programs for Southern and Eastern

10 For discussion, see D. Arner, *Financial Stability, Economic Growth and the Role of Law* (Cambridge University Press, 2007); R. Weber and D. Arner, "Toward a New Design for International Financial Regulation," 29 *U. Pa. J. Int'l L.* (2008) 391.

11 See *Proceedings and Documents of the United Nations Monetary and Financial Conference, Bretton Woods, New Hampshire, July 1–22, 1944*, (Washington D.C.: U.S. Governmental Printing Office, 1948).

12 See J. H. Jackson, *The Jurisprudence of GATT and the WTO, Insights on Treaty Law and Economic Relations* (2000), at 21–22.

European countries, and in competition with the efforts of the Soviet Union to build alternative arrangements. This left the World Bank to focus on developing (often postcolonial) countries – the role it continues to play today. Nonetheless, the design for monetary relations, with the IMF at the center of a system of fixed exchange rates based on the U.S. dollar and its link to gold, did function – arguably quite well – until the early 1970s. Finally, the BIS was not abolished – and continues to function today much as it functioned since its establishment in the interwar period.

During the Bretton Woods period (1945–1973), international economic relations were dominated both by the Cold War and by U.S. and Soviet interests. In the area of finance, although there was general support at the outset for an atomized international financial system, with limited cross-border capital flows (evidenced by the IMF Articles of Agreement, which only require current account convertibility – to support trade – and not capital account liberalization), this principle was violated to support interests of individual states, especially the United Kingdom. Nonetheless, capital flows remained largely limited until the 1970s, with the rise of the euromarkets.

2. INTERNATIONALIZATION OF FINANCE AND FINANCIAL LAW, 1973–1997

Following the gradual erosion of support for the underlying principle of limited capital flows combined with the unwillingness of the United States to sacrifice domestic interests in support of maintaining the fixed relationship between the U.S. dollar and gold at the heart of the Bretton Woods international monetary system, the Bretton Woods regime effectively ended in 1973 (with a general decision that it was impossible to return to the principle of fixed exchange rates and the decision to amend the IMF Articles of Agreement accordingly). This effectively ended the Bretton Woods international monetary regime and removed the central pillar supporting international macroeconomic stability. At the same time, commitment to atomized finance continued to erode, especially with decisions in Europe to move toward financial integration in support of economic integration. This gradual process, however, was not accompanied initially by the establishment of a new regime supporting international financial stability.

Since the end of the Bretton Woods international monetary system in 1973, financial markets have changed dramatically through a process of liberalization, internationalization, and globalization, undergirded by incredible technological changes. In response to the risks raised by increasing internationalization of finance, domestic central banks and regulators established informal committees hosted by the BIS. As finance continued to internationalize across the 1970s and 1980s, these initial efforts expanded beyond banking to a range of other areas, including securities and accounting. As a result of the 1980s debt crisis and other cross-border financial problems, these informal committees began to agree on common approaches to common problems, with such approaches implemented by means of domestic legal and regulatory systems – a network-based, soft law approach of which the 1988 Basel Capital Accord is the leading and most widely implemented example.[13]

During this period, the regime that replaced the Bretton Woods structure was based on principles of free trade, floating exchange rates, and international capital flows. Existing institutions continued but adapted to the new realities. Without its fundamental role in the international monetary system, the IMF focused on macroeconomic surveillance and related financial support for economic restructuring (essentially signaling an increasing role in development as opposed to international macroeconomic and monetary stability) and the World Bank continued to focus on developing countries. At the same time, the BIS began to take a quiet though influential role in serving as a meeting place for domestic central banking and financial authorities, laying the groundwork for the development of a new financial stability regime in the wake of the Asian financial crisis. Two other aspects also became significant during the period of internationalization of finance. First, this period witnessed the rise of the various "Groups," with the Group of 7 (G-7)[14] and the Group of 10 (G-10) eventually becoming the most significant fora for international economic dialogue, cooperation, and policy coordination. Second, it is during this period that the European Union was established, with commitments not only to free trade but also to integrated financial markets (underpinned by free movements of capital) and fixed exchange rate arrangements (eventually to be institutionalized as the single currency, the euro).

The international economic regime during this period could thus be characterized by the principles of free trade, floating exchange rates, free movement of capital, network-based cooperative and coordinative mechanisms, and competition in development (among both domestic and multilateral arrangements). Unlike the previous system, with the exception of trade and European arrangements (the legalization of both of which increased during this period), it was lightly legalized, with few formal obligations, a high level of generality, and

[13] "Transnational networks": See A. Slaughter, *A New Global Order* (Princeton University Press, 2004).

[14] The G-7 includes Canada, France, Germany, Italy, Japan, the United Kingdom, and the United States. The Group of Eight (G-8) also includes Russia. The European Union is also a member of both the G-7 and the G-8.

a general weakness or even absence of international delegation, with existing international organizations such as the IMF, World Bank, and Organization of Economic Cooperation and Development (OECD) weakening across the period. However, across the period, one can identify an increasing development of transnational network-based approaches in order to address common issues relating to finance, with increasing levels of domestic adherence to the informal approaches, arrangements, and standards agreed on, generally at the level of individual central banks and government or quasi-governmental agencies.[15]

As already noted, the major exceptions were the establishment of the WTO (marking the establishment of a new regime for international trade) and the European Union (marking a major deepening and strengthening of the regime for European integration) in the first half of the 1990s. In the area of finance, significantly, the WTO encompassed institutionalization and legalization of one of the principles of the new regime: financial liberalization, expressed as trade in financial services under the GATS and ancillary agreements relating to financial services. In Europe, the 1986 Single European Act and the 1992 Maastricht Treaty both formalized financial liberalization within Europe and also the move to fixed exchange rate arrangements at the regional level. Moves away from generalized commitment to floating exchange rates can also be seen in the widespread use of pegged exchange rate arrangements outside of the OECD, with developing countries in most cases seeking to maintain fixed exchange rate relations between domestic currencies and the U.S. dollar.

In addition, during the 1990s, as a further expression of the principle of financial liberalization, G-7 and G-10 nations sought to amend the IMF Articles of Agreement to include free movement of capital. In this way, whereas the 1970s was a period of regime disintegration and the 1980s a period of convergence toward principles underlying a new regime, the 1990s were marked by developed country efforts to legalize arrangements relating to the principle of financial liberalization and global finance.

At the beginning of the 1990s, as the United States assumed a truly hegemonic role for the first time since the late 1940s in the wake of the collapse of the Soviet Union, it sought to institutionalize and legalize a liberal economic and financial regime based on the Washington Consensus with the support of Europe, through WTO financial services provisions, amendments to the IMF Articles, and pressure (through international organizations and bilaterally) for

15 See J. Norton, *Devising International Bank Supervisory Standards* (Kluwer, 1995); J. Norton, "Comment on the Developing Transnational Network(s) in the Area of International Financial Regulation: The Underpinnings of a New Bretton Woods II Global Financial System Framework," 43 *Int'l Lawyer* (2009) 175.

free trade, floating exchange rates, and global capital flows (based on the U.S. dollar).

Unfortunately, during the 1990s, as finance became increasingly global, so did financial crises, especially in emerging market economies. In the 1990s, the deficiencies of the existing international institutions and arrangements for financial stability (the "international financial architecture") to deal with these changes came dramatically to light through the Mexican, East Asian, and other financial crises that followed. Since that time, countries, international organizations (especially the IMF, World Bank, and WTO), and regional arrangements gradually have been forced to come to grips with the increasingly globalized nature of finance and coordinate financial stability arrangements. Discussions both in these institutions and elsewhere have focused on whether there was a need to reform the existing international institutional arrangements – that is, whether there was a need for a "new international financial architecture"[16] to form the institutional basis of the emerging global financial stability regime.

3. INTERNATIONAL FINANCIAL LAW AND GLOBAL FINANCE, 1997–2008

Following the Asian financial crisis, a number of actions were taken to address these issues and to build on the initiatives undertaken after the Mexican financial crisis, centering on the IMF (transparency and liquidity), the World Bank (technical assistance), and international financial standards. In addition to these, the G-20 was also established[17] to serve a coordinating function. Overall, the result was the emergence of a new regime to support global financial stability.

First, the IMF acted to further enhance its role both in the provision of international liquidity and in encouraging transparency. Second, following the Mexican and Asian financial crises, the World Bank and the other multilateral

[16] For an overview, see R. Weber, "Challenges for the New Financial Architecture," 31 *Hong Kong L. J.* 241 (2001); M. Giovanoli, "A New Architecture for the Global Financial Market: Legal Aspects of International Financial Standard Setting," in M. Giovanoli (ed.), *International Monetary Law: Issues for the New Millennium* (2000), 3.

[17] As originally constituted, the G-20 was composed only of finance ministers and central bank governors from nineteen countries (Argentina, Australia, Brazil, Canada, China, France, Germany, India, Indonesia, Italy, Japan, Mexico, Russia, Saudi Arabia, South Africa, South Korea, Turkey, the United Kingdom and the United States), plus the European Commission and the European Central Bank (ECB), the Managing Director of the IMF, the President of the World Bank, and the chairs of the International Monetary and Financial Committee and Development Committee of the IMF and World Bank.

development banks (MDBs) increasingly focused on efforts to strengthen the domestic financial systems of their member countries.

In addition, the third major area of concern was the prevention of financial crises through the enhancement of the quality of individual financial systems. In response to an initiative at the Lyon Summit of the G-7 in June 1996, representatives of the G-10 countries and of emerging and transition economies jointly sought to develop a strategy for fostering financial stability through the analysis of experiences in previous crises and to elucidate basic standards and principles to guide individual economies in the development of stronger financial systems.[18]

Since the Mexican financial crisis, the concept of financial stability has become the primary target in preventing financial crises and reducing the severe risks of financial problems that do occur from time to time. "Financial stability," however, is not a clearly defined term but is generally seen as both the absence of financial crisis and the normal operation of financial intermediaries and markets. Marc Quintyn and Michael Taylor go one step further, suggesting that the financial sector plays a special and unique role in an economy and, as a result, "the achievement of *financial stability* . . . is now generally considered a *public good*,"[19] thus echoing one of the underlying principles of the Bretton Woods system. With financial stability as the agreed international objective, a system was developed to assist countries to achieve this goal.

The post-Asian crisis international strategy for the development of financial stability was a system of international financial standards. The system has the following primary characteristics: (1) development of an international consensus on the key elements of a sound financial and regulatory system by representatives of the relevant economies; (2) formulation of sound principles and practices by international groupings of technocratic authorities with relevant expertise and experience, such as the Basel Committee, the International Organisation of Securities Commissions, the International Accounting Standards Board, the International Association of Insurance Supervisors (IAIS), and the Joint Forum on Financial Conglomerates; (3) use of market discipline and market access channels to provide incentives for the adoption of sound supervisory systems, better corporate governance, and other key elements of

[18] G-10, Report of the Group of Ten (G-10) Working Party on Financial Stability in Emerging Markets, "Financial Stability in Emerging Market Economies: A Strategy for the Formulation, Adoption and Implementation of Sound Principles and Practices to Strengthen Financial Systems" (April1997). This framework was developed further in Group of 22 Systemically Significant Countries (G-22), "Reports on the International Financial Architecture" (October 1998).

[19] M. Quintyn and M. Taylor, "Regulatory and Supervisory Independence and Financial Stability," IMF Working Paper WP/02/46 (March 2002), at 8 (emphasis in original).

a robust financial system; and (4) promotion by multilateral institutions such as the IMF and the MDBs of the adoption and implementation of sound principles and practices. Importantly, however, the ultimate responsibility for policies to strengthen financial systems lies with the governments and financial authorities in the economies concerned.

Most generally, this system can be described as having four levels, incorporating both existing and new international institutions and organizations. At the first level, there is a structure that has mainly been established through political processes. The second level is international standard setting, largely of a technocratic nature. At the third level is implementation of standards – in principle a domestic process but with technical assistance through a variety of international, regional, and bilateral sources. The fourth level focuses on monitoring the implementation of standards.[20]

International standards and their development are the only truly new element of the international financial architecture to emerge from the series of financial crises culminating in the Asian financial crisis. The only new institution to emerge from discussions of the international financial architecture was the Financial Stability Forum (FSF).[21] The FSF was established to serve the role of the coordinator in the system of international standards and to promote standards. In addition to coordination and standard setting through the FSF, the established international financial institutions such as the IMF, World Bank, and BIS adhere to their mandate of standard setting, as well as implementation and monitoring. In addition to the international financial institutions, other formal international organizations such as the OECD are of importance. However, the WTO was not formally included. Finally, much standard setting takes place through various international financial organizations of varying levels of formality.[22] In addition to the FSF, the BIS plays an important role in coordination. It provides the secretariat for the FSF, as well

[20] This essential structure was affirmed by the G-7 Finance Ministers in the Communiqué from their Köln Summit in 1999 (G-7 Finance Ministers, "Report of the G7 Finance Ministers to the Köln Economic Summit," Cologne, Germany, June 18–20, 1999).

[21] The FSF, formed in 1999 in the wake of the Asian financial crisis, comprised financial authorities from developed financial systems (Australia, Canada, France, Germany, Hong Kong, Italy, Japan, Netherlands, Singapore, Switzerland, United Kingdom, United States, and ECB), and the major international financial institutions (BIS, IMF, and World Bank), international regulatory and supervisory bodies (Basel Committee, International Organization of Securities Commissions, International Association of Insurance Supervisors, and International Accounting Standards Board) and committees of central bank experts (Committee on the Global Financial System, and Committee on Payment and Settlement Systems).

[22] D. Zaring, "International Law by Other Means: The Twilight Existence of International Financial Regulatory Organizations," 33 *Tex. Int'l L. J.* 281 (1998).

as the Basel Committee, Committee on Payment and Settlement Systems, Committee on the Global Financial System, G-10, and the IAIS.

At the political level, prior to the current global financial crisis, the G-7 industrialized countries generally took the lead in establishing an operating framework for the process. In addition, the G-10 initiated efforts to elaborate the details. Finally, other groups such as the G-20 were also involved in various aspects.

In addition to the various organizations already discussed, foreign participation in domestic financial services is dealt with largely through bilateral, regional, and international negotiations, with the latter centered on the WTO. Although the WTO provides the international framework for foreign participation in financial services, unlike areas such as trade in goods, in the area of financial services the commitments made by members are exclusive rather than inclusive. Therefore liberalization is at the discretion of individual WTO members and remains quite limited in most cases. Moreover, since 1999, there has been essentially no progress in negotiations in this area.

Overall, at the onset of the global financial crisis of 2007–2009, the international financial regime addressed five central elements: macroeconomic cooperation and coordination through the G-7 (largely nonlegalized); trade in financial services through the WTO (largely legalized but of limited effectiveness); macroeconomic monitoring through the IMF (institutionalized but of limited legalization); financial stability through the FSF (institutionalized but of limited legalization); and development through the MDBs. Arguably, a new international financial regime had emerged, with a supporting institutional framework of mixed levels of legalization.

4. INTERNATIONAL FINANCIAL LAW AND THE GLOBAL FINANCIAL CRISIS

During 2008, for the first time since the 1930s, the world economy experienced a systemic financial crisis: On September 18, the international financial system was on the precipice of collapse and global credit markets essentially ceased to function for the following four weeks. Although the ultimate economic impact of the global financial crisis is still being resolved, following a series of dramatic events including the failure of major financial institutions and significant government interventions in the financial system around the world, it is now unlikely that either the global or any major domestic financial system will collapse, causing the onset of an economic depression of the sort unseen since the 1930s. The causes of the global credit crisis are now generally understood, however, and major initiatives are underway around the world to reform financial regulation, with far-reaching consequences for the future of global finance. In addition to the financial and economic story, the global financial crisis has also seen much activity in the area of financial law and regulation, at the domestic, regional, and international levels. Nonetheless, much of this activity has yet to move beyond the level of discussion and politics to the level of international law, international standards, or even international consensus.[23]

A systemic financial crisis can be seen as a play in five acts. During Act I, building excesses, the stage is set for the coming storm, typically with dramatic asset price appreciation, frequently combined with rapid growth in lending and increases in financial leverage. Act II, the initial phase, sees the top of the market, with peaks in asset prices, followed by initial declines. This phase is frequently characterized by general denial of the potential severity of the problem, though with an increasing level of realism among a minority of market participants. Act III, systemic financial crisis, sees some event – generally unanticipated by the majority – that sets off the systemic phase of the financial crisis, during which panic and confusion reign. Act III, however, is often quite short and acute, unlike Act IV, economic crisis, which can be long, even chronic. During Act IV, the effects of the systemic financial event and ensuing crisis, whether contained or not, move from the financial sector to the general economy, as finance ceases to be available, optimism turns to pessimism, and the economy begins to suffer. During this phase, realization gradually comes that, in the financial sector, the problems are not those of liquidity (as generally thought in earlier phases) but rather problems of solvency, requiring significant government intervention to address. At some point, however, in Act V, there will be a return to a "new normal."[24]

A. *Act I: Building Excesses*

In essence, the financial crisis of 2007–2009 resulted from an unprecedented period of excessive borrowing, excessive lending, and excessive investment incentivized by a series of significant economic and regulatory factors. Excessive borrowing and lending most directly arose in the context of the market for subprime residential mortgages in the United States, especially during 2005

[23] For detailed discussion, see D. Arner, "The Global Credit Crisis of 2008: Causes and Consequences," 43 *Int'l Lawyer* 91 (2009); D. Arner and M. Taylor, "The Global Financial Crisis and the Financial Stability Board: Hardening the Soft Law of International Financial Regulation?," *UNSW L. J.* (2009).

[24] See generally L. Laeven and F. Valencia, "Systemic Banking Crises: A New Database," IMF Working Paper 08/224 (September 2008).

and 2006. However, excessive borrowing and lending were prevalent in virtually all asset classes globally, including commercial real estate, corporate lending (especially for mergers and acquisitions and private equity transactions), commodities, and international (especially emerging markets) equities. These excesses were not limited to the United States; they were truly global, impacting almost every market and asset class. This broad-based excessive borrowing and lending was fueled by excessive investment from a wide range of investors around the world.

Excessive borrowing, lending, and investment were inextricably interconnected through a range of transaction structures derived from well-understood techniques of securitization. Excessive investment was largely the result of two economic factors: first, the period of low interest rates in Japan in the wake of the onset of its banking crisis at the beginning of the 1990s and in the United States following the bursting of the dot.com bubble in 2001; and second, the imbalances in saving and investment between the Anglo-American economies, especially the United States and United Kingdom, and the rest of the world, especially Japan, China, and the major oil-producing countries such as Russia and Saudi Arabia. The combination of low interest rates and large volumes of investment funds from outside the United States and the United Kingdom supported massive investment in debt securities in New York and London, which were designed to produce an appealing combination of perceived safety and attractive yields.

This combination of debt capital market technology, regulatory incentives, excessively low interest rates, and massive global investor demand set the stage for the crisis.

During this phase, only limited initiatives took place at the international level, and in fact, many of these, such as continued implementation of the Basel II Capital Accord and discussions regarding financial sector competitiveness, were not designed to address rising excesses but actually acted to unintentionally reinforce them.

B. *Act II: Initial Phase*

Toward the end of 2006, rising interest rates, subprime delinquencies, and downgrades of structured products began to shake confidence in the new financial paradigm. By summer 2007, the tide had turned, resulting in a freeze in markets in August 2007, significant equity market corrections, cuts in interest rates, and a seeming return to normalcy in the U.S. stock markets, with foreign equity and global commodities markets being simultaneously propelled to new heights as money moved out of credit and into other opportunities. At the same time, the failure of Northern Rock in the United Kingdom in September was followed by the beginning of the onset of the credit crisis globally as adverse selection, loss of confidence, and changes in investor preferences weakened global credit markets.

During this stage, in April 2008, the FSF met to discuss emerging issues and released a significant report, albeit one that would in many ways be overshadowed by subsequent events.[25] At the time and even today, these recommendations are central to the international framework for financial stability and, had they been implemented quickly, could perhaps have prevented the systemic phase of the crisis. At the same time, in the arena of politics rather than regulatory policy, the focus during this period was very much on blaming: blaming the United States and the United Kingdom for causing the "credit crunch" that had become the "subprime crisis," with many countries (especially in Continental Europe and emerging markets around the world) viewing themselves as having done well to avoid the excesses in London and New York.

C. *Act III: Systemic Financial Crisis*

Following the nationalization of Fannie Mae and Freddie Mac in the United States at the beginning of September 2008, on September 15, Lehman Brothers, the fourth-largest U.S. investment bank, filed for Chapter 11 bankruptcy protection, now the largest and most complex bankruptcy in history. More importantly, this event would come to be seen as the trigger for the subsequent systemic crisis. Around the same time, after pulling out of the bidding for Lehman Brothers, Bank of America agreed to acquire Merrill Lynch, the third-largest U.S. investment bank. Finally, the same weekend, American International Group, at the time the world's largest insurance company (with over U.S. $1 trillion in assets globally) and one of the largest counterparties in the global derivatives market, was rescued by the U.S. Treasury and Federal Reserve.

By Thursday, September 18, the series of events proved too much for the global financial system and it began to collapse. Most significantly, the collapse was triggered by uncertainty, loss of confidence, and adverse selection, but also by direct losses resulting from the collapse of Lehman. On September 18, the U.K. government announced that Lloyds TSB would take over HBOS, which otherwise would have failed. In the United States, the oldest money market fund, the Reserve Primary Fund, announced that it would have to close and

[25] FSF, "Report of the Financial Stability Forum on Enhancing Market and Institutional Resilience" (April 2008).

would not be able to pay its customers in full. This event, known as "breaking the buck," triggered a run on money market funds. At this point, panic set in in earnest, with market participants driving gold prices up by a record amount and short-term U.S. Treasury bills down to the lowest level since 1941 in a violent rush to safe assets. On September 18, the global financial system was collapsing. If it were to collapse, the global economy would follow, as had occurred during the Great Depression.

To stop or slow the collapse of the financial system, in addition to bolstering traditional short-term liquidity mechanisms, the Fed acted to increase liquidity dramatically. However, despite this, the financial death spiral continued. On September 20, to resuscitate the U.S. credit markets (which had suffered the financial equivalent of a heart attack and were now on liquidity life support provided by the Federal Reserve), then U.S. Treasury Secretary Paulson approached the U.S. Congress and asked for authorization to issue up to U.S. $700 billion of Treasury securities to finance the purchase of "troubled assets" under the Troubled Assets Relief Plan (TARP). This proposal essentially called a time-out in the financial crisis and the system went on hold (on continuing Federal Reserve life support) while the U.S. Congress discussed the plan. However, the bill was met with American public outrage. Had the plan been adopted quickly, it is possible (though certainly unknown) that the TARP may have prevented the credit crisis from becoming a systemic financial crisis, with consequent impact on the real economy.

Although the U.S. financial crisis did not worsen dramatically during the week of September 20, credit markets essentially did not function and it can be said that it was in this period that we witnessed the first systemic crisis in the U.S. financial system since the 1930s. At the same time, however, we did not see a systemic collapse of the financial system in September 2008, which we did see following 1929. However, as the discussions lengthened, individual financial institutions began to fail, most significantly Washington Mutual in the United States.

By this time, the financial crisis was taking its toll around the world. On September 29, to prevent major financial institution failures, the United Kingdom nationalized Bradford & Bingley; Belgium, Netherlands, and Luxembourg nationalized Fortis; Germany announced the first rescue of Hypo Real Estate; Iceland nationalized its third-largest bank, Glitnir; and in the United States, Wachovia, the sixth-largest U.S. bank, agreed to be sold to Citigroup in a deal brokered over the weekend by the Federal Reserve and the Federal Deposit Insurance Corporation. The same day, the U.S. House of Representatives rejected the TARP, driving what had been a systemic financial crisis into a potentially systemic economic crisis. On September 30, France and Belgium rescued Dexia, and Ireland announced a blanket guarantee of all deposits in its financial system.

During the week after the failure of the TARP in the United States, global stock prices dropped viciously and the credit crisis moved from a financial event to an economic event, as credit ceased to be available not only across the financial system but also across the economy and the public lost confidence in the financial system.

With significant impetus from these events, the U.S. Congress passed a new bill, signed by the President on October 3. By this time, however, the financial crisis had moved to the real economy. During the following week, domestic responses appeared rapidly, including most significantly a £400 billion (U.S. $600 billion) rescue package from the United Kingdom, focusing on three elements: capital, liquidity, and funding.[26] These elements would subsequently become central to the international response to the systemic crisis that was to emerge the following week.

During this phase, international activity focused on the G-7, the center of global economic and financial policy coordination for the previous two decades and also the forum comprising the major economies suffering from the systemic financial crisis in the global financial system. During the week of October 6–10, a comprehensive global response emerged, with an announcement from the G-7 on October 10.[27] Although it was not sufficient to prevent the systemic financial crisis or significant economic damage, the response was sufficient to resuscitate the U.S. and global financial systems. Clearly, the focus at this point was directly on addressing the systemic financial crisis and halting its collapse. The statement and plan was rapidly reaffirmed by the full membership of the IMF and World Bank,[28] as well as the FSF and the European Union, with actions directly following the agreed on approach.

In addition, on October 8, the world's major central banks announced their first globally coordinated interest rate cut, with the U.S. Federal Reserve, European Central Bank (ECB), Bank of England, Bank of Sweden, Swiss National Bank, and the Bank of Canada all cutting interest rates by 50 basis points and issuing a coordinated statement for the first time. Further, in the aftermath of the G-7 and IMF–World Bank–FSF meetings the following

[26] HM Treasury, "Financial Support to the Banking Industry," Press Notice 100/08 (October 8, 2008).

[27] G-7 Finance Ministers and Central Bank Governors, Plan of Action, Washington, D.C. (October 10, 2008).

[28] See the "Communiqué of the International Monetary and Financial Committee of the Board of Governors of the International Monetary Fund," IMF Press Release 08/240 (October 11, 2008).

weekend, the Federal Reserve dramatically increased the provision of dollar liquidity to the world's major central banks, agreeing on October 13 to provide unlimited dollar liquidity to the ECB, Bank of England, Swiss National Bank, and Bank of Japan.

In the realm of financial regulation, the FSF met again in October in the context of the G-7 and IMF–World Bank annual meetings.[29] Although it was significant in terms of content, this report was subsequently largely subsumed in the November 2008 G-20 leaders' statement.

At the same time, although not sufficient to prevent widespread economic consequences, this coordinated approach and subsequent actions at the domestic and international level have been sufficient both to prevent the collapse of the global financial system and to begin to return it to operation.

D. *Act IV: Economic Crisis*

As a result of the crisis, the governments around the world were forced to intervene dramatically to prevent the systemic financial crisis from becoming a systemic financial collapse, including the use of interest rate cuts, massive liquidity infusions, capital injections, guarantees, and asset purchases. At the same time, these actions, although sufficient to prevent the collapse of the global financial system and most domestic financial systems (Iceland being the exception), were not sufficient to prevent major adverse economic consequences, albeit less severe to date than those of the 1930s.

In this phase, the concern generally moved to both the realization of insolvency issues in major financial sectors (especially the United States and the United Kingdom) and the general realization that the financial crisis, even if contained, had triggered a serious economic problem for almost every economy in the world (a "Great Recession").

1. Group of Twenty: November 2008

On November 15, 2008, following two days of meetings in Washington, D.C., the leaders of the G-20 released their first statement.[30] In this declaration, the G-20 discussed the causes of the crisis, committed to supporting an open global economy, and defined a range of actions to be taken (under the supervision of G-20 finance ministers) to reform financial regulation to avoid future

[29] FSF, "Report of the Financial Stability Forum on Enhancing Market and Institutional Resilience: Follow-Up on Implementation" (October 2008).

[30] See G-20, Declaration: Summit on Financial Markets and the World Economy, Washington, D.C. (November 15, 2008; hereafter "G-20 Declaration").

crises. Although the majority of press and market attention focused on the various global economic aspects (and the general lack of tangible success in this respect), in many ways the most significant aspects relate to the reform of financial regulation, while at the same time avoiding overregulation. In this context, the G-20 established five main principles to guide reforms: (1) strengthening transparency and accountability; (2) enhancing sound regulation; (3) promoting integrity in financial markets; (4) reinforcing international cooperation; and (5) reforming the financial architecture. For each of these five principles, the leaders established a detailed action plan,[31] incorporating immediate actions (to be taken by March 31, 2009) and medium-term actions. The detailed action plan establishes the core content of the refinements to international financial regulatory standards to take place. In addition, the leaders tasked finance ministers to give highest priority to six areas: (1) mitigating against pro-cyclicality in regulatory policy; (2) reviewing and aligning global accounting standards, particularly for complex securities; (3) strengthening the resilience and transparency of credit derivatives markets and reducing their systemic risks, including by improving the infrastructure of the over-the-counter markets; (4) reviewing compensation practices as they relate to incentives for risk taking and innovation; (5) reviewing the international financial architecture; and (6) defining the scope of systemically important financial institutions and determining their appropriate regulation and oversight.

Although much of the detail had been previously addressed by the FSF, the November G-20 Declaration established the general framework for the content of financial regulation going forward.

2. Group of Twenty: April 2009

On April 2, 2009, the G-20 leaders met a second time in London to address issues relating to the financial crisis and resulting economic crisis. In their communiqué,[32] the leaders revisited many of the issues discussed in November 2008: "We face the greatest challenge to the world economy in modern times. . . . A global crisis requires a global solution."[33] To address the financial and economic crisis and prevent future crises, the leaders pledged "to do whatever is necessary" to (1) restore confidence and growth; (2) repair the financial system; (3) "strengthen financial regulation to rebuild trust"; (4) fund and

[31] G-20, Action Plan to Implement Principles for Reform, Washington, D.C. (November 15, 2008).

[32] G-20, The Global Plan for Recovery and Reform, London (April 2, 2009; hereafter, "G-20 Leaders' Statement."

[33] Id., paragraph 2.

reform the international financial institutions; (5) reject protectionism and promote global trade and investment; and (6) "build an inclusive, green, and sustainable recovery."[34]

As headline numbers, the G-20 committed to making available U.S. $1.1 trillion in international resources, including (1) trebling IMF resources to U.S. $750 billion; (2) approving a special U.S. $250 billion Special Drawing Rights allocation; (3) increasing MDB lending by over U.S. $100 billion; (4) making available U.S. $250 billion in trade finance; and (5) selling some IMF gold reserves to provide additional funding for poverty alleviation.

In relation to restoring growth and jobs, the G-20 first committed to fiscal expansion of U.S. $5 trillion by the end of 2010 and to "accelerate transition to a green economy"[35] and building long-term fiscal sustainability, price stability, and sustainable exit strategies.[36] Second, in relation to financial stability, the leaders committed to repair of their financial systems, including IMF assessments of all their financial sectors.[37] Third, in relation to money affairs, the leaders committed to refrain from competitive devaluation and promote a stable and well-functioning international monetary system backed by IMF assessments.[38]

In relation to financial regulation and supervision, the leaders committed to "build a stronger, more globally consistent, supervisory and regulatory framework for the future financial sector, which will support sustainable growth and serve the needs of business and citizens."[39] Significantly, the leaders committed to continued implementation of the November Action Plan, with substantial progress in all areas relating to financial regulation,[40] and also extended their commitments in nine major areas,[41] with finance ministers responsible for implementation and the IMF and FSF (renamed and reconstituted as the Financial Stability Board, or FSB) monitoring and reporting at the next G-20 Finance Ministers' Meeting to be held in autumn 2009.[42] Of these, the most

34 Id., paragraph 4.

35 G-20 Leaders' Statement, *supra* note 33, paragraph 6.

36 Id., paragraph 11.

37 Id., paragraph 10.

38 Id., paragraph 14.

39 Id., paragraph 13.

40 Id., paragraph 15. See G-20, "Progress Report on the Actions of the Washington Action Plan" (April 2, 2009).

41 G-20 Leaders' Statement, *supra* note 33, paragraph 15. See also G-20, Declaration on Strengthening the Financial System (April 2, 2009); G-20, "G20 Working Group 1 – Enhancing Sound Regulation and Strengthening Transparency: Final Report" (March 2009); G-20, "G20 Working Group on Reinforcing International Cooperation and Promoting Integrity in Financial Markets (WG2): Final Report" (March 2009).

42 G-20 Leaders' Statement, *supra* note 33, paragraph 16.

significant relate to the reform of the FSF into the FSB.[43] This is the foundation of reform of the system of international financial standards as opposed to their content, the focus of the Washington meeting. Second, the FSB and IMF were directed "to provide early warning of macroeconomic and financial risks and the actions needed to address them."[44]

In relation to strengthening global financial institutions, the G-20 provides detail of their headline funding commitments of an additional U.S. $850 billion to "support growth in emerging market and developing countries by helping to finance counter-cyclical spending, bank recapitalisation, infrastructure, trade finance, balance of payments support, and social support,"[45] with additional details provided in a second annex.[46] As a second element, the G-20 statement provides directions to address issues relating to the relevance, effectiveness, and legitimacy of the IMF and MDBs. Specifically, mandates, scope, and governance are to be reviewed and reformed "to reflect changes in the world economy and the new challenges of globalisation."[47] Better strategic oversight and decision making are mandated to enhance credibility and accountability.[48] The IFI Declaration (concerning international financial institutions) adds to these mandates strengthening cooperation and coordination and providing emerging and developing countries greater voice and representation.[49] Finally, the leaders commit to develop a charter for sustainable economic activity embodying a "new global consensus on the key values and principles that will promote sustainable economic activity."[50]

Following criticism of trade-related commitments from their November Summit, the G-20 April statement expands and hardens these. First, previous commitments to refrain from raising new barriers to investment or to trade in goods and services, imposing new export restrictions, or implementing WTO inconsistent measures to stimulate exports are reaffirmed and extended to the

43 Id., paragraph 15. On March 12, 2009, the FSF announced the expansion of its membership along these lines, with the inclusion of Argentina, Brazil, China, the European Commission, India, Indonesia, Mexico, Russia, Saudi Arabia, South Africa, South Korea, Spain, and Turkey. FSF, "Financial Stability Forum Decides to Broaden its Membership," Press Release (March 12, 2009).

44 G-20 Leaders' Statement, *supra* note 33, paragraph 15.

45 Id., paragraph 17.

46 G-20, Declaration on Delivering Resources through the International Financial Institutions, London, (April 2, 2009; hereafter, "G-20 IFI Declaration").

47 G-20 Leaders' Statement, *supra* note 33, paragraph 20.

48 Id.

49 G-20 IFI Declaration, *supra* note 47, p. 2.

50 G-20 Leaders' Statement, *supra* note 33, paragraph 21.

end of 2010, with any such measures to be promptly rectified.[51] Second, any negative impact on trade and investment of domestic policy actions including fiscal policy and action in support of the financial sector, including avoiding financial protectionism, particularly measures that constrain worldwide capital flows, especially to developing countries, is to be minimized.[52] These are supported by a commitment to notify the WTO promptly of any such measures; the WTO and other international bodies, within their respective mandates, are to monitor and report publicly on adherence on a quarterly basis.[53] Third, leaders commit to "take whatever steps possible to promote and facilitate trade and investment" and reiterate IFI commitments in relation to trade finance as already described.[54] Finally, they committed to completion of the Doha Trade Round.[55]

In looking forward, although they are limited, commitments relating to a fair and sustainable recovery highlight a number of significant issues and, one hopes, directions at the international level. Significantly, the leaders stressed that they were "determined not only to restore growth but to lay the foundation for a fair and sustainable world economy."[56] In this regard, they reaffirmed their commitment to meeting the Millennium Development Goals and to achieving development aid pledges.[57] In relation to climate change and sustainability, the leaders agreed that the overall objective is "transition towards clean, innovative, resource efficient, low carbon technologies and infrastructure" and tasked the MDBs to support this process,[58] and they reaffirmed commitment to address climate change "based on principles of common but differentiated responsibilities" with a successful completion of the UN Copenhagen Climate Change Conference to take place in December 2009.[59]

Overall, if the Washington communiqué provided the outline of the content of international financial regulation going forward, the London communiqué provides the outline of the system of international financial regulation as well as additional detail regarding content. At the same time, details of the reform of the IFIs such as the IMF are left for the next leaders' summit in September 2009 in Pittsburgh.

[51] Id., paragraph 22.
[52] Id.
[53] Id.
[54] Id.
[55] Id., paragraphs 23–24.
[56] Id., paragraph 25.
[57] Id., paragraph 26.
[58] Id., paragraph 27.
[59] Id., paragraph 28.

E. *Act V: Return to a New Normal?*

Perhaps as early as the autumn 2010 G-20 and FSB meetings, it may be possible to begin to see the outlines of the agreed on pattern for the international financial architecture and international financial regulation. At the same time, however, the pattern will take at least another year to work its way into systems of international institutions, treaties, standards, and domestic laws and regulations.

5. LOOKING FORWARD

As a result of the current global financial crisis, the post-Asian crisis financial stability regime system has been exposed as insufficient to meet the realities of global finance and its attendant risks. At the most fundamental level is the question that was addressed at Bretton Woods: On balance, should finance be global? Although the decision taken at Bretton Woods was in the negative, in the context of the global financial crisis, despite some misgivings, the consensus appears to be settling in favor of continued globalization of finance, albeit with enhanced mechanisms for prevention and resolution of problems that arise.

At the international level, the general elements that need to be addressed have not changed fundamentally, although their context has. To date, the outlines of a system of sorts appear to be emerging: (1) economic dialogue, policy cooperation, and coordination through the G-20, though with some role for the UN in the context of development and climate change; (2) trade (including in financial services) through the WTO; and (3) sustainable development coordination and assistance through the UN and MDBs, however with questions remaining regarding financial sector issues, macroeconomic restructuring, trade finance, climate change and food security issues.

In relation to macroeconomic policy and finance, whereas coordination is occurring via the G-20, macroeconomic assessment and surveillance for macroeconomic stability rest with the IMF. In the context of financial stability, international standards and coordination lie with the FSB, with implementation at the domestic and regional levels and monitoring and assessment currently with the IMF but likely to be shifted to some sort of peer review mechanism via the FSB. At the same time, major issues exist with respect to crisis management, both for liquidity and resolution of sovereign and global financial institution crises. In the context of liquidity, domestic arrangements have been supplemented with bilateral arrangements (through the U.S. Federal Reserve, the ECB and the People's Bank of China), regional arrangements (in Europe and Asia), with international liquidity support through the IMF.

Major issues, however, remain with respect to crisis resolution, with the current IMF-centered structure subject to major criticisms. At the same time, no arrangements exist for resolving crises of global financial institutions, such as Lehman Brothers.[60]

In this context, the discussion in many ways has followed the forms of global administrative law, with a range of approaches from a traditional hard law treaty-based approach centered on a formal international organization down to uncoordinated domestic responses. Although the latter have been found to be ineffective in the context of global finance (albeit not domestic finance under the Bretton Woods design), despite periodic proposals for a global financial regulator, a traditional international law–institution approach does not seem feasible at this time, even in the context of the European Union: Issues of domestic sovereignty continue to make a global regulator for global finance unlikely for the foreseeable future. In looking forward, on balance, it appears to make little sense to incorporate financial regulation into the WTO framework, both because the WTO system is already overburdened and also because of its focus on negotiated liberalization combined with dispute resolution, which is not overly useful in the context of financial regulation. At the same time, however, if amendments are to be undertaken to the IMF Articles of Agreement, then this would also present an opportunity to provide the Fund with a specific mandate and related tools in relation to financial regulatory surveillance. However, it is uncertain at this time whether actual amendment will be the path chosen – though for a variety of reasons beyond the scope of this article, this is probably in fact necessary though not politically simple, even in the present crisis environment.[61]

At the other end of the spectrum, purely soft law cooperative arrangements (such as the Basel Committee and the 1988 Basel Capital Accord) such as those that existed until 1999 have proven ineffective in preventing and resolving international crises such as the Asian financial crisis. Instead, the approach that has been adopted at the international level by the G2-0 is a further hardening of the precrisis system, through the strengthening of the FSF into the FSB, with a wider range of member commitments and strengthened peer review and external monitoring mechanisms.

However, what has become most interesting as the crisis has progressed is the realm of international relations. First, in the context of international economic dialogue, the G-7 seems to have been eclipsed by the G-20,

60 See D. Arner and J. Norton, "Building a Framework to Address Failure of Complex Global Financial Institutions," 39 *Hong Kong L. J.* (2009) 95.

61 See D. Arner and R. Buckley, "Redesigning the Architecture of the Global Financial System," 11:2 *Melbourne J. Int'l L.* (2010).

with developing countries (especially China) now being increasingly assertive across the international economic spectrum. Second, in relation to trade, the general principle of liberal trade has for the most part been widely reaffirmed throughout the crisis, though with certain exceptions relating to security issues (such as food and energy). At the same time, however, it seems that there is now no consensus and probably no motivating actor to lead further liberalization of trade in financial services; this principle has perhaps been a casualty of the crisis. Third, in relation to development, a new base set of principles may soon emerge, relating to sustainability, at Copenhagen in December. Fourth, in relation to financial stability, although global finance has been largely reaffirmed, countries are still unwilling to build effective mechanisms to address the problems that it brings, including an effective institutional framework for prevention through regulation, management through international liquidity arrangements, and effective mechanisms to resolve sovereign and firm crises when they arise in the future. Finally, in relation to investment, although support appears clear for both direct Greenfield and portfolio investment, acquisitions of major domestic enterprises or in strategic sectors look increasingly in doubt. The conclusion, then, must be that although the post-Asian crisis regime has been adjusted, at the present a comprehensive regime for financial stability has not yet emerged from the current global financial crisis.

PART IV

THE POLITICS OF DISPUTE SETTLEMENT IN INTERNATIONAL ECONOMIC LAW

11

Ruling Not to Rule

The Use of Judicial Economy by WTO Panels

Marc L. Busch and Krzysztof J. Pelc

1. INTRODUCTION

Despite the fact that panels at the World Trade Organization (WTO) exercise judicial economy in nearly half their rulings, little has been written on the subject.[1] This is surprising, because judicial economy is *the* issue-avoidance technique that panels use to avoid ruling on legal claims that they do not regard as being necessary to resolving the dispute at hand. Add to this that there are few hard and fast rules governing its use, and that litigants often appeal the panel's exercise of judicial economy, and we have all the makings of political intrigue. Indeed, observers agree that politics probably has a lot to do with it, though few venture a guess as to why judicial economy is practiced in some contentious cases but not in others. In this chapter, we seek to fill in this gap in the literature.[2] Our argument is that panels exercise judicial economy to limit the scope of the case law that results from their rulings, and they do so because of concerns raised by the wider membership, which has voice through third parties. Specifically, panels take those third parties siding with *both* the complainant and defendant – offering what we call mixed submissions – as a credible signal of the membership's ambivalence about the scope of a ruling.

[1] Notable exceptions include Jan Bohanes and Andreas Sennekamp, "Reflections on the Concept of 'Judicial Economy' in WTO Dispute Settlement," in G. Sacerdoti et al. (eds.), *The WTO at Ten: The Contribution of the Dispute Settlement System* (2006) 424; William Davey, "Has the WTO Dispute Settlement System Exceeded Its Authority? A Consideration of Deference Shown by the System to Member Government Decisions and its Use of Issue-Avoidance Techniques," 4 (1) *Journal of International Economic Law* (2001) 79; and brief mentions in Richard Steinberg, "Judicial Lawmaking at the WTO: Discursive, Constitutional, and Political Constraints," 98 (2) *American Journal of International Law* (2004) 247, at 269; Robert Hudec, "GATT Dispute Settlement after the Tokyo Round: An Unfinished Business," 13 (2) *Cornell International Law Journal* (1980) 145, at 189–192.

[2] This chapter draws on Marc Busch and Krzysztof Pelc, "The Politics of Judicial Economy at the World Trade Organization," 64 (2) *International Organization* (2010), 257.

Bringing data to bear on our argument, we find that an increase in the number of third parties offering mixed submissions increases the odds that the panel exercises judicial economy by as much as 67 percent.

2. JUDICIAL ECONOMY

The intuition of judicial economy is clearly set out by the Appellate Body (AB) in *US – Wool Shirts and Blouses*: "[a] panel need only address those claims which must be addressed in order to resolve the matter in issue in the dispute."[3] This means that, if a complainant argues X, Y, and Z, and the panel considers its rulings on X and Y sufficient to resolving the dispute at hand, it need not rule on Z. Where things get interesting is that the AB has explained that panels are *not* obliged to practice judicial economy under such circumstances, and that they should not get carried away if they do. First, in *US – Lead and Bismuth II*, the AB rejected the idea that "panels may *not* address any issues that need *not* be addressed in order to resolve the dispute between the parties."[4] Second, the AB has been especially worried that panels will be overly zealous in avoiding issues that are crucial to resolving the dispute, falling victim to what, in *Australia – Salmon*, it referred to as "false judicial economy."[5] In short, far from predetermining the use of judicial economy, WTO rules – and AB verdicts – give panels great latitude in this regard. Not surprisingly, some observers insist that panels could use judicial economy more than they do,[6] whereas others are struck by how often they use it.[7]

In *EC – Bed Linen* (EC stands for European Communities), an antidumping case brought by India, the panel reasoned that, "in light of considerations of judicial economy, it is neither necessary nor appropriate to make findings" on three of the complainant's claims,[8] a decision that was recorded without any comment by the AB.[9] This is what the AB had in mind in *US – Wool Shirts and Blouses*: Because, in the opinion of the panel, a review of further claims

[3] See WTO, "Report of the Appellate Body, United States – Measures Affecting Imports of Woven Wool Shirts and Blouses from India," WT/DS33/AB/R (1997), at 19–20.

[4] See WTO, "Report of the Appellate Body, United States – Imposition of Countervailing Duties on Certain Hot-Rolled Lead and Bismuth Carbon Steel Products Originating in the United Kingdom," WT/DS138/AB/R (2001), at 25–26.

[5] See WTO, "Report of the Appellate Body, Australia – Measures Affecting Importation of Salmon, " WT/DS18/AB/R (1998), at paragraph 223.

[6] Davey, *supra* note 1, at 70.

[7] Bohanes and Sennekamp, *supra* note 1, at 441.

[8] See WTO, "Report of the Panel, European Communities – Anti-dumping Duties on Imports of Cotton-Type Bed Linen from India," WT/DS141/R (2000), at paragraph 7.3(c).

[9] WTO, *supra* note 8, at fn. 6.

would not contribute much to the substance of the verdict, it was entirely reasonable for it to invoke judicial economy.

In *Argentina – Footwear (EC)*, by way of contrast, the panel did *not* invoke judicial economy. Here, Europe challenged an Argentine safeguard, and the panel completed an analysis of other issues it thought important. The AB strongly disagreed, perplexed by the panel's decision to examine claims of causation after having already found that there was *no* increase in imports, and *no* serious injury. In fact, the surprised AB observed that it "would be difficult, indeed, to demonstrate a 'causal link' between 'increased imports' that did not occur and 'serious injury' that did not exist."[10] Nevertheless, the AB added that it had found no error in the panel's views on causation, or on the Safeguard Agreement more generally. In short, the AB not only tolerates but promotes the use of judicial economy when it is appropriate. The question is, when is it appropriate?

Input on this is offered by the litigants, who often register a clear preference for or against judicial economy. Indeed, they routinely advise panels on its appropriateness and often appeal its use when they disagree with the panel's course of action. For their part, panels are seldom swayed by this lobbying. In *Korea – Paper*, for example, Indonesia spent a sizeable portion of its submissions arguing that the panel should not exercise judicial economy, warning that this would be false judicial economy.[11] The panel invoked it all the same. In *Mexico – Soft Drinks*, the defendant linked its argument about *jurisdiction* to the concept of judicial economy, pleading with the panel to exercise it, but to no avail.[12] By way of contrast, in *US – Zeroing (EC)*, the complainant insisted that the panel avoid exercising judicial economy, yet with no success.[13] As we show in the text that follows, litigants, in general, have fared poorly in this respect. Rather, it is certain third parties that are influential.

But does judicial economy really matter? After all, how big a deal is it for a panel to sidestep certain legal claims when the average dispute centers on eight arguments? The key is that judicial economy shapes the very contours of WTO law. This is because earlier rulings are used to justify current ones, such that a panel's decision not to rule on specific legal claims can have a substantial influence on the jurisprudence of the multilateral trade regime. Raj Bhala, for

[10] See WTO, "Report of the Appellate Body, Argentina – Safeguard Measures on Imports of Footwear," WT/DS121/AB/R (1999), at paragraph 145.

[11] See WTO, "Report of the Panel, Korea – Anti-dumping Duties on Imports of Certain Paper from Indonesia," WT/DS312/R (2005), at paragraph 6.24.

[12] See WTO, "Report of the Panel, Mexico – Tax Measures on Soft Drinks and Other Beverages," WT/DS308/R (2005).

[13] See WTO, "Report of the Panel, United States – Laws, Regulations and Methodology for Calculating Dumping Margins (Zeroing)," WT/DS294/R (2008).

example, goes so far as to argue that the widespread use of judicial economy is, itself, evidence that there is de facto stare decisis – or quasi-binding precedent – at the WTO.[14] Indeed, absent quasi-binding precedent, judicial economy would lose much of its meaning, and it would neither be the subject of such contention nor be resorted to nearly as often. He concludes that judicial economy is a "principle of self-restraint" by panels that has been affirmed by the AB "in a way strongly reminiscent of a common law court."[15]

The significance of judicial economy can further be gleaned from the institution's case law itself. In *Canada – Dairy*, for example, the question of whether to resort to judicial economy arose in the context of Articles 9.1 and 10.1 of the Agreement on Agriculture. Because Articles 9.1 and 10.1 "complement each other by focusing on different subsidy elements" and the borderline between them is "not always clear-cut,"[16] judicial economy could have been invoked to rule on one article and omit the other. The panel in this case repeatedly mentioned this possibility, but it chose to complete its investigation and make rulings on both articles – *despite the fact that no complainant had requested it to do so* – in anticipation that this would help the AB if appealed.[17] In the process of ruling on Article 9.1(c), the panel found that both payments in kind and payments through reduced input prices were payments under Article 9.1. Later, this interpretation was cited by the complainants and third parties (including Canada, against whom the original ruling was made) in *EC – Sugar*, and it became the basis for the ruling against the EC on Article 9.1(c) in that case. Had judicial economy been exercised by the panel in *Canada – Dairy*, that precedent would not have been available.

These disputes are compelling in light of our argument: In *Canada – Dairy*, where the panel did *not* exercise judicial economy, all third parties sided with the complainant, whereas in *EC – Sugar*, where the panel faced exactly the same choice but decided *not* to rule on Article 10.1, three third parties offered mixed submissions. More interesting still, the panel in *EC – Sugar* invoked the reasoning of the panel in *Canada – Dairy* over the logical link between Articles 9.1 and 10.1 in justifying its exercise of judicial economy with regard to Article 10.1.[18] This happened despite the fact that the panel in

[14] Bhala, Raj, "The Precedent Setters: De Facto Stare Decisis in WTO Adjudication (Part Two of a Trilogy)," 9 (1) *Journal of Transnational Law and Policy* (1999) 1, at 48.
[15] Ibid., at 49 and 51.
[16] See WTO, "Report of the Panel, Canada – Measures Affecting the Importation of Milk and the Exportation of Dairy Products," WT/DS103/R (1999), at paragraph 7.119(c).
[17] Ibid., at paragraph 7.119(e).
[18] See WTO, "Report of the Panel, European Communities – Export Subsidies on Sugar," WT/DS283/R (2004), at paragraph 7.371.

Canada – Dairy used this reasoning to draw the *opposite* conclusion, and chose to finish its analysis.

3. CONVENTIONAL WISDOM

The literature speculates that politics probably plays a role in panels' decisions to exercise judicial economy. Along these lines, William Davey explains that judicial economy is an appropriate means of avoiding "controversial issues" in rendering a decision.[19] Similarly, Reinhard Quick and Andreas Blüthner urge that judicial economy was "legally shocking" in *EC – Hormones*, chalking it up to the considerable controversy surrounding the health and safety standards at issue.[20]

Scholars have long examined ways in which states actively "signal their displeasure" with legal rulings, including threatening to renegotiate agreements, seeking outside options, or restricting the authority of the legal body itself.[21] Others urge that international institutions take it upon themselves to limit their rulings to preempt members from constraining their behavior. Arguments of this sort are commonplace in studies of the European Court of Justice (ECJ),[22] the United Nations Human Rights Committee,[23] and the WTO's AB, among others.[24] With respect to the WTO, Richard Steinberg refers to the concept of "strategic space" to denote the legal and political constraints that panels and the AB function within.[25] Steinberg goes so far as to suggest that the AB has an interest in learning about, and abiding by, these constraints, and that, to do

19 Davey, *supra* note 1, at 109.

20 Reinhardt Quick and Andreas Blüthner, "Has the Appellate Body Erred? An Appraisal and Criticism of the Ruling in the WTO 'Hormones Case'," 2 (4) *Journal of International Economic Law* (1999) 603, at 635.

21 Laurence Helfer and Anne-Marie Slaughter, "Why States Create International Tribunals: A Response to Professors Posner and Yoo," 93 *California Law Review* (2005) 1.

22 Geoffrey Garrett, Daniel Keleman, and Heiner Schulz, "The European Court of Justice, National Governments, and Legal Integration in the European Union," 52 (1) *International Organization* (1998) 149, at 150.

23 Helfer and Slaughter, *supra* note 21, at 56.

24 James McCall Smith, "WTO Dispute Settlement: The Politics of Procedure in Appellate Body Rulings," 2 (1) *World Trade Review* (2003) 65; Geoffrey Garrett and James McCall Smith, "The Politics of WTO Dispute Settlement," UCLA manuscript (2002); Daniel Kelemen, "The Limits of Judicial Power: Trade–Environment Disputes in the GATT/WTO and the EU," 34 (6) *Comparative Political Studies* (2001) 622.

25 The limits within which the panel operates can be seen as embodied in Article 3.2 of the Dispute Settlement Understanding: On one hand, the panel must "clarify the existing provisions of those agreements in accordance with customary rules of interpretation of public international law," and on the other, it cannot "cannot add to or diminish the rights and obligations provided in the covered agreements."

so, it needs to "obtain information on the preferences of members," although he does not pin down the means by which the AB accomplishes this.[26] What is lacking, then, is a better sense for how panels assimilate members' preferences, on the one hand, and an explanation of how WTO panels respond to this information, on the other. We argue that the answer to the first question can be found in the input of third parties, specifically those that offer mixed submissions; the answer to the second question rests on panels' use of judicial economy.

WTO scholars put judicial economy alongside other formal issue-avoidance techniques[27] like *non liquet* (i.e., asserting that the law is unclear) and *in dubio mitius* (i.e., adopting the least restrictive interpretation for the member in those cases in which the law is ambiguous). However, both these measures have been employed exactly once across all disputes.[28] By comparison, panels exercise some judicial economy in 41 percent of their rulings. Put simply, if issue-avoidance happens at the WTO, it happens through the use of judicial economy.

The literature on judicial economy that exists focuses mostly on its consequences for the dispute at hand. Observers voice concern, for example, about the combination of judicial economy and the AB's lack of ability to *remand* – that is, to send back to the panel for further consideration – a given ruling.[29] To be sure, in overturning the panel, the AB may, in the process, nullify its reason for invoking judicial economy. When this happens, the AB is not always able to go back and complete the analysis on a legal claim that the panel chose not to rule on, because the AB has no fact-finding ability of its own. Furthermore, because it cannot remand matters, this means that, on appeal, judicial economy sometimes leaves potentially valid claims unexamined, making the

[26] Steinberg, *supra* note 1, at 269.

[27] These should be distinguished from issue-avoidance techniques that need not be flagged as such by the panel. Judicial interpretation and textualism can play such a function, for example, but their use is not identifiable in a consistent manner across disputes (we thank Tomer Broude for bringing this to our attention). By contrast, the use of judicial economy must be identified as such by the panel.

[28] In *EC – Asbestos* and *EC – Hormones* (WT/DS135/AB/R and WT/DS26), respectively. See Joost Pauwelyn, "Cross-Agreement Complaints before the Appellate Body: A Case Study of the EC–Asbestos Dispute," 1 (1) *World Trade Review* (2002) 63. Hudec and Steinberg draw attention to the possibility of using *non liquet* at the WTO, but Pauwelyn insists that this is generally precluded by the Dispute Settlement Understanding. See Robert Hudec, "GATT Dispute Settlement," *supra* note 1; Steinberg, *supra* note 1; and Joost Pauwelyn, "The Role of Public International Law in the WTO: How Far Can We Go?," 95 (3) *American Journal of International Law* (2001) 535.

[29] Davey, *supra* note 1.

dispute more difficult to resolve, as occurred in *EC – Sugar*.[30] Other issues arise when panels choose the order in which they examine claims, because this can determine which claims are likely to be left unexamined in the event that judicial economy is employed.[31] The point to these observations is that judicial economy comes at a price; rather than serving as a means of *economizing* legal resources, as the term is typically taken to mean in the context of domestic courts, judicial economy is the subject of much discussion among parties to disputes, as the complainant and the respondent each argue for or against its use, and it is a frequent cause of appeals. Accordingly, reasoning over its exercise (or lack thereof) regularly takes up large sections of panel reports. Rather than economizing resources, then, judicial economy at the WTO is a means by which panels practice self-restraint in cases in which a broader ruling may be politically untenable. This is the point of departure for our argument.

4. ARGUMENT

Panels exercise judicial economy to limit the precedent set by a ruling where the wider membership is ambivalent about its scope. By precedent, we simply mean that rulings influence subsequent disputes by contributing to the body of WTO jurisprudence. This definition is not controversial; as David Palmeter and Petros C. Mavroidis explain it, "parties will continue to cite prior reports to panels, and panels will continue to take them into account by adopting their reasoning – *in effect, following precedent*."[32] Echoing this sentiment,

30 See WTO, "Report of the Appellate Body, European Communities – Export Subsidies on Sugar," WT/DS265/AB/R (2005); WTO, "Report of the Appellate Body, European Communities – Export Subsidies on Sugar," WT/DS266/AB/R (2005), at paragraph 341.

31 See, e.g., WTO, "Report of the Panel, India – Measures Affecting the Automotive Sector," WT/DS146/R (1998).

32 David Palmeter, David and Petros Mavroidis, *Dispute Settlement in the World Trade Organization: Practice and Procedure*, 2nd ed. (2004) at 56; emphasis added. See also William Davey, "The WTO/GATT World Trading system: An Overview," in P. Pescatore, W. Davey, and A. Lowenfeld (eds.), *Handbook of WTO/GATT Dispute Settlement*, Vol. 1 (1998) 7, at 79; John Jackson, "Designing and Implementing Effective Dispute Settlement Procedures: WTO Dispute Settlement, Appraisal and Prospects," in A. Krueger (ed.), *The WTO as an International Organization* (1998) 161, at 183; Norio Komuro, "The WTO Dispute Settlement Mechanism: Coverage and Procedures of the WTO Understanding," 29 (4) *Journal of World Trade* (1995) 5, at 37; Ernst-Ulrich Petersmann, "The Dispute Settlement System of the World Trade Organization and the Evolution of the GATT Disputes Settlement System Since 1948," 31 (6) *Common Market Law Review* (1994) 1157, at 1175; David Huntington, "Settling Disputes under the North American Free Trade Agreement," 34 (2) *Harvard International Law Journal* (1993) 407, at 435; and Ivo Van Bael, "The GATT Dispute Settlement Procedure," 22 (4) *Journal of World Trade* (1988) 67, at 69.

Steinberg adds that the importance of a ruling "lies not only in its implications for the national measures that are the subject of the decision, *but also in its precedential value*."[33] Bhala, as already noted, calls this de facto stare decisis, which, in contrast to de jure stare decisis, is followed for extralegal and quasi-legal factors, including custom and habit, rather than as a matter of legal requirement.[34] That said, he insists that *both* are "binding" sources of law, in that they establish a presumption that precedents will be followed in the future.[35]

The AB could not agree more, explaining in a highly important ruling that "[t]he reasoning in our Report in *United States – Shrimp* on which the Panel relied was not *dicta*; it was essential to our ruling. *The Panel was right to use it, and right to rely on it.* Nor are we surprised that the panel made frequent references to our Report in *United States – Shrimp. Indeed, we would have expected the Panel to do so*."[36] Similarly, in a highly anticipated comment on the role of precedent in WTO disputes, the AB explained in *US – Zeroing (Mexico)* that "following the Appellate Body's conclusions in earlier disputes is not only appropriate, but is what would be expected from panels, especially where the issues are the same."[37] Because the panel had strayed, in this regard, the AB went on to clarify that "failure to follow previously adopted Appellate Body reports addressing the same issues undermines the development of a coherent and predictable body of jurisprudence clarifying Members' rights and obligations under the covered agreements as contemplated under the DSU [Dispute Settlement Understanding]."[38] In sum, the practice of WTO law is such that, as Bhala quips, it is only "[o]ur intellectual rigidity [that] precludes us from admitting openly that the holdings of the Appellate Body – and, for that matter, panel – reports actually are a source of international law."[39]

Given that precedent matters, we present our argument in two steps. First, panels hold preferences over the results of their rulings. In the dispute at hand, they would prefer both to gain the litigants' compliance and avoid

33 Steinberg, *supra* note 1, at 254; emphasis added.

34 Bhala, *supra* note 14, at 3–4.

35 Ibid., at 9.

36 See WTO, "Report of the Appellate Body, Import Prohibition of Certain Shrimp and Shrimp Products – Recourse to Article 21.5," WT/DS58/AB/RW (2001), at paragraph 107; emphasis added.

37 WT/DS344/AB/R, "Report of the Appellate Body, United States – Final Anti-dumping Measures on Stainless Steel from Mexico," WT/DS58/AB/RW (2008), at paragraph 159.

38 Ibid., at paragraph 161.

39 Raj Bhala, "The Myth about Stare Decisis and International Trade Law (Part One of a Trilogy)," 14 (4) *American University International Law Review* (1999) 845, at 850–851.

appeal, or, in the alternative, have their findings upheld by the AB. Much of this depends on how the ruling is likely to impact the acquis of WTO case law. Because panel reports become part of the jurisprudence that governs dispute settlement, panels have to consider the broader ramifications of ruling on all of the litigants' arguments in establishing a broader or narrower precedent, not least because the AB has incentive to be politically savvy as well. If the panel addresses all the legal issues raised, then there is potentially more for the litigants to appeal, whereas if it addresses fewer, then the risk is that the litigants will make – and the AB may uphold – charges of false judicial economy.

In balancing the reasons for judicial economy with the risk of false judicial economy, panels look to input from third parties. As James McCall Smith observes, the AB encourages third party participation precisely "to gain access to valuable information regarding the views of the broader WTO membership."[40] At the panel stage, third parties with a "substantial interest"[41] in the dispute are permitted under Article 10 of the DSU to deliver both written and oral testimony during the first of (what is typically) two rounds of litigation, and thus have access to the first (of the two) submissions of the litigants.[42] The views expressed by third parties, which are recounted in both the interim[43] and final report, are to be taken into account by the panel in rendering a verdict. If the ruling is, in turn, appealed, DSU Article 17 gives those third parties that reserved rights at the panel stage the same access to proceedings before the AB. Members typically reserve third-party rights when they have a commercial stake in a dispute, but not one that is sufficient to commit the resources necessary to join as a co-complainant. All told, they participate in 65 percent of WTO disputes. Looking back over the past twenty disputes in our data set (which roughly coincides with China's entry into the WTO in 2001), the members who most frequently reserve third-party rights include the United States and the EC (100 percent), China (95 percent), Japan (66.7 percent), Chinese Taipei (62 percent), Mexico (47.4 percent), and Canada

[40] Smith, *supra* note 24, at 75 and 85.

[41] A "substantial interest" can include noneconomic factors, including simply having a stake in how the agreement is interpreted more generally. This is a lower "entry barrier" than in consultations, where the requirement is that the would-be third party have a "substantial trade interest."

[42] A few WTO members have taken to posting all of their submissions online, but this is the exception, not the rule. To gain access to the vast majority of submissions, a member must reserve third-party rights.

[43] The interim report, which precedes the final report, is issued only to the litigants and *not* third parties. It is intended to give the complainant(s) and defendant a preview of what is to come in the final report, the hope being that a "peek behind the curtain" will motivate a negotiated settlement.

(36.8 percent), though Australia, Brazil, Chile, Costa Rica, Colombia, Ecuador, Guatemala, Honduras, India, Korea, Norway, and Switzerland, among others, also make the list. Indeed, it is no exaggeration to say that if a developing country, in particular, has experience with WTO dispute settlement, it is as a third party.

Second, the most influential third-party input in this regard is *mixed*, rather than partisan, submissions. Third parties are typically partisan, siding with the complainant 56 percent of the time, versus 32 percent with the defendant. They can influence the direction of a ruling by endorsing either litigants' arguments. In *Dominican Republic – Cigarettes*, for example, the defendant decried the fact that "[i]t was not until the first meeting of the Panel that Honduras suddenly included all of the products in the complaint, *taking the idea from the written submissions of certain third parties*."[44] Conversely, in *EC – Sugar*, the panel listened to African, Caribbean, and Pacific (ACP) countries who, as third parties, argued for a protectionist regime that discriminated in their favor. Looking at all WTO disputes through 2002, one study finds that in cases that attract partisan third parties, the likelihood of a pro-complainant or pro-defendant ruling rises by one-half and one-third, respectively.[45]

However, another 12 percent of third parties are *not* partisan. Rather, they deliver mixed submissions, meaning that they support and critique both sides in the dispute, often on the exact same legal claim, or comment on how the panel should balance the competing arguments before it. These mixed submissions, which are offered in 20 percent of all disputes, are strikingly different from partisan submissions. This is not to say that these third parties are honest brokers, because they, like their partisan counterparts, tend to have a commercial interest at stake. Third parties giving mixed submissions are influential inasmuch as their ambivalence is a credible signal of the wider membership's sensibilities. To be sure, whereas partisan arguments reflect coalitional politics in the case at hand, and thus have an impact on who wins, mixed submissions indicate deeper questions about how a ruling would bear on future disputes.

Moreover, this input is informative precisely because it is *not* offered by honest brokers. The fact that third parties have a commercial interest at stake means that mixed submissions are costly for them to make, because they forego influence over a more encompassing legal victory in the dispute at hand – that is, one in which all of the legal arguments are ruled upon – that would

[44] See WTO, "Report of the Panel, Dominican Republic – Measures Affecting the Importation and Internal Sale of Cigarettes," WT/DS302/R (2004), at paragraph 4.351; emphasis added.

[45] Marc Busch and Eric Reinhardt, "Three's a Crowd: Third Parties and WTO Dispute Settlement," 58 (3) *World Politics* (2006) 446.

otherwise be of benefit to them. The trade-off for these third parties, in other words, is either raising the odds of gaining more trade liberalization (or for pro-defendant third parties, continued protection), and pushing for a narrower precedent, given concerns for its future implications as either a complainant or defendant. In short, mixed third-party submissions, given the underlying commercial interests, credibly signal the wider membership's ambiguity about points in law.

To illustrate what mixed third-party submissions look like, and flesh out the intuition of our argument, consider the following. In *Mexico – Telecoms*, for example, a case brought by the United States that called into question Mexico's regime for basic and value-added telecommunications services, ten third parties reserved rights, four of which provided submissions in time to be included in the panel's report. Of the four, three delivered decidedly mixed arguments: Brazil both challenged and gave weight to Mexico's positions, whereas the EC wavered between criticizing and embracing U.S. arguments. With twenty-two pages of its report dedicated to these third-party submissions, the panel reflected on how it had approached its "daunting task with the utmost prudence" and had "decided to exercise 'judicial economy'." In elaborating its decision, the panel likened judicial economy to the "constructive ambiguity" that "WTO negotiators sometimes praise . . . as a diplomatic means of enabling consensus on WTO rules." The point was that judicial economy had worked as intended: "Our legal findings are thus limited to . . . the very particular context of this bilateral dispute, and do not go beyond what we consider indispensable for deciding on the legal claims submitted to this Panel."[46]

In *EC – Biotech*, the United States and Canada, later joined by Argentina, brought suit against Europe's de facto moratorium on approving applications to sell genetically modified foods. The case attracted seventeen third parties, many of whom offered both written and oral submissions. *EC – Biotech* was said to raise an "extraordinarily wide range of factual, scientific and legal issues,"[47] many of which had little existing case law to draw on for a ruling. Moreover, health and safety cases are thought to be especially prone to controversy, because these measures are, by definition, contingent on constantly changing scientific findings and evolving risk assessment. Nevertheless, what

46 See WTO, "Report of the Panel, Mexico – Measures Affecting Telecommunications Services," WT/DS204/R (2004), at paragraph 7.3.

47 See WTO, "Report of the Panel, European Communities – Measures Affecting the Approval and Marketing of Biotech Product," WT/DS291/R (2006); WTO, "Report of the Panel, European Communities – Measures Affecting the Approval and Marketing of Biotech Product," WT/DS292/R (2006); WTO, "Report of the Panel, European Communities – Measures Affecting the Approval and Marketing of Biotech Product," WT/DS293/R (2006), at paragraph 5.15.

makes *EC – Biotech* so striking in the present context is that Australia, as a third party, was unusually candid about the goals of its written statement. In a perfect example of a mixed submission, Australia raised no specific legal issues, nor did it take any stance for or against either the complainant or the defendant, but instead it only registered its strong interest in the panel's assessment, and called for the panel to adopt "a measured approach" and to "limit its ruling and recommendations accordingly."[48] More telling still, Australia explicitly reminded the panel of its "considerable discretion to exercise 'judicial economy' in making an objective assessment of the matter before it,"[49] thus directly linking the novel and uncharted nature of the arguments at issue with the panel's option to exercise judicial economy. Finally, Australia ended its submission by calling for maximum participation by third parties in the dispute. In response, the panel did, in fact, expand third-party rights, giving all of them the opportunity to respond to the questions posed to the litigants. Importantly, the panel went on to exercise judicial economy with regard to a large number of claims by Canada and Argentina,[50] thus considerably limiting the reach of its ruling. Much as in *Mexico – Telecoms*, third parties were worried about what a broad ruling would mean for their own exposure to litigation in the future, and they wanted to ensure that the law would not fill in where the politics of genetically modified foods had fallen short.

Finally, in *Brazil – Tyres*, Europe challenged several measures under the defendant's import regime. For its part, the panel invoked judicial economy, sidestepping a number of these legal claims. On appeal, the AB affirmed the panel's right to invoke judicial economy, but nonetheless expressed surprise that it had done so in this case, commenting that "we have difficulty seeing how the Panel could have been justified in not addressing separate claims of inconsistency."[51] However, just as in *Argentina – Footwear (EC)*, the AB did not conclude that the panel had erred in this regard; it simply stated that it was surprised. We are not. The case drew nine third parties, seven of whom made partisan submissions, and two offered mixed submissions. One of these, Australia, told the panel that it would not make an assessment of Brazil's defense, but instead wanted to focus on the broader issues at hand concerning the interpretation of GATT (General Agreement on Tariffs and Trade) Article XX. As far as Australia was concerned, "each exception made under Article XX requires cautious weighing of Members' rights," and thus it

48 Ibid, at paragraph 5.5.

49 Ibid.

50 Ibid., at paragraphs 7.3377, 7.3384, 7.3394, 7.3405, 7.3422, and 7.3429.

51 See WTO, "Report of the Appellate Body, Brazil – Measures Affecting Imports of Retreaded Tyres," WT/DS332/AB/R (2007), at paragraph 257.

urged the panel to "evaluate carefully the factual evidence before it, including by drawing on expert opinion as necessary."[52] Likewise, Mexico did not take sides but instead reminded the panel that the issues at stake were complex and highly significant. As in *Mexico – Telecoms* and *EC – Biotech*, these mixed third-party submissions stood out against the backdrop of partisan third-party submissions, alerting the panel to the interests of the broader membership.

One possible objection might be that mixed submissions would *not* be costly if partisanship, rather than ambiguity, led third parties to prefer that the complainant win some claims and the defendant others. Put another way, it might be argued that mixed submissions are self-serving, rather than a signal of ambivalence, and as such are not costly for lack of a vested interest in a more encompassing legal victory. This concern is misleading for two related reasons. First, whereas we argue that judicial economy serves the purpose of third parties who are uncertain about how a ruling will impact their commercial interests, the same would *not* be true of third parties favoring the defendant on some arguments, and the complainant on others. Far from it: In recognizing that their allegiances are split, these third parties stand to benefit most if the panel renders a *mixed ruling*, that is, one that partly favors the complainant and partly favors the defendant, setting the particular precedents they would like to see established. This, rather than a decision *not to rule* on points of law over which they have clear preferences, is in their best interest.

Second, and following from this, mixed submissions, even if they could be traced to partisan preferences, do not improve the odds of securing a mixed *ruling* (or any type of ruling, for that matter). Previous research indicates that only pro-complainant or pro-defendant submissions help boost these odds; mixed submissions have no bearing on the direction of a ruling.[53] Mixed rulings are likely facilitated by coalitional politics among partisan third parties lining up on both sides of the dispute, a factor that we control for in our analyses. The point to make clear is that members with divided commercial interests benefit from mixed rulings, not judicial economy, and mixed third-party submissions (partisan or otherwise) do not help them in this regard.

In sum, our argument is that panels are likely to exercise judicial economy in those instances in which third parties offer mixed submissions, reflecting the wider membership's ambivalence about the precedential value of a ruling. By providing mixed submissions, these third parties, unlike their partisan counterparts, seek to define the contours of what they see as an acceptable

[52] See WTO, "Report of the Panel, Brazil – Measures Affecting Imports of Retreaded Tyres," WT/DS332/R (2007), at paragraphs 5.17 and 5.18.

[53] Busch and Reinhardt, *supra* note 45.

ruling. We hypothesize that the more third parties offer mixed submissions, the more likely the panel is to exercise judicial economy.

5. EVIDENCE

We compiled data on all 105 panel reports issued between 1995 and 2005.[54] This task is made easier by the fact that the exercise of judicial economy must be explained and identified as such by the panel in every case. As the AB clarified in *Canada – Autos*, a panel must always "address expressly those claims which it declines to examine and rule upon for reasons of judicial economy," and it went on to state that "[s]ilence does not suffice for these purposes."[55] For this reason, the coding of judicial economy is unambiguous. Of the 105 panel reports we examine, judicial economy is exercised in 42 reports.

Our main explanatory variables concern third parties and their submissions. We code for the number of third parties reserving rights in a dispute, and how many of those make submissions that are pro-complainant, pro-respondent, or mixed. Our coding is based on a careful reading of third-party arguments, building on the data set compiled by and updated for more recent disputes in our own data.[56] We code third-party submissions as mixed when they support or critiques both sides in the dispute, or comment on how the panel should balance the competing claims before it. Although the number of pro-complainant and pro-defendant third parties is sometimes as large as eighteen, the number of mixed third-party submissions in our data never exceeds three per case.

We also control for a number of case-specific attributes that might otherwise predispose the panel to exercise judicial economy. First, we include a count variable corresponding to the number of legal claims submitted by the complainant in each dispute. This is a necessary control for a number of reasons. Existing research, grounded in the literature on American courts, suggests that a high number of articles cited could be a proxy for the weakness of a case,

[54] In compiling instances of judicial economy, our task is made easier by the fact that the exercise of judicial economy must be explained and identified as such by the panel in every case. As the AB clarified in "Canada – Autos," a panel must always "address expressly those claims which it declines to examine and rule upon for reasons of judicial economy," and went on to state that "[s]ilence does not suffice for these purposes": See WTO, "Report of the Appellate Body, Report of the Panel, Canada – Certain Measures Affecting the Automotive Industry," WT/DS139/AB/R (2000), at paragraph 117. For this reason, the identification of judicial economy is unambiguous. Of the 105 panel reports we examine, judicial economy is exercised in 42 reports.

[55] See "Canada–Autos," *supra* note 54, at paragraph 117.

[56] Busch and Reinhardt, *supra* note 45.

reflecting a kitchen-sink approach to piling on claims against the defendant.[57] Under these circumstances, it might be easier for the panel to sidestep certain of the complainant's legal arguments. Moreover, the logic underlying judicial economy, whereby a ruling on a claim leads the panel to skip the reasoning on another, related claim, is more likely to be invoked as the number of submitted claims increases, whatever the merit of these claims. Indeed, panels would be hard pressed to exercise judicial economy in those instances in which a complainant presented a single claim. Finally, the number of claims brought by complainants has steadily risen since the inception of the WTO, and this variable takes this trend into account.

We also include a count of the number of members who have never previously served on a panel. The (untested) conjecture in the literature is that, on the one hand, new panelists may be more desirous of completing their analysis, so as to afford the AB more to work with in the event of an appeal. In this case, they may be less likely to invoke judicial economy than their more experienced colleagues. On the other hand, new panelists might also be more inclined to shy away from setting important precedents, in which case they may be more likely to invoke judicial economy.[58]

We also seek to account for the suspicion in the literature that more politically sensitive disputes lend themselves more readily to the practice of judicial economy. For example, nonviolation complaints, because they are about nullification or impairment resulting from measures that are not, themselves, in violation of WTO law, might be more likely to trigger the use of judicial economy.[59] Likewise, SPS (i.e., health and safety standards) cases and agricultural disputes are also viewed as being especially sensitive for political reasons, and thus panels might be more inclined to sidestep arguments levied by a complainant in these disputes.[60] These variables are among the foremost barometers of political discord in the empirical literature on WTO dispute settlement.[61]

57 Ibid.

58 For an examination of the relationship between panelist experience and dispute outcomes, see Marc Busch and Krzysztof Pelc, "Does the WTO Need a Permanent Body of Panelists?," 12 (3) *Journal of International Economic Law* (2009) 1.

59 Marc Busch and Eric Reinhardt, "Transatlantic Trade Conflicts and GATT/WTO Dispute Settlement," in E. Petersmann and M. Pollack (eds.), *Transatlantic Economic Disputes: The EU, the US, and the WTO* (2003) 465.

60 On SPS disputes, see Amelia Porges, "Settling WTO Disputes: What Do Litigation Models Tell Us?," 19 *Ohio State Journal on Dispute Resolution* (2003) 141. On agricultural disputes, see Christina Davis, *Food Fights over Free Trade: How International Institutions Promote Agricultural Trade Liberalization* (2003).

61 Busch and Reinhardt, *supra* note 45.

Given that some scholars have suggested that more powerful countries may be better able to make their preferences known to the panel, suggesting some distributional effects in panels' issue avoidance,[62] we add a dummy variable to indicate whether the United States or EC is a defendant. Defendants often support the use of judicial economy, as might be expected, and sometimes expend considerable effort trying to convince the panel to invoke it. Proceedings routinely feature defendants assuring the panel that a finding on a single claim is enough to "secure a positive solution" to the dispute. For instance, in *Mexico – Soft Drinks*, the defendant tried to convince the panel that it could invoke judicial economy to decline jurisdiction, an argument that the panel dismissed.[63] For this reason, we control for whether the United States or EC is the defendant, given the expectation that the two largest traders are likely to be particularly vocal in demanding judicial economy, and potentially more successful in this regard.

Another suspicion might be that a key influence is whether the United States or EC, as the *complainant*, asks for judicial economy. Indeed, in some cases, the United States and EC, as complainants, have vehemently argued for the panel to finish the analysis, sometimes even preempting a panel's mention of judicial economy. These arguments, as we already noted, are typically unsuccessful.

To get at the conventional wisdom even more directly, we include a variable for whether the United States or the EC, as the defendant, lost the case at hand. The logic is that, if panels are especially motivated to secure compliance in disputes involving the two largest members of the multilateral trade regime, then they may be more likely to exercise judicial economy to ease the burden of compliance for these defendants.

Likewise, to get at the concern discussed earlier about partisan mixed submissions, we include a control for the level of divisiveness among third parties. Here, the logic might be that some disputes are more likely to attract third parties with split commercial interests because of the number of unrelated issues being addressed by the dispute, for example. This might lead to greater divisiveness and bear on the prospects of judicial economy for reasons other than the wider membership's ambiguity about the resulting case law.

We also include the number of *co-complainants*, as some disputes have as many as eleven, and greater numbers could be revealing of the political nature of the case. For example, the argument might be that, even if a complainant's demands for judicial economy do not sway a panel, there might be strength

62 Helfer and Slaughter, *supra* note 21, at 50.

63 See "Mexico – Taxes on Soft Drinks," *supra* note 12.

in numbers, and thus more co-complainants could have some effect on the panel's likelihood of exercising judicial economy.

Finally, we also check for the impact of cases in which third parties join a dispute by claiming a *systemic* interest, rather than or in addition to a claim of a substantial interest, which any would-be third party must establish. Systemic interests are formally notified as such, making our coding straightforward; they are often registered along with claims of a substantial interest (as opposed to substituting for them) and, as previous research has shown, signal that third parties intend to raise broader – and potentially more axiomatic – concerns.[64] This, in turn, may tip off the panel that there is likely discord over the proper interpretation of a legal text, leading it to exercise judicial economy.

The results are striking. Mixed submissions hold a strong effect over the likelihood of observing judicial economy. Specifically, for an otherwise typical case, varying the number of third parties offering mixed submissions from zero to three, the odds of observing judicial economy increase by 67 percent. More conservatively, a move from zero to a single third party offering mixed arguments boosts the odds of judicial economy by an impressive 27 percent.

This contrasts markedly with the impact of partisan third-party submissions. Indeed, neither pro-complainant nor pro-defendant third parties exert a statistically significant effect on the panel's use of judicial economy. These results are consistent with the view that, although partisan third parties are influential in determining who *wins*, they are not with respect to the scope of the legal victory handed down.

Of the variables controlling for case characteristics, the only one we find to have any significant impact is whether the case includes SPS claims. Indeed, SPS cases are, on average, 36 percent more likely to result in judicial economy. Strikingly, agriculture cases, which are traditionally held to exhibit high political sensitivity,[65] do not show any effect. This dramatic difference between the effect of agricultural and SPS cases fits nicely with our story. Again, we do not make the claim that all politically sensitive issues increase the likelihood of judicial economy. Rather, panels use judicial economy in reaction to the broader ambivalence of the membership concerning the precedent at stake. In SPS cases, which rely in great measure on changing scientific findings and evolving risk assessment, this is more likely to be the case. A panel may thus wish to limit its ruling to the findings that are minimally necessary for resolution of the dispute, leaving any unresolved issues for later panels facing different political circumstances.

64 Busch and Reinhardt, *supra* note 45.

65 See, e.g., Davis, *supra* note 60.

Although the variation in the effect of political sensitivity fits nicely with our argument, our examination of how material power relates to panels' use of judicial economy yields some unexpected, and noteworthy, results. Given that some scholars have suggested that more powerful countries may be better able to make their preferences known to the panel, suggesting some distributional effects in panels' issue avoidance,[66] we examine the effect of powerful respondents in a dispute. Respondents often support the use of judicial economy, as might be expected, and sometimes expend considerable effort trying to convince the panel to invoke it. Similarly, we look at whether powerful *complainants* are able to sway the panel in its decision to exercise of judicial economy.

What we find should strike a cord with those who consider disputes brought against the United States and Europe as being of intrinsically more value to the membership as a whole. Despite the efforts by the panel to isolate itself from the influence of parties to the dispute in regard to judicial economy, as already shown, the presence of powerful defendants such as the United States and the EC *does* raise the likelihood of the panel exercising judicial economy. In fact, when either of these countries is the defendant, the odds that the panel exercises judicial economy surges from 26 percent to 51 percent. If one of the purported goals of the DSU is to "redress asymmetries of power,"[67] then this is disconcerting, because it suggests that panels are more prone to exercise judicial economy precisely in those cases in which the membership, as a whole, has the greatest interest in a fuller vetting of the issues at hand. By comparison, powerful complainants do not seem to have a significant impact. We can qualify these results somewhat, by showing that whether these powerful countries are winning or losing a case does *not* further affect the odds. In other words, although the presence of powerful defendants does raise the odds of judicial economy, panels do *not* appear to use judicial economy to lessen the burden of compliance on *losing* defendants, regardless of their economic power.

6. CONCLUSION

The use of judicial economy is *the* means by which WTO panels reveal themselves to be politically savvy. No other technique – not *non liquet* or *in dubio mitius* – comes close in this respect. Nevertheless, the exercise of

66 Helfer and Slaughter, *supra* note 21, at 50.

67 John Jackson, "International Law Status of WTO Dispute Settlement Reports: Obligation to Comply or Option to 'Buy Out'?," 98 (1) *American Journal of International Law* (2004) 109, at 118.

judicial economy is not simply correlated with controversial cases – far from it. Although there are many potential cues concerning the sensitivities surrounding a dispute, panels engage in issue avoidance under much more limited circumstances. In particular, third parties offering mixed, as opposed to partisan, submissions can more than double the odds of judicial economy. Rather than being about securing the litigants' compliance in the case at hand, judicial economy is about the membership's shaping how the institution handles disputes in the future, and this by limiting the scope of the case law that results. In that similar practices are evident on the part of institutions ranging from the ECJ to the International Court of Justice,[68] our results reach much further than the WTO.

The exercise of judicial economy is fascinating for several reasons. First, it is one of the only ways in which the *institution* can impose limits upon itself. Members have an assortment of safety valves to use in releasing the pressure of free trade in tough political times, such as safeguards. However, if a panel decides that it would be politically expedient to resort to a safety valve, its only real option is to exercise judicial economy. Although students of the ECJ and other institutions have long argued that courts can render politically informed rulings, the precise mechanism by which they do this, and under what conditions, has remained unclear.

Second, our results show that it is not just the direction of a ruling that matters, but its scope. This, after all, is what judicial economy is all about. The panel's choice to use judicial economy, or not, inspires such passion from members precisely because a ruling's reach bears directly on the institution's acquis of case law. Third parties offering mixed submissions grapple with how the case might impact their prospects not only as a complainant in the future, but also as a defendant.[69] If the content of a ruling were not sticky, third parties would care little about precedent and might, instead, be expected to be more partisan, worried only about shaping their side's prospects of prevailing. In this sense, the exercise of judicial economy is, itself, evidence that international courts matter, because members invest in shaping the *content* of the rulings rendered, and not just who wins.

68 See, e.g., Garrett, Keleman, and Schulz, *supra* note 22, at 150.

69 Marc Busch, "Overlapping Institutions, Forum Shopping, and Dispute Settlement in International Trade," 61 (4) *International Organization* (2007) 735.

12

The Politics of Competing Jurisdictional Claims in WTO and RTA Disputes

The Role of Private International Law Analogies

C. L. Lim and Henry Gao

1. INTRODUCTION

What is the relationship between the World Trade Organization (WTO) dispute settlement mechanism and the dispute settlement mechanism under a regional trade agreement (RTA)?[1] Even before the WTO was established, the North American Free Trade Agreement (NAFTA) had included a provision dealing explicitly with the relationship between its dispute settlement system and the one under the General Agreement on Tariffs and Trade (GATT), and any successor agreements. The problem is therefore not new, but only in recent years has it become more pronounced.

In the first years of the establishment of the dispute settlement mechanism (DSM), it was touted as an example of how an international dispute settlement system should be. It has compulsory jurisdiction; all WTO members had to accept the DSM as part of a single undertaking when they joined the organization. Moreover, with the newly introduced "negative consensus" rule, any WTO member can bring suit against another WTO member without risk of blockage, either at the point of panel establishment or subsequently in the adoption of panel reports. The WTO has an appeal system, in the form of the Appellate Body, whose reports are also saved from blockage by the Dispute Settlement Body (DSB), the supervisory political body comprising all the

[1] For the sake of consistency and clarity, we use the term "regional trade agreements" in this chapter to refer to both free trade agreements (FTAs) and customs unions (CUs) under GATT Article XXIV, as well as economic integration agreements under GATS (General Agreement on Trade in Services) Article V. The word "regional" carries no geographical connotations, and agreements between parties that are geographically remote from each other (such as the United States and Singapore) are also included.

Note: Generous support from Hong Kong University's Seed Funding for Basic Research Programme is gratefully acknowledged.

WTO members, because of the negative consensus rule.[2] It was not long after the establishment of the DSM that a problem that public international lawyers have been increasingly concerned with – the proliferation and fragmentation of international tribunals – started to have an impact on the DSM and its operation. This is a problem derived from the lack of rules ordering the relationship between different tribunals and the norms that they produce, and it is especially acute where such norms also exist in a relationship of conflict.[3]

In this regard, questions have arisen about the proper allocation of jurisdictional authority between the WTO's DSM and other dispute settlement bodies, such as the International Tribunal for the Law of the Sea.[4] At the same time, there has been much discussion in recent years about how one might define the substantive normative scope of trade law.[5] These questions have led to intense political controversy: Should other "values and policy objectives . . . 'trump the value of freer trade'"?[6] How do we overcome the fact that the "values shared by the current WTO members are not the same as in 1947"?[7] How should one approach the political question that every

[2] Dispute Settlement Understanding (DSU) Articles 6.1, 16.4, and 17.14. For the negative consensus rule, see John Jackson, "The WTO DSU: Misunderstandings on the Nature of Legal Obligation," 91 *Am. J. Int'l L.* (1997) 60. For the proposed alternative of a "consensus minus two" rule during the Uruguay Round negotiations, see John A. Ragosta, "Can the WTO DSB Live up to the Moniker 'World Trade Court'?", *L. Policy Int'l Bus.* (2000) 739.

[3] See, e.g., "Conclusions of the Work of the Study Group on the Fragmentation of International Law: Difficulties Arising from the Diversification and Expansion of International Law 2006," adopted by the International Law Commission at its Fifty-eighth session, A/61/10 (2006), paragraph 51; *Yearbook of the International Law Commission* (2006), Vol. II, Part Two; Tomer Broude, "Fragmentation(s) of International Law: On Normative Integration as Authority Allocation," in Tomer Broude and Yuval Shany (eds.), *The Shifting Allocation of Authority in International Law* (Oxford: Hart, 2008), 99.

[4] See "Chile – Measures Affecting the Transit and Importing of Swordfish," WT/DS193/1; G/L/37 (April 26, 2000); "Case between Chile and the European Community Concerning the Conservation of Swordfish Stocks in the South-eastern Pacific Ocean (Chile/European Community)," International Tribunal for the Law of the Sea, Order (December 11, 2008); discussed in C. L. Lim, "Free Trade Agreements in Asia and Some Common Legal Problems," in Yasuhei Taniguchi, Alan Yanovich, and Jan Bohanes (eds.), *The WTO in the Twenty-First Century: Dispute Settlement, Negotiations, and Regionalism in Asia* (Cambridge: Cambridge University Press, 2007), 434, 453.

[5] See the contributions in "Symposium: The Boundaries of the WTO," 96 *Am. J. Int'l L.* (2002) 1. Some scholars also note that there is a linkage between the integration of norms and the integration of authorities. See, e.g., Tomer Broude, "Principles of Normative Integration and the Allocation of International Authority: The WTO, the Vienna Convention on the Law of Treaties, and the Rio Declaration," *Loyola Univ. Chicago Int'l L. Rev.* (2009), available at SSRN: http://ssrn.com/abstract=1249432.

[6] Jose E. Alvarez, "Foreword," 96 *Am. J. Int'l L.* (2002) 1, 4.

[7] Debra Steger, "Afterword: The 'Trade and . . . ' Conundrum – A Commentary," 96 *Am. J. Int'l L.* (2002) 135, 144.

linkage "potentially raises strategic problems" because "a participant [i.e., state or WTO member] might perceive that the linkage will lead to a less favorable arrangement"? Finally, different solutions presented by different substantive norms or different tribunals are likely to present particular "dangers and costs," such as to "tilt too strongly toward the rich or toward the poor countries."[8]

Apart from the fragmentation and linkage problems, some scholars have noted that there is a correlation between the integration of norms and the integration of authority, thereby connecting issue-area politics with institutional politics.[9] Broude has previously argued that[10]

> the significance of authority fragmentation and the seriousness of the problems it presents largely depend upon the degree of norm fragmentation, and vice versa. Where substantive norms are integrated or harmonized rather than fragmented, identifying the proper forum for producing them or for making determinations based upon them is of less importance, because the room available to different fora for manoeuvring between different and potentially conflicting decisions is reduced. The normative commonality overcomes institutional differences.

This "interdependent" (i.e., substantive normative and jurisdictional) approach lies in contrast to that of Joel Trachtman, where Trachtman attempts to resolve the normative problem through a jurisdictional perspective instead.[11]

This chapter seeks out a further approach, which looks toward the development of choice-of-law principles. We believe this is different from and potentially superior to placing an undue emphasis on the substantive value differences that define norm fragmentation, an emphasis on a jurisdictional approach, or an emphasis on both. We attempt to seek ways of managing both norm and jurisdictional fragmentation by turning away from questions about both substantive norms and jurisdictional questions. By looking at the development of choice-of-law rules (i.e., second-order norms about the selection of substantive norms), we attempt to circumvent, or at least defuse, the intense political debate that has taken place over substantive values.[12] Our solution

[8] John H. Jackson, "Afterword: The Linkage Problem – Comments on Five Texts," 96 *Am. J. Int'l L.* (2002) 118, 124.

[9] Broude, "Fragmentation(s)," *supra* note 3 and Broude, "Principles," *supra* note 5.

[10] Broude, "Fragmentation(s)," op. cit., 105.

[11] See references to Trachtman, id., 105, footnote 21. For Trachtman's view that "[j]urisdiction is the core issue in all legal analysis," and his latest view on fragmentation and linkage issues, see Joel P. Trachtman, *The Economic Structure of International Law* (Cambridge, MA: Harvard, 2008), 26, 26–71, 196–207.

[12] For example, the connection between trade and environmental, labor, and human rights values in cases in which an RTA might handle these linkages differently from the WTO.

proposes a common set of choice-of-law rules that could be applied by different tribunals. The idea is that such choice-of-law rules – which invite formal, technical analysis – would lead to the application of the same substantive norms in each case in a relatively less politicized manner. This would reduce the risk of different results from different tribunals, which could in turn reduce the political tension inherent in jurisdictional clashes.

We focus here on the specific problem of RTA–WTO jurisdictional conflicts, but similar political problems of issue linkage and norm fragmentation can be found in this area as well. This is because different tribunals could approach the same problem differently even when the same substantive norms are contained in an RTA and a WTO covered agreement, all the more so when different substantive norms and linkages exist in two or more different agreements. Different RTA–WTO interpretations and rulings could also order the hierarchy of values differently, thereby giving different and controversial degrees of protection to free trade against other substantive, politically contested values. Likewise, RTA proliferation contributes to norm fragmentation amidst an increasingly varied and pluralistic WTO membership.

A. *WTO–RTA Disputes: The "Allocative Thesis" of Jurisdictional Authority*

In a previous article,[13] we addressed a related problem: Can and should panels and the Appellate Body apply RTA law? We argued that the WTO legal framework, at least in its current form, does not envisage the application of non-WTO rules and principles, including RTA rules. Therefore, the Dispute Settlement Understanding (DSU) should be revised to clarify two issues – (a) the jurisdiction of the WTO in the case of jurisdictional conflicts between WTO and RTA dispute settlement, and (b) whether WTO panels and the Appellate Body can apply RTA rules and principles both to the resolution of WTO–RTA jurisdictional conflicts and the substantive dispute between RTA parties.

In this chapter we attempt to take this discussion a step further. If WTO panels and the Appellate Body were to apply RTA rules and principles to resolve jurisdictional conflicts, on what basis would they have the authority to do so? Can it truly be said that because the WTO DSM contemplates the application of some public international law, such as the rules of the Vienna Convention

[13] Henry Gao and C. L. Lim, "Saving the WTO from the Risk of Irrelevance: The WTO Dispute Settlement Mechanism as a 'Common Good' for RTA Disputes," (2008) 11 *J. Int'l Econ. L.* 899.

on the Law of Treaties, it therefore also permits the application of RTA rules because these too are (conventional) public international law? In our previous article, we argued that such a view is simply too artificial.[14] For example, could a WTO panel apply an RTA jurisdictional rule, such as a "fork in the road" or *electa una via* clause (which says that a dispute resolved or in process before an RTA dispute settlement body can no longer be brought before the WTO)? We would argue that it should, but would this not be the outcome of private international law reasoning, rather than public international law?

In this chapter we discuss an even deeper problem. That problem has to do with the way we think about WTO–RTA conflicts. In particular, it relates to the source of our legal imagination. Much of the problem is brought about by looking at the issue in jurisdictional terms, and the jurisdictional problem is viewed in turn largely in "public international law" terms. Public international law, in the way it addresses the classic problem of competing state and criminal jurisdiction, establishes jurisdictional competence based on a number of principles. These include territorial, nationality, protective, and other principles. However, these principles do not allocate competence exclusively to a particular tribunal.[15] In contrast, private international law has better developed principles that not only furnish the courts with jurisdictional authority in the case of private law disputes with an international element (e.g., involving a foreign party) but also demarcate the authority of the various national courts that potentially have the jurisdiction to deal with the particular dispute. It does this through well-developed notions of judicial comity. The forum non conveniens doctrine is perhaps the prime example, because its salience is felt today both in civil law and common law jurisdictions worldwide.[16]

[14] Id., 912–920.

[15] This is not to say there are not other, specific rules that do, such as the double jeopardy (*ne bis in idem*) rule in international criminal law, and under Article 20 of the Rome Statute of the International Criminal Court, or the principle of complementarity under Article17 of the Rome Statute. See John T. Holmes, "The Principle of Complementarity," in Roy S. Lee (ed.), *The International Criminal Court: The Making of the Rome Statute* (Hague: Kluwer, 1999), 41.

[16] The origins of forum non conveniens in common law in England lie in Scots law; see *The Abidin Daver* [1984] AC 398; *Spiliada Maritime Corp. v. Cansulex Ltd.* [1987] AC 460. However, the European Court of Justice (ECJ) has rejected the application of *forum non conveniens; Owusu v. Jackson*, 2005 E.C.R. I-1383; Ralf Michaels, "Two Paradigms of Jurisdiction," 27 *Mich. J. Int'l L.* (2007) 1003, 1008. For criticism of the ECJ, see Adrian Briggs, "The Impact of Recent Judgments of the European Court on English Procedural Law and Practice," 124 *Revue de Droit Suisse* (2005) 231.

Comity does not establish jurisdictional authority. Instead it performs the task of resolving jurisdictional clashes. In contrast, public international law rules and principles – in the form of the *lex specialis, lex posterior,* and other rules – are often called upon to allocate jurisdiction. Even here, however, this is not the usual function of these principles in the public international law field. The *lex specialis, lex posterior,* and other rules are rules that were originally intended to resolve conflicts between substantive principles of international law (i.e., the problem of fragmented norms, as opposed to fragmented authority). Joost Pauwelyn's call for *public* international law to apply these rules to problems involving jurisdictional clashes between WTO and other dispute settlement systems therefore implicitly merges a jurisdictional and a choice-of-law problem.[17] To be sure, Pauwelyn does not explicitly address conflicts of jurisdiction between different international tribunals as such in these writings, as opposed to questions concerning the scope of what he calls the WTO's "substantive jurisdiction" (i.e., under the DSU and covered agreements). However, if true jurisdictional conflicts are not treated as being as important, and deserving of their own unique solutions as questions about the "substantive" jurisdiction of the WTO,[18] then there is a danger of a single set of principles being used both to decide what legal rules and principles the WTO panels and the Appellate Body should apply, and to address the problem of jurisdictional conflict between different tribunals.

For example, Pauwelyn's recent call for "forum exclusion clauses" raises the problem of how such RTA clauses relate to the WTO as, again, a question

[17] See Joost Pauwelyn, "The Role of Public International Law in the WTO: How Far Can We Go?," 95 (3) *Am. J. Int'l L.* (2001) 535, 538 ("no academic author . . . disputes that WTO rules are part of the wider corpus of public international law"), 544 (analyzing conflict rules in non-WTO treaties and the WTO treaty before concluding that "further rules on how to solve normative conflicts must be sought in general [i.e. public] international law"), 554 ("jurisdiction of WTO panels is limited to claims under WTO covered agreements . . . some WTO rules . . . explicitly confirm and incorporate pre-existing non-WTO treaty rules"), 555 (resting the authority of panels to apply "other," "non-WTO" rules on the notion of "implied jurisdiction"), and most importantly, 556 ("[t]he issue may arise as to whether a WTO panel has *jurisdiction* to hear WTO claims even though the underlying or predominant element . . . derives from other rules of international law"; emphasis added). See also Joost Pauwelyn, *Conflict of Norms in Public International Law: How WTO Law Relates to Other Rules of International Law* (Cambridge: Cambridge University Press 2003), esp. Chapter 8.

[18] Joel Trachtman, "Jurisdiction in WTO Dispute Settlement," in Rufus Yerxa and Bruce Wilson (eds.), *Key Issues in WTO Dispute Settlement: The First Ten Years* (Cambridge: Cambridge University Press, 2005), 132, 135 ("[t]he most important jurisdictional question regarding WTO dispute settlement is that of applicable law. The most prominent question here is the extent to which other international law is applicable within WTO dispute settlement").

of normative conflict. There is, in such solutions, a bias toward viewing jurisdictional conflicts as an extension of normative, treaty conflicts as opposed to the separate problem of how one tribunal should deal with another tribunal in practice. In such a scenario, two tribunals could still produce different outcomes based on conflicting answers given by the *lex posterior* and *lex specialis* rules,[19] precisely because public international law rules that allocate jurisdiction between different tribunals are underdeveloped.[20]

We call this danger of overreliance on public international law principles the "allocative thesis" because it would also decide on the allocation of jurisdiction. This would not be the result of the application of jurisdictional principles as such (general public international law has few such well-developed principles to speak of)[21] but what are essentially certain rule-selection principles (what Pauwelyn calls "conflict rules")[22] of public international law. Such rule-selection or "conflict" rules have traditionally been used by public international lawyers to resolve conflicts between competing, substantive treaty rules.

We believe the allocative thesis to be imperfect because of the traditional lack of well-developed principles in classical (public) international law that would serve the function of allocating jurisdiction.[23] That is why some commentators have pointed out that WTO panels should instead apply the doctrine of comity, following the recent practice of other international dispute

[19] Pauwelyn admits this problem; see Joost Pauwelyn, "Legal Avenues to 'Multilateralizing Regionalism': Beyond Article XXIV," in Richard Baldwin and Patrick Low (eds.), *Multilateralizing Regionalism: Challenges for the Global Trading System* (Cambridge: Cambridge University Press, 2009), 368, 378–379.

[20] Cf. Yuval Shany, *The Competing Jurisdictions of International Courts and Tribunals* (Oxford: Oxford University Press, 2003), Chapters 5 and 6, generally (hereafter, "*Competing Jurisdictions*").

[21] With the exception of the *non bis in idem* or "double jeopardy" rule, and specific treaty rules; see Ernst-Ulrich Petersmann, "Proliferation and Fragmentation of Dispute Settlement in International Trade: WTO Dispute Settlement Procedures and Alternative Dispute Resolution Mechanisms," in Julio Lacarte and Jaime Granados (eds.), *Inter-Governmental Trade Dispute Settlement: Multilateral and Regional Approaches* (London: Cameron May, 2004), 417, 474; Yuval Shany, *Competing Jurisdictions*, op. cit., 169 and Chapters 5 and 6, generally.

[22] Joost Pauwelyn, "How to Win a WTO Dispute Based on Non-WTO Law: Questions of Jurisdiction and Merits," 37 *Journal of World Trade* (2003) 997, 1003.

[23] With small exceptions such as the linking point doctrine in Dahm, *Zur Problematik des Voelkerstrafrechts* (1956), cited in *Attorney-General of the Government of Israel v. Eichmann* (1961) 36 I.L.R. 5 (District Court of Jerusalem), paragraph 31. But see also Shany, *Competing Jurisdictions*, op. cit., esp. Chapters 5 and 6. However, Shany's argument relies on principles that often are as much private international law as they are public international law principles. To that extent, his arguments support the present analysis – which is to draw the link more explicitly with private international law reasoning.

settlement bodies.[24] The argument is well taken here, but there is a major problem. It involves saying that the panels have an inherent authority to apply comity where the explicit provisions of the DSU may preclude doing so. In the *Mexico – Soft Drinks* case, the Appellate Body has come very close to saying that the DSU precludes the exercise of judicial comity.[25]

Although some people may find the Appellate Body's ruling too rigid, we take an alternative approach. As we explained earlier, the political and practical significance of the Appellate Body's ruling would be lessened if both the Appellate Body and an RTA dispute body were to apply the same body of law because of the application of common choice-of-law rules. A correlation between norm and authority fragmentation – such that norm integration results in a reduction of the significance of the fragmentation of authority – means that a solution may be sought *either* in the integration of norms *or* in the integration of authority.[26] We believe that a choice-of-law approach works toward norm integration, although it is not the same thing as (and is potentially less politically controversial than) the substantive integration of norms. We also believe that a choice-of-law approach receives some support in what the Appellate Body has said when it has had the occasion to rule on the issue.

In the next section, we turn to two cases which have touched directly on the issue. We believe our approach has some support in the reasoning of the WTO panels and the Appellate Body in these cases.[27]

24 Caroline Henckels, "Overcoming Jurisdictional Isolationism at the WTO RTA Nexus: A Potential Approach for the WTO," 19 *European Journal of International Law* (2008) 571; Pauwelyn, "Legal Avenues," op. cit., 381 ("[a] better solution is . . . to recognize each other's rules and rulings").

25 See WTO, "Mexico – Tax Measures on Soft Drinks and Other Beverages," Appellate Body Report, WT/DS308/AB/R (March 6, 2006; hereafter, "*Mexico – Soft Drinks*," Appellate Body Report).

26 Cf. Broude, "Fragmentation(s)", op. cit., 110.

27 We set aside another line of cases that really have more to do with whether a WTO member can seek unilateral redress notwithstanding Article 23 of the DSU. In *EC – Commercial Vessels*, the European Communities argued that Article 23 does not preclude unilateral redress but that it is merely an "exclusive jurisdiction" clause. The panel in *EC – Commercial Vessels* ruled that Article 23 in fact precludes unilateral redress, even if it is also an exclusive jurisdiction clause. Nonetheless, it seems that the panel was only responding to the defense raised by the European Communities in that case and did not consider, before it, a case involving a pending RTA case or RTA tribunal award. Indeed, on the facts of the case, the panel seems to have considered the exclusive jurisdiction rule to be a subset of the nonunilateral redress rule and not the other way round. See "EC – Measures Affecting Trade in Commercial Vessels," WT/DS301/R (April 22, 2005), paragraph 7.193 and, more generally, paragraphs 7.192–7.196. See also *US – Certain EC Products*.

2. THE *ARGENTINA – POULTRY* AND *MEXICO – SOFT DRINKS* CASES

A. Argentina – Poultry *(the "Chicken Case")*

1. "Jurisdictional Arguments": Estoppel, Res Judicata, and Others

RTA negotiators have specified the mechanism ("forum") for RTA dispute settlement, believing that they can "control" that question. Most negotiators in today's existing RTAs probably started out with some belief that they were in control of deciding where an RTA dispute should be heard. For example, NAFTA and the EFTA–Singapore FTA adopt the now common approach of including an *electa una via* clause, namely a clause that says a dispute can be brought either to the WTO or under the RTA's dispute system but that, once the choice is made, the party bringing the dispute should stick to that choice.[28] There is a similar clause in MERCOSUR's Protocol of Olivos.[29] Both this and other types of treaty clauses that attempt to preempt jurisdictional conflicts with the WTO and with other dispute settlement bodies may be found in the various RTAs; we have discussed this issue elsewhere.[30]

However, that is not always the end of the matter. The *Argentina – Poultry* case concerned the imposition of Argentinean antidumping duties on poultry imports from Brazil. In *Argentina – Poultry*, Brazil brought a dispute under the Protocol of Brasilia.[31] The Brasilia Protocol precedes the Protocol of Olivos, which had been signed but had not yet entered into force. Unlike the Olivos Protocol, the Brasilia Protocol does not contain an *electa una via* clause. A jurisdictional conflict arose when Brazil, having brought a dispute under the MERCOSUR dispute system (and lost), now attempted to bring the dispute before the WTO. Argentina argued that Brazil was precluded from doing so,[32] claiming that Brazil was acting in breach of the principle of good faith.[33]

[28] NAFTA, 17 December 1992, Article 2005; European FTA–Singapore FTA (June 26, 2002), Article 56.

[29] The Protocol of Olivos for the Settlement of Disputes in MERCOSUR (February 18, 2002), Article 1.

[30] Gao and Lim, op. cit., 907–909; reprinted in Debra Steger (ed.), *Redesigning the World Trade Organization for the Twenty-First Century* (Waterloo: Wilfrid Laurier University Press, 2009).

[31] See "Argentina – Definitive Anti-dumping Duties on Poultry from Brazil," Report of the Panel, WT/DS241/R 22 (April 22, 2003), Panel 2.10 (hereafter, "*Argentina – Poultry*").

[32] Id., 7.17–7.18.

[33] Argentina cited the doctrine in *US – Gasoline* that the GATT should not be read in clinical isolation from the rules of public international law; id., 7.20. Argentina also argued that

Brazil argued that it had not acted in bad faith as it was not, in the first place, precluded from bringing a second claim.[34]

Argentina replied that Brazil, by subsequently *signing* the Protocol of Olivos, had "consented" not to bring a second claim.[35] Brazil responded that the Olivos Protocol did not apply to disputes brought under the Brasilia Protocol.[36]

As for the third parties, Paraguay considered that Argentina's claim was res judicata.[37] Both the European Communities and the United States supported Brazil's case. The European Communities argued that estoppel could not be raised because Brazil had not consented not to bring a second dispute. Nor did Brazil renounce its right to bring a WTO claim by not bringing one earlier.[38] The United States argued that the panel can only apply the WTO's covered agreements, but cannot adjudicate upon an RTA dispute. Estoppel, if made out, would arise under MERCOSUR rules, not the WTO's rules. In any case, the United States reasoned that the conditions for estoppel had not been satisfied.[39]

The panel ruled that Brazil could bring the WTO case. The estoppel claim had not been made out because (1) Brazil had not clearly and unambiguously represented, expressly or by implication, that it would not bring a second dispute before the WTO, and (2) there was no evidence that Argentina actively relied on a representation by Brazil.[40] The panel also rejected the argument that Brazil was precluded from bringing a claim on the basis of res judicata. Although the panel acknowledged that the Olivos Protocol contained an *electa una via* clause, it accepted Brazil's argument that the Protocol of Brasilia applied, and that the Olivos Protocol had not entered into force.[41]

MERCOSUR's legal rules should be taken into account under Article 31.3.c of the Vienna Convention on the Law of Treaties; id., 7.21.

34 Brazil's argument turned on the construction of the estoppel doctrine, namely on whether there was a need to establish that Brazil expressly or impliedly consented not to bring a second claim. In any event, Brazil argued, the case before the WTO was "based on a different legal basis" and that the "object" of the two cases was different. This last was supported by Chile agreed, acting as third party; id., 7.25.

35 Olivos Protocol, Article 1.2.

36 *Argentina – Poultry*, op. cit., 7.22. That in effect is what the Olivos Protocol's *electa una via clause* – Article 1(2) – suggests, but it is unclear from the panel report whether the panel was in fact referring to this; cf., however, the EC's argument, id., paragraph 7.27 and footnote 49.

37 Id., 7.28–7.29. Argentina did not adopt this argument; id., 7.18.

38 Id., 7.27.

39 Id., 7.30.

40 Either to Argentina's detriment, or to Brazil's advantage; id., 7.37–7.39.

41 Id., 7.38.

2. Clarifying the Problem: The United States's Third-Party Arguments

The panel acknowledged that the general international law doctrines of estoppel and res judicata could have applied,[42] and interestingly did apply an RTA treaty rule contained in the Olivos Protocol[43] (i.e., the rule that the Olivos Protocol does not apply to cases arising under the Brasilia Protocol). What rule permits the panel to do so?

One answer is that the WTO DSU treats these principles as WTO rules.[44] Argentina argued that the estoppel doctrine was one such principle.[45] Moreover, there is GATT and WTO precedent discussing the estoppel doctrine.[46]

However, the United States as third party in the *Argentina – Poultry* case rejected this view, saying that the panel cannot apply the estoppel doctrine, as it is not authorized by the DSU to do so. The United States added that although GATT and WTO panels have on occasion discussed the doctrine of estoppel, it has been described in inconsistent ways and has never actually been applied by a panel. Likewise with res judicata; the United States's argument was that the res judicata argument would rest on a purported breach of the Brasilia Protocol (i.e., an RTA rule).[47]

42 The classic authority for the principle in modern international law is the Eastern Greenland case: *Legal Status of Eastern Greenland (Denmark v. Norway)*, (1933) PCIJ Reports, Series A/B, No. 53 (see also Anzilotti diss. op.). During the drafting of the relevant part of what became Article 38(1)(c) of the Statute of the International Court of Justice, the principles of estoppels and res judicata were considered to be general principles of international law; see the statement of Lord Phillimore (Great Britain), Permanent Court of International Justice, Advisory Committee of Jurists, *Procés verbaux of the Proceedings of the Committee* (June 16–July 24, 1920, L.N. Publication, 1920), 335. Lord Phillimore viewed it as a "maxim of law," and it was also viewed as necessary for resolving problems of *non liquet*. This last is a device used by international lawyers in recognition that gaps arise in the law. See Julius Stone, "*Non-liquet* and the Function of Law in the International Community," 35 *British Year Book of International Law* (1959) 124. See also D. W. Bowett, "Estoppel before International Tribunals and Its Relation to Acquiescence," 33 *British Year Book of International Law* (1957) 176. For the problem of applying equity generally as a source of international law, see O. A. Elias and C. L. Lim, "'General Principles of Law', 'Soft' Law and the Identification of International Law," 28 *Netherlands Yearbook of International Law* (1997) 3, 39–44.

43 For the argument that RTA rules are public international law rules, see "Saving the WTO", Gao and Lim, note 13.

44 Id.

45 *Argentina – Poultry*, op. cit., 7.20.

46 Panel Report, "EEC – Member States' Import Regimes for Bananas ("EEC – (Member States)," 3 (June 3, 1993), unadopted, DS32/R, paragraph 361; Panel Report, "Guatemala – Definitive Anti-dumping Measures on Grey Portland Cement from Mexico," WT/DS156/R (adopted November 17, 2000), footnote 791. Both *Bananas I* and *Guatemala – Cement II* were cited by the panel in *Argentina – Poultry*.

47 Argentina – Poultry, op. cit., 7.30. Paraguay, in contrast, considered res judicata to be a doctrine of international law contemplated by the DSU; id., 7.28.

To resolve such issues of jurisdictional conflict, we would therefore have to ask what rules and principles a WTO panel or the Appellate Body can apply under the DSU, and whether these are not confined largely to the rules of the covered agreements. A choice has to be made as to the "applicable law." This question is concealed insofar as a purported rule may be included under one of the WTO agreements or the DSU. Argentina had argued that estoppel is a WTO doctrine; this is an argument that the panel seemed to accept. One could argue, as Paraguay did, that WTO panels can apply public international law.[48] In either case, no question arises about whether the WTO panel can apply RTA rules. It was, at the end of the day, the United States's arguments which emphasized that what was being faced was really the application of RTA rules instead.

3. The Example of the "Article 3.2" Argument

Even the argument, which Argentina raised, that the WTO panel is bound by an RTA ruling was concealed in a similar way. As with the estoppel and res judicata arguments, there was a natural attempt to bring these arguments within the sources of WTO law and the scope of the DSU or the WTO's covered agreements. Although this serves an understandable forensic purpose in the context of what is, after all, a WTO panel dispute, such practical lawyering conceals rather than reveals the underlying problem.

In seeking to argue that the panel in *Argentina – Poultry* is bound by a MERCOSUR ruling, Argentina chose to advance a convoluted argument[49]: Article 3.2 of the DSU states the WTO members' recognition that the DSM should "clarify . . . [provisions in the covered agreements] . . . in accordance with customary rules of interpretation of public international law." In that regard, Article 31 of the Vienna Convention reflects such customary rules of treaty interpretation. Article 31.3(c) of the Vienna Convention on the Law of Treaties stipulates that, in interpreting an international treaty rule, one should take account of "any relevant rules of international law applicable in the relations between the parties." According to Argentina, that would include the MERCOSUR tribunal ruling. Therefore, DSU Article 3.2 requires the panel in *Argentina – Poultry* to take the MERCOSUR tribunal ruling into account.

48 We do not deny the usefulness of these doctrines, and that they should have a place in WTO law. See further Andrew D. Mitchell, "Good Faith in WTO Dispute Settlement," 7 *Melbourne J. Int'l L.* (2006) 14.

49 *Argentina – Poultry*, op. cit., 7.21.

In this way, the source of the purported rule requiring the panel to apply an RTA rule (i.e., the MERCOSUR ruling) is said to lie in the DSU; in other words, it is ultimately a WTO rule, not a RTA rule.

The panel, however, failed to see which WTO provision required interpretation in such a case.[50] Instead, what Argentina seemed to be asking was that the panel should rule in a certain way (i.e., adopt the MERCOSUR tribunal's ruling). Because panels are not even legally bound by the rulings of previous panels, the panel in *Argentina – Poultry* failed to see why it should be bound by a ruling of a non-WTO tribunal.[51]

4. The Question of the Application of RTA Rules

The United States' argument goes to the heart of the problem. Argentina was not only saying that the panel was "bound" by a non-WTO ruling: Argentina was asking for a non-WTO rule, which applied in the relations between Brazil and Argentina to be applied through the funnel of Article 3.2 of the DSU and Article 31.3(c) of the Vienna Convention on the Law of Treaties to a WTO dispute between Brazil and Argentina. The rule applying to Brazil and Argentina arose from their common membership of MERCOSUR. In effect, what Argentina was asking the panel to do was to apply RTA law; in this case, as determined by the MERCOSUR tribunal ruling.

Although the panel did not address the issue in this way, it did consider that had it not been for the nonfulfillment of the conditions for a finding of estoppel, the inapplicability of res judicata, and the inapplicability of the *electa una via* clause in the Olivos Protocol; it could have applied estoppel, res judicata, or an *electa una via* rule to resolve the dispute. This would have been on the basis either that the WTO requires the application of these doctrines,[52] or that WTO law chooses a "public international law" rule as the applicable rule. The panel did not actually say that a public international law rule could be "chosen" by WTO law (i.e., a WTO rule), but because these rules are inexplicit in the WTO agreements, such choice would logically have been the result of the operation of a choice-of-law rule.

It might be objected that the phrase "choice-of-law rule" is overly laden with meaning in the present circumstances. It suggests conflict-of-laws thinking (conflicts analysis), and this tends to "overread" the panel report whereas the

[50] See also the U.S. argument; id., 7.32.

[51] Id., 7.41.

[52] Cf. Mitchell, op. cit. (ultimately treating resort to good faith in *Argentina – Poultry* as a part of the inherent jurisdiction of the panel).

truth was that the panel did not even accept that a conflict existed. This admittedly is the case, but Argentina clearly saw a conflict. The objection rests ultimately on the doctrine of judicial economy. The better view, however, is that this is not a good example of the principle of judicial economy, which, properly defined, involves the choice by a panel of the contested measures that require solution in order to dispose of the case before it. The problem is one of characterization instead,[53] and we require a better example than the *Argentina – Poultry* case to view the problem in its proper light.

B. *The* Mexico – Soft Drinks *Case*

1. The Parties' Arguments

In *Mexico – Soft Drinks*, the Appellate Body took the issue further. It ruled that two clauses – the "no blockage" and "no delay" clauses in the WTO's DSU – prevented the panel and the Appellate Body from refusing to hear the case.

Mexico had argued that WTO panels have an "inherent" jurisdiction to decline to hear certain cases.[54] According to Mexico's arguments before the panel, the dispute involved the relationship between Mexico and the United States under NAFTA: "This dispute arises out of a dispute under the NAFTA regarding bilateral trade in sweeteners."[55] NAFTA presents an "available" forum "to hear all of the parties' claims together," and therefore the panel should decline to "exercise" its jurisdiction (i.e., stay its proceedings).[56] Mexico acknowledged that the WTO panel has prima facie jurisdiction, but that it also has the "implied jurisdictional power" to stay proceedings in favor of a tribunal constituted under Chapter 20 of NAFTA.[57]

First, Mexico cited the United States's own argument in a dispute brought under the GATT of 1947, the *US – Sugar Quota* case, in which the United States claimed that the dispute did not fall within the ambit of the GATT because the measure in question in that dispute "concerning sugar imports from Nicaragua were only one aspect of a larger State-to-State dispute."[58]

53 See further C. L. Lim, "Law and Diplomacy in World Trade Disputes," 6 *Singapore J. Int'l Comp. L.* (2002) 436, 463 (discussing disputes that "go towards legal characterization").

54 See "Mexico – Tax Measures on Soft Drinks and Other Beverages," Report of the Panel, WT/DS308/R (October 7, 2005), 4.185–4.187 (hereafter, "*Mexico – Soft Drinks*, Panel Report").

55 Id., 4.97.

56 Id., 4.98–4.101.

57 Id. 4.102–4.103.

58 Id., 4.104.

Quoting the United States's argument in that case, the GATT report makes this statement:[59]

> The United States was of the view that attempting to discuss this issue in purely trade terms within the GATT, divorced from the broader context of the dispute, would be disingenuous. The resolution of that dispute was certainly desirable, and would also result in the lifting of the action which Nicaragua had challenged before the Panel, but the United States did not believe that the review and resolution of that broader dispute was within the ambit of the GATT.

Second, NAFTA presented "the more appropriate forum" because "[t]he history, prior procedures, and substantive content of the bilateral sweeteners trade dispute demonstrate that the measures challenged by the United States before the WTO are inseparable from the non-WTO claims over which the Panel has no jurisdiction," and the United States would suffer no prejudice if the panel were to stay proceedings in favor of a NAFTA tribunal.[60]

The United States, however, adopted a different approach. It argued that Mexico's request for a preliminary ruling was, in effect, a request for a ruling:[61]

> Mexico's so-called "preliminary ruling" request . . . is not a request for a "preliminary ruling." If anything, it is a request for a "non-ruling" and there would be nothing "preliminary" about it. Mexico seeks to resolve the entire dispute on a definitive basis in this manner.

If this argument were accepted, it would have the effect of precluding all jurisdictional challenges. In fact, the United States was itself seeking to block the NAFTA proceedings. It was at this juncture that the United States presented an argument that would subsequently take hold in the Appellate Body. This was the theory that what is involved is not a conflicts issue at all, involving a choice of a "more appropriate" forum. Instead, it concerns the right of parties to seek justice before the WTO:[62]

> Let the United States present the situation plainly and clearly: Mexico admits that it imposed the . . . measure it does not contest is in breach of [GATT] Article III – to stop the displacement of Mexican cane sugar by imported . . . [high fructose corn syrup] . . . Mexico then claims that it has done so to coerce its desired solution to a bilateral dispute. And now Mexico wishes the Panel

59 See "US – Sugar Quota," GATT Panel Report (adopted March 13, 1984), BISD 31S/67, 3.10 and 3.11.

60 *Mexico – Soft Drinks*, Panel Report., op. cit., 4.105–4.108.

61 Id., 4.150.

62 Id.

to assist it in this WTO-inconsistent action by denying the United States its right to WTO dispute settlement."

The dispute is about the WTO obligations of the parties,[63] and as for Mexico's "more appropriate forum" argument,[64]

> [t]hat WTO Members may choose to settle disputes involving a mixture of WTO and non-WTO rules in other fora, as Mexico observes, hardly justifies a WTO panel refusing to exercise jurisdiction over the dispute for which it was established. . . . One party's determination that another forum is more "appropriate" similarly does not justify such a refusal to exercise jurisdiction.

In so arguing that it was entitled to a WTO ruling, the United States cited Article 7.2 of the DSU, which stipulates that panels "shall address the relevant provisions in any covered agreement or agreements cited by the parties" to a dispute, and Article 11, which requires an "objective assessment of the facts of the case," "an assessment of the applicability of and conformity with the relevant covered agreements" on the part of WTO panels, and the construction of the panel's own terms of reference.[65] In contrast, the power to stay proceedings is not found expressed anywhere in the WTO DSU.[66] It cited the case of *India – Quantitative Restrictions*, a case in which a "constitutional" argument concerning the "separation of powers" at the WTO (between the DSB and the Committee on Balance of Payments) was rejected in favor of the jurisdiction of panels and the Appellate Body.[67]

In its counterarguments, Mexico did not address the United States's argument that what it requested was not a preliminary ruling, arguing instead that the United States's theory tended to confine the work of the panel within bounds not contemplated by the DSU.[68] The DSU did not require the panel

63 Id., 4.154.
64 Id. 4.156.
65 Id. 4.151.
66 Id. 4.213.
67 Id., 4.156.
68 Canada as third party argued that the issue should be dealt with by way of a preliminary ruling, id., 5.10. It appears that Canada rejected the request for a stay of proceedings as it (mistakenly) considered the Mexican request to rest on an argument about judicial economy where Canada considered that this would constitute a misuse of the concept. However, Canada accepted the United States' argument that Articles 3.2 and 11 of the DSU, and the panel's terms of reference, require the panel to rule on the dispute, id. 5.12–5.18. The European Communities also rejected (what it considered to be) Mexico's judicial economy argument, but it also addressed the "more appropriate forum" argument in passing, pointing out that WTO disputes need not address a dispute between the two states comprehensively. The European Communities cited *Argentina–Poultry* in support of the argument that the WTO proceedings did not, and could not, resolve the dispute brought under MERCOSUR, id. 5.37. Guatemala also agreed with the

to issue a ruling finding a breach of a WTO obligation. It requires the panel to assist in the resolution of the dispute.[69] The panel should not therefore reward an attempt on the United States's part to engage in forum shopping instead.[70]

Most of these arguments on the part of Mexico and the United States were repeated before the Appellate Body.[71]

2. The Ruling of the Panel

The panel issued its preliminary ruling according to Mexico's request, but it rejected the view that it possessed the discretionary power to stay proceedings in favor of a NAFTA tribunal. It cited DSU Articles 3.1, 11, and 19.2. According to Article 3.1, the panel ruled that it was required to make "an objective assessment of... the applicability of and conformity with the relevant covered agreements." According to Articles 3.2 and 19.2, the panel ruled, a stay of proceedings would "diminish the rights and obligations of WTO members provided in the covered agreements."[72] Finally, the panel also cited Article 23 of the DSU, noting that the word "shall" where it stipulates that WTO members "shall have recourse" to WTO dispute settlement suggested that WTO members have a right to a WTO panel ruling.[73]

The panel made two further points. First, that it was ruling simply on whether it has the discretion to stay proceedings. A future panel may be *required* to stay proceedings by an RTA rule. In the present case, it was insufficient to argue that there was a broader dispute that could not comprehensively be handled by the WTO panel as opposed to NAFTA arbitration. Mexico had not argued that a NAFTA rule actually precludes the WTO panel from exercising its jurisdiction in this case or that the United States was legally precluded from bringing the WTO dispute.[74] In any case, the dispute before NAFTA

United States's argument that the DSU, because it exists to preserve the rights of the parties under the WTO agreements, requires panels to accept claims brought under it. Guatemala appears to have considered the right of the claimant to frame the legal issues under DSU Article 7 (panel's terms of reference) to be dispositive; id., 5.67–5.68.

69 Id., 4.313–4.321 (second written submission, Mexico), 4.410–4.417 (opening statement, second meeting, Mexico), and 4.470 (closing statement, Mexico).

70 Id. 4.295 (second written submission, Mexico). See also Mexico's description of the United States's long-standing attempts to block the establishment of a NAFTA panel, id., 4.388 (opening statement, second meeting, Mexico).

71 *Mexico – Soft Drinks*, Appellate Body Report, op. cit., 10–12 (Mexico), 21–24 (United States).

72 *Mexico – Soft Drinks*, Panel Report, op. cit., 7.5–7.8.

73 Id., 7.9.

74 Id., 7.10–7.13.

and the dispute before the WTO were not identical.[75] Second, if indeed the panel has the power to stay proceedings, it would nonetheless have refused a stay on these facts.[76] Mexico had not shown that a stay would lead to "better treatment" of the dispute, simply that it would have permitted Mexico to bring "another, albeit related" claim.[77]

In sum, an RTA rule could require a panel to stay its proceedings in favor of another tribunal. Unlike the allocative thesis, which would resolve the jurisdictional issue by invoking a general public international law principle– such as the *lex specialis* principle (the more specific treaty prevails),[78] the *lex posterior* principle (the later treaty prevails), estoppel, or res judicata – the panel in *Mexico – Soft Drinks* considered that a substantive RTA rule could constitute a "legal impediment" to a WTO panel ruling. In doing so, the *Mexico – Soft Drinks* panel entertained the future possibility of a panel ruling that an RTA tribunal constitutes a more appropriate forum on the basis of an application (i.e., choice) of RTA law.

3. The Appellate Body's Ruling

The Appellate Body disagreed with Mexico.[79] In particular, it upheld the panel's mandatory interpretation of the word "shall" in Article 7 of the DSU concerning the panel's terms of reference – "[p]anels shall address the relevant provisions in any covered agreement or agreements cited by the parties to the dispute."[80] As for DSU Article 11 – "a panel should make an objective assessment of the matter before it, including an objective assessment of the facts of the case and the applicability of and conformity with the relevant covered agreements" – the Appellate Body considered that too to be mandatory notwithstanding the word "should." Citing DSU Article 23, which states that WTO members *shall* have recourse to the WTO dispute settlement system, the Appellate Body in effect took the position that WTO parties cannot block a case brought by a complaining WTO member against another member.[81]

75 Id., 7.14–7.15.

76 Id., 7.18.

77 Id., 7.17 (the panel added that if this could constitute a factor, then there would be no end to the list of factors that could be taken into account).

78 In this case, a rule that would be more "specific" because it was "specific to the parties" (i.e. an *inter partes* rule).

79 *Mexico – Soft Drinks*, Appellate Body Report, op. cit., 40–57.

80 Id., 49.

81 Id., 52.

It seems to suggest that if WTO members approach the WTO for justice, they will get it *notwithstanding* the fact that a related dispute is also being heard under an RTA dispute system. The Appellate Body also gave a similarly broad reading in relation to DSU Article 3.3 – the "no delay" clause. The Appellate Body appears to treat an RTA dispute as nothing more than an excuse to delay WTO proceedings.[82]

Similarly, the Appellate Body reasoned that DSU Article 7 instructs a panel to address the provisions of the WTO's covered agreements. Again, one might disagree by saying that Articles 7 and 11 can just as easily be read to presuppose the panel's exercise of its jurisdiction, rather than mandating it to do so.

C. *Discussion: Politics and the Need for a Private International Law Approach*

Did RTA negotiators anticipate these rulings when they drafted their RTA dispute settlement clauses, which sought to determine the relationship between WTO and RTA dispute settlement beforehand? For a good number of RTAs negotiated before these Appellate Body cases, the answer is "probably not." Admittedly, in *Argentina – Poultry* the panel had been correct to ignore the Olivos Protocol's *electa una via* clause. It had found the Olivos Protocol to be inapplicable to the dispute in the first place. In *Mexico – Soft Drinks*, however, Mexico itself had failed to invoke NAFTA's *electa una via* clause, which in any case would probably not have applied to preclude the U.S. attempt to bring the dispute before the WTO according to its strict terms.[83] In *Argentina – Poultry* too the problem was compounded by an omission; the Protocol of Brasilia had failed to provide for WTO–RTA conflicts of jurisdiction (e.g., by way of an *electa una via* clause).[84]

The reason Mexico did not invoke NAFTA's *electa una via* clause in *Mexico – Soft Drinks* was almost certainly because the United States had sought to block NAFTA proceedings by refusing to appoint its own panelists.[85] In the case of MERCOSUR disputes, evidently countries like Argentina did believe – albeit wrongly – that the Olivos Protocol had filled in a lacuna in the MERCOSUR regime. Of the two rulings, the Appellate Body's *Mexico – Soft Drinks* is the more far reaching. It suggests that the Appellate Body is likely to ignore RTA dispute settlement even if an *electa una via* clause is invoked. If this is correct, then there is now the real risk of prolonged litigation in cases

82 Id.
83 NAFTA, Art. 2005.
84 *Poultry*, op. cit., para. 7.27 and footnote 49.
85 *Mexico – Soft Drinks*, Appellate Body Report, op. cit., paragraph 55.

in which a winning party would otherwise be justified in thinking that such cases should be confined purely to RTA dispute settlement. However, losing complainants will also have a second bite at the cherry. The real question, then, is this: Is this something the RTA negotiators would have welcomed, had they considered it? Disputes involving matters *not* included under one of the WTO's covered agreements – such as most investment disputes – are saved from this problem because WTO panels and the Appellate Body can only deal with disputes under one of the WTO's covered agreements (e.g., goods and services trade disputes).[86] However, there is a potentially high degree of overlap between RTA and WTO dispute settlement. It should be noted that to engage in so-called tit-for-tat litigation, WTO members that are also RTA partners do not require two disputes to be exactly identical. The legal character of the dispute may be beside the point, but the number of opportunities that exist to litigate roughly the same dispute, or issues related to the same dispute, is not. Saying, as the *Mexico – Soft Drinks* panel and Appellate Body did, that the two disputes must be identical, compounds the problem, for it encourages minute differentiations between the two disputes in order to justify the proliferation of trade litigation.[87]

The Appellate Body's ruling therefore encourages, rather than discourages, such litigation. Thus far there has been no case in which a panel or Appellate Body has declined exercise of its jurisdiction in favor of an RTA or other tribunal. In *Mexico – Soft Drinks*, the Appellate Body indeed ruled against having the authority to do so. The WTO has no response to the general problem of conflicting jurisdiction (i.e., authority fragmentation).

The picture is only slightly more encouraging in relation to the problem of norm fragmentation. The panel in *Argentina – Poultry* addressed the respective applicability of the Brasilia and Olivos Protocols. Had the Brasilia Protocol contained an *electa una via clause*, or had the Olivos Protocol applied to that case, things might have been different – the panel *could* also have declined the exercise of its jurisdiction. As for *Mexico – Soft Drinks*, the Appellate Body only said that it would not determine an RTA dispute, not that it will never apply an RTA rule.

Nonetheless, fragmentation operating at both the normative and jurisdictional levels could worsen bilateral relations between two countries. This was

86 See further Gao and Lim, "Saving the WTO," op. cit., 905–906 (on the exception of "mode 3" services disputes), and Lim, "Free Trade Agreements in Asia and Some Common Legal Problems," op. cit., 445–446 (on the investment/mode 3 services overlap).

87 *Mexico – Soft Drinks*, Appellate Body Report, 54. See also *Mexico – Soft Drinks*, Panel Report, op. cit., 7.14–7.15. However, it does at least demonstrate support for a litispendence rule; *cf.* Shany, *Competing Jurisdictions*, op. cit., 221–223, 239–245.

Mexico's view of the successful U.S. attempt to bring a WTO case in the *Mexico – Soft Drinks* dispute. Both norm and authority fragmentation are "political" because they contribute to international anarchy at the expense of international law. Norm fragmentation diminishes the prospects of a legal settlement by emphasizing the absence of common legal rules. Authority fragmentation erodes the authority of trade dispute settlement bodies by emphasizing their arbitrariness. Attempts at integration at both levels would likewise raise the political stakes. As Broude has also argued, norm integration not only involves "technical, lawyerly methods" but also has a "political meaning" because it not only aims for normative coherence but also represents a move "towards greater centralization and/or harmonization of authority." This could, in turn, heighten political controversy over jurisdictional authority, because attempts at the centralization or harmonization of norms means that one system is required to recognize and apply the norms of the other, thereby recognizing the existence of overlapping authority while asserting the authority to apply the norms of another system.[88]

The urgent need for an alternative approach should build on the willingness of panels and the Appellate Body to apply RTA rules while avoiding – that is, circumventing – the political controversy over fragmentation *and* integration. One approach is to recognize that the public law–private law distinction has proven unhelpful in this,[89] and that private international law analogies present the prospect of depoliticization through the application of a more neutral device – namely private international law's method of choice-of-law analysis. Choice-of-law analysis would avoid norm integration (i.e., a drive toward harmonization or unification) because it seeks agreement not over norms but the rules on the choice of applicable norms. In this regard, it could avoid the politics of norm integration by recalling the metaphor that (private) conflict of laws reasoning often resembles the impartial operation of a machine. Likewise, choice-of-law analysis – which involves a common technique shared by different jurisdictional authorities in selecting between diverse norms – could defuse political tensions over questions of overlapping authority. Simply put, it should matter less who applies a particular norm as long as that same norm is applied by all parties through the use of a common judicial technique.

88 Broude, "Fragmentation(s)", op. cit., 110–114.

89 Cf. Karen Knop, Ralf Michaels, and Annelise Riles, "Foreword: Transdisciplinary Conflict of Laws," 71 (3) *Law and Contemporary Problems* (2008); Duke Law School Public Law & Legal Theory Paper 252; Cornell Legal Studies Research Paper 09–015. Available at SSRN: http://ssrn.com/abstract=1413148.

3. THE PRIVATE INTERNATIONAL LAW ANALOGY

1. Some Inadequacies of Public International Law Solutions

Public international law solutions to jurisdictional clashes involve the invocation of general principles. Which was the later treaty? If the RTA is the later treaty, then it prevails to determine both jurisdiction and the applicable law. However, if a WTO agreement is the later treaty, then the WTO agreement prevails instead in order to determine both questions.[90] Similarly, the more specific treaty (or treaty rule) would prevail and determine both the jurisdictional question and the question of applicable law.[91] Alternatively the principle of res judicata may apply, and in the absence of an RTA treaty clause this means that the first award will prevail, or the public international law principle of estoppel. In *Mexico – Soft Drinks* Mexico had also raised the argument that he who comes to equity must come with clean hands, and because the United States had delayed proceedings by refusing to participate and had attempted to block the NAFTA arbitrator selection process, it cannot now argue that the case should be heard by the WTO.[92] As with estoppel, this argument seeks to apply equity to the question of competing jurisdictional authority. In doing so, it imports some of the difficulties concerning resort to equity under international law into the trade law field.[93]

The *lex posterior* and *lex specialis* rules were meant to resolve the problem of conflicting treaty rules in the field of public international law. The estoppel and res judicata doctrines, and indeed the application of equitable principles generally, were private law analogies that were intended to fill in gaps in the law because of the incomprehensive nature of the traditional sources of international law (i.e., custom and treaty). None of these public international law devices, which were meant to resolve public international law problems, were actually designed to meet the challenge of competing jurisdictional

[90] Because WTO and RTA rules are continuously being generated and regenerated – i.e. through successive amendments and Rounds of negotiation – the result is arbitrary, "checkerboard justice"; see Gao and Lim, "Saving the WTO," op. cit., 919; Ronald Dworkin, *Law's Empire* (Cambridge, MA: Belknap, 1996), 178–184. For the idea that the relationship between RTAs and WTO norms is "dynamic" in nature (i.e., that WTO norms are continuously being renegotiated and updated), see Pauwelyn, "Legal Avenues", op. cit., 397.

[91] Gao and Lim, "Saving the WTO from the Risk of Irrelevance," op. cit., 919–920.

[92] *Mexico – Soft Drinks*, Appellate Body Report, 55–56. See also *Mexico – Soft Drinks*, Panel Report, op. cit., 4.298–4.299 (Mexico), 4.468 (United States' reply).

[93] This is not to say that trade law generally, and WTO dispute settlement more specifically, cannot and should not account for equitable doctrines. See Elias and Lim, "General Principles," op. cit., 39–44 (addressing the "non-consensual," "subjective" nature of equitable doctrines in international law).

authority. The explanation is partly historical. There were few permanent courts and tribunals, and few organizations with established judicial settlement procedures in the field of public international law.

The attempt to force these public international law solutions has also meant that public international law ways of thinking currently play a dominant role in defining the problem of competing jurisdictional authority in the trade law field. They do so, as we have argued, by conflating two distinct questions. One of these has to do with the near absence of international law rules that properly allocate jurisdictional authority, as opposed to those that seek to prevent or resolve treaty conflicts. The other has to do with the potentially different sources of the applicable rules from the viewpoint of two competing trade law tribunals.

2. Analysis of the Current State of Trade Law Doctrine

In its current state of doctrinal development, trade law has produced a variety of possible solutions. According to the *Argentina – Poultry* panel, an *electa una via* rule may be applied, but only if the applicable law is an RTA *electa una via* clause, such as that which exists in the Olivos Protocol. The Argentinean argument that tribunal awards rendered under the Brasilia Protocol are final, and that the "legislative framework" of the Treaty of Asuncion, the Brasilia Protocol, and the principle of good faith prevent a second dispute from being brought to WTO dispute settlement, was not accepted by the *Argentina – Poultry* panel.[94] The panel in *Mexico – Soft Drinks* was faced with a different set of arguments raised by Mexico, which had argued that there is an inherent authority on the part of WTO panels to decline to hear a case while retaining their jurisdiction to do so. The essence of the Mexican argument was that the panel has discretion to choose to stay proceedings. In disagreeing that it has such a discretion, the panel did point out that in future cases another panel may be compelled to send the case to the NAFTA tribunal instead. According to this reasoning, such a future panel would not be able to choose whether to decline jurisdiction in favor of a NAFTA tribunal, but it may face a "legal impediment" in having or exercising jurisdiction in the case before it.

Thus, the two panels in *Argentina – Poultry* and *Mexico – Soft Drinks* were in agreement on some essential points. The difference seems to be that whereas the *Argentina – Poultry* panel was looking toward a RTA rule, the *Mexico – Soft Drinks* panel focused on the absence of discretion and was looking for

94 *Argentina – Poultry*, op. cit., 7.19.

an overriding mandatory rule *regardless of whether it was an RTA rule*. The theory that what is required is a mandatory rule received the support of the Appellate Body in the *Mexico – Soft Drinks* case. However, the Appellate Body, like the panel in that case, expressly left the possible, future exceptions to the *Mexico – Soft Drinks* ruling broadly undefined.

3. The Private International Law Analogy

These rulings are not necessarily inconsistent. At first glance, there is a difference between saying that there is a choice-of-law process involved (*Argentina – Poultry*) and that there is a mandatory rule involved (*Mexico – Soft Drinks*). However, mandatory rules are a commonplace thing in both the conflict of laws and international commercial arbitration. The Convention on the Carriage of Goods by Sea presents a mandatory rule in both fields.[95] Mandatory rules are also found in treaty rules such as the Rome Convention on the Law Applicable to Contractual Obligations.[96] The stipulations of the Sherman Act in the United States have been raised unsuccessfully as a mandatory rule in relation to arbitrability, though successfully in relation to the enforcement stage for international arbitral awards in the United States.[97] This is likewise the case with the concepts of lex fori in private international law and lex loci arbitri in international commercial arbitration. Whereas the concept of lex loci arbitri has been said to constitute a wider concept than lex fori (e.g., it comprises not only rules of evidence and judicial assistance but also the rule on the authority of the tribunal to

95 See, e.g., its implementation in the United Kingdom under the Carriage of Goods by Sea Act 1971, and application in *The Hollandia* [1983] 1 AC 565. It is implemented in the United States by the Carriage of Goods by Sea Act (COGSA), s. 3(8) (mandatory rule nullifying carriage contract clauses relieving carrier liability). See, e.g., *Indussa Corp. v. S.S. Ranborg* 377 F.2d 200 (2d Cir. 1967) (nonenforcement of foreign forum selection clause in bill of lading), *Vimar Seguros Y Reaseguros S.A. v. M/V Sky Reefer* 29 F.3d 727 (1st Cir. 1994) (foreign arbitration clause); Elizabeth Clark, "Foreign Arbitration Clauses and Foreign Forum Selection Clauses in Bills of Lading Covered by COGSA: Vimar Seguros Y Reaseguros S.A. v. M/V Sky Reefer," *Brigham Young Univ. L. Rev.* (1996) 483; Symeon C. Symeonides, "Choice of Law in American Courts in 1995: A Year in Review," 44 *Am. J. Comp. L.* (1996) 181. See further, *Fireman's Fund Insurance Co. v. M.V. DSR Atlantic*, 131 F.3d 1336 (9th Cir. 1997); *Central National-Gottesman, Inc. v. M.V. "Gertrude Oldendorff"*, 204 F. Supp.2d 675 (S.D.N.Y. 2002).

96 Rome Convention on the Law Applicable to Contractual Obligations 1980, Article 3(3), [1980] OJ L266. See further, Peter North, *Essays in Private International Law* (Oxford: Clarendon, 1993), 23, esp. 43–46.

97 *Mitsubishi Motors v. Soler Chrysler-Plymouth*, 473 U.S. 614, 105 S.Ct. 3346, 87 L.Ed.2d 444 (1985).

determine its own jurisdiction),[98] the principle is similar. Lex fori is mandatory, whereas lex loci arbitri is said to exist alongside the parties' choice of lex arbitri.[99]

According to the United States, the *Argentina – Poultry* panel faced squarely the question of the application of RTA law. If this is correct, then logic would demand to know what *further* rule permits such a choice to be made. The answer, according to the public international law mindset, is that RTA rules are a part of public international law because treaty rules are also "public international law." In other words, insofar as the WTO DSU (an international treaty) permits recourse to international law, WTO panels can apply RTA rules. The argument is something of a stretch, and that is why we have argued elsewhere[100] for (1) an express clause in the DSU authorizing WTO panels and the Appellate Body to apply RTA rules, and (2) a corresponding rule in future RTAs permitting these WTO bodies to do so.[101] The *Mexico – Soft Drinks* panel too did not preclude the application of an RTA "forum selection" rule (which would involve the operation of a "hidden" choice-of-law process). Admittedly, this was because NAFTA's *electa una via* clause was not raised in argument, yet the panel did go on to make this observation:[102]

> Mexico did not argue, nor is there any evidence on record to indicate, that there are legal obligations under the NAFTA or any other international agreement to which Mexico and the United States are both parties, which might raise legal impediments to the Panel hearing this case or to the United States bringing its complaint to the WTO. Indeed, when specifically questioned on this point by the Panel, Mexico responded that there was nothing in the NAFTA that would prevent the United States from bringing the present case to the WTO dispute settlement system.

This led the panel to conclude that it "makes no findings about whether there may be other cases where a panel's jurisdiction might be legally constrained."[103]

On appeal too, the Appellate Body had pointed out that the two disputes were not identical, precisely because the issues that could be raised before NAFTA

98 Compare Adrian Briggs, *Conflict of Laws* (Oxford: Clarendon, 2002), Chapter 2; Alan Redfern and Martin Hunter, *Law and Practice of International Commercial Arbitration* (London: Sweet & Maxwell, 2004), 2–10.

99 Redfern and Hunter, *International Commercial Arbitration*, op. cit., 2–12.

100 Gao and Lim, "Saving the WTO," op. cit.

101 *Ibid.*

102 *Mexico – Soft Drinks*, Panel Report, op. cit., 7.13.

103 Id., 7.10.

arbitration showed no cause of action at the WTO.[104] Although Mexico had argued that another forum would be more suitable because certain causes of action do not exist at the WTO, the Appellate Body saw no reason that resolution of the dispute could not therefore be divided between two tribunals. This was the "identical dispute" requirement in operation.[105] Second, the Appellate Body left room for a res judicata doctrine, noting that in this case a NAFTA tribunal had not yet handed down an award. Third, Article 2005.6 of Chapter Twenty of NAFTA contains the following clause:

> Once dispute settlement procedures have been initiated under Article 2007 or dispute settlement proceedings have been initiated under the GATT, the forum selected shall be used to the exclusion of the other, unless a Party makes a request pursuant to paragraph 3 or 4.

This clause was not invoked.[106] As with the panel ruling, the Appellate Body therefore concluded that "we express no view as to whether there may be other circumstances in which legal impediments could exist that would preclude a panel from ruling on the merits of the claims that are before it."[107] In other words, *Mexico – Soft Drinks* could be read so as to allow the application of a non-WTO rule, such as an RTA forum selection rule, so long as such a rule is mandatory.

Where would these legal impediments lie? The res judicata doctrine is consistent with both public and private international law analysis.[108] So is Mexico's argument that the United States, having prevented the establishment of the NAFTA tribunal, could not now invoke WTO law. Mexico had cited the *Chorzow Factory Case (Germany v. Poland)* in public international law – that a party cannot take advantage of its own wrong. In public international law, that is a general principle of law "generally accepted in the jurisprudence of international arbitration, as well as by municipal courts."[109] In private international law, however, it is an appeal to equity such as in a request for an antisuit injunction.[110] The *electa una via* clause is trickier. Because customary international law generally lacks the operation of the *lis alibi pendens* doctrine,[111] that

[104] *Mexico – Soft Drinks*, Appellate Body Report, op. cit., 54.

[105] Id.

[106] Id.

[107] *Id.*

[108] Shany. *Competing Jurisdictions*, op. cit., 223–226, 245–254.

[109] *Chorzow Factory Case (Germany v. Poland) (Indemnity)*, PCIJ, Series A No. 9 (1927) at 31. See further, Humphrey Waldock, "General Course on Public International Law," 106 *Recueil des Cours* (1962-II) 54.

[110] See, e.g., Briggs, 202, citing *Airbus Industrie GIE v. Patel* [1999] 1 AC 119.

[111] Shany, *Competing Jurisdictions*, op. cit., 239–244.

and similar doctrines would usually have to be provided for by treaty.[112] Many RTAs now include an *electa una via* clause. In one important sense, an *electa una via* clause serves a similar purpose as the *lis pendens* doctrine in private international law – that is, it seeks to prevent a second set of proceedings to be brought where one set of proceedings has already been triggered.[113] The operation of a *lis pendens* doctrine, say under custom or as a general principle of law recognized by civilized nations,[114] is, however, potentially broader in scope because an *electa una via* clause would depend on the specific treaty drafting language. If the NAFTA clause is truly a *lis pendens* clause, then it would be more akin to a creature of private rather than public international law.

However, NAFTA Article 2005.6 is Janus-faced: It is also informed by public international law doctrine. NAFTA's framers knew that the WTO dispute settlement system would come into existence and had, it seems, sought to preempt jurisdictional clashes with a *lex specialis* rule in the form of a NAFTA treaty rule that would provide for such an eventuality. Nonetheless, that clause presupposes not only that NAFTA tribunals will recognize and apply the clause, but also that WTO panels and the Appellate Body will, or at least might, do so. The framers probably presupposed a choice of an RTA rule in light of the absence of an express WTO rule (i.e., notwithstanding the contrary view in some circles that the WTO *may* contain an exclusive jurisdiction rule).[115] If that is true, then they probably saw the choice as being governed by treaty law, operating under public international law's *lex specialis* doctrine. The WTO's covered agreements, however, came into existence after NAFTA. Had NAFTA's framers also considered that the WTO's DSU would be the later treaty under another public international law doctrine – that is, the *lex posterior* doctrine? Even if they had not, would the *lex posterior* doctrine not point

[112] Id., 218–222.

[113] Id., 23 (*electa una via* encompasses both concepts of *lis alibi pendens* and res judicata). For the characterization of *electa una via* as an extension of the abuse of rights doctrine, see Petersmann, op. cit., 474. Part of the difficulty lies in comparative law; the *lis alibi pendens* doctrine may have different meanings in different legal systems; see Michaels, "Two Paradigms," op. cit., 1062 (explaining that, in U.S. law, the doctrine applies only at the recognition stage). As Michaels points out too, the European concept of *lis alibi pendens* operates ex ante and seeks to prevent parallel proceedings from being brought; id. In that sense, it is difficult to distinguish the doctrine from the intended effect of an *electa una via* clause.

[114] Cf. *Certain German Interests* (1925) PCIJ (Ser. C) No. 9-I, 82 (Germany, oral pleadings); *Certain German Interests* (1925) PCIJ (Ser. A) No. 6, 19–20. Discussed further, *id.*, 239–240. Whether the broad use of *electa una via* clauses may lead toward the establishment of a firm litispendence rule under customary international law is a good question.

[115] Shany, *Competing Jurisdictions*, op. cit., 183–184.

against the application of RTA law?[116] In other words, public international law doctrines could point in both directions. This tends to suggest that the clause was intended to codify or introduce the *lis pendens* doctrine so as to fill a gap in international public law and that its source therefore lies as much in private international law thought as in public international law analysis.

Other "impediments" could include the operation of a doctrine of comity.[117]

All this leaves the Appellate Body's invocation of the "mandatory" aspects of DSU Articles 7 (terms of reference), 11 (function of panels), 23 (with its "no blockage" aspects), and 3.3 (no delay clause). There is no reason to suppose that they have unlimited scope, and so what we are concerned with here is the precise bounds of these mandatory rules: the precise definition and scope of the exceptions to them.

4. The Private International Law Analogy versus the Allocative Thesis

It is here that the greatest difficulty with the private international law analogy presents itself. In the course of rejecting Mexico's argument that the United States was seeking to take advantage of its own wrong in bringing a WTO dispute after having "illegally" prevented the NAFTA tribunal from being constituted, the Appellate Body considered that, had it entertained Mexico's objection, it would be ruling on a "non-WTO" (i.e., NAFTA) dispute.[118] This appears to deny the scenario envisaged in the *Argentina – Poultry* case, namely the application of an RTA rule by a WTO panel or Appellate Body. However, this objection to the application of an RTA rule may be addressed in a number of ways.

First, one can distinguish between the inability of a WTO panel or Appellate Body to apply a substantive RTA rule, and its inability to apply an RTA "conflicts" rule. A res judicata or *electa una via* clause in the RTA, such as in the Olivos Protocol,[119] or the *electa una via* clause in NAFTA, could be applied by a WTO panel or the Appellate Body. The Appellate Body in *Mexico – Soft Drinks*, although rejecting its own power to decide a NAFTA dispute, nonetheless leaves open the question of the application of an RTA conflicts

[116] See Pauwelyn, "Legal Avenues," op. cit., 378–379 (arguing that international law "does not offer a clear response" and that such conflicts would have to be approached on a case-by-case basis).

[117] Henckels, op. cit.

[118] *Mexico – Soft Drinks*, Report of the Appellate Body, op. cit., 56.

[119] Cf. Olivos Protocol, Article 1(2) (*electa una via*) and Article 26(1) (res judicata).

rule by pointing out that the *electa una via* clause in NAFTA had not been invoked in *Mexico – Soft Drinks*. At best, what the Appellate Body may have ruled out is the power of WTO panels and the Appellate Body to apply a substantive as opposed to a conflicts rule in an RTA.

In other words, the private law analogy would hold *even if* the *Mexico – Soft Drinks* ruling were to be taken to constitute a bar to the direct application of a substantive RTA rule. After all, a res judicata or *lis pendens* rule in a RTA is also a conflicts rule that both panels in *Argentina – Poultry* and *Mexico – Soft Drinks*, as well as the Appellate Body, have accepted. In theory, it is therefore open to the Appellate Body to find that a RTA rule which operates as a conflicts rule chooses the application of RTA law. We can imagine a clause in an RTA which says that in the case of a jurisdictional conflict, another tribunal may apply the RTA's substantive rules – thereby leaving it to the WTO panel or the Appellate Body to decide on whether the RTA rule is applicable to the dispute before it. Such a clause may be cumbersome and confusing, but it offers a plausible solution.

The better view may be that the Appellate Body says nothing about whether it can apply a substantive RTA rule, so long as it does not actually rule on the RTA dispute. This is also the logic of the Appellate Body's pronouncement in *Mexico – Soft Drinks* that the two disputes were not identical. A difficulty arises only in those instances in which the two disputes are identical and the Appellate Body has the option of applying a substantive RTA rule and claiming and exercising the jurisdiction to do so. In effect, it could end up ruling on the RTA dispute. Compare the allocative thesis, which would seek out the *lex specialis*, or a later treaty rule – a WTO or RTA rule – and allocate jurisdiction on the basis of that rule. By doing so it assumes that the one forum that has exclusive jurisdiction will therefore simply apply one set of treaty rules to the exclusion of other treaty rules. The Appellate Body's refusal to rule on a "non-WTO" dispute is a version of the allocative thesis, which means that it will generally resist deciding points of RTA law because it tends to treat WTO rules as *lex specialis*. Is such a "judicial" policy sound?

Considering that the WTO is threatened by the proliferation of RTAs, the better policy may be that panels and the Appellate Body should revisit their power to apply RTA rules. An RTA "conflicts" clause such as that suggested earlier which points a WTO panel toward the application of a substantive RTA rule, by supplying the express permission of the RTA parties for the panel or Appellate Body to apply RTA law, will also encourage the application of RTA rules. That is one illustration of how private, not public, international law thinking could help to dispel some of the fears about the "politics" of competing jurisdictional claims, a matter that we turn to in our conclusion.

Unfortunately, such a clause is not only cumbersome, it is confusing. The better view should be that the Appellate Body has not (yet) precluded the application of substantive RTA rules. Our argument is that the Appellate Body should push beyond the allocative thesis. In order to do this, what trade law needs is a choice-of-law method of analysis.

Previous approaches would seek to resolve RTA and WTO jurisdictional clashes by turning to comity as a jurisdictional doctrine or public international law in the form of the *lex specialis* and other rules. In the first case, no answer is given to whether a WTO panel or the Appellate Body may apply RTA rules because the question is framed purely as a problem involving the proper allocation of jurisdiction. In the second case, no answer is given either because the method of resolving the problem simply presupposes that one treaty should apply to the exclusion of the other – that is, either the RTA or a WTO agreement, whichever is the later or more precise treaty. What we are proposing is a need to close a fundamental gap in the proposals that currently exist for resolving the problem of WTO and RTA jurisdictional clashes.

4. CONCLUSION

In the course of rejecting Mexico's arguments, the panel in *Mexico – Soft Drinks* expressed the following view:[120]

> We understand Mexico's argument to be that the United States' claims in the present case should be pursued under the NAFTA, not because that would lead to a better treatment of this particular claim, but because it would allow Mexico to pursue another, albeit related, claim against the United States. The Panel fears that if such a matter were to be considered then there would be no practical limit to the factors which could legitimately be taken into account, and the decision to exercise jurisdiction would become political rather than legal in nature.

In this regard, resort to public international law principles already implies a "public" legal dispute requiring a "public" legal solution. There is no doubt that WTO and trade law disputes generally are public international disputes insofar as the legal subjects are oftentimes sovereigns or their "delegates."[121] Nevertheless, there is no reason to think that public international law analysis

[120] *Mexico–Soft Drinks*, Panel Report, op. cit., 7.17.

[121] This is one explanation of Hong Kong's status as an independent customs territory, and there have also been common law pronouncements to this effect applying the "delegation theory" at common law to other territories (e.g., Chinese Taipei). See further, C. L. Lim, "Non-recognition of Putative Foreign States (Taiwan) under Singapore's State Immunity Act," 11 *Asian Yearbook Int'l L.* (2003–2004) 3, 4–7.

should have a monopoly over trade law reasoning. Indeed, the panel in *Mexico – Soft Drinks* refused to accept Mexico's "larger dispute" argument (in this case, between two sovereigns), citing the tendency to thereby "politicize" the jurisdictional issue. This is understandable because jurisdictional disputes, as conceived in the public international law field, concern clashes of penal jurisdiction between states, and state consent is typically the basis for the legal personality of international organizations, as well as their dispute settlement processes. State interests are often, though not always, implicated in WTO and RTA jurisdictional disputes.

At the same time, such treaty-based disputes (i.e., involving the WTO as a treaty-based organization and RTAs) consist of parties that are both governed by WTO and RTA law. It might be objected that such treaty conflicts are not analogous to true conflicts in the private international law sense, where there is a need to choose between entirely different personal laws between the parties.

Nonetheless, it is precisely because RTA disputes are typically "larger," in that they involve the bilateral relations of the parties, that resort to private international law concepts may prove more suitable to the task of resolving jurisdictional clashes. Our approach seeks to defuse the political tensions surrounding trade disputes generally and WTO–RTA jurisdictional clashes in particular in two related ways.

First, it recognizes that WTO and RTA disputes may operate in slightly different political contexts. Whereas third-party dispute settlement generally is meant to depoliticize bilateral legal disputes between countries and "ring-fence" such disputes from crossing into other issues involving the relationship between the two countries, the decision to bring a complaint is political and often implicates the bilateral relationship. Indeed, this can be observed even in the more mature RTA tribunals, such as what happened under NAFTA before the *Mexico – Soft Drinks* case was brought to the WTO. Although disputes in the WTO are not always immune from political influence and ill feeling, the fact that the WTO has almost universal membership and that WTO rulings are formally adopted by all WTO members in the DSB acts as a check against bilateral political spillovers.

Second, turning to private international law devices and analogies, especially rethinking res judicata, estoppel, and other criteria such as the requirement that the two disputes should be identical, mandatory rules, and legal impediments to the exercise of WTO jurisdiction, would mean resorting to rules and principles that, by their nature, are psychologically less "political" than the corresponding rules under international economic law or even public international law. Compared with public international law rules, private international law rules provide a softer, less intrusive model of normative integration. As Broude argues, normative integration that creates fewer pressures toward authority integration has a much better chance of being adopted by tribunals and thus a better prospect of attaining its normative goals.[122] Hopefully, conflict of laws–based thinking can ultimately point the way through the layers of international agreements and enable us to realize what trade is, ultimately, really about – transactions between private firms and the activities of private individuals who trade in order to improve their lives.

Third, there is a typical consideration that is usually taken to justify the forum non conveniens doctrine that the panel in *Mexico – Soft Drinks* overlooked. There is no reason that, in the absence of express agreement, the claimant should be favored over the defendant in its choice of forum.[123] WTO panels and the Appellate Body may need to grapple with such questions in the future concerning the need to do justice between the parties where the circumstances may be such that the issue cannot so easily be evaded by invoking mandatory WTO rules and policies. As the authorities stand at present, the Appellate Body's position seems to be that the parties have agreed to WTO dispute settlement and such agreement cannot be obviated by pleading that the dispute could be brought elsewhere. Nevertheless, it can be seen how tenuous the Appellate Body's ruling is. It was no coincidence that Mexico's arguments were based in large part on equity, and there is no sign that the issue will disappear anytime soon. A deeper engagement with highly developed private international thinking on the matter seems warranted in those cases in which the relevant public international law rules may be too ill developed to handle such questions.

Finally, the allocative thesis as applied by the WTO Appellate Body presently relies on public international law doctrine to determine both jurisdiction and applicable law. In doing so, it will divide up jurisdiction between the two tribunals, or it will allocate (exclusive) jurisdiction to an RTA tribunal on the basis of a *lex specialis* or later treaty rule in the RTA. Neither of these options helps the WTO to address the proliferation of RTAs and the continued politicization of jurisdictional clashes. The WTO as a multilateral body that is not concerned with the overall bilateral relationship between the two parties could seek to defuse this growing political problem by turning toward private international law analogies. There is no reason in either policy or principle that should preclude WTO panels and the WTO Appellate Body from exercising their jurisdiction while applying RTA rules, because a proper law analysis points toward the application of an RTA rule.

[122] Broude, op. cit.

[123] Briggs, *Conflict of Laws*, op. cit., 94.

It might be asked, by what authority can WTO panels and the Appellate Body resort to such analogies or other private international law devices? One answer is that they can do so on the same basis on which the doctrines of res judicata, *lex specialis*, and other principles have been discussed by panels and the Appellate Body: Not that they are public international law principles per se, but because they are principles of legal reasoning based ultimately on logic, experience, and the developing practice and jurisprudence of WTO dispute settlement.[124]

[124] See further, on such principles of legal reasoning and their status in public international law debate, Elias and Lim, "General Principles," op. cit., 31–34. See also Hersch Lauterpacht, *Private Law Sources and Analogies of International Law: With Special Reference to International Arbitration* (London: Longmans 1927), 215–296.

PART V

LINKAGES BETWEEN INTERNATIONAL ECONOMIC LAW AND FOREIGN POLICY

13

The Politics of Rules of Origin

Moshe Hirsch

1. INTRODUCTION

The political economy literature of international trade posits that external trade policies are closely linked with domestic and foreign political processes.[1] Rules of origin (ROOs) aim to determine whether a particular trade concession (e.g., duty-free import) will be applied to a given product in international trade. Certain features of ROOs make them particularly susceptible for employment as an instrument of foreign and domestic policies.

The increasing political employment of ROOs was one of the principal factors leading to the inclusion of this topic in the Uruguay Round agenda[2] and the formulation of the 1994 World Trade Organization (WTO) Agreement on Rules of Origin. As elaborated in the subsequent text, that initial agreement is

1 See, e.g., Nagire Woods, "International Political Economy in the Age of Globalization," in John Baylis and Steve Smith (eds.), *The Globalization of World Politics: An Introduction to International Relations*, 3rd ed. (Oxford University Press, 2006), 325, 326. On the link with domestic politics, see Helen V. Milner, B. Peter Rosendorff, and Edward D. Mansfield, "International Trade and Domestic Politics: The Domestic Sources of International Trade Agreements and Institutions," in Eyal Benvenisti and Moshe Hirsch (eds.), *The Impact of International Law on International Cooperation* (Cambridge University Press, 2004), 216. See also David N. Balaam and Michael Veseth, *International Political Economy*, 2nd ed. (Prentice-Hall, 2000) 4–6; J. H. Jackson, W. Davey, and A. O. Sykes, *Legal Problems of International Economic Relations*, 4th. ed. (West, 2002), 38–39.

2 See, e.g., E. Navarro Varona, "Rules of Origin in the GATT," in E. Verlmust, P. Waer, and J. Bourgeois (eds.), *Rules of Origin in International Trade* (University of Michigan Press, 1994), 355, 263; W. Keijzer, "GATT Agreement on Rules of Origin: Its Purposes and Implications from a European Community Perspective," in J. H. J. Bourgeois, F. Berrod, and E. G. Fournier (eds.), *The Uruguay Round Results: A European Lawyers' Perspective* (European University Press, Brussels, 1995) 331, 335. On the negotiations leading to the 1994 Agreement on ROOs, see Moshe Hirsch, "Commentary on the Agreement on Rules of Origin," in Rudiger Wolfrum and Peter-Tobias Stoll (eds.), *WTO – Trade in Goods* (Brill, the Netherlands, 2010).

not effectively coping with the widening political employment of ROOs. This chapter analyzes the political utilization of ROOs and offers some proposals to strengthen future agreement in this sphere.

2. RULES OF ORIGIN: MAJOR AIMS AND KEY PRINCIPLES

Rules of origin primarily serve as a differentiating mechanism for distinguishing between products according to their place of production. These rules are indispensable for the operation of international trade regimes that promote liberalization on a reciprocal basis. Under the WTO agreements, as well as bilateral and regional trade agreements (RTAs), trade concessions are granted only to products manufactured in states that undertake to grant concessions to products of other contracting states. Consequently, the operation of such "discriminatory" regimes necessitates a differentiating mechanism to identify products manufactured in contracting states (which are eligible for preferred treatment), to the exclusion of products manufactured in noncontracting states. In addition, in those instances in which a contracting party does not comply with its obligations under the trade agreement, effective retaliatory measures are of significant importance to maintaining the regime's credibility in the long run.[3] Efficient retaliatory machinery presupposes the existence of a differentiating mechanism to make a distinction between products manufactured in "cooperative" and "noncooperative" parties. Current trends, and particularly the rapid proliferation of RTAs (mainly free trade area agreements),[4] indicate that the importance of ROOs is likely to grow in the coming decade.

The determination of origin does not present special difficulties when the product is wholly manufactured in a single state. However, with the increasing trend that has been labeled the "global factory," most final products in contemporary international commerce involve factors of production from more than one country. In such cases, ROOs are designed to identify which of the states involved is the "originating state." The general principle widely accepted in international trade law is that the state where the "last substantial

[3] On the significance of retaliatory measures for compliance with international rules, see Moshe Hirsch, "Compliance with International Norms in the Age of Globalization: Two Theoretical Perspectives," in Eyal Benvenisti and Moshe Hirsch (eds.), *The Impact of International Law on International Cooperation* (Cambridge University Press, 2004), 166, 185–186.

[4] See, e.g., J. A. Crawford and R. V. Fiorentino, "The Changing Landscape of Regional Trade Agreements," WTO Discussion Paper 8 (2005), available at http://www.wto.int/english/res_e/booksp_e/discussion_papers8_e.pdf.

process"[5] or "sufficient working or processing" was carried out is the originating state.[6]

The principle of the "last substantial process" is vague and leaves wide discretion to national customs authorities. Three additional tests are widely employed to define the general principle more precisely: (1) a change in tariff classification, requiring the product to change its tariff heading under the Harmonized Commodity Description System (Harmonized System) in the originating state; (2) a domestic content test, requiring a minimum percentage of local value added in the originating state (or setting the maximum percentage of value originating in nonmember states); and (3) manufacturing operations, prescribing that the product must undergo specific processing operations in the originating state.[7]

3. ROOs AS A FOREIGN POLICY INSTRUMENT

Foreign policy factors often play a significant role in the formation and enlargement of RTAs. States occasionally form or join RTAs to promote geopolitical objectives such as supporting political partners or coalition building.[8] Consequently, RTAs have also been investigated by political scientists. The neofunctional approach is one of the most influential political science theories of international integration. This theory (and particularly its intellectual ancestor, the functional approach) is widely associated with the economic and political integration processes in Europe after World War II.[9] Whereas the functional

5 Article 3 of Annex D.1 of the 1973 International Convention on the Simplification and Harmonization of Customs Procedures, 950 U.N.T.S. 269 (hereafter "Kyoto Convention"). The Kyoto Convention was amended in 1999 and the former Annex D.1 was transferred to Annex K. Article 3 that restates the principle of substantial transformation appears under the title "Recommended Practice." See the Protocol of Amendment to the International Convention on the Simplification and Harmonization of Customs Procedures (June 26, 1999).

6 The term "last substantial process" is often used in global contexts and the term "sufficient working or processing" is widely used in regional or bilateral trade agreements.

7 Article 3 of Annex D.1 to the Kyoto Convention, *supra* note 5. These tests are also included in Article 2(a) of the 1994 WTO Agreement on Rules of Origin.

8 See, e.g., Schiff and Winters, *supra* note 27, at 187–207; R. Bhala, *Modern GATT Law* (Sweet and Maxwell, 2005), 568–569; M. Gibbs and S. Wagle, *The Great Maze: Regional and Bilateral Free Trade Agreements in Asia* (Wiley, 2005), 51–53; John Whalley, "Why Do Countries Seek Regional Trade Agreements?," NBER Working Paper 5552 (1996), 18–20; Oli Brown et al., *Regional Trade Agreements: Promoting Conflict or Building Peace?* (International Institute for Sustainable Development, 2005); OECD, *Regionalism and the Multilateral Trading System*, *supra* note 63, at 2.

9 On the important role of functional and neofunctional theories in the establishment and evolution of the European Union, see Cornelia Navari, "Functionalism versus Federalism: Alternative Visions of European Unity," in Philomena Murray and Paul Rich (eds.), *Vision of European Unity* (Westview,1996), 63.

approach emphasizes the final aims of reduction of interstate conflicts and promotion of peace, the neofunctional approach embraces a general utilitarian perspective that may promote a wider range of additional goals.[10]

ROOs may promote the foreign policy interests of a country or economic block. The link between foreign policy and ROOs is prominent in those instances in which a trading party is required to determine the origin of products manufactured in territorially disputed areas (including goods produced in an area controlled by a government not recognized by all countries).

ROOs are relevant to territorial disputes because the origin of goods is commonly defined on a territorial basis. Ordinarily, only products that are manufactured within a particular state are eligible to benefit from the preferences accorded to that state. Consequently, the determination of origin of a product may involve a prior decision regarding whether the particular product has been manufactured within or outside the exporting state. A similar question arises with regard to the competence of unrecognized governments to issue valid certificates of origin. In such cases, the determination of origin by the importing country may be affected by its foreign policy position regarding the status of the disputed area, or that of the relevant government.

Trading parties that are required to determine the origin of products manufactured in disputed areas may pursue either a practical or political approach.[11]

10 In accordance with the neofunctional approach, the process of increasing interdependence generates complex problems that individual states cannot deal with effectively. Thus, the point of departure for cooperative arrangements is the shared need of the relevant parties to further their interest in a collective manner. The neofunctional approach suggests that, in the first stage, states' policymakers identify a cooperative framework that is plausible to further the interests of involved parties. It is desirable to begin with international cooperation in relatively "low key" and apolitical sectors (such as technical or environmental sectors) that should be of importance for the parties involved. Once the cooperative efforts in such "low political" spheres generate benefits for both parties, interest groups are expected to exert pressure on national leaders to expand integration to additional sectors, not necessarily apolitical ones. The gradual process of broadening integration ("the spillover") is expected to generate further gains for involved states, thus enhancing the prospects of closer political association. Political spillover also requires a process of loyalty transference toward a new institutional center, whose organs possess or demand jurisdiction over the relevant cooperative activities. On the neofunctional approach, see Walter Mattli, *The Logic of European Integration: Europe and Beyond* (Cambridge University Press, 1999), 23–28; Ben Rosamond, *Theories of European Integration* (Palgrave Macmillan, 2000), 50–73. On the functional approach, see Mattli, *Logic*, at 21–23; Rosamond, *Theories*, at 31–42; Charles Pentland, "Functionalism and Theories of International Political Integration," in A. J. R. Groom and Paul Taylor (eds.), *Functionalism: Theory and Practice in International Relations* (Crane, Russak, 1975), 9. It is noteworthy that neofunctionalism identifies certain linkage mechanisms but makes no assumptions as to the inevitability of the cumulative integrative process; Mattli, *Logic*, at 26–27.

11 For a detailed analysis of these alternative approaches, see Moshe Hirsch, "Rules of Origin as Trade or Foreign Policy Instruments? The European Union Policy on Products Manufactured

The practical approach considers the issue of origin from a commercial perspective and seeks to minimize the role of political factors in the operation of ROOs. Under this approach, the application of ROOs should not be based on the legal rules regarding sovereignty, acquisition of territory, or international recognition, but rather on factual factors like de facto control and ensuing international responsibility. Support for the practical approach is found in Article XXVI (5) of the General Agreement on Tariffs and Trade (GATT),[12] as well as in the practice of GATT members regarding the accession of Portugal to the GATT in 1961 (with respect to the status of "some of its overseas provinces" in India)[13] and the application of the GATT to Antarctica.[14] As to ROOs included in regional arrangements, the European Union (EU) applied the practical approach with regard to goods imported from the disputed territory of Taiwan.[15]

in the Settlements in the West Bank and the Gaza Strip," 26 *Fordham Journal of International Law* (2003), 572, 576–584.

[12] Article XXVI(5)(a) of the General Agreement provides as follows: "Each government accepting this Agreement does so in respect of its metropolitan territory *and of the other territories for which it has international responsibility*, except such separate customs territories as it shall notify to the Executive Secretary to the CONTRACTING PARTIES at the time of its own acceptance" (emphasis added); see General Agreement on Tariffs and Trade, in *The Results of the Uruguay Round of Multilateral Trade Negotiations* (WTO, 1994), 7. See also *Guide to GATT Law and Practice: Analytical Index*, 6th ed. (WTO, Geneva, 1994), 852–853, 858.

[13] When Portugal sought to accede to the GATT in 1961, the question regarding the application of the General Agreement to some of its "overseas provinces" generated concerns in India. The representative of India sought clarification of the relationship between Portugal and these territories. The GATT Executive Secretary replied that "[h]e was satisfied that in adopting the text which was proposed . . . the CONTRACTING PARTIES would not be taking any position with respect to the international status of these territories. *Contracting parties were concerned only with what was relevant to the General Agreement, which were the trading arrangements proposed with respect to these territories and not their status in international law.* Therefore, the approval of this protocol would not, in [his] view, in any way affect or conflict with whatever decisions might be taken or had been taken by the General Assembly of the United Nations, on these legal matters" (emphasis added); see *GATT Law and Practice*, *supra* note 12, at 852.

[14] Following the issuance of a list of countries and territories where the GATT was effective, the United States formally stated in 1965 that it did not recognize the claims of sovereignty regarding the territory of Antarctica and reserved all rights with respect to that territory. See *GATT Law and Practice*, *supra* note 12, at 852.

[15] The EU and its member states do not recognize the Republic of China (Taiwan) as a sovereign state. Rather, they consider it a province of the State of China. Notwithstanding this nonrecognition, EU law allows the import of some products from Taiwan to the EU accompanied by a certificate of origin issued by the competent Taiwanese authorities (and not necessarily by the People's Republic of China). See, e.g., EU Commission Regulation 1084/95, Article 2, O.J. L 109/1 (1995), abolishing the protective measure applicable to imports of garlic originating in Taiwan and replacing it with a certificate of origin. See also Stephan Talmon, "The Cyprus Question before the European Court of Justice," 12 *European Journal of International Law* (2001) 727, 747–748.

The political approach considers the issue of origin from an international political perspective, and it underlines the involved questions of sovereignty and recognition. This approach accords considerable importance to prior determination regarding sovereignty or recognition with regard to a particular territory, and this earlier stage overshadows the process of determination of origin. Under this approach, the state that is identified as the sovereign state is the state of origin, and only the recognized government is authorized to issue certificates of origin. In addition to recourse to various sources of international law (including relevant decisions of international institutions), domestic tribunals that deal with questions of sovereignty or recognition are likely to take into account the political position adopted by their own governments in the particular cases. Thus, the political approach is significantly more likely to be influenced by the political position of the relevant institution with regard to the disputed territory. Support for the political approach is found in case law of the EU Court regarding certificates of origin for products manufactured in the northern part of Cyprus, as well as in the practice of the EU with respect to the origin of goods produced in the West Bank and the Gaza Strip.

In the *Anastasiou I* case, the principal question posed to the European Court of Justice (ECJ) was whether the 1972 Association Agreement between the European Economic Community and Cyprus should be interpreted as precluding acceptance by the EU member states of products from the northern part of Cyprus – when accompanied by certificates of origin issued by authorities other than the competent authorities of the Republic of Cyprus. The ECJ refused to accept certificates of origin issued by the institution established in the northern part of Cyprus, "which is recognized neither by the Community nor by the Member States; the only Cypriot State recognized is the Republic of Cyprus."[16]

The EU policy regarding goods produced in the Israeli settlements in the West Bank and the Gaza Strip well illustrates the political approach.[17] The

[16] Minister of Agriculture, Fisheries and Food, ex parte S.P. Anastasiou (Pissouri) Ltd. and Others, Case C-432/92, [1994] *E.C.R.* 3087, 3131–32. See also "The International Practice of the European Communities: Current Survey re Cypriot Import Certificates," 7 *European Journal of International Law* (1996) 120; Nicholas Emiliou, "Current Survey: Cypriot Import Certificates – Some Hot Potatoes," 20 *European Law Review* (1995) 202; Talmon, *supra* note 15.

[17] For a detailed analysis of this controversy, see Hirsch, "Rules of Origin as Trade or Foreign Policy Instruments?", *supra* note 11; Guy Harpaz, "The Dispute over the Treatment of Products Exported to the European Union from the Golan Heights, East Jerusalem, the West Bank and the Gaza Strip – The Limits of Power and the Limits of the Law," 38 *Journal of World Trade* (2004) 1049. Christian Hauswaldt, "Problems under the EC – Israel Association Agreement: The Export of Goods Produced in the West Bank and the Gaza Strip under the EC – Israel Association Agreement," 14 *European Journal of International Law* (2003) 591.

principal contentious question was whether goods produced in Israeli settlements in these areas were entitled to the trade benefits provided for in the 1995 European Union–Israel Association Agreement. The European Commission examined the question and concluded that these products are not eligible for preferential treatment under the agreement.[18] The European Commission explained that the principal question was whether Israeli settlements were part of the State of Israel.[19] The answer provided by the European Commission to this question was that "[a]ll relevant United Nations Security Council Resolutions lead to the conclusion that neither Israeli settlements in the West Bank and Gaza Strip, nor East Jerusalem and the Golan Heights can be considered as part of the State of Israel."[20]

The question regarding the origin of goods produced in the Israeli settlements in the West Bank was recently addressed by the ECJ in the Brita Case. Although the Legal Opinion delivered by the ECJ Advocate General clearly adopted the political approach (emphasizing the legal status of the West Bank),[21] the ECJ was careful not discuss issues pertaining to sovereignty over this area. The ECJ, like the Advocate General, was of the view that products manufactured in a settlement in the West Bank should not be considered as originating in Israel, but it preferred to base this conclusion on the relationships between the two parallel trade agreements concluded by the EU with Israel and the Palestine Liberation Organization.[22]

Whereas the link between ROOs and foreign policy is evident with regard to products manufactured in disputed territories, it is less manifest (and often hidden) with regard to ROOs favoring producers in two contracting parties, to the detriment of producers located in third parties. Thus, for example, India argued in the case concerning the United States and ROOs for textile products that the particular U.S. origin requirement on textile products provided an advantage to goods of concern for the European Commission, which it did not provide to goods of concern for developing countries such as

[18] See Notice to Importers; Imports from Israel into the Community (November 23, 2001), O.J. C 328/04 (2001).

[19] Implementation of the Interim Agreement on Trade and Trade-Related Matters between the European Community and Israel 7, SEC (1998) 695 final (June, 1998).

[20] The communication cites several resolutions of the Security Council, General Assembly, and other declarations issued by the EU. This straightforward logic led the commission to the conclusion that "[p]referential access to Community markets for exports originating in Israeli settlements . . . would contravene agreed rules of origin." Ibid., at 8.

[21] Case C-386/08, *Brita GmbH v. Hauptzollamt Hamburg-Hafen* (Opinion of Advocate General, October 29, 2009), paragraphs 109–111.

[22] Case C-386/08, *Brita GmbH v. Hauptzollamt Hamburg-Hafen* (February 25, 2010), at paragraphs 46–53.

India.[23] Similarly, certain origin requirements included in the United States–Singapore Free Trade Agreement (2003)[24] enable businesses operating in third parties (especially Indonesia) to take advantage of certain provisions of this free trade agreement (FTA). This special origin mechanism was influenced by the geostrategic goals of both contracting countries.[25]

As discussed in greater detail in Section 6, although some political objectives are desirable, it is clear that unrestrained political employment of ROOs presents some significant hazards, particularly the undermining of the predictability and stability of trade relations.

Special ROOs may be employed as instruments to promote desirable political interests. Cumulation of origin allows producers in one contracting party to use nonoriginating materials or labor from other countries without losing the preferential status of the final product. This mechanism effectively expands the geographic area from which factors of production may be drawn, and it moderates the restrictive impacts of regular ROOs.[26] Establishing a cumulation arrangement between several parties provides a significant incentive for producers located in those parties' territories to cooperate and reap the benefits of cumulation in their trade with third parties.

Establishing cumulation rules between former belligerents is of particular importance because commercial cooperation may well ameliorate the level of conflict and constitute a precursor to the development of cooperation in other spheres.[27] A network of commercial links between individuals and corporations located in areas susceptible to armed conflicts sets a higher "price" for any party considering the possibility of a conflict. This outcome of cumulation is likely

[23] See WTO "United States – Rules of Origin for Textiles and Apparel Products" (June 20, 2003), Panel Report, WT/DS243/R, at paragraph 6.258. See also paragraph 6.244.

[24] United States–Singapore Free Trade Agreement (May 6, 2003), available at http://www.ustr.gov/new/fta/Singapore/final/2004–10-15-final.pdf.

[25] On the Integrated Sourcing Initiative under the United States–Singapore Free Trade Agreement, see John Coyle, "Rules of Origin as Instruments of Foreign Economic Policy: An Analysis of the Integrated Sourcing Initiative in the U.S.–Singapore Free Trade Agreement," 29 *Yale Journal of International Law* (2004) 545, 554–561.

[26] On various cumulation arrangements, see Antoni Estevadeordal and Kati Suominen, "Rules of Origin: A World Map" (November 14, 2003) (Centre William Rappard World Trade Organization), 4–5, available at http://www.wto.int/english/tratop_e/region_e/sem_nov03_e/estevadeordal_paper_e.pdf.

[27] On trade as a means of reducing frictions between antagonistic countries, see Maurice Schiff and Alan Winters, *Regional Integration and Development* (The World Bank, Washington, D.C., 2003), 188–195. For a survey of empirical studies on the link between international economic integration and political conflicts, see Edward Mansfield and Brian M. Pollins, "Interdependence and Conflict: An Introduction," in Edward Mansfield and Brians M. Pollins (eds.), *Economic Interdependence and International Conflict: New Perspectives on an Enduring Debate* (University of Michigan Press, 2003), 1. See also Galia Press-Barnathan, "The Neglected Dimension of Commercial Liberalism: Economic Cooperation and . . . ", 43 *Journal of Peace Research* (2006) 261.

to strengthen the prospects for peace in embattled areas.[28] Such cumulation mechanisms have been established by the United States[29] and three Middle Eastern countries.

The 1997 agreement between Jordan and Israel, as well as U.S. legislation, allow cumulation of origin between Jordan and Israel vis-à-vis the United States regarding products manufactured in designated Qualifying Industrial Zones (QIZs).[30] Following a similar agreement concluded between Israel and Egypt in 2004, the U.S. Trade Representative designated four QIZs in Egypt in 2005.[31] These arrangements enable producers in Jordan and Egypt to export products to the United States duty free if the products contain inputs from Israel. These special origin rules are designed to broaden support for the Middle East peace process, because Jordan and Egypt are the two Arab countries that have signed peace treaties with Israel.[32]

[28] On expanding trade relations between Afghanistan and Pakistan as an instrument to promote peaceful relations between these countries, see, e.g., "Afghanistan, Pakistan Pledge Cooperation on Trade," 13(1) *Bridges Weekly Trade News Digest* (January 14, 2009), available at http://ictsd.net/i/news/bridgesweekly/37793/.

[29] On possible origin rules regarding goods manufactured by South and North Korean producers, see Annex 22-B of the 2007 United States–South Korea Free Trade Agreement, available at http://www.ustr.gov/Trade_Agreements/Bilateral/Republic_of_Korea_FTA/Final_Text/Section_Index.html. See also "South-Korea/ US: FTA Jumps Major Hurdles," *International Herald Tribune* (April, 3, 2007), available at http://www.iht.com/articles/2007/04/03/news/oxan.0403.php. I am grateful to Prof. Sungjoon Cho, who kindly provided me with these materials and discussed with me this topic.

[30] See the 1997 Agreement between Israel and Jordan on Irbid Qualifying Industrial Zone (unpublished; on file with author); U.S.–Israel Free Trade Area Implementation Act of 1985, Sec. 9, 19 *U.S.C. Sec.* 2112; Proclamation No. 6955 of the President of the United States of America. See also Office of the United States Trade Representative, *United States–Israel Free Trade Area Implementation Act*; Designation of Qualifying Industrial Zones, 65(239) *Fed. Reg.* 77688–89 (December 12, 2000). Subsequently, the United States Trade Representative (USTR), on behalf of the President, designated 13 QIZs in Jordan. See also Mary Jane Bolle, Alfred B. Prados, and Jeremy M. Sharp, *Qualifying Industrial Zones in Jordan and Egypt* (Congressional Research Service Report for Congress, 2006), available at http://www.au.af.mil/au/awc/awcgate/crs/rs22002.pdf; Joshua Ruebner, *U.S.–Jordan Free Trade Agreement* (Congressional Research Service Report for Congress, 2001), available at http://digital.library.unt.edu/govdocs/crs/permalink/meta-crs-2010:1; Joel Singer, "The Qualifying Industrial Zone Initiative – A New Tool to Provide Economic Assistance to Middle Eastern Countries Engaged in the Peace Process," 26 *Fordham International Law Journal* 547 (2003); Coyle, *supra* note 25, at 573–574.

[31] "US, Egypt, Israel Sign 3-Way Trade Pact; May Fall Foul Of WTO," 8(43) *Bridges Weekly Trade News Digest* (December 15, 2004), available at http://ictsd.net/i/news/bridgesweekly/7789/; Bolle, Prados and Sharp, *supra* note 30, at 4; Shmuel Rosner, "U.S. Designates New Qualifying Industrial Zone in Egypt," *Haaretz Daily News* (November 1, 2005), available at http://www.bilaterals.org/article.php3?id_article=3021; Coyle, *supra* note 25, at 573–574.

[32] Bolle, Prados, and Sharp, *supra* note 30, at 1, 6; Coyle, *supra* note 25, at 574–146; Rueber, *supra*, at 38; Singer, "Qualifying Industrial Zone Initiative," *supra* note 30.

4. ROOs AND DOMESTIC POLITICS

Political economy analysis of international trade argues that an international effort to reduce protectionism must involve the operation of *reciprocal* trade regimes. The underlying rationale for this approach is to avoid "free riding": The benefits of free trade are *not* to be accorded to all states. Trade concessions are to be granted only to products manufactured in states that undertake and implement similar concessions for products of other contracting states. Existing trade barriers vis-à-vis noncontracting parties are to be maintained.[33] As already noted, the operation of such "discriminatory" regimes require ROOs to identify products manufactured in contracting states (which are eligible for preferred treatment), to the exclusion of products manufactured in noncontracting states. From this perspective, ROOs function as "gate keepers" in discriminatory trade regimes.[34]

In reality, however, ROOs often fall prey to domestic protectionist pressures. ROOs are increasingly employed as an instrument *to increase* trade barriers vis-à-vis producers located in countries that do not participate in the mutual trade regime. The main objective of ROOs in such cases is to increase the consumption of local inputs (materials and labor) by restricting access of third parties' suppliers into the preferential market. The apparent motive of this move is to "compensate" local manufacturers for the losses expected to arise following the implementation of trade liberalization toward the contracting parties. Setting more restrictive ROOs generates an enhanced incentive for local producers to employ factors of production originating in the territories of the contracting states,[35] at the expense of foreign

33 On reciprocal trade agreements as an instrument to reduce protectionism see, e.g., Peter Moser, *The Political Economy of the GATT* (Verlag Ruegger, Grusch, 1990), 25, 39; Hoekman and M. Kostecki, *The Political Economy of the World Trading System* (Oxford University Press, 1995); M. J. Trebilcock and R. Howse, *The Regulation of International Trade*, 3rd ed. (2005), 6–8. For an analysis of the GATT–WTO system from this perspective, see Jagdish Bhagwati, *Protectionism* (MIT Press, 1988), 35–37, 40; Arie L. Hillman, *The Political Economy of Protection* (Hardwood Academic Publishers, Switzerland, 1989), 121–123.

34 For a detailed political economic analysis of ROOs, see Moshe Hirsch, "International Trade Law, Political Economy and Rules of Origin: A Plea for a Reform of the WTO Regime on Rules of Origin," 36 *Journal of World Trade* (2002) 171.

35 The terms "local" and "domestic" refer here to the territories of the contracting states, and "foreign" refers to the territories of noncontracting states. This terminology is based on the assumption that the preferential arrangements include rules of either "bilateral cumulation" or "multilateral cumulation." Cumulation rules allow each party to the arrangement to use factors of production originating in the territories of the other contracting parties without infringing upon the ROOs. See, e.g., Article 404 of the North American Free Trade Agreement (NAFTA), 32 *International Legal Materials* (1983) 289. In the absence of such cumulation rules, the

suppliers.[36] Generally, as more local materials and processes are employed in the manufacture of a product, the likelihood of meeting the origin requirements increases. Thus, the inclusion of more stringent ROOs in a preferential agreement generates a greater incentive for producers to use more local materials and intermediate components.[37]

Numerous cases of utilizing ROOs as an instrument of domestic protectionism are documented in the international trade literature.[38] Prominent examples are the origin requirements from the North American Free Trade Agreement (NAFTA) that were shaped with the intention of increasing local sourcing of tomatoes[39] and textiles,[40] and the change of the European Commission's ROOs applied to photocopiers – with the apparent intention of "targeting" Ricoh producers in the United States.[41] These reports of employing

aforementioned effects of ROOs operate only with regard to the territory of each contracting party.

36 On this impact of ROOs, and its inefficient consequences (in terms of reallocation of resources) in detail, see Moshe Hirsch, *The Asymmetric Incidence of Rules of Origin: Will Progressive and Cumulation Rules Resolve the Problem?*, 32 *Journal of World Trade* (1998) 41, 44–45.

37 For a comparative analysis of the levels of restrictiveness of ROOs, see Antoni Estevadeordal and Kati Suominen, "Mapping and Measuring Rules of Origin around the World," in *Regional Trade Agreements* (Oxford University Press, 2006), 69, 93–99.

38 See, e.g., Olivier Cadot, Jaime De Melo, and Alberto Portugal-Pérez, "Rules of Origin for Preferential Trading Arrangements: Implications for the ASEAN Free Trade Area EU and U.S. Experience," World Bank Policy Research Working Paper 4016 (2006), 15, available at http://.com/abstract=940247; Schiff and Winters, *supra* note 27, at 79–80.

39 The ROOs regarding tomato catsup in NAFTA are more stringent than those included in the former Canada–United States FTA. The apparent aim of this change was to increase the share of Mexican tomato producers in the U.S. market, at the expense of their competitors from Chile. David Palmeter, "Rules of Origin in Regional Trade Agreements," in Paul Demaret, Jean-Francois Bellis, and Gonzalo Garcia Jimenez (eds.), *Regionalism and Multilateralism after the Uruguay Round* (European Inter-University Press, Brussels, 1997), 341, 343–345.

40 NAFTA ROOs regarding textiles and apparel are restrictive, with the intention of encouraging Canadian and Mexican textile manufacturers to use costlier U.S. fabrics, instead of less expensive Asian ones. Joseph A. LaNasa III, "Rules of Origin under the North American Free Trade Agreement: A Substantial Transformation into Objectively Transparent Protectionism," 34 *Harvard International Law Journal* (1993) 381, 397–399.

41 Exports from the Ricoh plant in the United States significantly increased following the imposition of antidumping duties by the European Community on imported photocopiers from Japan. The new ROOs essentially described the operations carried out by the Ricoh producer in the United States, and provided that such operations do *not* confer U.S. origin. Consequently, photocopiers produced in the United States were considered as originating in Japan, and they were subject to antidumping duties. Edwin A. Verlmust, "Rules of Origin as Commercial Policy Instruments – Revisited," 26 *Journal of World Trade* (December 1992) 61, 66–67; Anna Murphy, *The European Community and the International Trading System*, Vol. II (Center for European Policy Studies, Brussels, 1990), 50–51. See also Jeri Jensen-Moran, "Trade Battles as Investment Wars: The Coming Rules of Origin Debate," 19 *The Washingtonian Quarterly* (1995) 239, 242–243.

ROOs as a tool of protectionism are supported by the results of statistical studies.[42]

5. WHY ARE ROOS MORE SUSCEPTIBLE TO POLITICAL PRESSURES?

The international trade literature shows that ROOs are increasingly employed as instruments of foreign and domestic policies. ROOs are more susceptible to political pressure than many other trade measures because of three principal factors: the nontransparent nature of most origin requirements, increasing legal restrictions on the application of other trade barriers, and a relatively weak legal regime.

A. *Veiled Protectionism*

Political economy studies show that policymakers are inclined to prefer trade protectionist measures that are less transparent. Regularly, nontariff barriers (NTBs) are not immediately discernable by the losers from protectionism policies, and the extent of the incurred losses is less detectable.[43] Employing less transparent trade measures decreases the likelihood of opposition to these measures by other segments of the population. Most ROOs are formulated in a complex and technical form. Though origin requirements are formally accessible to the public in most states, their level of complexity often requires special expertise to assess their impact upon a particular sector of the economy. Practically, ROOs and their economic impact are not comprehensible to most citizens, journalists, and policymakers.[44]

Policymakers who seek to employ trade measures for political purposes are more prone to use ROOs because their technical content and restrictive impact are hardly known to the public. Still, the likely implications of new

[42] Kerry A. Chasl, "Protecting Free Trade – Political Economy of Rules of Origin," 62 *International Organization* (2008) 507; Antoni Estevadeordal, "Negotiating Preferential Market Access: The Case of the North American Free Trade Agreement," 34 *Journal of World Trade* (2000) 141, 151.

[43] Hillman, *supra* note 33, at 73–74; Daniel Y. Kono, "Optimal Obfuscation: Democracy and Trade Policy Transparency," 100 *American Political Science Review* (2006) 369. See also Hirsch, "The Political Economy of Rules of Origin," *supra* note 34, at 182–183.

[44] The statement made by the Canadian Trade Minister before the Canadian parliament regarding NAFTA's ROOs well illustrates this factor: "Rules of origin are very, very complex. You don't want to know about them. They are terrible things to deal with." As cited in John P. Simpson, "North American Free Trade Agreement – Rules of Origin," 28 *Journal of World Trade* (1994) 33.

ROOs are well known to experts within the interested industrial sectors, and also to the policymakers who prescribe them.

B. *Increasing Legal Restrictions on the Application of Other Trade Barriers*

Domestic and external demands for protectionism are not removed whenever certain international trade agreements direct parties to reduce or eliminate certain trade barriers. When one route of protection is restricted or blocked, the demand for protection is simply channeled to other available routes. Under the "Law of Constant Protectionism" (as defined by Bhagwati), "[i]f you reduce one kind of protection, another variety simply pops out elsewhere. (You then have a Displacement Effect, not evidence of any increase in protectionism pressure)."[45] Thus, as tariffs have been intensely reduced in the recent GATT–WTO rounds, and resorting to various NTBs has been significantly curtailed over the past three decades, restrictive ROOs are increasingly needed as a substitute for traditional trade barriers.

C. *Weak Legal Regime*

The third factor that explains why ROOs are more susceptible to political pressures is the lack of an effective legal regime to restrain the employment of ROOs for political aims. The regulation of ROOs under WTO auspices is still in its infancy, and initial steps were only taken in the recent Uruguay Round. As elaborated in Section 7, the scope of the current WTO ROOs Agreement is considerably limited and some of its important rules are vague. Thus, the existing global ROOs regime does not effectively curb the political use of ROOs.

6. THE PERILS OF THE POLITICAL EMPLOYMENT OF ROOs

It is well known that the rules included in RTAs, as of international law in general, are not shaped in a political vacuum and some political influences are inevitable.[46] Generally, such political impacts are more legitimate (and

[45] Bhagwati, *Protectionism*, *supra* note 33, at 53. This effect was also confirmed by a statistical study that focused on the interaction between the employment of tariffs and NTBs. Edward D. Mansfield and Marc L. Bush, "The Political Economy of Nontariff Barriers: A Cross-National Analysis," 49 *International Organization* (1995) 723, 739–740.

[46] On the various interactions between international law and international politics, see, e.g., Louis Henkin, *How Nations Behave: Law and Foreign Policy*, 2nd ed. (Columbia University Press, 1979), 88–98.

visible) in the process of design of RTAs' legal rules than in the process of their implementation. International trade rules, once they have been agreed upon by the RTA's members, are fundamentally different from changing patterns in foreign policy. Although international law interacts with international politics in various respects, it retains (and should retain) an essential autonomy from political processes.[47]

International legal rules aim, inter alia, to enhance certainty and predictability in a particular realm of international interaction. These attributes of rules of law are vital to the development and expansion of the international economic system. The recent trend of increasing "legalization" (or "rule oriented diplomacy")[48] is noticeable in the multilateral trading system,[49] as well as in world politics in general.[50] Although international trade rules are inevitably influenced to a certain degree by foreign and domestic policies, the unrestrained politicization of ROOs (and particularly in the implementation stage) is bound to undermine certainty in the international economic system.

Foreign policy goals are modified over time, and it is not desirable that inconsistent ROOs will be implemented in different periods. The application of different ROOs that follow different political policies is likely to weaken predictability for producers and traders, destabilize trading relations, and hinder long-term development of international trade. These significant considerations suggest that the political employment of ROOs should be restrained.[51]

These important considerations are emphasized by the WTO ROOs Agreement clarifying that ROOs are designed to facilitate the flow of international trade in a predictable manner,[52] and it affirms the need to ensure that origin requirements are "applied in an impartial, transparent, predictable, consistent and neutral manner."[53]

47 See Andrew Hurrel, "International Law and the Changing Constitution of International Society," in Michael Byers (ed.), *The Role of Law in International Relations* (Oxford University Press, 2000), 327, 331.

48 See John H. Jackson, *The World Trading System: Law and Policy of International Economic Relations*, 2nd ed. (MIT Press, 1997), 109 et seq.

49 See, e.g., Arie Reich, "From Diplomacy to Law: The Juridicization of International Trade Relations," 17 *Northwestern Journal of International Law & Business* (1997) 775.

50 See Kenneth W. Abbott et al., "The Concept of Legalization, International Organization," 54 *International Organization* (2000) 401–419; Miles Kahler, "Conclusions: The Causes and Consequences of Legalization," 54 *International Organization* (2000) 661–683.

51 As discussed in Section 8, it is not suggested that all policy-oriented ROOs should be prohibited.

52 The second and sixth preambular paragraphs of the WTO Agreement on Rules of Origin, *The Legal Texts – The Results of the Uruguay Round of Multilateral Trade Negotiations* (1994), 241. See also, Hirsch, "Commentary on the Agreement on Rules of Origin," *supra* note 2, Section B.

53 The sixth preambular paragraph of the 1994 WTO Agreement, *supra* note 52.

7. THE WTO LAW AND POLITICALLY MOTIVATED ROOs

The GATT–WTO law on ROOs is still in its formative stage. The 1947 GATT assumes the identification of origin of traded goods, but its provisions address this issue only to a limited extent. GATT provisions largely allow individual contracting parties to determine their own origin rules and do not specify how ROOs are to be applied.[54] The major international treaty that addressed ROOs until 1994 was prepared under the auspices of the Customs Cooperation Council (the forerunner of the current World Customs Organization). Annex D.1 of the 1973 Kyoto Convention[55] laid out several central principles regarding the determination of origin in international trade. The convention prescribed the substantial transformation principle[56] and presented three specific, alternative criteria to implement this principle. Thus, the Kyoto Convention left the parties with discretion regarding the employment of three alternative tests.[57] The proliferation of RTAs, as well as the increasing employment of ROOs as an instrument to raise trade barriers, resulted in a series of discussions between several major trading powers, and the topic of ROOs was included in the Uruguay Round agenda.[58]

The scope of the 1994 ROOs Agreement is significantly limited and it applies only to *nonpreferential* ROOs. The definition of ROOs in Article 1(1) of the ROOs Agreement unequivocally excludes preferential ROOs from the scope of the agreement. Thus, ROOs included in RTAs are not covered by the agreement's provisions and are addressed only in the declaration contained in Annex II. When the negotiations on the future ROOs agreement were opened, Japan, the United States, and some other countries suggested applying the agreement to both preferential and nonpreferential ROOs.[59] The

54 See, e.g., Articles I:1, II:1(b), (c), III:2 and 4, XI:1 and XIII:1, and Article VIII:1(c) of the GATT. Article IX of the GATT refers to "marks of origin" and Subsection (1) essentially applies the most-favored-nation obligation with regard to marking requirements. Article IX(2) vaguely guides the members to "reduce to a minimum" the difficulties caused by marks of origin to the commerce and industries of exported countries. See also Article VIII(1)(c) of the GATT; and P. Mavroidis, *The General Agreement on Tariffs and Trade: A Commentary* (Oxford University Press, 2005), 278.

55 Annex D.1 of the Kyoto Convention, *supra* note 5.

56 Standard 3 of Annex D.1 of the Kyoto Convention, *supra* note 5.

57 The Kyoto Convention was amended in 1999 and the former Annex D.1 was transferred to Annex K. See Article 3. Protocol of Amendment to the International Convention on the Simplification and Harmonization of Customs Procedures (June 26, 1999).

58 See, e.g., J. Croome, *Reshaping the World Trading System* (Kluwer, The Hague, 1999), 164–165.

59 On the position of Japan, see Note by the Secretariat, MTN.GNG/NG2/16 (March 13, 1990), Group of Negotiations on Goods (GATT), Negotiating Group on Non-Tariff Measures, Meeting of 14–15 February 1990, at paragraph 17. On the position of the United States, see Statement by the United States Delegation, Multilateral Trade Negotiations, MTN.GNG/NG2/W/51

European Communities (EC) opposed this proposal and suggested that the agreement be applied only to nonpreferential arrangements.[60] The European Communities explained that preferential arrangements were often based on special relations and the parties should have the freedom to formulate ROOs for such arrangements.[61] The final text of Article 1 and Annex II of the ROOs agreement reflected the compromise that was reached prior to the Brussels Ministerial Meeting in December 1990.[62]

The nonapplication of the ROOs agreement to origin requirements included in RTAs is of major significance. The recent decade has witnessed an unprecedented wave of growth in the number and scope of RTAs. Though some kinds of RTAs have existed for centuries, their number, as well as the world share of trade covered by RTAs, has been steadily increased over the past ten years. Nearly all countries belong to at least one RTA, and some are party to numerous agreements. RTAs already account for almost half of all world trade, a figure expected to increase if all the RTAs currently in the pipeline are implemented.[63] As Hoekman and Kostecki state, "[r]ules of origin have been problematical mostly in the context of preferential trade agreements: exactly the arena where WTO rules do not apply."[64]

(December 22, 1989), Group of Negotiations on Goods (GATT), Negotiating Group on Non-Tariff Measures, Rules of Origin, 30 November 1989, at p. 3. Hong Kong and Israel also supported this position. Communication from Hong Kong, Multilateral Trade Negotiations, MTN.GNG/NG2/W/41 (September 15, 1989), Group of Negotiations on Goods (GATT), Negotiating Group on Non-Tariff Measures, Rules of Origin; Note by the Secretariat, Multilateral Trade Negotiations, MTN.GNG/NG2/16 (March 13, 1990), Group of Negotiations on Goods (GATT), Negotiating Group on Non-Tariff Measures, Meeting of 14–15 February 1990.

60 Communication from the European Communities, MTN.GNG/NG2/W/55 (February 5, 1990), Group of Negotiations on Goods (GATT), Negotiating Group on Non-Tariff Measures, Rules of Origin, paragraph 1.

61 Keijzer, "GATT Agreement on Rules of Origin," *supra* note 2, at 331, 336; Croome, *supra* note 58, at 165.

62 See P. Brenton and H. Imagawa, "Rules of Origin, Trade and Customs," in L. De Wulf and J. B. Sokol (eds.), *Customs Modernization Handbook* (The World Bank, Washington, D.C., 2005), 183, 188.

63 OECD, *Regionalism and the Multilateral Trading System* (2003), 1–2, available at http://www.oecd.org/LongAbstract/0,3425,en_2649_37431_8895923_1_1_1_1,00.html. See also Crawford and Fiorentino, "The Changing Landscape of Regional Trade Agreements," *supra* note 4.

64 Hoekman and Kostecki, *Political Economy*, *supra* note 33, at 104. Similarly, Lawrence makes this statement: "The major abuses perpetrated by the emerging regional arrangements relate to their use of rules of origin and antidumping provisions." See Robert Z. Lawrence, "Regionalism and the WTO: Should the Rules be Changed?," in Jeffrey J. Schott (ed.), *The World Trading Organization System: Challenges Ahead* (Institute of International Economics, Washington, D.C., 1996), 41, 52.

Preferential ROOs are addressed in the declaration included in Annex II of the ROOs agreement, but the declaration's provisions are significantly more lenient than those applied by the agreement to nonpreferential ROOs. This weakness arises not only from the nonbinding nature of the declaration but also from a comparison of the content of the rules applied to preferential and nonpreferential ROOs.

The main part of the declaration on preferential ROOs (Articles 3 and 4 of Annex II) applies some rules of conduct to preferential ROOs.[65] Although there are some parallels between the content of the rules applied to preferential and nonpreferential ROOs (though the former are not binding), it is noteworthy that some significant disciplines that are applied to nonpreferential ROOs are *not* applied by the declaration regarding preferential ROOs. Most prominently, the declaration does not state that members should not employ preferential ROOs as instruments to pursue trade objectives;[66] that they should not create preferential ROOs that restrict, distort, or disrupt international trade;[67] that they should administer preferential ROOs in a consistent, uniform, impartial, and reasonable manner;[68] and that preferential ROOs should reflect the widely accepted principle of substantial transformation.[69]

As to nonpreferential ROOs, Part II of the ROOs agreement defines two distinct periods with two different sets of applicable rules: the transition period (i.e., until the harmonization of ROOs is completed – addressed by Article 2) and the post-transition period (addressed by Article 3). During the transition period the Members generally retain a wider measure of discretion regarding the determination and application of ROOs, as compared to the post-transition period.

The ROOs agreement prohibits the employment of ROOs for foreign policy and domestic political aims. As to the transition period, Article 2(b) prohibits the utilization of ROOs as an instrument to promote trade objectives. The term "trade objectives" refers here to protecting the domestic industry against import competition or favoring imported products of one member over imported

65 For a detailed analysis of Annex II of the ROOs Agreement, see Hirsch, "Commentary on the Agreement on Rules of Origin," *supra* note 2, Section J.

66 See Article 2(b) that is applied to the transition period, and Article 9(1)(d) of the Agreement that is applied to the harmonization work program.

67 See Articles 2(c) that is applied to the transition period, and Article 9(1)(d) of the Agreement that is applied to the harmonization work program.

68 See Article 2(e) that is applied to the transition period, and Article 9(1)(e) of the Agreement that is applied to the harmonization work program.

69 See Article 3(b) of the Agreement that is applied to the post-transition period, and Article 9(1)(b) that is applied to the harmonization work program.

goods of another.[70] Thus, this provision corresponds to two of the GATT's main obligations: the prohibition against favoring domestic products to the detriment of imported products (the national treatment principle),[71] and the prohibition against favoring products of one member over goods of another (the most-favored-nation principle).[72] Like Article 2(b), Article 2(d) of the ROOs agreement also prohibits two kinds of discrimination: discrimination in favor of domestic producers and discrimination in favor of producers in one member state over those in another member state. However, whereas Article 2(b) focuses on the *use* of ROOs (and prohibits their employment as an instrument to promote trade policies), Article 2(d) places the emphasis on the stringency of the origin requirements themselves. The first part of Article 2(d) prohibits the application of ROOs that are more stringent than those applied to determine whether or not a good is domestic, and this ban parallels the prohibition of Article III of the GATT. The second part of Article 2(d) prohibits ROOs that discriminate between the WTO members, and this ban corresponds to the prohibition under Article I of the GATT.[73]

As to disciplines during the post-transition period (upon implementation of the results of the harmonization work program): Generally, most rules included in Article 2 (and applied during the transition period) are also included in Article 3 and will continue to be applied after the transition period. These rules relate, inter alia, to the prohibition against discrimination in favor of domestic producers or between Members.[74] The ROOs agreement's provisions regarding the disciplines applied during the current (transition) period were interpreted in a restrictive manner in the only WTO decision that addressed the ROOs agreement.[75]

70 United States – Rules of Origin for Textiles and Apparel Products United States – Rules of Origin for Textiles and Apparel Products, *supra* note 23, at paragraph 6.40.

71 Article III of the GATT, *supra* note 12.

72 Article I of the GATT, *supra* note 12.

73 See also Mavroidis, *supra* note 54, at 125.

74 See Article 3(c) and Article 2(d) of the ROOs Agreement, *supra* note 23.

75 See, e.g., the panel's analysis of the question concerning the application of the second clause of Article 2(d) not only to the "same" products but also to "like" products. United States – Rules of Origin for Textiles and Apparel Products, *supra* note 23, at paragraph 6.246–6247. In addition, the panel refrained from endorsing the universally recognized principle of the "substantial transformation" (though it was careful not to reject it). The panel stated in that regard "[w]e see no requirement in Article 2 that Members need to confer origin on the country where a significant, or even the most significant, economic contribution to a final good has been made." United States – Rules of Origin for Textiles and Apparel Products, *supra* note 23, at paragraph 6.75. The panel further clarified in a note that its finding on the specific argument of India does not contradict the substantial transformation principle: "[I]t is our understanding that, under the widely recognized substantial transformation criterion,

8. CONCLUDING REMARKS AND THE FUTURE ROOs AGREEMENT

The preceding sections have revealed that ROOs are more susceptible to political pressures and that they are increasingly employed to promote foreign and domestic political interests. Though some of those political objectives are desirable, the unrestrained political employment of ROOs embraces some significant hazards, particularly the undermining of the predictability and stability of trade relations. Consequently, it is suggested to further restrain the involvement of political considerations in the formulation and implementation of ROOs. As already noted, the current global regime on ROOs is still in its infancy, and the provisions of the present ROOs agreement do not effectively address the risks of increasing political utilization of origin requirements.

To effectively cope with the present challenges of the widening political use of ROOs, it is desirable that the future ROOs agreement would include strengthened and clear disciplines to curb trading parties' discretion with regard to nonpreferential ROOs. More importantly, it is of significant importance that the future global instrument in this field will also be applied to ROOs included in RTAs (which are more vulnerable to political utilization).

Even without the application to RTAs of the future WTO ROOs Agreement, future WTO tribunals may apply Article XXIV(5)(b) of the GATT (applicable to RTAs) to curb politically motivated ROOs.[76] Although the declaration on preferential ROOs is not legally binding, its provisions may influence the interpretation given by the WTO organs to Article XXIV GATT regarding ROOs included in regional agreements.

The future ROOs regime should not prohibit every employment of origin requirements for foreign policy purposes. As already noted, cumulation of origin arrangements between former belligerents may well lower the level of conflict and enhance economic cooperation between producers and traders

a substantial transformation may, in some instances, be said to occur in situations where the transforming process adds little value, or even where it decreases the value of the transformed good." United States – Rules of Origin for Textiles and Apparel Products, *supra* note 23, at Footnote 193 (in paragraph 6.75).

[76] Under Article XXIV(5)(b) of the GATT, regulations of commerce maintained in each of the constituent territories of free trade areas or customs unions and applied to the trade of non- parties should not be higher or more restrictive than the corresponding regulations of commerce existing in the same constituents territories prior to the formation of the free trade area or customs union. See also J. J. Barcelo, "Harmonizing Preferential Rules of Origin," Cornell Legal Studies Research Paper Series (2006), 21–23; *GATT Law and Practice, supra* note 12, at 746–747. See also Article XXIV(b)(8) of the GATT.

from the rival countries. Such desirable (though discriminatory) ROOs may be legalized by a "waiver" under Article IX (3) of the WTO Agreement[77] or under a special exception clause to be included in the future agreement on ROOs.

[77] See, e.g., P. Van Den Bossche, *The Law and Policy of the World Trade Organization: Text, Cases and Materials*, 2nd ed. (Cambridge University Press, 2006), 114–115, 142–143; James Harrison, "Legal and Political Oversight of WTO Waivers," 10 *Journal of International Economic Law* (2008) 411.

14

The Politics of Divestment

Perry S. Bechky

Divestment[1] is back. Notably associated with the anti-apartheid movement,[2] when "as many as 140 states, cities, and localities" in the United States divested from South Africa over twenty years,[3] divestment largely faded from public view with the end of apartheid. Even when Massachusetts and various cities took up the cause of promoting democratization in Burma during the 1990s, they restricted government procurement of goods and services rather than divesting shares.

[1] In this chapter, I use the word "divestment" to describe investment-related actions motivated principally by concern for noneconomic objectives. "Divestment" in this sense can involve selling shares in a target company, refusing to buy new shares, and engaging with management to change the behavior of concern. Although "divestment" and "engagement" are often regarded as opposing strategies, I treat them together on the ground that it is prudent to try to persuade management before selling shares and appropriate to sell shares when management fails to respond to shareholder concerns.

[2] The economic sense of the word "divestment" apparently first acquired the political connotations of interest here during the anti-apartheid movement. See "Princeton to End Credit in R.O.T.C.; Faculty Also Votes to Set Up Black Studies Program," *New York Times* (March 4, 1969) ("students have demanded divestment of $127-million in university investments in 29 American companies with dealings in South Africa"). The first usage with this connotation in the *Compact Oxford English Dictionary* (2nd ed. 1991), also concerning South Africa, is – surprisingly – nine years later.

[3] Cleveland, "*Crosby* and the 'One-Voice' Myth in U.S. Foreign Relations," 46 *Vill. L. Rev.* (2001) 975, at 995 and note 140.

Note: I presented an earlier version of this chapter at the biennial conference of the International Economic Law Interest Group of the American Society of International Law, when I was a Visiting Assistant Professor at the University of Connecticut School of Law. I am grateful to the conference organizers for inviting me to participate; to the University of Connecticut for funding my participation; to Jack Kirkwood, Orde Kittrie, Adam Sterling, conference participants, and the editors for their helpful comments; and to Patrick Mott and Nicole Trask for their research assistance. All mistakes are my own. The information in this chapter is updated through February 1, 2010.

State and local divestment emerged again to prominence (if not at 1980s levels) in response to the horrors of Darfur. By the end of 2008, twenty-seven states and the District of Columbia had divested from Sudan, as had twenty-two cities.[4] In December 2007, Congress enacted an unprecedented federal law – the Sudan Accountability and Divestment Act (SADA) – authorizing states to divest, within important bounds, from companies that do business in Sudan.[5] The Darfur movement also sparked wider interest in divestment.[6] Most notably, at least nineteen states and the District of Columbia have divested from companies investing in Iran's energy sector.[7]

The media are showing renewed interest in divestment as well. The word "divestment" appeared in 18 articles in the *New York Times* in 2005, more than in any year since 1990, the year South Africa released Nelson Mandela from prison. The *Times*' median annual use of the word since 2005 (13 articles per annum) is greater than during any five-year period since 1980, except for the height of the anti-apartheid movement in the late 1980s (61 articles per annum). Similarly, the word appeared in the industry newspaper *Pensions & Investments* over five times more since 2005 than in the preceding decade (295 articles to 52).[8]

Divestment also surfaced during the 2008 U.S. Presidential Election campaign. Barack Obama and John McCain spoke in favor of divestment from Iran.[9] Mr. Obama, Mr. McCain, and Sarah Palin announced that they had divested their personal assets from Sudan, while Joseph Biden confirmed that

4 See Sudan Divestment Task Force, Divestment Statistics, available at http://sudandivestment.org/statistics.asp (last accessed on October 2, 2009), listing divesting jurisdictions.

5 See Pub. L. No. 110-174, § 3(b) (2007).

6 See Dobris, "SRI – Shibboleth or Canard (Socially Responsible Investing, That Is)," 42 *Real Prop. Prob. & Tr. J.* (2008) 755, 758 and note 12 (describing Darfur as a "specific-event catalyst" fueling interest in divestment).

7 See S. Rep. No. 111–99 (2009), at 6.

8 These data are based on a year-by-year search for the word "divestment," using the search engines on www.nytimes.com and www.pionline.com. These data are both overinclusive and underinclusive: they omit articles containing synonyms and even closely related words (e.g., divest) and they capture some noise (e.g., articles using "divestment" to describe ordinary commercial transactions or referring back to the anti-apartheid movement).

9 After Mr. McCain called for divestment from Iran, Mr. Obama retorted, "I was interested to see Senator McCain propose divestment as a source of leverage.... It's a good concept but not a new one; I introduced legislation over a year ago." John McCain, Speech to the AIPAC Policy Conference 2008 (June 2, 2008), at 10; Barack Obama, Speech to the AIPAC Policy Conference 2008 (June 4, 2008), at 8. Both speeches are available at http://www.aipac.org/about_AIPAC/Learn_About_AIPAC/12161.htm (last accessed on February 16, 2010). Faced with the prospect of endorsing a policy already associated with his opponent, Mr. McCain seems to have stopped speaking publicly about divestment for the remainder of the campaign.

he owned no investments in companies targeted for divestment.[10] Ms. Palin also invoked divestment in an effort to substantiate her competence to handle foreign policy – not an insignificant challenge when running against the Chairman of the Senate Foreign Relations Committee to be a "heartbeat away from the presidency." In their much-anticipated vice presidential debate, Ms. Palin responded to Mr. Biden's call for a "no-fly zone" in Darfur by agreeing with his proposal and claiming to lead an effort to enact divestment legislation in Alaska as a second policy regarding Darfur.[11] Ms. Palin thus effectively claimed that the job of governor today includes, to some extent, foreign affairs. This claim – unlike some of Ms. Palin's other claims to foreign policy experience[12] – did not attract significant public criticism. The silence is telling. Criticism, even "mock[ery]," should have followed if the American public accepted the traditional dualist notion that foreign affairs is the exclusive preserve of the federal government – a field in which the states "do[ ] not exist," according to the Supreme Court's hoary phrase.[13]

To be fair, the data show a downtick in interest in divestment in 2009. This downtick raises the question of whether divestment is bound again for obscurity after a brief second life. Recognizing the wisdom of Yogi Berra's warning that "It's tough to make predictions, especially about the future," one might

[10] See Sudan Divestment Task Force, "Governor Sarah Palin Divests from Sudan, Joins Senators Obama and McCain" (October 10, 2008), available at http://sudandivestment.org/statistics.asp (last accessed on October 2, 2009). For additional details, see also Mullins, "Obama Sells Investment with Link to Sudan," Wall Street Journal (May 16, 2007), available at http://blogs.wsj.com/washwire/2007/05/16/obama-sells-investment-with-link-to-sudan/ (last accessed on February 16, 2010); Rood, "McCain Urges Sudan Divestment – after Wife Dumps Her Holdings," ABC News, available at http://www.abcnews.go.com/Blotter/ story?id=4861297 (last accessed on February 16, 2010).

[11] See "Transcript: The Vice-Presidential Debate" (October 2, 2008), available at http://elections.nytimes.com/2008/president/debates/transcripts/vice-presidential-debate.html (last accessed on February 16, 2010). Ms. Palin's claim to leadership on divestment had the disadvantage of "significant omissions or exaggerations," in the judgment of the fact-checker at *The Washington Post*, because "[t]he legislative record shows that her administration was late in embracing the [divestment] campaign . . . and that it initially opposed the divestiture." See "Palin Team Opposed Divesting of Holdings to Protest Darfur," *Washington Post* (October 4, 2008), at A6 (awarding "two Pinocchios" on a scale of zero to four). After the election, Ms. Palin introduced new Sudan divestment legislation and secured the endorsement of the board of the Alaska Permanent Fund, but then resigned with the bills still pending before the state legislature.

[12] Ms. Palin's early effort to claim relevant experience by virtue of Alaska's proximity to Russia was "mocked," a problem that she admitted but then compounded by defending her claim on the ground that, when "Putin rears his head and comes into the air space of the United States," he flies over Alaska. See "Transcript: Katie Couric Interview of Sarah Palin," CBS Evening News (September 25, 2008; on file with author).

[13] See *United States v. Belmont*, 301 U.S. 324, 331 (1937): "[I]n respect of our foreign relations generally, state lines disappear. As to such purposes, the State of New York does not exist."

nevertheless be so bold as to predict that divestment has a future. A short-term dip might be explained by national absorption with the Great Recession, which has immersed governors and state legislatures in economic and budgetary crises, as well as a pause by activists early in the Obama Administration.[14] By contrast, the Sudan and Iran movements demonstrated the feasibility of successful divestment campaigns outside the original anti-apartheid context. Indeed, these campaigns showed that divestment can attract support in both "red" and "blue" states and can avoid the legal problems – domestic and international – that plagued Massachusetts' procurement restrictions regarding Burma. Establishing foreign policy credentials is a recurring challenge for governors seeking national office – although the successful candidacies of Governors Carter, Reagan, Clinton, and Bush show that the challenge is not insuperable. Other governors (and state legislators) are likely to conclude that divestment offers an attractive way to build their own foreign policy resumes – unless their power to do so is curtailed by the courts or the political branches of the federal government. In this regard, Robert Ahdieh aptly invokes the "endowment effect": "[O]nce states and localities have been empowered to act against states such as Sudan, it may be difficult to strip them of that power. As with coffee mugs, so with legislative authority."[15]

If divestment is to remain a feature of our political landscape, we may witness a shift toward the states of a power traditionally associated with the federal government. Depending on the extent and nature of that shift, it could have significant implications for the contemporary conception of federalism. These implications would not be limited to the United States, because the states can influence the ways in which the federal government interacts with the rest of the world.[16] In a recent article, I described and (within limits) celebrated the potential of state divestment, deployed wisely and occasionally,

[14] David Barron recently described this as the risk of "easing off" and warned against the possibility that "the creative local activism [of progressives] of recent years may give way to passivity" with the Democrats' success in the national elections of 2006 and 2008. See Barron, "Foreword: Blue State Federalism at the Crossroads," 3 *Harv. L. Pol'y Rev.* (2009) 1, at 6.

[15] See Ahdieh, "Foreign Affairs, International Law, and the New Federalism: Lessons from Coordination," 73 *Mo. L. Rev.* (2008) 1185, at 1210 note 113, citing Korobkin, "The Endowment Effect and Legal Analysis," 97 *Nw. U. L. Rev.* (2003) 1227, at 1236.

[16] John Kincaid goes so far as to suggest that "constituent diplomacy" by subnational governments in federal systems challenges the "classic unitary, univocal conception of the nation-state and, thereby, the international order built upon that conception" and, together with the rise of nonstate actors in international affairs, could require "a redefinition of the nature and role of the nation-state and a recognition of the fact that the cartelistic international arena is a pluralistic interorganizational arena." See Kincaid, "Constituent Diplomacy in Federal Polities and the Nation-State: Conflict and Co-operation," in H. J. Michelmann and P. Soldatos (eds.), *Federalism and International Relations: The Role of Subnational Units* (1990), at 54, 74.

to contribute valuably to the domestic political process for the formulation of foreign policy. As an instrument of democratic process, state divestment may call public and federal attention to an underattended concern, influence societal attitudes about that concern, and build domestic political support for a more vigorous national response thereto.[17] So, for example, state divestment may induce the federal government to impose new or tougher economic sanctions against a target country.

SADA is a remarkable federal embrace of state divestment, expressly authorizing, for the first time, state actions that some contend intrude unconstitutionally into the foreign relations prerogatives of the federal government. At the same time, SADA establishes federal bounds within which states are at least encouraged (if not required) to act. Acknowledging that state participation in the domestic process of formulating foreign policy has its costs, my previous article welcomed SADA's approach of bounded authorization and presented SADA as a case study for a new, "dialogic" understanding of federalism.[18] This conception of federalism rejects the antiquated notion that our nation does and must speak with only one voice about international matters in favor of a more pluralistic vision that both more accurately describes the reality of our national political processes and more fully accords with our democratic values, while still preserving ultimate federal control over foreign relations.

Nevertheless, in granting unprecedented federal approval to state divestment, SADA leaves unanswered questions about the theoretical underpinning for doing so. Did Congress "merely" move responsibility for divestment from the federal box to the state box in a traditional dualist model of federalism? Or did Congress challenge dualism itself by legitimizing a degree of concurrent responsibility on matters of foreign affairs? In other words, did Congress embrace a view about the role of the states in domestic and transnational discourse? Where might such a view lead?

This chapter strives to answer these questions. In so doing, it examines SADA together with other recent political developments, including the election of Barack Obama as President and Congress' ongoing consideration of SADA-like legislation to authorize state divestment from Iran.

Part 1 situates divestment in its constitutional and political contexts. Part 2 examines the extent of congressional support for dialogic federalism, as

[17] See generally Bechky, "Darfur, Divestment, and Dialogue," 30 *U. Penn. J. Int'l L.* (2009) 823.

[18] See Powell, "Dialogic Federalism: Constitutional Possibilities for Incorporation of Human Rights Law in the United States," 150 *U. Penn. L. Rev.* (2001) 245. Among the variety of adjectives found in the federalism literature, I use "dialogic" here as best capturing the vertical, horizontal, and transnational conversations that state divestment is capable of furthering, while also offering a nice antidote to the flawed "one voice" metaphor.

evidenced in the Sudan and Iran bills. Part 3 concludes with a look forward at the continuing politics of divestment.

1. DIVESTMENT IN CONTEXT

A. *The Constitutional Context of Divestment*

1. Contemporary Constitutional Theory

Federalism is often conceived as a dualist exercise in the vertical division of legal authority between the national and state governments, with each occupying "exclusive and non-overlapping spheres of authority."[19] Federalism today, however, is not so much about dividing power into neat boxes labeled "federal" and "state" as it is about managing concurrent exercises of power. The literature is replete with adjectives that capture the contemporary spirit of federalism: collaborative, cooperative, dialectic, dialogic, dynamic, interactive, polyphonic.[20]

Federalism is a conversation.[21] This conversation takes place among governments that share concurrent authority in many areas, sometimes cooperatively and other times contentiously.[22] This conversation serves constitutional values, including democratic participation values[23] and at least the hope that conversation will improve policy through competition in the marketplace of

[19] See Schapiro, "Toward a Theory of Interactive Federalism," 91 *Iowa L. Rev.* (2005) 243, at 246–250 (criticizing "dual federalism" and advancing "interactive federalism" as a better alternative, descriptively and normatively).

[20] See Ahdieh, *supra* note 15, at 30.

[21] So, for example, David Shapiro concludes his "dialogue" about the merits of federalism with the observation that "the true genius of American federalism lies in the continuing, and constitutionally assured, basis for dialogue – for moral, political, economic, and social debate over the merits of the allocation of power (both in general and in specific instances) among the various branches of government." David Shapiro, *Federalism: A Dialogue* (1995), at 140.

[22] See Schapiro, *supra* note 19, at 246 (citing "narcotics trafficking to securities trading to education" as examples where federal and state laws regulate the very same conduct); Ibid. at 249 ("Polyphony accepts a substantial role for dissonance as well as harmony."). For a new look at "how the state's status as servant, insider, and ally" under a cooperative approach to federalism "might enable it to be a sometime dissenter, rival, and challenger" to the federal government, see Bulman-Pozen and Gerken, "Uncooperative Federalism," 118 *Yale L. J.* 1256 (2009).

[23] See Duchacek, "Perforated Sovereignties: Towards a Typology of New Actors in International Relations," in Michelmann and Soldatos, *supra* note 16, at 1, 9 ("In all federal democratic frameworks, of course, elected officials of non-central governments and their staffs have always tried to have an influence or significant role in all federal policy-making, including the conduct of relations with foreign nations. Such lobbying... has always been consistent with both democratic and federal theory and practice"); Kincaid, *supra* note 16, at 73 ("Constituent diplomacy enhances the participation not only of state and local officials but also of citizens in national-policy-making.... [It] thus contributes to the democratization of national political processes by adding new voices to foreign-policy-making").

ideas. State action may likewise prioritize problems, identify potential solutions, and "generally prod[ ] the federal government into action."[24] This is all familiar in domestic matters, where Justice Brandeis famously described state legislatures as laboratories of democracy,[25] but it runs directly counter to the dominant metaphor of U.S. foreign relations law: that the nation speaks with "one voice" in its foreign relations, with the President as its "sole organ."[26]

A dialogic view of federalism recognizes that the federal government has the dominant role in making foreign policy, but this role has not been and need not be to the complete exclusion of the states. To the contrary, the federal government may tolerate, encourage, and even listen to and benefit from state expression of foreign policy preferences and priorities. The states may influence the democratic process of making foreign policy through attention getting, norm changing, and door opening; they may even assist the federal government in pursuing its foreign policy objectives.[27]

2. Constitutional Doctrine

The anti-apartheid movement, which included divestment as a key locus, helped place opposition to apartheid on the national agenda. Congress certainly knew of state divestment from South Africa. It debated whether to expressly allow or ban divestment in the Comprehensive Anti-Apartheid Act of 1986, ultimately doing neither.[28]

24 See Schapiro, "Not Old or Borrowed: Truly New Blue Federalism," 3 *Harv. L. Pol'y Rev.* (2009) 33, at 51 ("Blue state federalism consists in the states becoming actively engaged in these areas and generally prodding the federal government into action. The state measures are designed to complement federal efforts and generally require action by the federal government to achieve fully the desired ends. Blue state federalism empowers the states; it does not diminish the authority of the federal government."); see also Bechky, *supra* note 17, at 847–861 (describing divestment as an instrument of democratic process).

25 *New State Ice Co. v. Liebmann*, 285 U.S. 262, 311 (1932) (J. Brandeis, dissenting): "To stay experimentation in things social and economic is a grave responsibility. Denial of the right to experiment may be fraught with serious consequences to the nation. It is one of the happy incidents of the federal system that a single courageous State may, if its citizens choose, serve as a laboratory; and try novel social and economic experiments without risk to the rest of the country."

26 See, e.g., *United States v. Curtiss-Wright Export Corp.*, 299 U.S. 304, 320 (1936) (describing the "President as the sole organ of the Federal government in the field of international relations"); *Japan Line, Ltd. v. County of Los Angeles*, 441 U.S. 434, 452–453 (1979) (holding that a California tax impeded the nation's ability to "speak with one voice"); *Crosby v. National Foreign Trade Council*, 530 U.S. 363, 381 (2000) (stating that Massachusetts' Burma law "compromise[s] the very capacity of the President to speak for the Nation with one voice in dealing with other governments"). For description and criticism of the "one voice" jurisprudence, see generally Cleveland, *supra* note 3; see also Bechky, *supra* note 17, at 865–881.

27 These themes are further developed in Bechky, *supra* note 17, at 847–861.

28 See Cleveland, *supra* note 3, at 1001–1002, discussing legislative history of the Comprehensive Anti-Apartheid Act.

This congressional avoidance left the question of the propriety of state divestment to the courts. The leading case upheld Baltimore's divestment ordinances against, inter alia, the three main challenges brought against state actions affecting foreign relations: preemption by federal statute; the "dormant" effects of the Foreign Commerce Clause; and intrusion into an exclusive zone of federal control over foreign relations (also known as the "dormant foreign affairs power").[29] That decision, however, was rendered by a state court (the Maryland Court of Appeals) and cannot be regarded as definitive. In the year 2000, the Supreme Court emphasized that it had never ruled on the constitutionality of state divestment. In a case brought against Massachusetts's Burma procurement law by the National Foreign Trade Council (NFTC), a leading business group, the Supreme Court held that a federal Burma statute implicitly preempted Massachusetts' law. The Supreme Court left unaddressed the lower court's constitutional holdings that the law also violated both the dormant Foreign Commerce Clause and the dormant foreign affairs power.[30] A 2003 decision striking down California's Holocaust Victim Insurance Relief Act further suggested that the Supreme Court would find preemption readily when state action allegedly interferes with federal foreign policy.[31]

Two years later, Illinois passed the first Sudan-specific state law. The Illinois law provided, inter alia, for divestment from Sudan of assets controlled by both the state and city governments. The NFTC sued. The federal district court in Chicago grounded its divestment holding on precedents in the Seventh Circuit concerning the relationship between state and city governments. The court struck down the Illinois law, but its reasoning suggested that it would uphold a revised statute that limited divestment to state-controlled assets, omitting city-controlled assets. The court also held that another part of the Illinois law, concerning banking services, intruded into the exclusive federal realm of foreign affairs, distinguishing that provision from divestment.[32]

These lower-court decisions provide a nondefinitive degree of support for the constitutionality of state divestment absent SADA-like federal authority,

[29] See *Board of Trustees of Employees' Retirement System v. Mayor of Baltimore City*, 562 A.2d 720, 726 (Md. 1989).

[30] See *National Foreign Trade Council v. Natsios*, 181 F.3d 38 (1st Cir. 1999), *aff'd sub nom. Crosby v. National Foreign Trade Council*, 530 U.S. 363 (2000). For further discussion of these decisions and their significance for contemporary divestment, see Bechky, *supra* note 17.

[31] See *American Insurance Association v. Garamendi*, 539 U.S. 396 (2003).

[32] See *National Foreign Trade Council, Inc. v. Giannoulias*, 523 F. Supp. 2d 731, 742-45 (N.D. Ill. 2007). Illinois proceeded to enact new divestment legislation intended to conform with *Giannoulias* by omitting the provisions on city divestment and banking services. See 15 *Ill. Comp. Stat. Ann.* 520/22.5 (West, 2007).

as does a Reagan-era opinion of the Office of Legal Counsel.[33] Nevertheless, it also must be acknowledged that current doctrine casts some constitutional clouds over divestment – clouds that should neither be overstated nor ignored. The Sudan Divestment Task Force developed model divestment legislation, which was adopted by nineteen of the twenty-seven divesting states, designed to minimize difficulties under current constitutional doctrine.[34] For example, the task force's model legislation has several provisions to minimize conflict with federal policy, as well as other provisions to assure potential targets of fair process. Moreover, in practice, the task force recommended divestment from only a handful of companies with significant operations in Sudan, known as the "Highest Offenders."[35]

B. *The Political Context of Divestment*

Business opposition to U.S. economic sanctions is generally led by the NFTC and a coalition it organized called USA*Engage. The business groups offer two main arguments against sanctions: They don't work, and they hurt U.S. businesses and their employees.[36] These might be characterized as the "effectiveness" and "economic" objections. A third objection – "unilateralism" – draws much of its initial force from its relationship with the other two: If U.S. sales to a target country are replaced by sales from competitors elsewhere, that weakens both the effectiveness of the sanctions and the position of U.S. companies vis-à-vis their competitors. Proponents of sanctions, recognizing both the costs of unilateralism and the difficulties of securing multilateral cooperation with U.S. sanctions initiatives, sometimes advocate "extraterritorial" application of U.S. sanctions as a means of squaring the circle. This is where the unilateralism objection acquires its own independent bite, generating arguments that extraterritoriality causes diplomatic controversy, violates international law (whether customary law or particular treaties such as the World Trade Organization Agreements), and risks retaliation against U.S. businesses.

In its public objections to SADA, the NFTC seemed to acknowledge important differences between divestment and other sanctions. Critically, the U.S.

33 See "Constitutionality of South African Divestment Statutes Enacted by State and Local Governments," 10 *U.S. Op. Off. Legal Counsel* (1986) 49.

34 See Sudan Divestment Task Force, "Targeted Sudan Divestment: Model Legislation" (2008; on file with author).

35 See Sudan Divestment Task Force, "Sudan Company Rankings" (2008; on file with author).

36 For a good introduction to the business community's concerns about sanctions policy, see the Web site of USA*Engage (www.usaengage.org).

business community did not seem to perceive any real economic threat from divestment from Sudan – at least when the divestment was limited to a handful of companies, as under the Sudan Divestment Task Force model legislation adopted in most of the states divesting from Sudan. Indeed, because U.S. law already bars U.S. companies from conducting most business with Sudan, only one U.S. company has been named as a Highest Offender.[37] The Iran divestment movement likewise builds on existing U.S. sanctions against Iran, thus focusing on divestment from third-country companies doing business in Iran already barred for U.S. companies. This is a key difference between today's major divestment movements and their anti-apartheid predecessor, which developed in the absence of federal sanctions against South Africa and largely targeted U.S. companies. The only claim of economic harm in the NFTC's testimony opposing passage of SADA was that mutual funds would be burdened with compliance challenges.[38] The NFTC's actions seem to confirm its priorities: Although the NFTC sued Massachusetts over its procurement restrictions and Illinois over its statute with both divestment and procurement provisions, it has not challenged any pure divestment law. More proactively, the NFTC facilitated a meeting between its member companies and divestment advocates to foster dialogue about Sudan.[39]

Nor does the "unilateralism" of divestment pose any real threat. It does not jeopardize the competitiveness of U.S. companies. It has not provoked any significant diplomatic controversy. Europe and Japan swiftly challenged the Helms–Burton Act against Cuba, the Iran and Libya Sanctions Act, and the Massachusetts–Burma law under the World Trade Organization's dispute settlement procedures, but they have not challenged any of the state divestment laws.

Absent a substantial objection to divestment itself, at least in its limited contemporary manifestations, NFTC opposition seems motivated mainly by an interest in setting markers to constrain future state-level sanctions – especially procurement restrictions like the Massachusetts–Burma law and the Illinois banking provisions. Those constraints would be optimized by a constitutional

37 See Vivienne Walt, "U.S. Oil Firm Pulls out of Sudan," *Fortune* (September 14, 2007), discussing Weatherford's designation as a Highest Offender and subsequent decision to terminate a foreign subsidiary's activities in Sudan.

38 Written Statement of William A. Reinsch before the Senate Committee on Banking, Housing, and Urban Affairs, S. Hrg. 110-933 (2007), at 91; see also Cummings, "NFTC and USA*Engage Express Disappointment over House Approval of Iran Divestment Bill" (October 14, 2009), available at http://www.nftc.org/newsflash/newsflash.asp?Mode=View&id=236&articleid=2919&category=All (last accessed on February 16, 2010), stating objections to the Iran Sanctions Enabling Act without mention of any economic harm.

39 Interview with Adam Sterling (September 26, 2009).

theory that forbids state sanctions, thereby limiting to one the number of regulators on matters affecting foreign relations. As a result, NFTC objections to divestment focus on "one voice" constitutional arguments treating divestment as a state intrusion into exclusive national prerogatives. This understanding of the nature of the business community's interest in divestment suggests that the NFTC will continue to oppose any shift toward dialogism, preferring that any divestment authorization rest on the narrowest possible theory in an effort to maintain constraints minimizing the number and variety of state sanctions.

Conversely, divestment advocates will often lack any real interest in challenging "one voice." If an advocate's objective is to secure either state divestment from a particular target or express federal approval of such divestment, the prospects for success are likely to be maximized by hewing to prevailing constitutional doctrine. According to Adam Sterling, former executive director of the Sudan Divestment Task Force, "[w]e never intended to confront 'one voice.' Targeted divestment could be done within the 'one voice' frame."[40]

2. DIVESTMENT IN CONGRESS

A. *Divestment from Sudan*

In January 2007, Representative Barbara Lee of California – where the "targeted approach" was initially developed[41] – introduced the first federal bill to authorize state divestment from Sudan.[42] Just two weeks after the court decision in the Illinois case, Senator Richard Durbin of Illinois introduced a parallel bill in the Senate.[43] These bills drew widespread support: The Lee bill passed the House of Representatives by a vote of 418 to 1, and the Durbin bill attracted 32 cosponsors, including then-Senator Obama.

After the House passed the Lee bill, Senate Democrats tried for quick passage in the Senate as well, but Senate Republicans (presumably in coordination with the Bush Administration) insisted on fuller consideration in the Senate Banking Committee.[44] That led to the introduction of a new – and

[40] Ibid.

[41] Ibid.

[42] See the Darfur Accountability and Divestment Act, H. Rep. 180 (110th Cong. 1st sess., introduced January 4, 2007).

[43] See the Sudan Divestment Authorization Act, S. 831 at § 3 (110th Cong. 1st sess., introduced March 8, 2007).

[44] See Schor, "Shelby Blocks Fast Track for Darfur Bill," *The Hill* (August 15, 2007).

ultimately successful – bill sponsored solely by the Chairman, Senator Christopher Dodd.[45] The Banking Committee report confirms that the statute's purpose was "to address the issues raised in the Illinois case and the issue more broadly, by clearly authorizing divestment decisions made consistent with the standards it articulates."[46]

SADA authorizes the states to divest – within important bounds – from companies that do business in Sudan.[47] The key provision of this unprecedented statute provides

> Authority to Divest – Notwithstanding any other provision of law, a State or local government may adopt and enforce measures that meet the requirements of subsection (e) to divest the assets of the State or local government from, or prohibit investment of the assets of the State or local government in, persons that the State or local government determines, using credible information available to the public, are conducting or have direct investments in business operations described in subsection (d).[48]

In authorizing (but not requiring) states to divest from Sudan, Congress left to each state the decision *whether* to divest state-controlled assets from Sudan. Should a state decide to divest from Sudan, it also has considerable discretion to decide *how* to do so. As the aforementioned provision makes clear, however, SADA also bounds its authority to divest in various respects intended to ensure the compatibility of state actions with federal policy.[49]

SADA defines a space where a particular form of state expression is plainly authorized under particular circumstances, even though that speech concerns international matters. SADA thus seems to move past the dualist notion that our nation only and necessarily speaks with one voice toward respect for the possibilities offered by welcoming a multiplicity of voices, while still preserving the ultimate dominance of the federal voice.

Although SADA resonates with the theory of dialogic federalism, it is not clear whether Congress intended to embrace this theory when enacting SADA.

45 This is not to say that Senator Dodd's staff wrote the bill alone or that they ignored the views of other actors. To the contrary, I understand that the Dodd bill reflected a serious effort to accommodate the views of a number of active participants, including (at the least) the Bush Administration, Committee Republicans, Senator Durbin, Representative Lee, the NFTC, and the Sudan Development Task Force.

46 S. Rep. No. 110–213, at 3 (2007).

47 Pub. L. No. 110-174, 21 Stat. 2516 (2007).

48 See SADA § 3(b).

49 See SADA §§ 3–5, 12; see also Bechky, *supra* note 17 (describing six limitations on SADA's authority to divest).

At the least, Congress seems to have wished not to be seen to embrace it. SADA includes this declaration:

> It is the sense of Congress that the United States Government should support the decision of any State or local government to divest from . . . a person that the State or local government *determines poses a financial or reputational risk*.[50]

The Banking Committee report explains that it put this language in the statute to make clear that divestment is "conducted for purposes of mitigating a 'financial or reputational risk'" in light of "the Constitutional concerns about states' enacting legislation which touches on international relations."[51] The report further refers to "balancing" the states' proprietary interests against the "singular" federal authority to conduct foreign policy.[52] This, needless to say, is not the language of foreign relations multipolarism. It suggests, rather, a continuing adherence to dualism – albeit with a (still notable) willingness to assign divestment to the state side of the federal–state divide.

Nevertheless, the committee report language cannot be accepted as the final word on this question. As the Bush Administration argued in opposition to SADA,[53] the statute's operative language does not require any showing of "financial or reputational risk" as a condition of the authority to divest, or otherwise limit the grounds on which a state may decide to divest. Congress could have limited SADA's authority to divestment done for the express purpose of mitigating risk – as Congress permits state regulation of nuclear plants depending upon the state's stated regulatory purpose[54] – or to divestment where the state makes certain factual determinations about risk. It did not do so.

50 See SADA § 3(a); emphasis added.

51 S. Rpt. 110-213, at 6; Ibid. at 1, 4.

52 S. Rpt. 110-213, at 3.

53 See *Negative Implications of the President's Signing Statement on the Sudan Accountability and Divestment Act: Hearing before the H. Comm. on Financial Serv.*, H. Rep. 110-87 (2008), at 67–68 (reprinting letter from Brian Benczkowski, Principal Deputy Assistant Attorney General, U.S. Dept. of Justice, to Richard Cheney, President of the U.S. Senate, giving the Department of Justice's views on SADA): "This hortatory provision [about financial or reputational risk] provides virtually no limits on the State and local divestment the bill says the United States Government 'should support.' But the operative divestment authorization that follows it, which contains no limitations on the motivations covered by the bill, is even broader."

54 In *Pacific Gas & Electric Co. v. State Energy Resources Conservation & Development Comm'n*, 461 U.S. 190 (1983), the Supreme Court held that the Atomic Energy Act did not preempt California's regulation of nuclear plants, reasoning that Congress occupied the field of nuclear safety, but left states free to regulate nuclear plants "for purposes other than protection against radiation hazards." Ibid. at 210–216, quoting 42 U.S.C. § 2021(k). Indeed, the court "accept[ed] California's *avowed* economic purpose as the rationale" for the statute at issue rather than

Moreover, the word "singular" ought not be read too far. Taken literally, it would mean that states could not send trade missions abroad, could not open overseas commercial offices, could not form sister-city relationships, could not pass resolutions or make other symbolic statements about foreign affairs, and so forth. Yet, states do all of this – and more – quite routinely, often with the federal government's support.[55] It is simply implausible that the Senate Banking Committee meant to endorse, sub silentio, the complete abolition of all this state involvement in foreign affairs.

Three aspects of SADA's legislative history shed light on the political choices made by Congress.

First, the Durbin bill – like the Lee bill in the House of Representatives – did not include the risk-based language ultimately found in SADA. To the contrary, it affirmatively embraced the language of federalist dialogue. It expressed the "sense of the Congress" that states should be permitted to divest as "an expression of opposition to the genocidal actions and policies of the Government of Sudan."[56] The Durbin bill also would have expressly authorized state divestment with fewer bounds on the authority than are contained in SADA.[57]

Second, according to Adam Sterling, the Sudan Divestment Task Force's position "evolved over time" as it came to stress "financial and reputational" concerns about doing business with Sudan together with "moral" concerns. In his judgment, this strategy helped both to overcome pension fund objections to state divestment legislation and to respond to the "slippery slope" argument from businesses concerned about the volume and variety of social concerns. He considered it "easy to show the significant reputational risks" presented by doing major business with a regime declared by the U.S. Government to be committing genocide.[58]

Third, SADA passed over the "grave constitutional" objections of the Bush Administration. The administration contended that SADA unconstitutionally and unwisely enabled states to "interfere with national foreign policy":

> [T]he bill purports to transfer to State and local governments, in a way that raises both constitutional separation of powers and federalism questions,

"become embroiled in attempting to ascertain California's true motive," because "inquiry into legislative motive is often an unsatisfactory venture." Ibid. at 216 (emphasis added).

55 Examples are available at Bechky, *supra* note 17, at 841–842.

56 S. 831, *supra* note 43, at § 3.

57 Ibid. at § 5(a): "Notwithstanding any other provision of law, any state may adopt measures to prohibit any investment of State assets in the Government of Sudan or in any company with a qualifying business relationship with Sudan, during any period in which the Government of Sudan, or the officials of such government are subject to sanctions authorized under . . . Federal law or executive order."

58 Interview with Adam Sterling (September 26, 2009).

> foreign policy authority that the Constitution places, for very good reasons, with the Federal government. We strongly object to this effort because it raises concerns under a long line of Supreme Court cases and because it could jeopardize, rather than strengthen, the robust and carefully calibrated response to the crisis in Darfur that the Federal government is pursuing. . . .[59]

The Bush Administration's invocation of separation of powers is notable. Its objections were not only vertical but horizontal. In other words, it took the position that the exclusion of states from participation in foreign affairs is constitutionally fixed and the U.S. Congress is powerless to adjust it even when Congress (with the President's signature or over his veto) concludes that allowing state participation is in the national interest. The Bush Administration conceded that Congress can resolve concerns involving statutory preemption and the dormant Foreign Commerce Clause, but it questioned whether "federal legislation could remove any Federal preemptive force that flows from the Constitution's grant *to the President* of certain foreign affairs powers under Article II."[60]

The Bush Administration similarly challenged Congress to explain why states should be allowed to participate in the making of foreign policy when they lack relevant expertise. It warned of the dangers of "effectively converting State actions – which States are already taking – into federally protected privileges, thereby undercutting the Supremacy Clause and the President's powers thereunder." It raised the camel's nose argument: "Such authorization would set a dangerous precedent, making it easier to pass similar legislation in other cases."[61]

The administration persisted with its constitutional objections to the extent that President Bush ultimately signed SADA subject to a signing statement, which maintained that SADA "purports" to authorize state divestment but will be "construe[d] and enforce[d]" by the executive branch to preserve the federal government's "exclusive authority to conduct foreign relations."[62]

The legislative history of SADA thus shows support for a dialogically premised bill by the House and a third of the Senate, strenuous opposition by the Bush Administration, a convergence of views by business and activist groups toward an approach focused on reputational and financial risk, and

59 See Benczkowski letter, *supra* note 53, at 67.

60 Ibid. at 67, 69 (emphasis added, punctuation omitted).

61 Ibid. at 63–64 (letter from Jeffrey T. Bergner, Assistant Secretary for Legislative Affairs, U.S. Department of State, to Senator Harry Reid, giving the views of the State Department on SADA, October 22, 2007).

62 "Statement by President George W. Bush upon Signing S. 2271," 43 *Weekly Comp. Pres. Doc.* 1646 (December 31, 2007).

ultimate passage of a different bill lacking any express commitment to the dialogical view. There appears to be no information in the public record explaining the new language put forth in the Banking Committee bill and the committee report. In the circumstances, it seems not unreasonable to surmise that the Banking Committee decided to advance a bill capable of minimizing conflict with the Bush Administration and securing Republican backing to enact a divestment-authorizing statute, without regard to its theoretical basis.

B. *The Politics of Divestment from Iran*

As a senator, Barack Obama was the primary sponsor of a Senate bill designed to authorize states to divest from companies investing in the Iranian energy sector. The Obama bill would have obliged the Treasury Department to publish a list of companies investing more than $20 million in the Iranian energy sector,[63] because that in turn was the threshold at which the Iran Sanctions Act (ISA) requires the President to impose federal sanctions unless he certifies that a waiver is "important to the national interest."[64] The Obama bill thus reflected both congressional interest in invigorating presidential use of ISA and an effort to align federal and state policies by tying the states' authority to divest to federal sanctions.

The Obama bill was premised on a congressional "finding" that "[p]olicy makers and fund managers may find moral, prudential, or reputational reasons to divest" from Iran.[65] The words "moral . . . reasons" suggest a more open embrace of state involvement with matters international than does SADA's reference to "financial or reputational risk." They acknowledge and legitimize state divestment not merely to protect states' own narrow business interests, but to condemn unacceptable foreign conduct and thereby participate in transnational discourse about ending that conduct.

Representative Barney Frank, the Chairman of the House Financial Services Committee, introduced a parallel to the Obama bill. The House of Representatives passed the Frank bill in July 2007, by a vote of 408 to 6. The Frank bill went beyond the Obama bill in two important respects. First, while keeping the recognition that states may divest for "moral" reasons, the House-passed bill added that "[i]t is the policy of the United States to support the decision of state governments, local governments, and educational institutions to divest from . . . persons that have investments of more

63 Iran Sanctions Enabling Act, S. 1430 (110th Cong. 1st sess., introduced May 17, 2007).

64 Iran Sanctions Act, 50 U.S.C. § 1701 note, §§ 4(d)(1), 5(a), 9(c).

65 S. 1430, *supra* note 63, § 2(10).

than $20,000,000 in Iran's energy sector." The House did not limit this "support" with any language about the states' motives for divestment. Indeed, the operative language went still further, authorizing divestment from any company "having an investment in, or carrying on a trade or business . . . in or with, Iran."[66] The House committee report explained that this bill "allows State and local governments to develop their own criteria with regard to the companies from which they will divest . . . irrespective of the list provided by the Federal government."[67]

Like the Durbin bill on Sudan, the Obama bill faced procedural obstacles in the Senate, which led to a new bill sponsored by Chairman Dodd. In July 2008, the Banking Committee approved the Comprehensive Iran Sanctions, Accountability, and Divestment Act, or CISADA, by a vote of 19 to 2. CISADA echoed SADA in more than just name. Evidently drawing on the lessons of SADA's success over Bush Administration objections, the Banking Committee crafted CISADA's divestment provisions from the SADA mold. CISADA thus followed the SADA formulation connecting the "sense of Congress that the United States Government should support" state divestment to cases of "financial or reputational risk." As with SADA, the operative language was not tied to risk, but neither did it make the apparently open-ended commitment of the House-passed bill. Instead it tied the authority to ISA's $20 million threshold – except that CISADA applied this threshold to banks providing financing at that level, as well as investors themselves, reflecting a preference to expand ISA long favored by its proponents.[68]

The Banking Committee report on CISADA repeated the SADA report's language about "balance" between the states' interests as investors and the "singular" federal control over foreign relations, stressing the theme of divestment as a tool of risk management.[69] It added an unmistakable response to President Bush's SADA signing statement: "[T]he Committee has concluded that, with respect to each of these challenges [statutory preemption, dormant foreign commerce, and dormant foreign affairs], Congress and the President have the constitutional power to authorize States to enact divestment measures, and Federal consent removes any doubt as to the constitutionality of those measures."[70]

66 Iran Sanctions Enabling Act, H.R. 2437, §§ 2(10), 4 (110th Cong. 1st sess., as passed July 31, 2007).
67 H.R. Rep. No. 110–277 (2007), at 7.
68 Comprehensive Iran Sanctions, Accountability, and Divestment Act, S. 3445, § 202 (110th Cong. 2nd sess., introduced August 1, 2008).
69 S. Rep. No. 110–443 (2008), at 2, 4, 5, 8.
70 Ibid. at 5.

The House then passed CISADA, but the Senate did not act on it – a result perhaps not too surprising during the first general election campaign in U.S. history to pit two sitting senators against each other.

Through 2008, then, congressional consideration of divestment from Iran seemed to confirm the evidence of SADA. Once again, the House and a substantial number of senators (thirty-seven cosponsored the Obama bill) supported a dialogically grounded approach to divestment, but the Senate Banking Committee advanced a less openly dialogic bill apparently in an effort to maximize prospects for passage despite the objections of the Bush Administration. Both times, the House accepted the risk-based approach that emerged from the Senate Banking Committee.

In January 2009, Barack Obama took office as President of the United States. In his efforts to address Iran's nuclear program, President Obama pursued diplomacy with Iran – apparently with the twin objectives of trying in good faith to resolve the matter diplomatically while also laying the groundwork to persuade the UN Security Council about the necessity for multilateral sanctions against Iran should diplomacy fail. President Obama continued this "dual-track approach" even after Iran violently oppressed protestors and new disclosures emerged about Iran's nuclear program. The President's speech accepting the Nobel Peace Prize in December 2009 nicely illustrates his effort to find balance between multilateral sanctions and diplomatic outreach, as he appears to speak all at once to Iran, the international community, and domestic critics:

> Those regimes that break the rules [of international law] must be held accountable. Sanctions must exact a real price. Intransigence must be met with increased pressure – and such pressure exists only when the world stands together as one. One urgent example is the effort to prevent the spread of nuclear weapons. . . . [I]t is also incumbent upon all of us to insist that nations like Iran and North Korea do not game the system. Those who claim to respect international law cannot avert their eyes when those laws are flouted. Those who care for their own security cannot ignore the danger of an arms race in the Middle East or East Asia. Those who seek peace cannot stand idly by as nations arm themselves for nuclear war. . . .
>
> Let me also say this: the promotion of human rights cannot be about exhortation alone. At times, it must be coupled with painstaking diplomacy. I know that engagement with repressive regimes lacks the satisfying purity of indignation. But I also know that sanctions without outreach – and condemnation without discussion – can carry forward a crippling status quo. No repressive regime can move down a new path unless it has the choice of an open door. . . . There is no simple formula here. But we must try as best we can to balance isolation and engagement, pressure and incentives, so that human rights and dignity are advanced over time.

It did not take long for President Obama to be confronted with the views of Senator Obama on U.S. sanctions against Iran. Even with President Obama's fellow Democrats in control of both Houses, congressional patience for diplomacy with Iran is thin – and Iran strained it during 2009. In April, two bills intended to disrupt sales of refined petroleum to Iran expressly quoted then-Senator Obama's earlier support for such sanctions.[71] In July, the Senate urged the President to impose new U.S. sanctions unless Iran started negotiations by late September and ended its nuclear program within sixty days thereafter.[72] In October, the Senate Banking Committee held a hearing on Iran sanctions, during which it became evident both that the Obama Administration did not favor new sanctions legislation at that time and that the Banking Committee intended to push forward regardless.[73] Weeks later, the Banking Committee marked up a new Iran sanctions bill – here called "CISADA 2" – which passed the Committee quickly and unanimously.[74] In December, the House passed its refined petroleum sanctions bill, 412 to 12. In January 2010, the Senate passed CISADA 2 under its "unanimous consent" procedure – deferring the Obama Administration's concerns about the "timing and content" of the bill to be addressed, if at all, in a House–Senate conference committee.[75]

To be sure, the main thrust of congressional interest is directed at federal sanctions against Iran rather than SADA-like approval of state divestment. Still, bills authorizing divestment from Iran have moved through Congress as well. In March, Chairman Frank introduced an Iran divestment bill reminiscent of the Frank and Obama bills of 2007.[76] In May, Senator Sam Brownback (who had been the principal cosponsor of the Obama bill in 2007) introduced a parallel bill in the Senate.[77] The House passed the Frank bill in October,

71 See Iran Refined Petroleum Sanctions Act, S. 908, § 2(a)(4-6) (111th Cong. 1st sess., introduced April 28, 2009); Iran Refined Petroleum Sanctions Act, H.R. 2194 (111th Cong. 1st sess., introduced April 30, 2009).

72 National Defense Authorization Act for Fiscal Year 2010, S. 1390, § 1232(b)(2) (111th Cong. 1st sess.).

73 See, e.g., Bogardus, "Dem Senators Frustrated with State Dept. on Iran," *The Hill* (October 7, 2009) 16; "Steinberg Says Administration Still Undecided on Iran Sanctions," *Inside U.S. Trade* (October 9, 2009), 2009 WLNR 19948777. The administration's position is best reflected in the exchange with Senator Corker, and the Senate's appetite for quick action is evidenced in comments by Senators Bayh, Brownback, Bunning, Dodd, Schumer, and Menendez. Transcript, *Federal News Service* (October 6, 2009), at 2, 4, 6, 25–28, 35–36, 38–39.

74 Comprehensive Iran Sanctions, Accountability, and Divestment Act, S. 2799 (111th Cong. 2nd sess., introduced November 19, 2009); S. Rep. No. 111-99, at 1.

75 See Letter from James Steinberg, Deputy Secretary of State, to John Kerry, Chairman of the Senate Foreign Relations Committee, December 11, 2009 (on file with author), expressing the State Department's concerns about CISADA 2; 156 Cong. Rec. (28 Jan. 2010), at S324, S326 (remarks of Senator Dodd, noting the administration's "lingering concerns").

76 Iran Sanctions Enabling Act, H.R. 1327 (111th Cong. 1st sess., introduced March 5, 2009).

77 Iran Sanctions Enabling Act, S. 1065 (111th Cong. 1st sess., introduced May 18, 2009).

414 to 6. The Brownback bill, as with the Durbin and Obama bills before it, was replaced by the divestment provisions of a new Banking Committee bill, CISADA 2. With the Senate's recent passage of CISADA 2, both Houses have voted to authorize state divestment from Iran – subject, of course, to final reconciliation of the bills and presentment to President Obama.[78]

The Frank and Brownback bills include the language legitimizing a "moral" basis for state divestment.[79] The Banking Committee seemed poised to omit these words in favor of the less dialogic, risk-based path of SADA and the original CISADA bill. The Committee Report on CISADA 2 employs familiar language about "balance" between the "singular authority" of the federal government over foreign affairs and "risks to profitability, economic well-being, and reputations" arising from the states' management of their investment portfolios.[80] The report even appears to suggest that CISADA 2 limits states to divesting only for reasons of risk management.[81]

In fact, however, CISADA 2 does not limit the authority to divest in this way. Indeed, it includes the Frank and Brownback language acknowledging "moral" reasons for state divestment.[82] It passed the Senate by unanimous consent. The Senate thus took a step away from its previous reliance on risk management as an explanation for authorizing states to divest. This step better aligns the bill's stated premises with its operative language, allowing a peek behind the veil drawn by the Banking Committee as part of the effort to secure passage of SADA.[83]

78 As this chapter goes to press, President Obama signed CISADA 2 into law as Public Law 111-195, with the divestment provisions discussed here intact.

79 H.R. 1327, *supra* note 76, § 2(2); S. 1065, *supra* note 77, § 2(2).

80 *See* S. Rep. No. 111-99, at 7; see also id. at 2 ("to reduce the financial or reputational risk"); 6 ("prudential or reputational reasons to divest from companies that accept the business risk" of dealings with Iran); 11 ("prudential and economic reasons," including "reputational and financial risks").

81 Id. at 7: "The Committee believes it has struck an appropriate balance by targeting State action in such a way that permits State divestment measures based on risks. . . ."

82 S. 2799, *supra* note 74, § 202: "It is the sense of Congress that the United States Government should support the decision of any State or local government that for moral, prudential, or reputational reasons divests from, or prohibits the investment of assets of the State or local government in, a person that engages in investment activities in the energy sector of Iran, as long as that country is subject to economic sanctions imposed by the United States."

83 I am presuming, of course, that the Senate's addition of the word "moral" was purposeful. Cf. Frankfurter, "Some Reflections on the Reading of Statutes," 47 Colum. L. Rev. (1947), at 527, 545–546: "The pressure on legislatures to discharge their responsibility with care, understanding and imagination should be stiffened, not relaxed. Above all, they must not be encouraged in irresponsible or undisciplined use of language. In the keeping of legislatures perhaps more than any other group is the well-being of their fellow-men. Their responsibility is discharged ultimately by words."

Why did the Senate take this step toward a more openly dialogic rationale for divestment? The public record is silent. CISADA 2 moved quickly through committee and the full Senate, with a minimum of public debate. Issues about divestment necessarily predominated in the consideration of SADA, but divestment attracted relatively little attention in discussions about the larger CISADA 2 bill. Neither the State Department nor the NFTC mentioned divestment in their statements opposing CISADA 2.[84]

One might ask whether the move toward dialogism reflects President Obama's own personal policy preferences. Besides the evidence of his legislative record and his statements and actions during the 2008 campaign, we have this passage from his memoir *Dreams from My Father*:

> I got involved in the [anti-apartheid] divestment campaign [at Occidental College]. . . . I found myself drawn into a larger role – contacting representatives of the African National Congress to speak on campus, drafting letters to the faculty, printing up flyers, arguing strategy. . . . When we started planning the rally for the trustees' meeting, and somebody suggested that I open the thing, I quickly agreed . . . .
>
> "There's a struggle going on," I said. . . . "It's happening an ocean away. But it's a struggle that touches each and every one of us. . . . A struggle that demands we choose sides. . . . It's a choice between dignity and servitude. Between fairness and injustice. Between commitment and indifference. A choice between right and wrong."

Let us assume that this passion endures, that it extends beyond apartheid to current-day Iran, that President Obama is willing to allow states to act on that passion even if such actions complicate his own high-stakes diplomatic outreach to Iran, and that he is also willing to tolerate the risk that similar complications may arise in our relations with other countries should new divestment campaigns emerge.[85] Even so, this is not enough. After all, a SADA-like bill would achieve express authority for state divestment from Iran. President Obama's commitment would have to extend beyond divestment itself to the nonoperative language in his Iran bill or Senator Durbin's Sudan

[84] See Steinberg letter, *supra* note 75; Cummings, "Business Community Voices Strong Opposition to Iran Sanctions Bills" (January 26, 2010), available at http://www.nftc.org/newsflash/newsflash.asp?Mode=View&id=236&articleid=2974&category=All (last accessed February 15, 2010).

[85] In mentioning the risks of state divestment for the president's foreign policy, one should not lose sight of the possibility that state divestment might in fact strengthen the president's position by, for example, signaling to foreign actors the depth of public support for that position. See Bechky, *supra* note 17, at 869–870; H.R. Hrg. 111-13 (2009), at 80 (quoting Chairman Frank).

bill – to the very idea that states may divest for "moral . . . reasons" or as "an expression of opposition" to Iranian policy.

In fact, there is reason to believe that the Obama Administration might be more open than was the Bush Administration to sharing with the states a degree of power on matters touching upon foreign relations – as, indeed, the Reagan and Clinton Administrations were.[86] Claims of broad executive power were a hallmark of the Bush Presidency. In its first year, the Obama Administration wrestled with how far to roll back these claims – showing, at times, a greater willingness to accept constraints on executive action and to share power with other actors, while still securing the institutional interests of the United States and the Executive Branch.[87] With regard to CISADA 2, the Executive Branch's institutional priorities lie in preserving its dominant position in foreign policy generally and minimizing the bill's impact, in its substance or timing, on the president's diplomatic initiatives. President Obama's past personal support for an earlier bill containing certain language would seem an unlikely basis for the Executive Branch to instigate legislative amendments inviting freer challenges on a central matter of foreign policy than Congress itself previously had been willing to endorse. That prospect seems remote, even if we imagine that an Obama Administration addressing the issue on a blank slate might have opposed the Durbin bill less vigorously than the Bush Administration actually did (or not at all) and so might have negotiated different language for SADA and the committee report.

Instead, CISADA 2's step toward dialogism may reflect the efforts of supporters of the Brownback bill. Senator Brownback himself cast his support for state divestment in, inter alia, moral terms: "[D]ivestment serves as a way

[86] See "Constitutionality of South African Divestment Statutes," *supra* note 33 (Reagan Administration; finding constitutional states' divestment and procurement laws); Brief for the United States as Amicus Curiae Supporting Respondents, *Natsios v. National Foreign Trade Council*, U.S. S.Ct. No. 99–474, 2000 WL 14805 (Clinton Administration; opposing Massachusetts' procurement restrictions, but recognizing the legitimacy of various state measures, possibly including divestment). By contrast, the Bush Administration's amicus brief in *Garamendi* stressed the exclusive prerogatives of the president without acknowledging the legitimacy of any state measures touching foreign relations. See Brief for the United States as Amicus Curiae Supporting Petitioners, *American Insurance Association v. Garamendi*, U.S. S.Ct. No. 02-722.

[87] In one notable early example, the Obama Administration shifted the legal basis for holding the Guantánamo detainees from a claim of inherent presidential power to a construction of the statute authorizing use of military force in Afghanistan. This approach maintained a legal basis for continuing to hold the detainees while the administration works toward closing Guantánamo, while also sharing power over detainee policy with a Congress capable of amending the statute. See Brief for the United States, In re Guantánamo Bay Detainee Litigation, D.D.C. Misc. No. 08-442 (March 13, 2009), at 1 ("the Government is refining its position with respect to its authority to detain those persons who are now being held at Guantanamo Bay").

of fulfilling our minimum moral obligation towards the victims of oppression from brutal regimes, like that in Tehran."[88] Senator Robert Casey, the principal cosponsor of the Brownback bill, nicely captured its dialogic spirit:

> I call on my colleagues to listen to legislatures in so many states across the country who have passed divestment measures. The American people do not want anything to do with investing in this regime. Let's send a strong message to this regime and the international community that a nuclear-armed Iran is unacceptable.[89]

This is not to say that the election of President Obama is irrelevant to the addition of the "moral" language to CISADA 2. Supporters of the Brownback and Frank bills often quoted then-Senator Obama or otherwise claimed that the Obama bill evidenced the President's personal support.[90] Aligning CISADA 2 with the Obama bill may well have been part of the political strategy to secure passage of the bill.

3. A LOOK FORWARD: THE CONTINUING POLITICS OF DIVESTMENT

The political evidence through 2008 suggested that the U.S. House of Representatives was prepared to legitimize a degree of concurrent state responsibility on matters of foreign affairs, but the U.S. Senate as a whole was not yet prepared to do so and the House was willing to accept the less dialogic language capable of securing Senate passage. It should be recognized that this difference in approach flows less from a genuine commitment by either chamber to a particular theory of federalism than to the institutional differences between the chambers. The Senate finessed the question to facilitate enactment of

88 Written Statement of Sam Brownback before the Senate Committee on Banking, Housing, and Urban Affairs, "Minimizing Potential Threats from Iran" (October 6, 2009), at 2, available at http://banking.senate.gov/public/index.cfm?FuseAction=Hearings.Hearing&Hearing_ID=23f97300-5b76-483b-9225-aa14a2a82e79 (last accessed February 16, 2010).

89 Written Statement of Robert Casey before the Senate Committee on Banking, Housing, and Urban Affairs, "Minimizing Potential Threats from Iran" (October 6, 2009), at 6, available at http://banking.senate.gov/public/index.cfm?FuseAction=Hearings.Hearing&Hearing_ID=23f97300-5b76-483b-9225-aa14a2a82e79 (last accessed February 16, 2010).

90 For example, Senator Brownback said, "And lest any of my colleagues worry about where our President stands on this, you can rest easy. In the last Congress, then-Senator Obama and I introduced almost this very same bill." He then quoted then-Senator Obama and added, "I could not have said it better than the President." Brownback Statement, *supra* note 88, at 3. Likewise, Senator Casey said, "When President Obama was in the Senate, he introduced an earlier version of this legislation. It was right in 2007, and it is right now." Casey Statement, *supra* note 89, at 5. See also H.R. Hrg. 111-13 (2009), at 5–6, 20, 29–30, 77–78 (statements of Rep. Erik Paulsen and Professor Orde Kittrie).

SADA, and it had reasons of prudence and precedent to continue to do so. This finesse pointed to the possibility that Congress would retain a nominal commitment to dualism in foreign affairs, while allowing an important degree of dialogism to develop in fact.

A year later, however, the Senate took its own step toward a more open embrace of dialogism. It did so notwithstanding the institutional interests of both the Executive Branch and the business community. Admittedly, it may have done so based on particular political calculations in the unusual circumstance where President Obama himself had recently sponsored similar legislation as a senator. Whatever the reasons, however, if Congress finally enacts legislation authorizing states to divest from Iran and legitimizing moral concerns as the basis for so doing, that may supplant SADA's less openly dialogic approach as a precedent should Congress contemplate authorizing state divestment again in the future.

Regardless, questions of the politics of divestment will endure. The politics of divestment, when they can be separated from the politics of a particular foreign-policy controversy, are the politics of federalism – with an added touch of the politics of separation of powers. In other words, they are the politics of sharing power in a complex and ever-evolving polity. On such enduring questions of U.S. politics, all answers are transitory.

More generally, although this chapter has emphasized the role of divestment in fostering dialogue within the United States, it should be seen that a divestment strategy entailing shareholder engagement backed by the possibility of selling shares also opens channels for transnational dialogue. These channels supplement, not replace, traditional *inter*national dialogue. They build upon the established and uncontroversial channel of investor–company communication, as well as the trends toward both greater inclusion of social responsibility discourse in such communication and greater involvement by nonstate actors in shaping international norms.

This transnational dialogue will not be cost free, of course. As within the United States, transnational discussion of moral and political controversies should be expected to generate frictions and coordination challenges for national governments. By way of example, the Norwegian Government Pension Fund – Global has divested in recent years from a number of European, Israeli, and U.S. companies when it has concluded that the companies were likely to continue activities it deemed unacceptable, including selling certain weapons and causing environmental harm.[91] In managing the inevitable

[91] Information about the fund, its ethical guidelines, and the reasons it has divested from various companies is available at http://www.regjeringen.no/en/dep/fin/Selected-topics/The-Government-Pension-Fund/Ethical-Guidelines-for-the-Government-Pension-Fund–Global-.html?id=446948 (last accessed February 16, 2010).

controversies, it should be borne in mind that it is undesirable and impracticable to force investors to make and hold investments against their will, that divestment will have little impact on share prices unless the objections motivating it are widely shared, and that the disagreement underlying the divestment would still exist even if it had to be expressed by different means. In other words, the real source of controversy is not divestment itself, but the underlying differences in interests, policies, laws, values, and perceptions that give rise to the divestment – and divestment, deployed wisely, may contribute positively to the transnational discourse that is so vital to addressing such differences.

Index